# DATA MODEL PATTERNS

The Morgan Kaufmann Series in Data Management Systems
*Series Editor: Jim Gray, Microsoft Research*

# DATA MODEL PATTERNS

## *A Metadata Map*

David C. Hay
*Essential Strategies, Inc.*

AMSTERDAM • BOSTON • HEIDELBERG • LONDON
NEW YORK • OXFORD • PARIS • SAN DIEGO
SAN FRANCISCO • SINGAPORE • SYDNEY • TOKYO

Focal Press is an imprint of Elsevier

MORGAN KAUFMANN PUBLISHERS

ELSEVIER

| Publisher | Diane D. Cerra |
| Assistant Editor | Asma Stephan |
| Editorial Intern | Marisa Crawford |
| Publishing Services Manager | George Morrison |
| Project Manager | Marilyn E. Rash |
| Cover Design | Hannus Design |
| Cover Image | *Aristotle with a Bust of Homer*, 1653 (Oil on canvas) |
| | Rembrandt Harmensz van Rijn (1606–1669 Dutch) |
| | Metropolitan Museum of Art, New York, USA |
| Composition | Cepha Imaging Pvt. Ltd. |
| Technical Illustrations | Dartmouth Publishing Inc. |
| Indexer | Kevin Broccoli |
| Interior printer | Courier Westford |
| Cover printer | Phoenix Color Corp. |

Morgan Kaufmann Publishers is an imprint of Elsevier.
500 Sansome Street, Suite 400, San Francisco, CA 94111

This book is printed on acid-free paper.

Library of Congress Cataloging-in-Publication Data

Hay, David C., 1947-
  Data model patterns : a metadata map / David C. Hay.
    p. cm.
1. Data warehousing. 2. Metadata. I. Title.
  ISBN-13: 978-0-12-088798-9 (pbk.: alk. paper)
  ISBN-10: 0-12-088798-3 (pbk.: alk. paper)

  QA76.9.D37.H38 2006
  005.74–dc22                                    2006011123

For information on all Morgan Kaufmann publications, visit our Web site at www.mkp.com or www.books.elsevier.com

Printed and bound by CPI Group (UK) Ltd, Croydon, CR0 4YY

Transferred to Digital Print 2011

## Working together to grow
## libraries in developing countries

www.elsevier.com | www.bookaid.org | www.sabre.org

ELSEVIER    BOOK AID International    Sabre Foundation

To my mother, Henrietta Hay, who taught me the value of
a well-written sentence and to appreciate good writing.

To Aristotle, the father of data modeling

CHRONO-SYNCLASTIC INFUNDIBULA—*Just imagine that your Daddy is the smartest man who ever lived on Earth, and he knows everything there is to find out, and he is exactly right about everything, and he can prove he is right about everything. Now imagine another little child on some nice world a million light-years away, and that little child's Daddy is the smartest man who ever lived on that nice world so far away. And he is just as smart and just as right as your Daddy is. Both Daddies are smart, and both Daddies are right.*

*Only if they ever met each other they would get into a terrible argument, because they wouldn't agree on anything. Now, you can say that your Daddy is right and the other little child's Daddy is wrong, but the Universe is an awfully big place. There is room enough for an awful lot of people to be right about things and still not agree.*

*The reason both Daddies can be right and still get into terrible fights is because there are so many different ways of being right. There are places in the Universe, though, where each Daddy could finally catch on to what the other Daddy was talking about. These places are where all the different kinds of truths fit together as nicely as the parts in your Daddy's solar watch. We call these places chrono-synclastic infundibula.*

. . .

*Chrono (KROH-no) means time. Synclastic (sin-CLASS-tick) means curved toward the same side in all directions, like the skin of an orange. Infundibulum (in-fun-DIB-u-lum) is what the ancient Romans like Julius Caesar and Nero called a funnel. If you don't know what a funnel is, get Mommy to show you one.*

—Kurt Vonnegut Jr.

From The Sirens of Titan, © copyright 1988
by Kurt Vonnegut
Used by permission of Dell Publishing,
a division of Random House, Inc.

# CONTENTS

# PREFACE

## ABOUT METADATA

Twenty years ago, when I started working as a consultant with the Oracle Corporation, I learned a particular style of data modeling. I had done database design for many years before that, and often illustrated my designs with drawings. The particular flavor of modeling I learned at Oracle, however, was very different. For the first time, I was modeling the structure—the language—of a company, not just the structure of a database. How does the organization understand itself and how can I represent that so that we can discuss the information requirements?

Thanks to this approach, I was able to go into a company in an industry about which I had little or no previous knowledge and, very quickly, understand the underlying nature and issues of the organization—often better than most of the people who worked there. Part of that has been thanks to the types of questions data modeling forces me to ask and answer. More than that, I quickly discovered common patterns that apply to all industries.

It soon became clear to me that what was important in doing my work efficiently was not conventions about *syntax* (notation) but rather conventions about *semantics* (meaning). This was the source of my first book, *Data Model Patterns: Conventions of Thought*. I had discovered that nearly all commercial and governmental organizations—in nearly all industries—shared certain semantic structures, and understanding those structures made it very easy to understand quickly the semantics that were unique to each.

The one industry that has not been properly addressed in this regard, however, is our own—information technology. This is at least partly because the patterns that address most businesses are not as helpful to the understanding this one. Where a business model represents the semantics of a business, what we need are models that represent semantics itself. We need models of the models we use to describe the business. This is more difficult.

Our industry also has not been properly addressed for the same reason many companies do not have data models: we have not seen the need. Just as the idea of modeling an organization's data seems a little too arcane for many business people, so too the idea of modeling information technology data seems too strange for many of us. But the need is definitely there. Just as it is essential for an organization to better understand the underlying nature of its data (and through that the underlying nature of its own structure) if it is to acquire and use systems successfully to meet its customers' needs, so too is it essential for us to understand the underlying nature of our data (and through that the underlying nature of our industry's own structure) if we are to be successful in producing information systems products for our customers.

As you will see, some of the semantic patterns are in fact the same for information technology as they are for any other industry. Most notably, people and organizations are components of the information technology world, just as they are at the heart of any business. Similarly, locating programs and data in the information technology world is not that different from locating products and customers in the business world. Beyond these topics, however, the model in this book is very different from a typical commercial model. Whereas a business is concerned with modeling products and processes, our model is concerned with modeling the *concepts for describing* a product or process.

Aristotle called his work "Meta" physics, simply because it was the one he wrote after writing the one on physics, the word *meta* being Greek for "after". This book could also be about a "meta" model simply because I am creating it after years of creating business models. But it is more than that. Because of the strange nature of Aristotle's metaphysics, the word *meta* came to mean "above" or "beyond". Because of the strange nature of this model, I am sure no one will argue against applying the word in this more cosmic sense.

## ABOUT THIS BOOK

The "data" in *metadata* means that this description of our industry will be expressed as a data model. The concepts are presented here using semantic data constructs. But data are not the sole *subject* of this model. The book is intended to be more *comprehensive* than prior efforts, in that it will cover more facets of our industry. Because this is a comprehensive view of metadata, a comprehensive view of the world is required. The book describes not just the structure of data modeling but also models of activities, people and organizations, locations, events and timing, and motivation.

Yes, those of you familiar with John Zachman's Framework for Enterprise Architecture will recognize these topics. They are the what, how, who, where, when, and why columns in his approach to understanding the body of knowledge that is the information systems development world. These columns indeed form the basis for chapters in the book.

While the model is intended to be comprehensive, by the way, I am acutely aware that it probably is not comprehensive enough. First, not all rows are covered. To model the builder's world (the fifth row) requires a model of every different programming language, brand of relational database, and new tool for addressing business rules and other areas. Those models alone would require several books this size. It seems reasonable, therefore, to start "small".

Second, as suggested by the title of the book, these really are just patterns for modeling metadata. This is not a comprehensive design for a "metadata repository". Rather, this model is an attempt to identify the most fundamental and widely applicable concepts that must be present in such a repository. I am acutely aware of the fact that if you are building a repository in a particular environment you will need more specific details in many areas. My only hope is that this model will make it clear where to add those details.

In addition to addressing the columns in John Zachman's Architecture Framework, this book addresses the different points of view taken by various people in the systems development process: the CEOs, the people who run the business, the information architects, the designers, the builders, and the users of systems. By addressing the different perspectives described in the framework, this book should be more *comprehensible* than previous efforts, as well. It describes metadata as seen by business owners, system architects, and designers—in their terms.

Because each row of the Architecture Framework described here represents a particular perspective, and the part of the model describing that row is presented in terms of language appropriate to that perspective, both business metadata and technical metadata are included. Each is intended to be readable and understandable by its intended audience. Moreover, the model is presented one small piece at a time to ensure that the structures described can be understood by any educated—even if not technologically savvy—reader.

The subject of the book is a single *conceptual data model* (an *entity-relationship model*) of the metadata that control systems development and management. It is a conceptual data model in that it is a unified description of the business we are in, not of a specific database design. Indeed, it is not the design of a metadata repository at all, although it does describe what should be in such a repository, and any designer would be well advised to understand it thoroughly before taking on such a design. It is fundamentally an architect's model.

This book itself uses a particular vocabulary (as close to educated English as possible) to describe the concepts contained here. One of the things described, however, is itself the idea of vocabulary. This means that the models used are themselves examples of what is being described. (For those who, in spite of your author's best efforts, do not find the meaning of the models intuitively obvious, all the entity classes and attributes presented are defined both in the text and in the glossary at the back of the book.)

When a company develops a data model of its operations, the model is a useful product for the development of a new database. The effort of producing the model itself, however, often reveals to the people involved profound insights into the nature of their business. These insights often represent a direct benefit to the enterprise, over and above any improved systems obtained from the model. It gives them the opportunity to understand the *implications* of what they do for a living—on their systems, their colleagues, and on the business as a whole.

So, what you have here is a model of the principal concepts behind what we do when we try to improve the information management of an organization. The interesting thing is that once we understand these concepts the major controversies that have plagued our industry for the last couple of decades (such as object-oriented versus relational, the entity-relationship diagram versus the UML class model, and so forth) become less heated. It turns out that there is no real disagreement about the merit of any particular technological change, but only on the perspectives of the contenders. Understand these differences of perspective, and the arguments disappear.

What the model in this book shows is just what such technological changes mean. Does this new tool change the way we write programs? Does it change the way we construct (or carry out) processes? Does it change how we analyze requirements? Correctly placing the technology in the framework goes a long way toward understanding its significance—and, indeed, increases our ability to implement it effectively.

For example, UML has been trumpeted as a great innovation in modeling. It is true that it is more expressive in some areas than has been seen before. But it is important to understand what is really new about it and what is simply a new notation for things that can also be represented in other ways. The models in this book should make this distinction clear.

This book is intended for the data management community—data administrators, database administrators, data modelers, and the like. But it should also be useful to system developers, helping them to more readily understand both the meaning of what they are doing and where that fits into the larger scheme of things. It should also be useful in an academic setting for teaching any and all of these people. This may be asking a lot, but it would be valuable also if information technology managers at least understood the broad strokes of these models, again to ensure that they understand the context of what they are doing.

The model in these pages attempts to show the information processing world from many different perspectives. With luck, perhaps we actually have a chrono-synclastic infundibula.

## ACKNOWLEDGMENTS

I must begin by expressing my thanks to Allan Kolber, who not only encouraged me throughout this effort but provided invaluable insights into the Zachman Framework, and in particular into the real meaning of the Business Owner's View. I still reserve the right to disagree with him on specifics, but his insights have been vital to this book.

And of course thanks go to my Business Rules Group colleagues who provided a wonderful place for the incubation of ideas on business rules and the Architecture Framework. Their movement to become collaborators in the Business Rules Team has been a significant step forward, and I appreciate the publication of the "Semantics of Business Vocabulary and Business Rules". I sincerely hope that this book can be a proper complement to that work. In particular, Cheryl Estep has spent many hours helping clarify where my work has diverged from the Business Rule Team's efforts.

Please note that I have borrowed extensively from early drafts of the BRT work. While I want to give them credit for members' contributions, any errors of interpretation or divergence from the eventual final draft are entirely my responsibility.

Thanks must also go to Bob Seiner for publishing *The Data Administration Newsletter* (*www.tdan.com*) faithfully for all these years. In addition to providing the world with a wonderful source of knowledge about all things data administration, it provided me with a wonderful vehicle for exploring the ideas that ultimately resulted in this book.

Thanks to Meiler Page-Jones for writing the best book I have found about object-oriented design [Page-Jones 2000]. It was clear enough to form the basis for my model of object orientation.

From ANSI to John Zachman, I am always indebted to all the authors in my bibliography (and others) who have formed the intellectual basis for anything I may have done here.

I am fortunate to have been able to present this model to various organizations. I want to thank The Texas Modeling and User Group in particular, and specifically Lee Leclair for his insightful comments. Also my thanks to the Information Resource Management Association of Canada for their hospitality; especially the comments of Dorothy Russel, Kerel Vitrofsky, and Deborah Henderson were most helpful. Comments from the Boston and Rochester DAMA chapters are also appreciated. The people attending the Metadata 2005 Conference in London were also helpful in showing me some remaining errors in the model.

None of this would have been possible without the help of Diane Cerra, my advocate at Morgan Kaufmann, and Marilyn E. Rash, the project manager/editor who put it all together. In addition, the quality of the book was immeasurably improved by the suggestions from all the people who graciously gave of their time to review the contents of the manuscript: James Bean, Charles Betz, Malcolm Chisolm, Michael Eulenberg, Dagna Gaythorpe, Terry Halpin, Mike Lynott, Dave McComb, Ken Orr, and Graeme Simseon.

And of course, as always, thanks to my wife, Jola, and to Pamela and Bob, for being there.

# FOREWORD

Marcel Proust wrote that the real voyage of discovery lay not in finding new landscapes, but in having new eyes. In the information systems field, parts of the landscape change so rapidly that we can easily overlook the value that can be found in fresh perspectives. This is particularly true of systems specification, where advances have more often come from new ideas than from new technologies.

Systems specification is traditionally discussed in terms of its processes. Neophytes are taught the stages and tasks; debate centers on the merits of the different methodologies. Yet information systems professionals learned a long time ago that although process analysis might be the most obvious approach to understanding a business, it is not the only one. Looking at data—the *what* rather than the *how*—not only complements the process perspective, but also arguably results in a deeper, more concise and more stable description. Data modelers regularly achieve insights that process modelers miss.

In this book, Dave Hay brings the perspective of an expert data modeler to the business of systems specification. His starting point is the Zachman Framework for Enterprise Architecture, which itself owes its longevity at least in part to a focus on artifacts rather than activities.

This book begins with some insightful and practical adjustments to the Framework. It is hardly surprising that after some twenty years, reflective users should have some suggestions for improvement, and it would be disappointing if purists saw these changes as anything other than a confirmation of the Framework's continuing relevance and adaptability. Dave then sets out, in considerable detail, the structure of the information used in each of the relevant cells. In keeping with his philosophy of data modeling, he seeks to describe rather than prescribe, to illuminate established approaches rather than proposing his own.

The result is a comprehensive picture of what constitutes an information systems specification, from business requirements to logical design. Dave calls it "an enterprise data model of the IT industry"—a description of the data that systems professionals need to do their jobs. Whatever methodology we use, and regardless of whether we document the data or convey it informally, these are the things we need to know. For users of the Zachman Framework, the information here provides a clear "next level down". For information systems practitioners, students, and academics in general, it offers a perspective likely to be of continuing value even as methods and technologies change.

The language of the book is data modeling—and this is one of its particular strengths. The use of data models, rather a reliance on text and examples, provides a level of completeness and rigor missing in much of the other works in the field. Dave's background as a working data modeler is evident in the content and presentation of the models, and in the examples he uses to illustrate them. Readers of his earlier books on data model patterns and systems specification will know that he brings to the task a unique combination of subject matter knowledge and data modeling expertise.

Read this book, therefore, not only to gain a "new eye" on information systems specification, but also to see how an expert modeler uses the language of data modeling to represent and communicate a complex and important domain.

Graeme Simsion
*Simsion & Associates and the*
*University of Melbourne*

# ABOUT METADATA MODELS

*There once was a fellow named Corey*
*Whose career was not covered in glory*
*He had a bad day*
*When he just couldn't say*
*Me-ta-da-ta Re-pos-i-TOR-y.*

## WHAT ARE METADATA?*

During the 1990s, the concept of *data warehouse*\*\* swept the information technology industry. After many years of trying, it appears finally to be possible for a company to store all of its data in one place for purposes of reporting and analysis. The technology for doing this is still new, and the first attempts have had mixed results, but the effort has been quite serious.

One of the problems that arose from this effort was the realization that if a senior executive is going to ask a giant database a question it is necessary to know just what is in the database and what types of questions to ask. In addition to the data themselves, therefore, it is necessary to keep data about the data. The term coined for "data about data" during the 1990s was *metadata*.

Since then, numerous books and magazine articles have been published on this subject, but most have focused on why metadata are important and on technologies and techniques for managing them. What these publications have left out is a clear

---

\*Ok, it's true. I studied Latin in high school and have always held that *data* is the plural form of the word *datum*. I realize that I may be swimming against the current, but, hey! It's my book!

\*\*Key words and phrases, shown in bold italic font, are defined in the glossary at the back of the book.

description of exactly *what* the stuff is. After a decade, there is still no simple, clear description of metadata in a form that is both comprehensive enough to cover our industry and comprehensible enough that it can be used by people. This book is an attempt to produce such a description.

As with all buzzwords, once invented the term metadata has taken on a life of its own. It is variously described as:

- *Any data about the organization's data resource* [Brackett 2000, p. 149].
- *All physical data and knowledge from inside and outside an organization, including information about the physical data, technical and business processes, rules and constraints of the data, and structures of the data used by a corporation* [Marco 2000, p. 5].
- *The detailed description of instance data. The format and characteristics of populated instance data: instances and values, dependent on the role of the metadata recipient* [Tannenbaum 2002, p. 93].

Several significant points come out of these definitions. First, as Mr. Marco pointed out there is a difference between *business metadata* and *technical metadata*. The business user of metadata is interested in definitions and structures of the language as terms for the types of information to be retrieved. The technician is concerned with the physical technologies used to store and manage data. Both of these points of view are important, and both must be addressed.

Second, the subject is concerned with more than just data. It is, as Mr. Brackett said, "*any* data about an organization's data resource." Once you have started looking at the structure of an organization's data, you have to also account for its activities, people and organizations, locations, timing and events, and motivation.

Third, as Ms. Tannenbaum pointed out, the "meta" aspect of the question is a matter of point of view. There is metadata relative to the data collected by the business. There is also *meta-metadata*, which is used to understand and manage the metadata.*

---

*While delivering a lecture on cosmology one day, Sir Arthur Eddington gave a brief overview of the early theories of the universe. Among others, he mentioned the American Indian belief that the world rested on the back of a giant turtle, adding that it was not a particularly useful model as it failed to explain what the turtle itself was resting on. Following the lecture, Eddington was approached by

| | | | | |
|---|---|---|---|---|
| **This Book (Meta-metadata)** | Elements of metadata (metadata model) | **Objects:** "Entity Class" "Attribute" | **Objects:** "Entity Class" "Attribute" "Role" | **Objects:** "Table" "Column" | **Objects:** "Program module" "Language" |
| **Data Management (Metadata)** | Data about a database (a data model) | **Entity class:** "Customer" **Attributes:** "Name" "Birthdate" | **Entity class:** "Branch" "Employee" **Attributes:** "Employee.Address" "Employee.Name" **Role:** "Each branch must be *managed by* exactly one Employee" | **Table:** "CHECKING_ ACCOUNT" **Columns:** "Account_number" "Monthly_charge" | **Program module:** ATM Controller **Language:** Java |
| **IT Operations (Instance Data)** | Data about real-world things (a database) | **Customer Name:** "Julia Roberts" **Customer Birthdate:** "10/28/67" | **Branch Address:** "111 Wall Street" **Branch Manager:** "Sam Sneed" | **CHECKING_ ACCOUNT. Account_number:** = "09743569" **CHECKING_ ACCOUNT. Montly_charge:** "$4.50" | **ATM Controller:** Java code |
| | Real-world things | Julia Roberts  | Wall Street branch  | Checking account #09743569  | ATM Withdrawal  |

*Fig. 1–1: Data and metadata.*

This last point is illustrated in Figure 1–1. Here, the bottom row shows examples of things in the world that are often described in information systems. "Julia Roberts" is a real human being. The "Wall Street branch" of a bank is a physical place were business is performed. Checking account "09743569" is a particular account held in that bank by a particular customer (Julia Roberts, for example). The customer of that account may then perform an actual "ATM Withdrawal" at a specific time.

The next row up shows, in the first three columns, the data that might describe those three things: (1) A Customer has the name "Julia Roberts" and the "Birthdate" of "10/28/67". (2) A Branch has the address "111 Wall Street" and a manager, "Sam Sneed". (3) The checking account has an account number "09743569" and a monthly charge, "$4.50". In the fourth column, the first row from the

an elderly lady. "You are very clever, young man, very clever," she forcefully declared, "but there is something you do not understand about Indian cosmology: it's turtles all the way down!"

bottom shows that a particular program, called here "Java code", is responsible for a "Withdrawal Transaction". These are the things that would concern a person managing data for a banking business. Note that each of the terms was described as to what it was: customer name, branch manager, account number, and so forth.

The third row from the bottom collects those descriptors and labels them in turn. This is to create what we in the data administration world call the *metadata*. There are two components to these labels. First are the names of the things of significance being described by the business data, such as the entity classes "Customer" and "Branch". Second, each of these is in turn described by attributes, such as "Name", "Address", and "Birthdate". We also discover, in the case of the bank branch, that there is really an additional entity class, "Manager", and that it is related to "Branch". ("Each Branch must be managed by exactly one Employee.")

In the checking account column, we see that a checking account is actually the subject of a table in a database. The table is called "CHECKING_ACCOUNT" and has columns "Account_number" and "Monthly_charge". The ATM program described in the second row simply as "Java code" is actually a program module with the name "ATM Controller" written in the language "Java". As we can see, the metadata row itself encompasses several different types of objects ("Entity class", "Attribute", "Table", "Column", "Program module", and "Language"). The assignment of this book, represented by the top row, is to show how these objects relate to one another.

Metadata don't just describe data. They describe how the organization understands not only its data, but also its activities, people and organizations, geography, timing, and motivation. Yes, metadata describe the entity classes and attributes of an entity-relationship model, and the tables and columns by which these are implemented in a computer system. They also provide, however, structure for describing the activities of the organization and the computerized processes that implement these activities. They describe who has access to data, and why. They describe the types of events and responses that are the nature of an organization's activities. They describe where the data and processes are, and they describe the motivation and business rules that drive the entire thing. So, from all of this comes the following definition of metadata.

Metadata *are the data that describe the structure and workings of an organization's use of information, and which describe the systems it uses to manage that information.*

One anomaly has revealed itself in the line between business data and metadata. The information about what constitutes a legal value for a product category or an account type in the business model is often captured in separate reference tables. To reflect these validation structures, a typical data model often has many "type" entity classes (ACCOUNT TYPE, STATUS, DAY OF THE WEEK, and so on) describing legal values for attributes. These are part of the business data model.

But because they are in fact constraints on the values of other attributes in the same data model, they are also included in the category of metadata. Where a table designer would be required to specify the domain of a column, the data modeler (who is instructing the designer) must now provide the values that constitute that domain. Here you have business data acting as metadata.

Be aware, of course, that even this line between business data and metadata is not as clear-cut as it seems. PRODUCT TYPE, for example, is about reference data that constrain many attributes in a business model. Even so, specification of the list of product types is very much the domain of the business, not the data administrator. This plays both the roles of business data and metadata. Probably more in the metadata manager's domain would be PRODUCT CATEGORY. There should be relatively fewer of these, and the list should be relatively stable.

## IN SEARCH OF METADATA

*Metadata repository* is a pretentious term for nothing other than a computerized database containing metadata to support the development, maintenance, and operations of a major portion of an enterprise's systems. Among other things, such a repository can be the foundation for a data warehouse.

The idea has been interpreted in many different ways over the past thirty years or so. The first metadata repositories were the *data dictionaries* and *copy libraries* that accompanied programs in the 1970s and 1980s. A data dictionary was simply a listing of the fields contained in a record of a particular type in the files of a traditional mainframe data processing application. *Sometimes* this was accompanied by definitions of the meanings of each file and field. A copy library is a file containing data definition sections to be used for more than one program (typically COBOL programs, but other languages used copy libraries as well). Specific programs would then make use of the copy library to get their data specifications. This was rarely accompanied by a definition of each term in the program code.

The IBM user group GUIDE addressed the issue of how to organize data dictionary and copy library data with white papers on a "Repository Data Model" in 1987 and 1989 [GUIDE 1987, 1989]. Since the 1980s, *computer-aided systems engineering (CASE)* tools have always captured descriptions of the structures they create and manage in an organization, and some CASE tool vendors have made available models of their own underlying data structures. (Typically these are models of data and activities as captured in data and function models and the documentation behind them) Even now, the business information gathered during requirements analysis is typically the first component of metadata captured in any development project.

Along the same lines, "encyclopedias" have been developed to support other types of tools such as *extraction, transfer, and load (ETL)* facilities. During the 1980s and early 1990s, IBM expended enormous effort toward developing a universal metadata management tool called Repository Manager MVS (RM/MVS). This tool was the centerpiece of the AD/Cycle tool activity that IBM developed as a part of the CASE movement. IBM worked with a number of CASE partners and other organizations in an attempt to build a universal, end-to-end metadata management schema for all of application development from planning through operations.

Various software vendors have attempted to improve communications between CASE tools, which has required them to model the internal structure of metadata. This structure is usually proprietary, however, and these vendors have not been motivated to publish their versions. In recent years, with the advent of the data warehouse movement, the literature about metadata repositories has proliferated. There is a plethora of books and magazine articles describing the importance of metadata and their significance to corporations operating in the twenty-first century.

Ms. Tannenbaum's and Messrs. Brackett's and Marco's original books (alluded to previously in this chapter) contain the definitions cited previously, and are currently the best available on the subject of metadata and their significance to modern commerce. But while they describe the importance and implications of metadata their descriptions of what should be in a metadata repository don't present a complete model.

Ms. Tannenbaum does present a list categorizing what should be included [Tannenbaum 2002], but she does not attempt to model these. In his 2000 book Mr. Marco presents a simple model, but even he concedes that this is only a starting point. His latest book [Marco and Jennings 2004] is a better version of a practical metamodel for a data warehouse design, but as such it misses much that could be included: it does not go far enough to address the underlying structure of our industry as a whole.

Several companies in the 1990s offered metadata repository products, each consisting of an empty database and tools for manipulating the metadata such a database could contain. These products, however, only described some of the required information—largely just table and column structures, along with the ability to keep track of the history of updates.

The Meta Data Coalition (MDC) attempted to develop a more comprehensive model of metadata, and in 1999 published its model, the Object Information Model. It was extremely convoluted and abstract, however, and very difficult to understand. The MDC has since been absorbed into the Object Management Group (OMG), and the combined organization has now published the *Common Warehouse Metamodel (CWM)* and the *Meta Object Facility (MOF)*. These are described by John Poole and his colleagues in *Common Warehouse Metamodel* [Poole et al. 2002]. A more detailed description can be found on the OMG's web site at *http://www.omg.org/cwm/*.

The CWM is intended to be a model of business metadata, whereas the MOF is intended to be a meta-metadata model of metadata themselves. Although much better than the MDC model, both models suffer from being developed in an object-oriented design environment and focusing on elements that are appropriate to defining an object-oriented design, not to displaying the concepts themselves to the public. Both have many abstractions that serve their design purposes but confuse the presentation of the core concepts. These models are not really accessible to those who just want to see how to represent concepts such as business rules, entity classes and relationships, or functional hierarchies. So where does all this leave us? What *should* we include in a metadata repository?

## THE ARCHITECTURE FRAMEWORK*

Because the model presented here is intended to represent the information management industry as a whole, an *Architecture Framework* is needed to organize

*This section is based on a similar description of the Architecture Framework in your author's book *Requirements Analysis: From Business Views to Architecture* [Hay 2003].

the body of knowledge concerned. The Architecture Framework used here is based on John Zachman's 1987 and 1992 Enterprise Architecture Framework [Zachman 1987; Sowa and Zachman 1992].

The *Zachman Framework* consists of a matrix in which the rows represent perspectives different people have on an information technology project and the columns represent what they are seeing from each perspective. The latter includes data, activities, motivation, and so forth. (The Architecture Framework used here is concerned with the same matrix, but differs slightly in its definition of rows from Mr. Zachman's version. Even so, the principal concepts are the same. This is further explored below.)

It turns out that everything we want to know about an information system is contained in one or more of the cells in this matrix, and the set of cells represents a very useful basis for organizing this book. Each part of the model presented here describes the content of one or more of these cells. After this introductory chapter, one chapter will address each column.

The Architecture Framework is diagrammed in Figure 1–2. The rows in the framework represent the perspectives of different actors in the system development process, and the columns represent the things viewed from each perspective. Although the concepts are the same, some of the names of rows are different from those used by Mr. Zachman in his original paper.

## The Rows

Each *row* in the Framework represents the perspective of one of the categories of players in the systems development process, whereas each column represents a different aspect of the process. The perspectives are:

- *Scope (Planner's View):* This defines the enterprise's direction and business purpose. This is necessary in order to establish the context for any system development effort. It includes definitions of the boundaries of system or other projects.
- *Model of the business (Business Owner's View):* This defines—in business terms—the nature of the business, including its structure, processes, organization, and so forth. There are usually multiple business owners' views of a given enterprise, and these may overlap or even contradict each other. These business owners' views may be classified into two groups.

| | Data (What) | Activities (How) | Locations (Where) | People (Who) | Time (When) | Motivation (Why) |
|---|---|---|---|---|---|---|
| Objectives/ Scope (Planner's View) | List of things important to the enterprise | List of functions the enterprise performs | List of enterprise locations | Organization approaches | Business master schedule | Business vision and mission |
| Enterprise Model (Business Owner's View) | Language, divergent data model | Business process model | Logistics network | Organization chart | State/ transition diagram | Business strategies, tactics, policies, rules |
| Model of Fundamental Concepts (Architect's View) | Convergent e/r model | Essential data flow diagram | Locations of roles | The viable system, use cases | Entity Life History | Business rule model |
| Technology Model (Designer's View) | Database design | System design, program structure | Hardware, software distribution | User interface, security design | Event processing | Business rule design |
| Detailed Representation (Builder's View) | Physical storage design | Detailed program design | Network architecture, protocols | Screens, security coding | Timing definitions | Rules specification program logic |
| Functioning System | *(Working System)* | | | | | |
| | Databases | Program inventory, logs | Communications facilities | Trained people | Business events | Enforced rules |

*Fig. 1–2: The Architecture Framework.*

    ◦ *Views of the tangible current nature of the business:* Most people in a business are concerned with the specific organization, computer systems, forms, and procedures required to carry out a business the way it exists now. This view of the world constitutes what the American National Standards Institute in 1975 called the "external schema" [ANSI 1975].

    ◦ *A single view of the underlying nature of the business:* Individual things seen by each business owner are usually examples of more general and fundamental things. This view is relatively abstract, although it is not yet structured to use as the basis for designing computer systems. This is the beginning of the "conceptual" schema (model) of the business [ANSI 1975].

       The essence of this row is its capture of the *semantics* of the organization. That is, this row is about the vocabulary of the business as seen by business owners.

- *Model of the fundamental concepts (Architect's View):* This perspective sees the underlying structures of Row Two rendered in a more disciplined fashion, completing the conceptual model of the business. This is still without reference to any particular technology.

  For example, business owners' views of business rules encompass all constraints that might be imposed on a business, whereas the Architect's View is only of constraints that affect the updating of data or the processes of doing such updating. A Business Owner's View of data can include many-to-many relationships, relationships among three or more entity classes (*n-ary relationships*), and *multi-valued attributes*.* The architect's perspective eliminates all of these.

  Mr. Zachman originally called Row Three the "Information Designer's View" because of its role in making the structures suitable for automation. The word *designer*, however, has the connotation of applying technology to the solution of a problem, even though this row really simply represents the final stage in describing the enterprise as rigorously as possible. It is the architect of a building project who describes its structure with emphasis on design as opposed to the technology. For this reason, it seems more appropriate to call this the "Architect's View."

---

*Multi-valued attributes are those that can take on more than one value for a row, such as using Address as an attribute when it can have more than one value for a person.

- *Technology model (Designer's View):* This describes how technology may be used to address the information-processing needs identified in the rows described above. Here, object-oriented databases are chosen over relational ones (or vice versa), types of programming languages are selected (third- or fourth-generation, object-oriented, and so on), program structures are defined, user interfaces are specified, and so forth.

    The previous three views are views of the business. This is the first view that is of information technology.

    The ANSI view of data called this the "internal" schema [ANSI 1978], but in later years this has taken on the name "physical model." Indeed, even Mr. Zachman calls this perspective "the Builder's View." This is unfortunate, in that it is the next row that seems more appropriately the domain of the "builder" and all things "physical." This fourth row is about the *design* of new artifacts, not their *construction*.

- *Detailed representations (Builder's View):* The builder sees the details of a particular language, database storage specifications, networks, and so forth.

    Mr. Zachman called this the "subcontractor's view".

- *Functioning system (Inventory View):* Finally, a new view is presented to the organization in the form of a new system. This is the view of actual computer systems installed in particular places, along with their databases. A single system design from Row Four may be implemented in numerous functioning systems.

## The Columns

Each *column* in the Architecture Framework represents an area of interest for each perspective. The columns describe the dimensions of the systems development effort. These are:

- *Data:* Each of the rows in this column addresses understanding and dealing with the things of significance to an enterprise, about which information is to be held. In Row One, this is about the most significant objects treated by the enterprise. In Row Two, it is about the language used—terms, facts, and definitions—and in Row Three it is about specifically defined entity classes and their relationships to each other. Row Four concerns the representation of data by computer software and database management systems. This may be in terms of tables and columns, object classes, or the artifacts of any other system development approach. In Row Five, this is about the way data are physically stored on the computer with a particular data management technology. This row is described in terms of table spaces, disk drive cylinders, and so forth. Row Six is about the physical inventory of databases.

- *Activities:* The rows in the second column are concerned with what the enterprise does to support itself. In Row One, these are the overall functions of the business. In Row Two, these are the physical processes used to carry out those functions. In Row Three, they are the essential activities underlying the Row Two processes. Row Four concerns the workings of programs, and the Row Five perspective is of the specifics of programming languages. Row Six is about the physical inventory of program code.

- *Locations:* This column is concerned with the geographical distribution of the enterprise's operations and how its elements communicate with one another. In Row One, it is concerned with the parts of the world where the enterprise operates. In Row Two, it is concerned specifically with the enterprise's various offices and how they are related to each other. In Row Three, it is concerned with the roles played in each location, and how they communicate with those in other locations. Row Four is about the design of computer networks and communications, whereas Row Five is about the protocols and particular components of a communications network. Row Six is about the physical components and locations of each node in the networks, and the communications facilities that link them.

- *People:* This column describes who is involved in the business and in the introduction and management of technology. Row One addresses the enterprise's attitudes and philosophy concerning the management of human resources. Row Two is concerned specifically with people's responsibilities for the Row Two artifacts of language, processes, and the like. Row Three addresses stewardship for definitions and architecture. Row Four is concerned with the design of man/machine interfaces, including issues of security and access, whereas Row Five (in conjunction with the activities column) is concerned with the programming of those interfaces. Row Six is about the trained people interacting with systems in a secure and effective environment.

- *Time:* This column describes the effects of time on the enterprise. This includes annual planning at Row One, business events at Row Two, and data-related events at Row Three. Row Four translates the data-related events into system triggers. Row Five is concerned with the implementation of those triggers. Row Six is about keeping track of actual events.

- *Motivation:* As Mr. Zachman originally described this column, it concerned the translation of business goals and strategies into specific ends and means. This has since been expanded to include the entire set of constraints (business rules) that apply to an enterprise's efforts, because it is these constraints that often determine why people do what they do. Row One is concerned with the enterprise's vision and mission. Row Two addresses its goals, objectives, strategy, and tactics, as they are translated into business policies and business rules. Row Three addresses the specific articulation of system constraints in terms of their effects on data. Row Four is about the design of the programs that will implement those effects (along with constraints applied to activities), and Row Five is about the construction of those programs. Row Six is the collection of programs (including database management systems) that implement the rules.

## METAMODELS AND THE FRAMEWORK

Each framework cell, then, contains a description of some aspect of an enterprise from a particular point of view. Typically, this description is rendered in the form of one or more models, although most of the Row One artifacts are simply lists. Descriptions of these descriptions (models or lists) are metadata. The model that is the subject of this book, then, is a model of these descriptions.

This book is organized by column, but the underlying model is organized by row. That is, each perspective yields a model that encompasses all framework cells (row/column intersections) in that row. In presenting a cell, concepts of the model will be introduced as "belonging" to that cell in that column, but it will almost always be shown in the context of concepts from cells in other columns in the same row.

Because of the overlap between columns, it will be a little tricky presenting them in sequence. In some cases, concepts will have to be introduced before introducing the column they apply to. Patience is required.

For the most part, there is not the same degree of overlap between rows. Most of the concepts are the domain of one perspective only. There are exceptions, however. First, the Data Column in Row Two is concerned with the idea of

BUSINESS CONCEPT. In Row Three, ENTITY CLASS and ATTRIBUTE are shown as subtypes (examples) of BUSINESS CONCEPT. There are a few other cases of inter-row overlap as well. More commonly though, in each column there are examples of entity classes simply linking concepts from different rows (such as ATTRIBUTE COLUMN MAPPING between the attributes described in Row Three and the columns of Row Four).

The model presented in this book is itself an artifact of the data column, where the "enterprise" involved is the set of people involved with the development, maintenance, and operation of information systems. It is a cross between an external Business Owner's View and the conceptual Architect's View. It is first an architect's conceptual model, in that it follows all of the data modeling disciplines of normalization and it is represented entirely in terms of binary relationships.* Among other things, this entails resolving many-to-many relationships. It is also a coherent, unified view—a single model of the entire range of metadata management elements.

The model also resembles a Business Owner's View, however, in that it is entirely in the language of the metadata manager and the system developer. It uses abstractions from these terms only rarely, and where abstraction is necessary the rationale (and result) is explained. This model provides a vocabulary for discussing metadata, and the terms of this vocabulary are defined both in the text and in the glossary at the back of the book.

This book's model sets out to describe metadata for all columns for Rows Two through Four of the Architecture Framework. That is, it presents diagrams of the portion of each column that reflects, in succession, the Business Owner's View, the Architect's View, and the Designer's View. In addition, it will cover Row Six (the Functioning System) of the Data, Activities, Location, and Motivation columns. To establish context, occasionally references will be made to models of other rows.

All of this should demonstrate that the cells of the framework are not tidy. In some cases the differences between rows are nothing other than the content of the models. In others, the metamodel of a column makes use of elements from other perspectives on the same column. In still other examples, a diagram may describe elements from more than one column. Specifically, the model is organized as outlined in the following sections.

---

*Binary relationships, in this context, are relationships between only two entity classes.

## Data

Data consists of the following:

- *Row Two* is concerned with the language of the business. It deals with concepts, facts, words, and symbols. This part of the model is derived from the seminal work by the Business Rules Team, in conjunction with the Object Management Group [OMG 2007].
- *Row Three* is about the entity-relationship model (the "conceptual" data model). That is, it is concerned with entity classes, attributes, and relationships that describe the things of significance to a business in rigorous terms. These are in fact sub-types of the concepts described in Row Two.
- *Row Four* describes the structure of data as used for a particular technology. In the first three rows, the nature of the business is being described, whereas in Row Four models are of design artifacts—relational database tables, object-oriented design classes, and so forth. The tables or classes in this row are fundamentally different from the entity classes that appear in Row Three.

  The technology chosen affects the metamodel on this row. The model of relational database design is different from the model of object-oriented classes. Note that the modeling notation UML was originally intended as a way to model object-oriented designs in Row Four. That some of the symbols in a UML class diagram can also be used to create a Row Three entity-relationship diagram does not change the fact that the meaning of a Row Three model is fundamentally different from that of a Row Four model.
- *Row Six* describes the actual instances of tables and columns that constitute a real database.

## Activities

Activities consist of the following:

- *Row Two* describes both the functions (in a function hierarchy) of a business (without regard to timing or mechanism) and the particular business processes (with mechanisms, participants, and timing) that carry out those functions.
- *Row Three* models essential system processes with sequence and timing, but without mechanisms. Most significantly, the *essential data flow diagram*

models the way data are passed from one process to another and the transformations performed by each process.

- *Row Four* describes computer processing according to the technique being employed. Here you will see references to program modules, their structures, and the data they use and produce.
- *Row Six* is about the inventory of actual program modules and the log of their runs.

## Locations

Locations consist of the following:

- *All rows:* This model makes use of the business model for geography, but links the relevant concepts there to concepts in the metamodel for each row of the framework. In the world of metadata we are concerned with where activities take place, where data are captured and catalogued, and so forth, just as in the business model we are concerned with where people live, facilities are located, and production takes place. Distinctions between rows have to do with the types of things in each location.

## People and Organizations

People and organizations consist of the following:

- *All rows:* Similarly, the model for people and organizations at a meta level makes extensive use of business-level concepts. In the repository, we want to record who is responsible for an entity class or program module, just as in the business we want to know who is responsible for a product or contract. Again, the only distinctions across levels are about what each person or organization is responsible for.

## Timing

Timing consists of the following:

- *Rows Two and Three* are both concerned with the *state-transition diagram*— showing the states an entity class (or business concept) can go through and the events that trigger those state changes. In Row Three we add references to an *entity life history*, and revisit the *essential data flow diagram*.

- *Row Four* has its own model, describing the triggers for program elements.

## Motivation

Motivation includes the following:

- *Rows One and Two* are the model of *motivation* in the running of a business. Row One describes the enterprise's *vision* and *mission*, while Row Two is concerned with *goals, objectives, strategies, tactics, business policies*, and *business rules*. Note that the business objectives may include business requirements for new systems.
- *Row Three* is the model of *constraints* on data, including domains. Business rules are translated into constraints on the values of attributes, the existence of relationships, and the existence of entity class occurrences. These constraints may in turn serve as the basis for system requirements.
- *Row Four* is the model of how program modules implement the system requirements defined for Row Three. This includes referential integrity and uniqueness constraints usually managed by a database management system, as well as other constraints that must be implemented by stored procedures and other programs.
- *Row Six* is about the enforcement of data quality procedures in real databases.

## THE NOTATION: OBJECT AND ENTITY CLASSES

The model of a metadata repository is a graphic representation of the structure of a body of data. As such, it may be represented by any of the techniques available for describing data structure. These include various forms of entity-relationship modeling, information engineering, UML, and so forth. Before getting into the details of the metamodel, it is worth exploring the issue of notation. Because the metadata being presented are in fact data, let's delve into the Data column of the Architecture Framework to explore the concepts behind a data model.

## Class Model (UML)

UML is becoming a popular notation for representing models of data.* In a UML class diagram, we can represent an *object class* as the definition of a business object—a thing of significance to an organization about which it wishes to capture information. The UML class diagram in Figure 1–3 shows an example of a model we might prepare to describe the sales business. The boxes ("Customer", "SalesOrder", "LineItem", and "ProductType") represent object classes; that is, things of significance to the business about which it wishes to hold information.

Within each object class box are listed *attributes*, describing the information to be captured about each object class. For example, "Customer" is described by "Name", "Shipping address", and "Billing address". For each occurrence of Customer, each attribute must have at least one value, but may have no more than one, as indicated by "[1..1]". Each of these is of data type "string", meaning that its value will be a piece of text. Note that both "Description" and "Unit cost" for the object class ProductType are shown with the designator "[0..1]", which means that an occurrence of ProductType can have no value for either of those two attributes, if appropriate.

Note that usually the object classes are related to each other in pairs, as indicated by the lines between them. A line connecting two boxes means that an occurrence of one object class is associated in some way to occurrences of another object class. The relationship names are intended to be read in each direction as, for example, "Each Customer may be *the buyer in* one or more SalesOrders", and "Each SalesOrder must be *from* one and only one Customer".

In this book, for clarity, a convention has been applied to relationship names that is not usually followed by practitioners of UML. Each role name is designed to be part of a structured sentence that exactly conveys the optionality and cardinality constraints.

```
Each

<object class name 1>

must be (if the first character next to the second entity class is "1")
(or)
```

---

*There are at least six different types of models in UML. The "class" diagram, representing data structure, is but one of them.

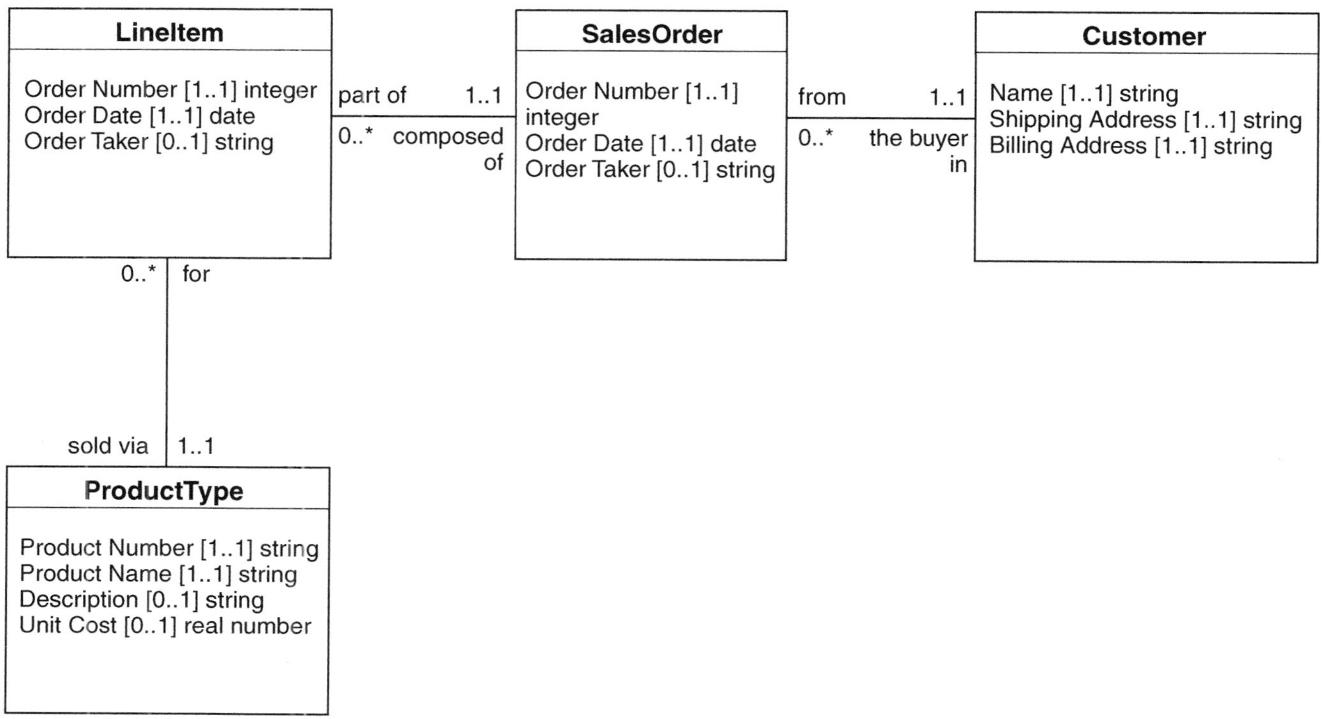

**LineItem**

Order Number [1..1] integer
Order Date [1..1] date
Order Taker [0..1] string

**SalesOrder**

Order Number [1..1] integer
Order Date [1..1] date
Order Taker [0..1] string

**Customer**

Name [1..1] string
Shipping Address [1..1] string
Billing Address [1..1] string

**ProductType**

Product Number [1..1] string
Product Name [1..1] string
Description [0..1] string
Unit Cost [0..1] real number

part of    1..1

0..*    composed
        of

from    1..1

0..*    the buyer
        in

0..*    for

sold via    1..1

*Fig. 1–3: A UML class diagram.*

```
may be (if the first character next to the second entity class is "0")

<role name>

one or more (if the second character next to the second entity class
            is "*")
(or)
one and only one (if the second character next to the second entity
                 class is "1")

<object class name 2>
```

For example, each role may be read as follows: "Each Customer may be *the buyer in* one or more SalesOrders", and "Each SalesOrder must be *from* one and only one Customer".*

With that introduction, let's begin modeling the language we will use to create the model of the language we will use. Figure 1–4 shows the beginning of an object model of object modeling.** In this model, ObjectClass is itself an example of an object class, as is Attribute.

An *attribute* is the definition of a piece of information *about* an object class. In a UML diagram, attributes are shown inside each of the object class boxes as text. Because ObjectClass is itself an object class in this model, it has

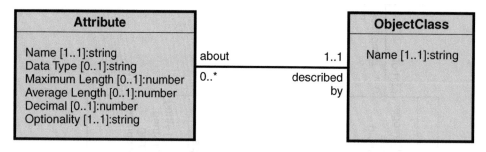

*Fig. 1–4: Object Classes.*

---

*Note that this book adopts the convention that the relationship names and multiplicity indicators ("[1..1]", "[0..*]", and so on) are to be read in a clockwise direction.

**Recursion (see *Recursion*).

attributes—well, one, at least (its "Name"). This is shown in Figure 1–4, along with the type of data the attribute can contain—in this case, "string". In addition, the "[1..1]" next to "Name" means that it is mandatory and that it can have no more than one value.* That is, for every occurrence of ObjectClass there must be exactly one value for "Name".

Because it is a thing we are interested in, "Attribute" is also an example of an object class on the diagram. Attribute also has attributes, which include its "Name", as well as its "Data Type", "Maximum Length", "Average Length", "number of Decimal places", and "Optionality". Again, "Name" is mandatory, as is "Optionality", but other attributes may have either zero or one value for each—they are optional. This is shown by the "[1..1]" next to the mandatory attributes and "[0..*]" next to the optional ones. Because we are building a conceptual business model in a relational environment, in practice each attribute is constrained to have no more than one value, indicated by the "[..1]" part of the annotation. UML does permit relaxing that constraint and allowing multiple values for each instance of an attribute, but your author does not.

If the model in Figure 1–4 were converted into a relational database design, you would have a table called ObjectClasses, and the occurrences would be shown (as in Table 1–1) with the names "ObjectClass" and "Attribute". You would also have a table called Attributes (as is also shown in Table 1–1). Columns of the table Attributes are "Name" (from the table ObjectClasses), "Name", "Data Type", "Maximum Length", and so forth.

*Table 1–1: Object classes and attributes.*

| Object Classes | | Attributes | | | |
|---|---|---|---|---|---|
| Name | Object Class (Name) | Name | Data Type | Max. Length | ... |
| ObjectClass | ObjectClass | Name | String | 15 | |
| Attribute | Attribute | Name | String | 15 | |
| | Attribute | Data Type | String | 10 | |
| | Attribute | Maximum Length | Number | 3 | |
| | Attribute | ... | | | |

*Because these are very common, the notations "0..*" and "1..1" are often abbreviated to "*" and "1", respectively.

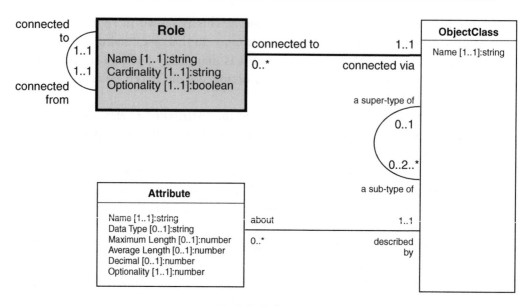

*Fig. 1–5: Roles.*

Object classes may be associated with each other. As we saw previously, an *association* is represented graphically in UML by means of an annotated line between the object classes.

Each half of the association (going in one direction) is a *role*. "Role" is then another object class in our metamodel, as shown in Figure 1–5. One attribute of Role is "Cardinality", which is the maximum number of occurrences of an associated class that may be related to an occurrence of the class playing the role. Another attribute is "Optionality", a binary variable determining whether or not an occurrence of the role must be present in the first place. Each role, of course, must have a "Name".

Optionality in the model drawing is represented by the first half of the symbols next to the box representing the object class playing the role. As we saw before, the character "1" in the initial position means that each occurrence of the opposite object class *must be* associated with at least one occurrence of the adjacent object class. Thus, the role is *mandatory*. (The Optionality attribute for the Role takes the value "False"). The character "0" means that each occurrence of the opposite object class *may be* associated with no occurrence of the adjacent object class.

That is, the role is *optional*. (The Optionality attribute for the Role takes the value "True"). Using the metamodel itself as an example, "each Role must be *connected to* one and only one ObjectClass", but "each ObjectClass may or may not be *connected via* one or more Roles".

Cardinality in the model drawing is represented by the second half of the symbols next to each object class box. The character "1" in the second position means that each occurrence of the opposite object class may be associated with *no more than one* occurrence of the adjacent object. (That is, the Cardinality attribute of the Role takes the value "1"). The character "*" means that each occurrence of the opposite object class may be associated with *one or more* occurrence of the adjacent object class. (The Cardinality attribute of the Role takes the value "*", or a particular number.) For example, in Figure 1–5 "each Role *must be connected to one and only one* ObjectClass", but "each ObjectClass *may be connected via one or more* Roles".

In the model, then (as we saw previously), each attribute must be associated with exactly one "[1..1]" occurrence of ObjectClass. Each ObjectClass may be associated with zero, one, or more "[0..*]" occurrences of Attribute. Similarly, each ObjectClass may be *connected via* one or more Roles, each of which must be *connected to* another Role, which in turn must be *connected to* the same or another ObjectClass.

The same symbols apply to attributes. As we saw previously, the "[1..1]" next to "Name" means that Name must have exactly one value for any occurrence of Attribute. The "[0..1]" next to "Data Type" means that an occurrence of Attribute may exist without a value for Data Type, but it can have no more than one value. Thus, Optionality is an attribute of Attribute, but Cardinality is not.*

A *sub-type* is an object class that contains some of the occurrences of a *super-type* object class. That is, the occurrences of a super-type may be categorized into two or more sub-types. For example, the object class "Person" might have as sub-types "MalePerson" and "FemalePerson". Figure 1–5, then, shows that each object class may be a *super-type of* two or more other object classes (zero, two,

---

*Because data modeling usually takes place in a relational environment, multi-valued attributes are not permitted. That is, an attribute may not have a cardinality of anything but 1, so there is no need for an explicit attribute "Cardinality" (the second part is always "..1"). UML does allow it, however, so the model could be made more complete by adding the attribute.

or more). Each object class, in turn, may be a *sub-type of* one and only one other object class (zero or one).*

## Entity-Relationship Model

So much for object classes and associations. Suppose you are one of those old-fashioned people who still models with entity classes and relationships. What does that model look like? Figure 1–6 shows an object model of entity-relationship modeling.

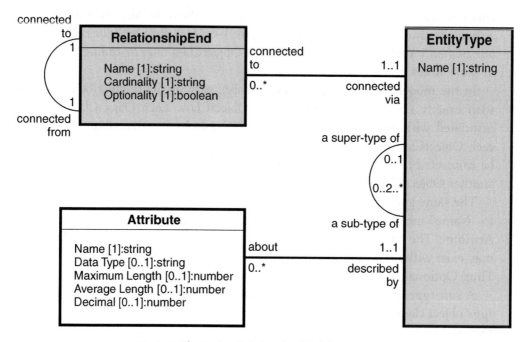

*Fig. 1–6: The Entity-Relationship Model version.*

*Yes, some would assert that an object class may be a sub-type of *more than one* other object class, but it is my contention that this adds unnecessary complexity and that it can be avoided by approaching the model from a different direction. It is therefore not used in this model. I of course cannot prevent you from making this relationship "many-to-many," should you want to. Be sure to add an intersect object class.

Specifically:

- Each EntityType may be *described by* one or more Attributes. (Each attribute must be *about* one and only one EntityType.)
- Each EntityType may be *connected via* one or more RelationshipEnds, where each RelationshipEnd must be *connected to* one and only one other Relation-shipEnd. This second RelationshipEnd, then, must be *connected to* another EntityType.
- Each EntityType may be *a super-type of* two or more other EntityTypes (Each EntityType may be *a sub-type of* one and only one other EntityType).

Funny thing about the metamodel of entities and relationships: with a couple of names changed, Figure 1–6 (a metamodel of entity types and relationship ends) looks just like Figure 1–5's metamodel of objects and roles. This is not a coincidence. They in fact represent the same things.

An object class model (at least as far as we have determined so far) *is* in fact an entity-relationship model. Both an entity type and an object class represent the definition of a kind of thing of significance to the business about which it wishes to hold information. The two models are enough alike that a UML repository model itself can be represented as an entity-relationship diagram.

Note, however, that UML class notation has other features not appropriate to a conceptual architect's model. It departs from entity-relationship modeling when it describes not business objects but system objects. It also has numerous symbols (not appropriate to entity-relationship modeling) that describe object-oriented design considerations. These include symbols for *composition*, *association navigation*, and so forth.

Figure 1–7 shows the entity-relationship diagram (ERD) that is a version of our model. It makes use of a notation from the Structured Systems Analysis and Design (SSADM) method [Eva 1994], sponsored by the British Government, and used widely in Europe. It is the entity-relationship notation used by the Oracle Corporation in its Designer CASE tool, and it is available in IKAW Corporation's CWD4ALL tool.

The entity class names have been changed in an attempt to bring the language of the object-oriented and entity-relationship worlds together. This has been done without loss of meaning. A "type" of entity can as easily be called a "class" of entity, and each end of a relationship does indeed describe one "relationship role".

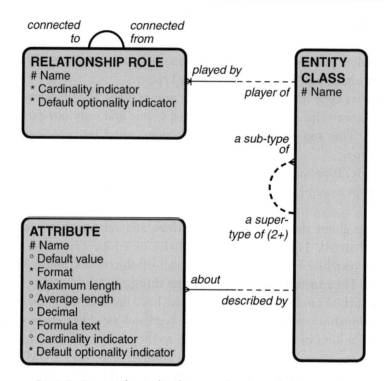

*Fig. 1–7: Entity-relationship diagram of entity and object classes.*

UML and entity-relationship *notations* are of course different. There are three main differences between the two approaches.

First and most obviously, the typography and the graphics (syntax) are different. The entity-relationship notation shown here has been chosen to improve the readability of the diagrams for nontechnical viewers. This is important if the models are to be presented to the user community for validation. For example, the world at large expects to see spaces between words in names.

Instead of the first character "0" in the relationship notation, you see a *dashed line half* adjacent to the first entity class. This means that the relationship is optional ("may be" in the previous association sentences). Instead of the first character "1", you see a *solid line half* adjacent to the first entity class. This represents a mandatory relationship ("must be" in the previous sentence examples).

Instead of the second character "*" you see a "crow's-foot" symbol for "one or more". Absence of a crow's-foot represents the second UML character "1" and stands for "one and only one". Entity class names are in all capitals, and spaces are inserted between words.

These differences have no affect whatsoever on the content (semantics) of the model. Consequently, the syntax for reading relationships in an entity-relationship diagram is now as follows.

```
Each

<entity class 1>

must be (if the line next to the first entity class is solid)
(or)
may be (if the line next to the first entity class is dashed)

<role>

one or more (if a "crow's-foot" appears next to the second entity
            class)
(or)
one and only one (if a "crow's-foot" does not appear next to the
                 second entity class)

<entity class 2>
```

So, using the metamodel as an example, each ENTITY CLASS may be *described by* one or more ATTRIBUTES and each ATTRIBUTE must be *about* one and only one ENTITY CLASS. Also, the model says that each ENTITY CLASS may be *connected via* one or more RELATIONSHIP ROLES and that each RELATIONSHIP ROLE must be *connected to* one and only one ENTITY CLASS. As before, each RELATIONSHIP ROLE must be *connected to* exactly one other RELATIONSHIP ROLE that must itself be *connected to* one and only one ENTITY CLASS.

A second difference between the entity-relationship notation and UML is in the information represented about each attribute. Because these models are for exposition only, and not the basis for design, it is not necessary to describe the data type for each attribute on the picture. To do so unnecessarily clutters the diagram.* (Of course, that information should be captured in the repository that supports the drawings.)

It is useful, however, to be able to see if values for an attribute are required, and thus next to each attribute name is still an "optionality" symbol. If the symbol is an asterisk (*) or an octothorpe (#), every occurrence of the entity class must have a value for the attribute (equivalent to 1.. in UML). If the symbol is an open circle (o), an occurrence of the entity class may or may not have a value for the attribute in question (equivalent to 0.. in UML). Again, because this is a normalized conceptual model—and in no case can an attribute have more than one value—there is no reason for ERD notation to show that the second half of the UML cardinality notation ("..1" and "..*").

The entity-relationship model is more expressive than the UML model in the area of identifiers. In object-oriented design, every object class is assumed to have an object identifier (OID) to identify occurrences of a class. Therefore, there is no requirement to explicitly designate attributes or roles as identifying. In the relational word supported by entity-relationship models, however, the identifier of an entity instance is very important, in that it is expected to consist explicitly of visible attributes or relationships.

Figure 1–7 shows an octothorpe (#) next to "Name" in each of the entity classes. This means that in each case the attribute is at least partially responsible for identifying instances of the entity class. For example, it is assumed here that every ENTITY CLASS will be given one unique name. In the case of RELATIONSHIP ROLE, however, it is possible that more than one RELATIONSHIP ROLE occurrence may have the same name. In this case, a mark is also made across the relationship to ENTITY CLASS to indicate that it is necessary to specify the ENTITY CLASS involved, (as well as its Name) to uniquely identify each occurrence of the RELATIONSHIP ROLE.

The one place where the entity-relationship model is not quite as expressive as a UML class diagram is in describing complex cardinality. The UML version can assert that "each ENTITY CLASS may be a super-type of *two or more* ENTITY CLASSES." The standard entity-relationship notation can say only that an ENTITY CLASS may be a super-type of *one or more* other ENTITIES. It cannot constrain the statement to *two* or more. For purposes of this model, however, our notation has been modified to show just that.

---

*It is noteworthy that different tools for producing UML class models show different types of information about each attribute.

Which notation to use has been the basis for extensive debates in the information technology industry over the years. Different notations have been developed to serve different purposes and different audiences. Where the UML class diagram is a notation for communicating with object-oriented developers, entity-relationship diagramming was specifically designed to support the discussion of concepts with business people untutored in data modeling. For this reason it is somewhat more accessible to the casual reader. Because the purpose of this book is to explain concepts, rather than to provide a schematic for building a system, this is the notation used here.

The UML class diagram, then, is not a grand new conceptualization of the system development process. The notation is simply another way of creating conceptual entity-relationship models. What is new is its ability to represent object-oriented designs.* In coming chapters, the various types of models available under the umbrella of UML, as well as the additional notations of the class model, are addressed in this metamodel.

## LEVEL OF ABSTRACTION

It is possible to model anything at varying degrees of abstraction. Anytime one tries to create a data model, the question arises as to how abstract to make it. Make it too abstract and it makes no sense to the people who want to understand it. Make it not abstract enough, and it is vulnerable to changes in the business. Achieving exactly the right balance is as much art as science.

Ultimately, the model of all metadata could be a variation on the one shown in Figure 1–8. Here, all things of interest in the model are represented simply as THING. Each THING must be *an example of* one and only one THING TYPE, where a THING TYPE is the definition of a class of THINGS.

Each THING may be related to another THING, as shown by the relationship that each THING may be *on one side of* one or more THING RELATIONSHIPS, each of which is *to* another THING. Similarly, each THING TYPE may be *on one side of* one or more THING TYPE RELATIONSHIPS, each of which is *to* another THING TYPE.

---

*For a more comprehensive comparison of many different notations for doing entity-relationship models, see Appendix B of David C. Hay's *Requirements Analysis: From Business Views to Architecture* [Hay 2003].

Each THING TYPE may be *the object of* one or more ATTRIBUTE ASSIGNMENTS *of* a ATTRIBUTE. That is, knowledge of the type of THING something is tells you what characteristics should be collected for it. The actual value *of* an ATTRIBUTE *for* a THING is shown in Figure 1–8 as ATTRIBUTE VALUE, which not surprisingly must be *of* an ATTRIBUTE and *for* a THING.

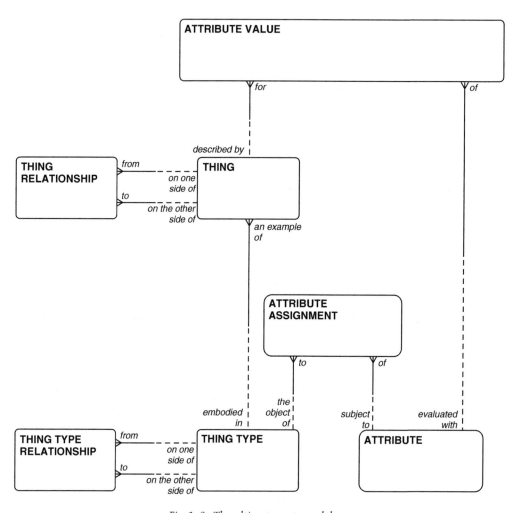

*Fig. 1–8: The ultimate metamodel.*

This model can actually describe *anything* we might want to include in our repository. In this case, it could represent entity classes, classes, program units, people, concepts, and the like.

The concrete models we know, then, could each be considered *views* of this more abstract model. For example, an ENTITY CLASS could be defined as "a THING that is *an example of* the THING TYPE 'entity class'." Another view could define ATTRIBUTE as "a THING which is *an example of* the THING TYPE 'attribute'." A THING TYPE RELATIONSHIP would be defined from THING TYPE "entity class" to THING TYPE "attribute" with the name "described by". Another THING TYPE RELATIONSHIP would be defined from THING TYPE "attribute" to THING TYPE "entity class" with the name "about".

Actually, the model in Figure 1–8 could made even more abstract by showing it as consisting only of THING and THING RELATIONSHIP. After all, the association of THING to THING TYPE is itself simply an association between two higher-level THINGS.

In effect, all entity classes contained in this book are but views of the entity classes in Figure 1–8.* It is perfectly reasonable, then, for a metadata repository to have a *physical* structure based on the abstract model of Figure 1–8. This allows the tool managing the repository to have the maximum flexibility in addressing future requirements. As a description of our metadata business, however, it does not tell us very much about what is really going on. When people go to a repository for information, they will want to use a vocabulary considerably richer than this. They will be seeking information about the definition of a *business term*, when a *program* has been run, or how *data* are constrained.

It is important, therefore, to present users of the repository with a set of views in a vocabulary more appropriate to their needs. For this reason, in this book we must produce a model that is not quite as abstract as that presented in Figure 1–8. In preparing this book, your author has worked hard to reach the right level of abstraction. It is for you, the reader, to determine whether he has been successful.

---

*But you don't have to know that in order for them to make sense.

# DATA

*The kinds of question we ask are as many as the kinds of things which we know. They are in fact four:*

*1. whether the connexion of an attribute with a thing is a fact,*
*2. what is the reason of the connexion,*
*3. whether a thing exists,*
*4. what is the nature of the thing.*

*Thus when our question concerns a complex of thing and attribute and we ask whether the thing is thus or otherwise qualified—whether, e.g., the sun suffers eclipse or not—then we are asking as to the fact of a connexion.*

—Aristotle [350 BCE]
Posterior Analytics

## Data and the Architecture Framework

The Data column of the architecture framework is concerned with *what* is significant to an organization from the six points of view.

- The *planner* looks at aggregate groups of major things of significance that are the domain of the business.
- The *business owner* is concerned with the nature of the business itself, in terms of the tangible things that constitute the organizational environment. Both the planner and the business owner are also responsible for defining the language used by the business. The metamodel for Row Two, then, is concerned with the concepts behind the business and facts that link them, along with the means of describing those concepts.

- The *architect* is concerned with the structural elements of the enterprise that will be the basis for automating it. The third row is the conceptual entity-relationship model that codifies the enterprise's language and gives it a rigorous structure suitable for use in information processing.
- The *designer* uses the architect's rigorous structure as the basis for defining how data management technology can be used to solve specific problems. Row Four is concerned with relational tables and columns, object-oriented classes, or other approaches for using a particular data manipulation technology.
- The *builder* defines places for data on a particular data storage medium.
- The *functioning system* consists of an inventory of physical databases.

Figure 2–1 shows the architecture framework, with the cells to be discussed in this chapter (for the Business Owner, the Architect, the Designer, and the Functioning System) highlighted.

## THE BUSINESS OWNER AND BUSINESS RULES

The Business Rules Group (formerly the GUIDE Project on Business Rules) published a paper in 1995 describing categories of business rules [Business Rules Group 1995]. The paper essentially addressed the Architect's View of business rules, concentrating on how to capture and organize them for eventual implementation in an information system.

Among other observations, that paper included recognition that a business rule at Row Three is best understood as a statement that defines or constrains *data* about an enterprise. To be sure, some rules are more appropriately described in terms of *events* and *activities*, but a preponderance of them are best expressed in terms of permissible states of data. The categories identified by the Business Rules Group paper are:

- *Terms (and the business concepts these terms describe):* The definition of a business term is itself a rule that describes how people think and talk about things. Thus, according to this view the definition of terms (that is, their underlying business concepts) establishes a category of business rule. For example, this can be a term used in a data model (such as *product type*) or one simply used in the business, such as *prestige client*.

| | Data (What) | Activities (How) | Locations (Where) | People (Who) | Time (When) | Motivation (Why) |
|---|---|---|---|---|---|---|
| **Objectives/ Scope** (Planner's View) | List of things important to the enterprise | List of functions the enterprise performs | List of enterprise locations | Organization approaches | Business master schedule | Business vision and mission |
| **Enterprise Model** (Business Owner's View) | Language, divergent data model | Business process model | Logistics network | Organization chart | State/ transition diagram | Business strategies, tactics, policies, rules |
| **Model of Fundamental Concepts** (Architect's View) | Convergent e/r model | Essential data flow diagram | Locations of roles | The viable system, use cases | Entity Life History | Business rule model |
| **Technology Model** (Designer's View) | Database design | System design, program structure | Hardware, software distribution | User interface, security design | Event processing | Business rule design |
| **Detailed Representation** (Builder's View) | Physical storage design | Detailed program design | Network architecture, protocols | Screens, security coding | Timing definitions | Rules specification program logic |
| **Functioning System** | _(Working System)_ | | | | | |
| | Databases | Program inventory, logs | Communications facilities | Trained people | Business events | Enforced rules |

_Fig. 2–1: The Data Column._

- *Facts:* These link terms. Both the nature and operational structure of an organization can be described in terms of the facts that relate the enterprise's terms to one another. To say that a customer can place an order, for example, is a fact; and is therefore a business rule. Facts can be documented as natural language sentences or as relationships, attributes, or generalization structures in a graphical model. For example, a fact may be expressed in a sentence, such as "Each product instance may be located in one or more sites."
- *Derivations:* These are business rules (including laws of nature) that define how knowledge in one form may be transformed into other knowledge, possibly in a different form. Calculations for product cost and profitability are examples of this category.
- *Constraints:* Every enterprise constrains behavior in some way, and this is closely related to constraints on what data may or may not be updated. These include business constraints such as those controlling to whom you will issue credit, and data constraints such as those on the values data elements can take [Business Rules Group 1995, p. 6].

In the Business Rules Group paper, terms and facts are called *structural assertions*, whereas constraints are called *action assertions*. Derivations are a separate category, although the results of derivations are *derived facts* (structural assertions). For the most part, structural assertions (terms and facts) are data-column artifacts—which can be represented in entity-relationship (or object) models—whereas action assertions (constraints) are motivation-column artifacts which for the most part cannot be represented in an entity-relationship model. Derived terms (attributes) are structural assertions that can be presented in a data model, although the logic of their derivations cannot.

Since publication of that original paper, the Business Rules Group has teamed with other organizations and the Object Management Group to form what they call the "Business Rules Team".* Their charge was to attempt to deal in more detail with the Data and Motivation columns not from the Architect's View (Row Three) but from the Business Owner's View (Row Two). They set out specifically with the practical objective of describing the characteristics of a language that could be

---

*The Business Rules Team now includes vendors as members, whereas the Business Rules Group did not.

used both to describe a business in business owners' terms and (using formal logic) to convey that meaning in a rigorous way to be useful to technology designers. From this work, they have come up with some significant insights into the role language plays in the manipulation of both business concepts and technology. The result of this effort was adopted as a standard by the Object Management Group in 2007 [OMG 2007].

One of the conclusions the group came to was that terms and facts are not, strictly speaking, business rules. First, it is the *business concepts* behind the terms that are important. Second, the definition of a set of facts (*fact types*, actually, but more on that later) is more useful for understanding the nature of an enterprise than the facts themselves. Neither of these, strictly speaking, are business rules. Instead, the Business Rules Team asserts that business rules (the former action assertions) are built on fact types, which in turn are built on the business concepts behind terms.

Another term for this first major category—structural assertion—is *universe of discourse*. This consists of the *business concepts* that are the meaning behind the terms and fact types, each of which is the definition of a category of facts.

Terms, concepts, and fact types are the domain of the Data column of the Business Owner's View at Row Two of the architecture framework. These will be described more rigorously in the following section. Row Two business rules (and the data and database management system constraints that follow from them) fall under the Motivation column, and are more fully explored in Chapter Seven.

## ROW TWO: BUSINESS TERMS, CONCEPTS, AND FACT TYPES

Examination of Row Two begins with a description of the concrete and tangible (albeit often narrow) world seen by each business user. This view describes specific occurrences of things (e.g., "the A-26 lathe"), and is often intertwined with current systems (e.g., "My job is to look at the Framis report and determine which items need maintenance"). The first step from here is to generalize these observations into structures that apply more widely. The generalized structure in the example, then, might be "Pieces of equipment" and "Determine maintenance requirements".

These structures are still unconstrained, however. The model here may include *many-to-many relationships*, *ternary (and higher-order) relationships*, *multi-valued attributes*, and other *normalization* issues. These constraints are added in Row Three models.

In the Data column, Row Two is primarily concerned with the *semantics* of an organization. Semantics is the branch of philosophy concerned with meaning [Kemerling 1997–2002a], and the assignment here is to determine what the business *means* when it uses certain language. Semantics has recently been explicitly recognized as an important field in the development of knowledge-based systems, and indeed, even when unrecognized as such, it has always been important in developing any system capable of working smoothly in an organization. When you discuss the way parts of an organization communicate with one another, you are discussing semantics.

## Terms and Concepts

Figure 2–2 shows that for our purposes a BUSINESS TERM is defined to be *the use of* a single WORD or PHRASE *to represent* a single BUSINESS CONCEPT.* A BUSINESS CONCEPT is simply something we understand to exist or to be the case. In this context, a BUSINESS CONCEPT is an aspect of an enterprise's operations or environment. It may be about something tangible or it may be an abstract idea generalized from particular instances. It is the set of BUSINESS CONCEPTS that give meaning to our language.

This may be something we data modelers characterize as an entity class (such as "Product"), an attribute of such a class (such as "color"), or an instance of a class (such as "IBM ThinkPad Model T24"). More significantly, however, it may also be something of importance to the business that is not necessarily included in our data model (such as "ICD 10", the medical world's catalogue of diseases, or *completion*—an oil industry term for the part of a well with holes in it, through which oil passes from the ground to the well).

A PHRASE may be *composed of* one or more WORDS. A WORD may be *a part in* one or more PHRASES. A WORD USAGE, then, is the use *of* one WORD *in* one PHRASE. Whereas in conventional language *term* is nearly equivalent to *word* or *phrase*, the

---

*As described previously, major parts of this section are inspired by the work of the Business Rules Team [BRT 2005]. The results shown here, however, are my own.

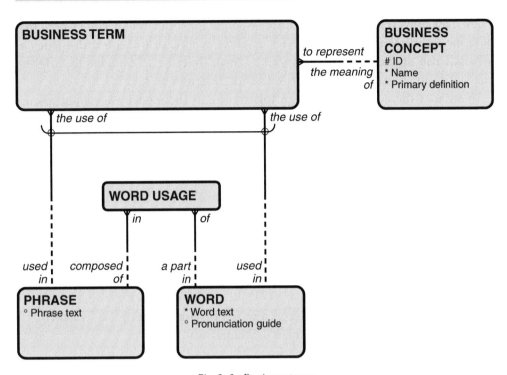

*Fig. 2–2: Business terms.*

constrained definition of BUSINESS TERM used here allows us to deal with the fact
that the same BUSINESS CONCEPT may be described by many different WORDS or
PHRASES (*synonyms*) and the same WORD or PHRASE may represent many BUSINESS
CONCEPTS (*homonyms*).

For example, *client, customer,* and *account* are often synonyms. Alternatively,
*facility* in an oil company is a large complex of equipment assembled to perform a
function, whereas *facility* in a bank is an internal agreement to extend a specified
amount of credit to a particular customer.* These are homonyms. Thus, it is very
useful to constrain a BUSINESS TERM to be the assignment of a single word or
phrase to just one meaning.

The BUSINESS TERMS we are concerned with here may be *the use of* any words
commonly used to describe the organization and its workings (such as *product*).

---

*And of course in the United States, the "facilities" in a restaurant mean something else altogether.

They may, however, also be the industry-specific (or company-specific) words that describe technical aspects of processes or other aspects of the enterprise (such as a bank's use of the word "instrument", which describes a completely different concept from an orchestra's use of the word "instrument").

Note that there is an anomaly in this model: in the model, we cannot discuss instances of BUSINESS CONCEPT without using words to do so. Hence, "Name" shows up as a perfectly reasonable attribute. In fact, however, no language can be used to refer to a BUSINESS CONCEPT that is not in terms of the WORDS and PHRASES that are *used in* the BUSINESS TERMS that are *to represent* the BUSINESS CONCEPT. Indeed, it is important to state that a BUSINESS CONCEPT has an existence independent of our ability to describe it.

> **Business Rule***
>
> At the very least, each BUSINESS CONCEPT must be *represented by* the BUSINESS TERM, which is *the use of* a WORD or PHRASE that is equivalent to the value of the BUSINESS CONCEPT's "Name" attribute.

Neither BUSINESS CONCEPTS nor the WORDS used to describe them exist in isolation. People must use them. In Figure 2–3, each BUSINESS CONCEPT must be *the shared understanding of* a SEMANTIC COMMUNITY. That is, concepts are only recognized if a group of people does so. A SEMANTIC COMMUNITY is the set of people who agree on the meaning of a set of BUSINESS CONCEPTS, such as oil well wranglers or data modelers.**

In Figure 2–4, a SPEECH COMMUNITY is defined as any group of people who are *part of* a SEMANTIC COMMUNITY and who are *speakers of* a particular LANGUAGE. At a general level, this could be "The population of the United Kingdom" or simply "English speakers", but it could also be as specific as a particular dialect.

---

*As should become evident in this book, business rules are very different things from what is normally displayed in a data model. This requires us to document them separately. The Metadata Model portrayed in this book has just as many business rules behind it as would be expected in any corporate model of comparable size. So, here, we add them to the text in this form.

**Well, some data modelers.

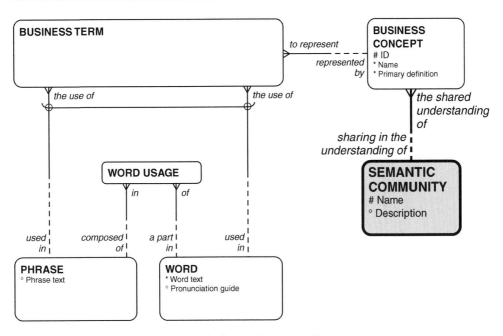

*Fig. 2–3: Semantic communities.*

Hence, a SPEECH COMMUNITY may be *composed of* one or more other SPEECH COMMUNITIES.

By definition, all members of a SPEECH COMMUNITY are *speakers of* the same LANGUAGE and *part of* the same SEMANTIC COMMUNITY. In Figure 2–4, each BUSINESS TERM is shown to be *in the language of* exactly one SPEECH COMMUNITY. Even if a WORD or PHRASE (such as "FORTRAN") exists in multiple languages (and therefore in multiple SPEECH COMMUNITIES), its use in each of these constitutes a separate BUSINESS TERM.

Similarly, each BUSINESS TERM is also shown in Figure 2–5 to be *in* exactly one SYMBOL CONTEXT, where a SYMBOL CONTEXT provides a scope for the BUSINESS TERM. For example, in a rental car company the word "site" means different things in the context of a rental than it does in the context of a repair.

To summarize, a BUSINESS TERM is the use of a single WORD or PHRASE in the language of a particular SPEECH COMMUNITY to represent a single BUSINESS CONCEPT in a particular SYMBOL CONTEXT.

As shown in Figure 2–6 (see page 44), in addition to a BUSINESS TERM's representing a BUSINESS CONCEPT, an ICON (which is *the use of* a GRAPHIC) can do this

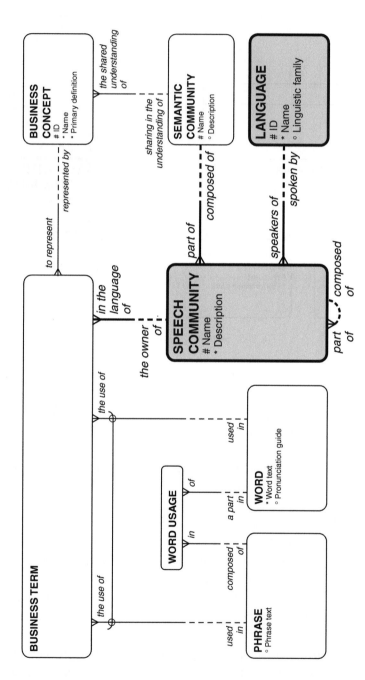

Fig. 2-4: Speech communities.

42

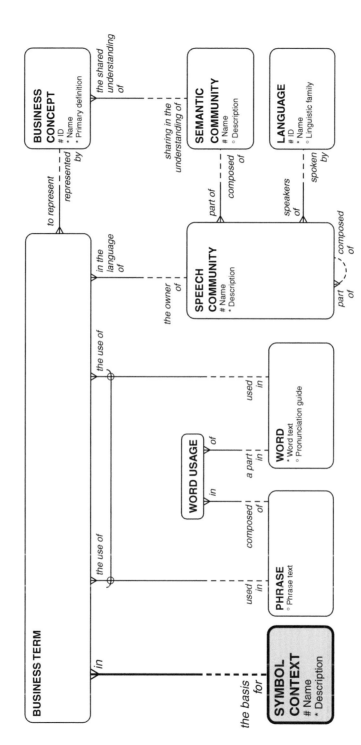

Fig. 2–5: Symbol contexts.

43

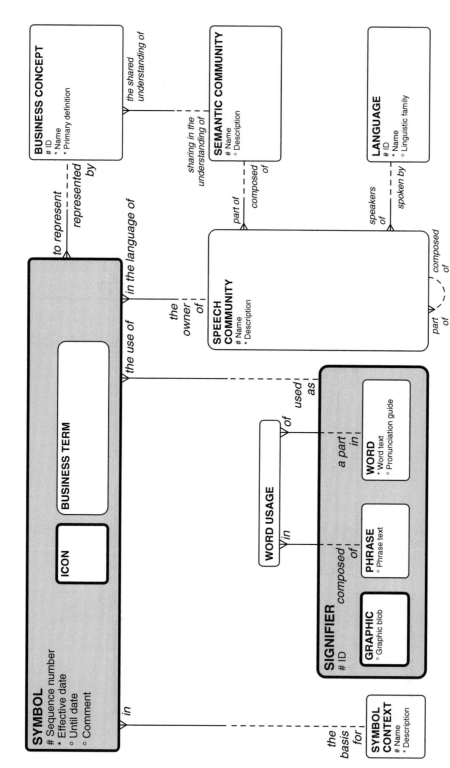

Fig. 2–6: Symbols and signifiers.

44

as well. BUSINESS TERM and ICON are shown in the figure as sub-types of SYMBOL. This means that the representation of a BUSINESS CONCEPT may be represented by an ICON as well as by a TERM.

Indeed, the entity class SIGNIFIER has been added to encompass GRAPHIC, WORD, and PHRASE. In other words, a SYMBOL is defined as *the use of* a SIGNIFIER *to represent* a BUSINESS CONCEPT *in* a SYMBOL CONTEXT and *in the language of* a SPEECH COMMUNITY. For example, the GRAPHIC ≻— can be *used for* the ICON "Crow's-foot", which (in the SYMBOL CONTEXT of "Information Engineering Entity-relationship Models") is *to represent* the BUSINESS CONCEPT with the *primary definition* "upper limit is more than 1".

### Business Rules

1. Each ICON must be *the use* (only) *of* one and only one GRAPHIC (not a WORD or PHRASE).
2. Each BUSINESS TERM must be *the use* (only) *of* one and only one WORD or PHRASE (not a GRAPHIC).

## Ontologies

A set of SYMBOLS constitutes a *vocabulary* for an organization or SEMANTIC COMMUNITY. Another word for vocabulary is *ontology*. This term is derived from the branch of philosophy concerned with identifying, in the most general terms, the kinds of things that actually *exist* [Kemerling 1997–2002b]. That is, an ontology is a representation of a body of knowledge. The assignment of a systems analyst is to compile an ontology that represents the semantics of the organization. What are the things that exist in that organization?

According to McComb [2004], ontology "is closely related to semantics, the primary distinction being that ontology concerns itself with the organization of knowledge once you know what it means. Semantics concerns itself directly with what something means." In Figure 2–7, each SYMBOL may be *subject to* one or more ONTOLOGICAL CLASSIFICATIONS, each of which must be *into* an ONTOLOGY. Each ONTOLOGY, in turn, must be *defined by* one SEMANTIC COMMUNITY.

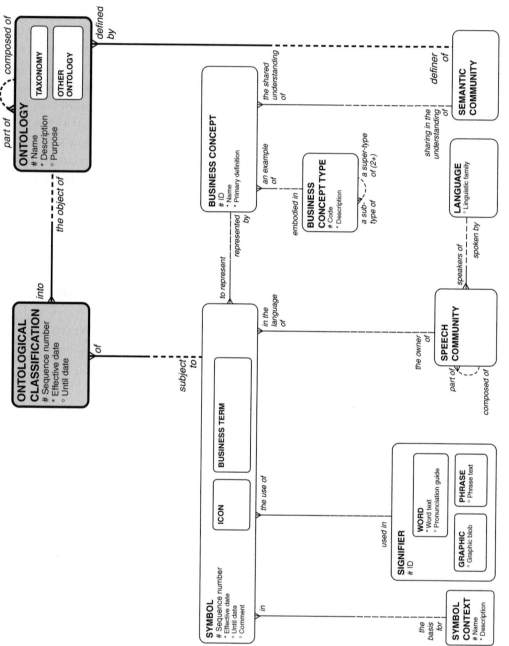

Fig. 2-7: Ontologies.

**Business Rule**

Any ONTOLOGY that is an ONTOLOGICAL CLASSIFICATION *of* a SYMBOL must be *defined by* the same SEMANTIC COMMUNITY that is *sharing in the understanding of* a BUSINESS CONCEPT *represented by* the SYMBOL. In other words, the SEMANTIC COMMUNITY that defines an ONTOLOGY must be the same SEMANTIC COMMUNITY that is the source of all the SYMBOLS in the ONTOLOGY.

The first assignment of any systems analyst is to reconcile the language of the different SEMANTIC COMMUNITIES within an organization. This is challenging, but it is aided by the fact that most industries have a basic vocabulary common to most companies in that industry. One thing the semantic approach in the information processing industry is beginning to do is to codify these industry vocabularies. Ontologies are beginning to appear on the World Wide Web in a form that allows them to be incorporated into company ontologies.*

Indeed, there is movement afoot to make ontologies a fundamental part of the Web. From the beginning, Tim Berners-Lee (the web's inventor) envisioned that eventually it would go beyond its original objective of being a *collaborative medium* to the objective of being a *semantic web*—understandable, and thus *processable*, by machines. That is, a semantic web is "a machine-processable web of smart data, [where] smart data is data that is application-independent, composeable, classified, and part of a larger information ecosystem (ontology)" [Daconta et al. 2003, p. 4]. The semantic Web is expected to do this by including ontologies to support techniques for searching not only the tags of documents but the text of documents themselves. A search for a topic would find not only documents explicitly identified as being on that topic but also those whose text referred to it.

A particular type of ontology is called *taxonomy*. This is a hierarchical organization of concepts. The most commonly known of these is biological classification of the structure of life itself. This is described in terms of phylum, family, genus, species, and so on. Unfortunately, many areas of interest in an enterprise do

---

*For example, for a geographic ontology see *http://www.getty.edu/research/conducting_research/ vocabularies/tgn/index.html*.

not lend themselves easily to a hierarchical representation, convenient though it may be.

## Propositions

A PROPOSITION is an assertion that may be true or false. PROPOSITIONS link concepts together. It is propositions that describe what a business does and how it does it.

Each PROPOSITION links BUSINESS CONCEPTS together. That is, each PROPOSITION must be *composed of* two or more PROPOSITION ELEMENTS, each of which must be *about* a BUSINESS CONCEPT. This is shown in Figure 2-8.

Also note that in Figure 2-8, each PROPOSITION must be *an example of* exactly one PROPOSITION TYPE, which is itself a kind of BUSINESS CONCEPT. And just as each PROPOSITION must be *composed of* two or more PROPOSITION ELEMENTS, so too must each PROPOSITION TYPE be *composed of* two or more PROPOSITION TYPE ELEMENTS. Since PROPOSITION TYPE is an example of a BUSINESS CONCEPT, it seems appropriate to identify a BUSINESS CONCEPT ELEMENT, that is a component in (*part of)* a BUSINESS CONCEPT. This is the super-type of PROPOSITION TYPE ELEMENT.

The truth of all PROPOSITIONS of a particular PROPOSITION TYPE may be

- *Deontic* – This is an assertion of obligation (something is required to be so), or permission (Something is permitted to be so). This is the realm of Business Rules.
- *Alethic* – This is an assertion of necessity (Something must be true), or possibility (Something is possible). This is the realm of physics.
- *Epistemological* – This is an assertion that something is known to be the case. Epistomological propositions are presented in a typical data model.

This is represented by the PROPOSITION TYPE attribute "Modal type".

An attribute of PROPOSITION ELEMENT is "Predicate" where a predicate is "something that is affirmed or denied of the subject in a proposition in logic" [Merriam-Webster 2005]. The PROPOSITION "The sun will rise tomorrow," consists of two PROPOSITION ELEMENTS. One connects to the BUSINESS CONCEPT "tomorrow" with the predicate "will rise". The other connects to the BUSINESS CONCEPT "The sun" with the predicate <subject>, signifying that "The sun" is the subject of the PROPOSITION.

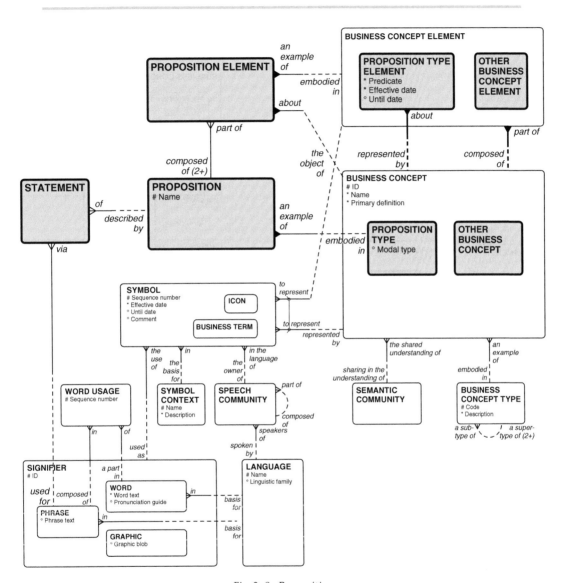

*Fig. 2–8: Propositions.*

## Fact Types

A FACT is a PROPOSITION that must always be true. Thus, the metamodel in Figure 2-9 shows that FACT is a kind of PROPOSITION. A FACT might be that

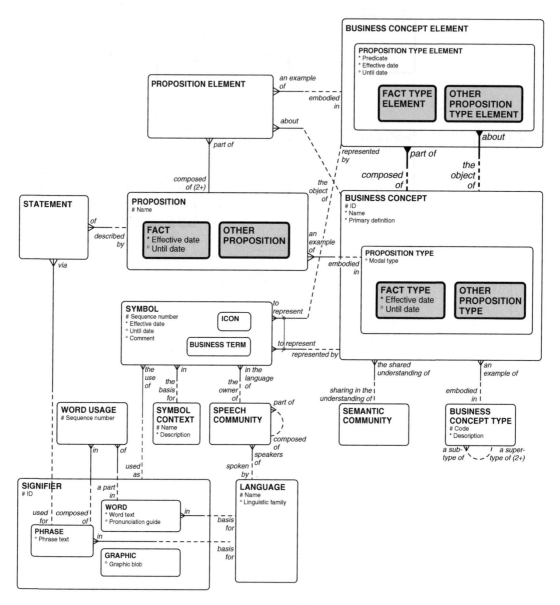

*Fig. 2–9: Facts.*

"Charlie was assigned to Project Z on January 14, 2005". This links together the BUSINESS CONCEPT "Charlie" with BUSINESS CONCEPTS "Project Z" and "January 14, 2005", using the predicates "was assigned to" and "was assigned on," respectively.

Each FACT must be *composed of* two or more PROPOSITION ELEMENTS, each *about* one BUSINESS CONCEPT.

A *fact type* is the definition of a set of similar kinds of facts. Each FACT TYPE must be *composed of* two or more FACT TYPE ELEMENTS, each *descriptive of* a BUSINESS CONCEPT. An attribute of FACT TYPE is "Predicate".

FACTS and FACT ELEMENTS might include:

– Order 359823-A was placed by MacDonalds..

> → Predicate: <subject>; Business concept: "Order 359823-A"
> → Predicate: "was placed by"; Business concept: "MacDonalds"

– Order 359823-A was placed on June 23, 2005.

> → Predicate: <subject>; Business concept: "Order 35923-A"
> → Predicate: "was placed on"; Business concept: "June 23, 2005""

– Product Type 33 is identified by part number "33"..

> → Predicate: <subject>; Business concept: "Product Type 33"
> → Predicate: "is identified by"; Business concept: "part number 33""

Instances of FACT TYPES might include such statements as:

– An "order" is *placed by* a "customer"..

> → Predicate: <subject>; Business concept: "order".
> → Predicate: *placed by;* Business concept: "customer"..

– "Order Date" is *an attribute of* ORDER.

> → Predicate: <attribute>; Business concept: "order date".
> → Predicate: *an attribute of*: Business concept: ORDER.

–  "Part number" is *an identifier of* PRODUCT TYPE.

   →  Predicate: <subject>; Business concept: "Part number".
   →  Predicate: *an identifier of*; Business concept: PRODUCT TYPE.

–  And so forth.

## Characteristics

One kind of FACT TYPE, as shown in Figure 2–10, is CHARACTERISTIC. A CHARAC-TERISTIC is something you can measure about one or more BUSINESS CONCEPTS. The fact that a particular CHARACTERISTIC is about a particular BUSINESS CONCEPT is shown on the model as a CHARACTERISTIC ASSIGNMENT, a kind of FACT TYPE ELEMENT.

The specification of an instance of a BUSINESS CONCEPT is in its use of a specified set of CHARACTERISTICS. "Amount of disk space", "Amount of memory", "Length", and "Width" are CHARACTERISTICS that could be applied to computers and other things. For example, a CHARACTERISTIC ASSIGNMENT might link the CHARACTERISTIC "Amount of random-access memory" to the OTHER BUSINESS CONCEPT "Laptop computer".

An example of CHARACTERISTIC and CHARACTERISTIC ASSIGNMENT was shown in the abstract model in Chapter One. There it was used to describe a THING TYPE, and to collect VALUES for THINGS.

Note the attributes of CHARACTERISTIC ASSIGNMENT "Essential indicator" and "Delimiting indicator". If Essential indicator is "True", this CHARACTERISTIC is required for instances of the BUSINESS CONCEPT that it is linked to via CHARACTER-ISTIC ASSIGNMENT. If Delimiting indicator is "True", values of this CHARACTERISTIC will distinguish one instance of the BUSINESS CONCEPT from another.

### Business Rule

The "Delimiting indicator" may not be set to "True" unless "Essential indicator" has been set to "True".

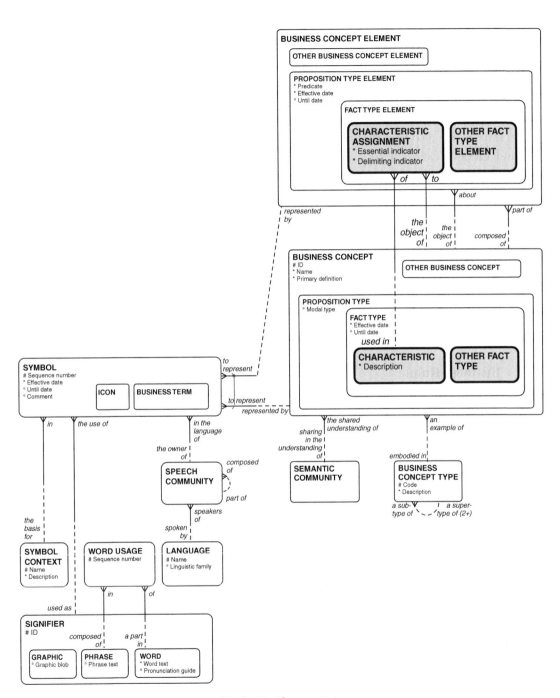

Fig. 2–10: Characteristics.

This reveals the problem of trying to include general concepts and specific concepts in the same model. It is true that CHARACTERISTIC is a kind of BUSINESS CONCEPT, and CHARACTERISTIC ASSIGNMENT is a kind of BUSINESS CONCEPT ELEMENT. It is also true that the relationship between CHARACTERISTIC ASSIGNMENT and CHARACTERISTIC ("of") is in effect a *sub-type* of the relationship between BUSINESS CONCEPT ELEMENT and BUSINESS CONCEPT ("*part of*").

Similarly, the relationship role "each CHARACTERISTIC ASSIGNMENT must be *to* one and only one BUSINESS CONCEPT" is a sub-type of "each PROPOSITION TYPE ELEMENT must be *about* one and only one BUSINESS CONCEPT". The problem is that the names of the relationships really should be different, but it is impossible to show both without appearing redundant. Both are shown here for the sake of clarity, and this is not the only place where this has come up.* As an alternative, the following business rule can be recorded if the redundant relationships are not shown.

> ### Business Rule
>
> Each BUSINESS CONCEPT ELEMENT that is a CHARACTERISTIC ASSIGNMENT must be *part of* one and only one BUSINESS CONCEPT that is a CHARACTERISTIC.

## Resources

Where does the information represented by these SYMBOLS (BUSINESS TERMS and ICONS) come from? Typically it is initially recorded on some sort of document: a specification, videotape, e-mail, and so on. Figure 2–11 shows RESOURCE to be *the source of* one or more SYMBOLS. A RESOURCE is any collection of a set of SYMBOLS.

Because each SYMBOL may also be *created from* one or more RESOURCES, the "intersect" entity class RESOURCE TOPIC is defined to be the fact that a particular SYMBOL was referred to in one RESOURCE. That is, each RESOURCE ELEMENT must be *part of* exactly one RESOURCE, and *a reference to* exactly one SYMBOL. Note that

---

*Anyone wanting to use a CASE tool to create a default database design from this model should beware.

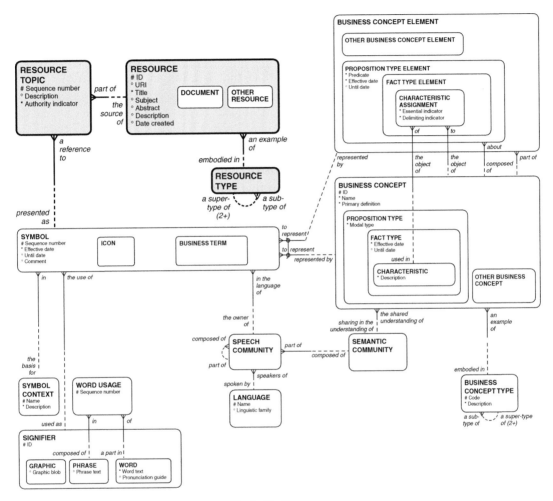

*Fig. 2–11: Resources.*

an attribute of resource element is "authority indicator", denoting whether this particular resource is the authoritative source of the definition for this symbol (business term or icon).

Attributes of RESOURCE include:

- *Uniform resource identifier (URI):* A way of identifying the resource.
- *Title:* Text that names the resource.

- *Subject:* Text that briefly describes the primary purpose of the resource.
- *Abstract:* A description, no more than a couple of paragraphs in length, of the content of the resource.
- *Description:* An alternative to an abstract that is a longer description of the resource.
- *Date created.*

Each RESOURCE must be *an example of* exactly one RESOURCE TYPE, but the list of possible RESOURCE TYPES is far more extensive than simply the DOCUMENT shown as a sub-type of RESOURCE (although again that is one example of RESOURCE TYPE). The identification and definition of BUSINESS CONCEPTS could also be caused by an event of some sort, or even the carrying out of a service. Dublin Core is an organization attempting to standardize the metadata describing documents. It has identified the following RESOURCE TYPES.

- Document

    → Collection
    → Data Set
    → Image
    → Interactive Resource
    → Moving Image
    → Physical Object
    → Software
    → Sound
    → Still Image
    → Text (a document) [DCMI 2004]

- Other Resource Types

    → Event
    → Service

Each RESOURCE TYPE may be *a super-type of (2+)* other RESOURCE TYPES. Note that each RESOURCE may be *the source of* one or more SYMBOLS, each of which could in principle be in a different LANGUAGE. In most cases, though, it is more likely that all SYMBOLS *presented as* a RESOURCE are in one LANGUAGE. This, however, is not shown in the model.

In Figure 2–12, RESOURCE STRUCTURE is the fact that one RESOURCE is related to another in a specified way. That is, the RESOURCE STRUCTURE is *an example of* one RESOURCE STRUCTURE TYPE. Currently, candidate RESOURCE STRUCTURE TYPES (again, from the Dublin Core) are:

→   A reference to
→   The source of
→   Bibliographic citation
→   Conforms to
→   Structure
→   Has format of
→   Replacement for
→   Required by
→   Updated version of
→   Derived from [DCMI 2005]

Others are certainly possible.

## Authorship

Figure 2–13 introduces the entity class PARTY, which is more fully described in Chapter Five. It has grey boundaries because it "belongs" to a different column than the one we are discussing here.*

The entity class PARTY refers to a PERSON or ORGANIZATION that is of interest in some way to the enterprise. In the more expanded view presented in Chapter Five, a PARTY can, for example, be a PERSON who is an employee or an ORGANIZATION that is a vendor. That is, the principal sub-types of PARTY are PERSON (any human being of interest) and ORGANIZATION (any enterprise, government agency, or other group of people organized for a purpose).

PARTY is significant here because a PARTY may be involved in the creation of one or more RESOURCES. Because a RESOURCE may also be worked on by one or

---

*Throughout the book you will see examples like this of entity classes borrowed from other chapters. In each case, there will be a brief definition where it is first introduced, but you should go to its home chapter to get a fuller description.

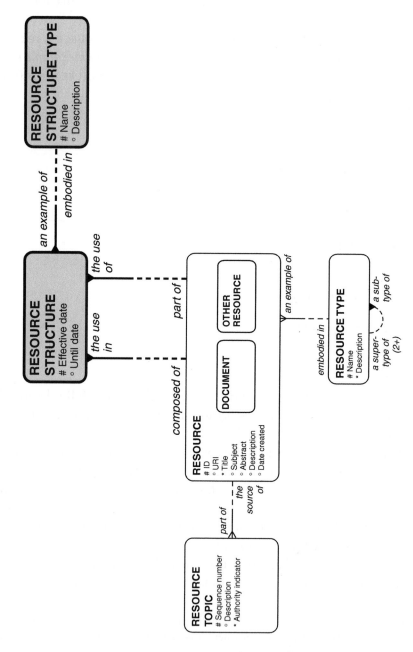

*Fig. 2–12: Resource structures.*

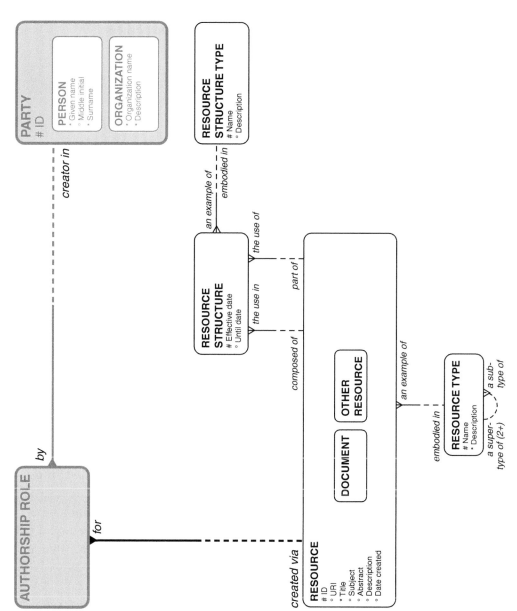

Fig. 2–13: Authorship roles.

59

more PARTIES, AUTHORSHIP ROLE is defined as the fact that a particular PARTY was involved in creating a particular RESOURCE. According to the Dublin-Core/ISO standard, the following are kinds of AUTHORSHIP ROLE, among others.

- Author
- Contributor
- Publisher
- Rights Holder [ISO 2003]

## Document Distribution

A RESOURCE is inherently abstract. It is the expression that can be copyrighted, independently of its physical manifestation. In particular, its existence is a collection of descriptions of SYMBOLS. Its physical embodiment is shown in Figure 2–14 as COPY. That is, each RESOURCE must be *embodied in* at least one (and potentially more) COPY. A COPY may be a PHYSICAL COPY (such as a book or journal) or a VIRTUAL COPY, such as an e-mail or web site.

SITE is another example of an entity class that is more fully defined in another chapter—in this case Chapter Four. A SITE is a location designated for a particular purpose, such as a house, an office, or a warehouse.

Each COPY is sent to one or more PARTIES and/or one or more SITES. Specifically, a RESOURCE DISTRIBUTION is the fact that a particular COPY was sent, at a particular time, *to* either a specific PARTY or *to* a SITE (when the PARTY involved was not identified).

## Coverage

Figure 2–15 shows GEOGRAPHIC LOCATION, another entity class borrowed from Chapter Four. A GEOGRAPHIC LOCATION is a place on the Earth's surface with clearly identified boundaries, such as a state or province, a sales region, or a surveyed plot of land. The figure also shows that each RESOURCE may be *used to describe an aspect of* one or more COVERAGES, where a COVERAGE is the fact that a resource is about a particular GEOGRAPHIC LOCATION. That is, a COVERAGE must be *by* a RESOURCE and *of* one GEOGRAPHIC LOCATION.

A GEOGRAPHIC LOCATION is either a GEOGRAPHIC AREA (shown) or a GEOGRAPHIC POINT (described in Chapter Four). A GEOGRAPHIC AREA, in turn, is either a GEOPOLITICAL AREA (such as a city, state, country, and so on), a MANAGEMENT

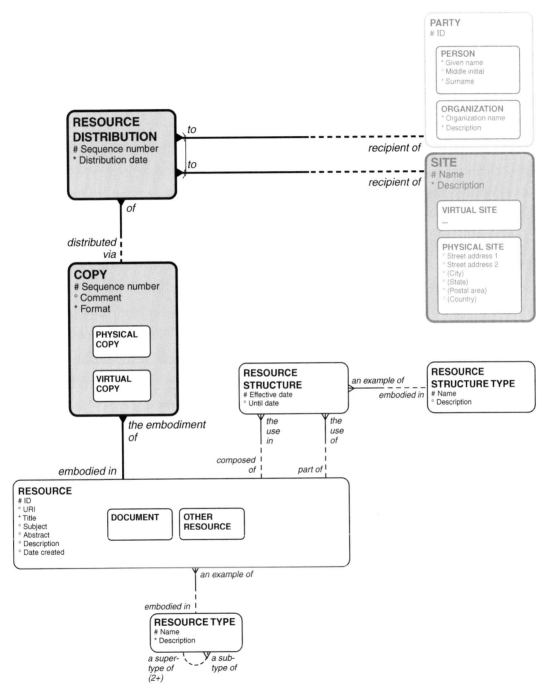

*Fig. 2–14: Resource distribution.*

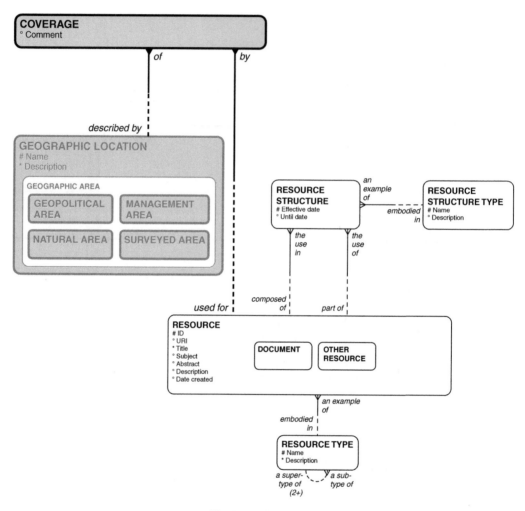

*Fig. 2–15: Coverage.*

AREA (whose boundaries are defined by the enterprise, such as "Southwestern Sales Region"), a NATURAL AREA (such as a habitat or a lake), or a SURVEYED AREA (whose boundaries are specifically measured in terms of townships, sections, and so on). Of these, only GEOPOLITICAL AREA and MANAGEMENT AREA are usually of interest in the metadata arena, but any of them could be described by a RESOURCE.

## The Dublin Core

The Dublin Core, referred to previously, has obtained ISO certification for a basic standard set of attributes required to describe a resource for data. As you can see, the complete model is a bit more complex than a simple set of attributes describing a document, but all of the Dublin/ISO attributes are in fact covered by this model, as shown in Table 2–1 [ISO 2003; DCMI 2005]. Additional attributes specified by the Dublin Core as "Other Elements and Element Refinements" are also covered by this model, most of them in the form of RESOURCE STRUCTURE TYPES.

*Table 2–1: Dublin Core equivalents.*

| Dublin Core Term | Metadata Element |
|---|---|
| Contributor | *Created via* AUTHORSHIP ROLE/ *that are an example of* AUTHORSHIP ROLE TYPE Contributor |
| Coverage | *To describe an aspect of* COVERAGES/ *of a* GEOGRAPHIC LOCATION |
| Creator | *Created via* AUTHORSHIP ROLES/ *an example of* AUTHORSHIP ROLE TYPE Creator |
| Date | RESOURCE: Date Created |
| Description | RESOURCE: Description |
| Format | *Embodied in* COPY: Format |
| Identifier | RESOURCE: ID; RESOURCE: URI |
| Language | *The source of* RESOURCE ELEMENTS/ *a reference to* ASYMBOL/ *in the language of* a SPEECH COMMUNITY/ *speaker of* a LANGUAGE* |
| Publisher | *Created via* AUTHORSHIP ROLES/ *an example of* AUTHORSHIP ROLE TYPE Publisher |
| Relation | *Part of* ARESOURCE STRUCTURE/ *the use of* another RESOURCE |
| Rights | *Created via* AUTHORSHIP ROLES/ *an example of* AUTHORSHIP ROLE TYPE Rights holder |
| Source | *Part of* RESOURCE STRUCTURE/ *an example of* RESOURCE STRUCTURE TYPE Source |
| Subject | RESOURCE: Subject |
| Title | RESOURCE: Title |
| Type | RESOURCE TYPE: Name |

*Read "/" as that is (are)...
Note: *Each line in the table should be read as if this phrase precedes it:* "Each RESOURCE *may be* ...".

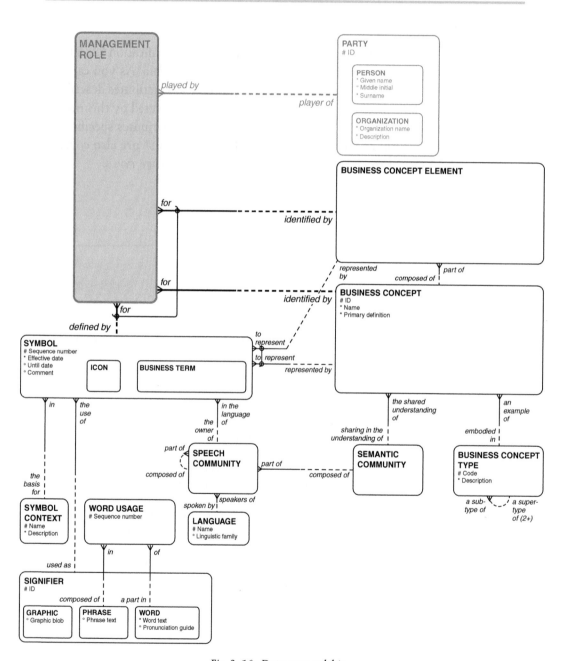

*Fig. 2–16: Data stewardship.*

## Data Stewardship

Chapter Five takes up in detail the issue of the roles people, organizations, jobs, and so on play in managing metadata. Here, however, the specific responsibility for defining the representation (SYMBOLS) of BUSINESS CONCEPTS is shown in Figure 2–16. In the diagram, MANAGEMENT ROLE is the fact that a PARTY has a specific role to play in managing either a BUSINESS CONCEPT or a SYMBOL. That is, if the metadata are to be maintained reliably someone must be assigned responsibility for doing so. Note that both PARTY and MANAGE-MENT ROLE are more fully described in Chapter Five, which is about people and organizations.

## ROW THREE: THE ENTITY-RELATIONSHIP DIAGRAM

In general, the models for the rows of the architecture framework are different, linked only by entity classes that connect one row's concepts to those of another row. These entity classes show how the elements in one row are derived from those in another row. For example, each TABLE ENTITY CLASS MAPPING (described in the following section on Row Four) portrays the fact that one entity class is part of the basis for defining one table.

An exception to this is in the Data column between the Business Owner's View and the Architect's View. Because the notion of BUSINESS CONCEPT is so all-encompassing, and because an entity-relationship diagram is in its own way trying to represent the nature of the business, it is more appropriate to designate the major components of an entity-relationship diagram as *instances* of BUSINESS CONCEPT and FACT TYPE. To be sure, the mapping approach could also be taken, but that would require mapping from BUSINESS CONCEPT and/or FACT TYPE to virtually every element of the Row Three model. In the author's judgment, the sub-type approach will more effectively reveal exactly what each of these elements really is.

In reading this chapter on the entity-relationship model, note that some elements of such a model really are constraints. These include unique identifiers, cardinality and optionality, domains, and derived attributes. For this reason, they are discussed not here but in Chapter Seven, under the section on Row Three constraints.

## Sample Entity-Relationship Model

Figure 2–17 shows a sample business model that embodies the concepts we have just seen. ENTITY CLASSES include:

— PARTY
— PERSON
— ORGANIZATION
— ORDER
— SALES ORDER
— PURCHASE ORDER
— LINE ITEM
— SERVICE TYPE
— PRODUCT TYPE

As we have already seen, by the conventions of this notation ATTRIBUTES for each ENTITY CLASS are shown inside their respective ENTITY CLASS boxes. PARTY is described by the attribute "ID"; PERSON is described by "Given name", "Middle initial", and "Surname"; and so forth. Each attribute is marked with a symbol representing its "Default optionality indicator". A circle means that the attribute is optional, and an asterisk means that it is mandatory. An octothorpe (#) means that it participates in the ENTITY CLASS's unique identifier, and is therefore mandatory. (To learn about unique identifiers, see Chapter Seven.)

Relationships composed of two ASSOCIATIVE ROLES link the main ENTITY CLASSES: ORDER and PARTY, ORDER and LINE ITEM, LINE ITEM and PRODUCT TYPE, and LINE ITEM and SERVICE TYPE. Note the arc between the two *for* roles from LINE ITEM. Each LINE ITEM must be *for* either one PRODUCT TYPE or one SERVICE TYPE, but not both.

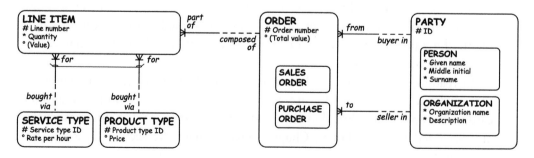

*Fig. 2–17: Sample entity-relationship model.*

This is an example of an exclusion constraint. In UML and Object Role Modeling notations, a broad range of interrelationship constraints are available, but in the notation used here only the "exclusive or" constraint is possible. The metamodel for this constraint is discussed in Chapter Seven.

## Entity Classes and Attributes

In the world of requirements analysis data modeling, we create data models in order to capture the BUSINESS CONCEPTS that refer to classes of things (including abstract things) about which an organization wishes to capture and hold information. Data models also describe the elements of that information, and relationships between them. These are examples of the BUSINESS CONCEPT called ENTITY CLASS (the definition of a thing), ATTRIBUTE (a descriptor of a thing), and RELATIONSHIP ROLE (which links things together). The metamodel for this was introduced in Chapter One, consisting of ENTITY CLASS, ATTRIBUTE, and RELATIONSHIP ROLE. Figure 2–18 shows how that model fits into the scheme of BUSINESS TERMS, BUSINESS CONCEPTS, and BUSINESS CONCEPT ELEMENTS.

BUSINESS TERMS include the names of ATTRIBUTES, ENTITY CLASSES, and OTHER BUSINESS CONCEPTS as well as INSTANCE NAMES. The names of instances of ENTITY CLASS and ATTRIBUTE are clearly examples of WORDS and PHRASES *used as* BUSINESS TERMS *to represent* them. Each of these must be *to represent* an occurrence of an ENTITY CLASS or an ATTRIBUTE. For example, "Colorado" is a word *used as* an INSTANCE NAME for the ENTITY CLASS that is STATE. ("State" is a word *used as* an ENTITY CLASS NAME for the entity class STATE. Note that "Name", an attribute of BUSINESS CONCEPT, will be the first OTHER BUSINESS TERM *to represent* any BUSINESS CONCEPT.)

Of course, there is all the rest of the language used by the enterprise that will not appear in an entity-relationship model at all, and this comprises all the WORDS and PHRASES *used as* OTHER BUSINESS TERMS *to represent* OTHER BUSINESS CONCEPTS or BUSINESS CONCEPT ELEMENTS.

### Business Rules

1. An ENTITY CLASS NAME must be specifically to represent only an ENTITY CLASS, not any other kind of BUSINESS CONCEPT or BUSINESS CONCEPT ELEMENT.

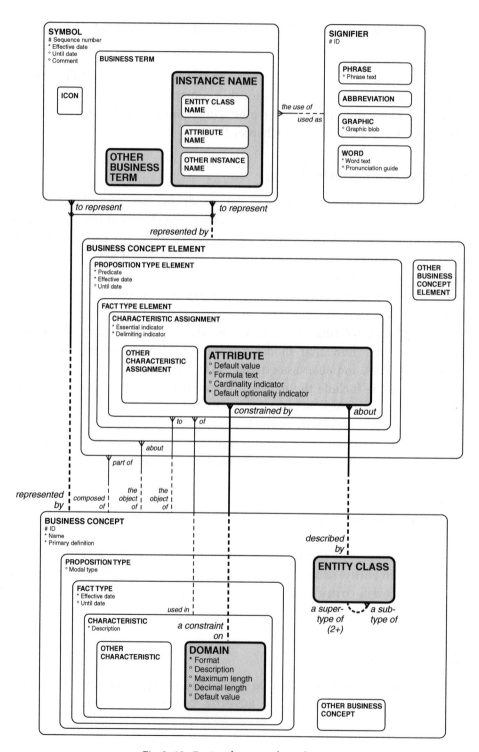

*Fig. 2–18: Entity classes and attributes.*

2. An ATTRIBUTE NAME must be specifically to represent only an ATTRIBUTE, not any other kind of BUSINESS CONCEPT or BUSINESS CONCEPT ELEMENT.

Note that ATTRIBUTE is shown as a kind of CHARACTERISTIC ASSIGNMENT (a FACT TYPE ELEMENT) *of* a CHARACTERISTIC that is a DOMAIN. That is, each ATTRIBUTE must be *constrained by* a DOMAIN. What this is saying is that a DOMAIN is a CHARACTERISTIC in the abstract, which can be assigned to many ENTITY CLASSES.

An ATTRIBUTE is the fact that a particular DOMAIN applies to a particular ENTITY CLASS. Often we are not aware of the domain when we say that PRODUCT has "Name", "Length", and "Width" as attributes, but it is there. It is the definition of what we mean by the attribute. It can be as simple as specification of a format or as complex as a calculated constraint, but implicitly or explicitly it is there. Note that DOMAIN is highlighted. It is actually documented more fully as a constraint in Chapter Seven.

We have already seen that the relationship "each CHARACTERISTIC ASSIGNMENT must be of one CHARACTERISTIC" is a more specific sub-type of the relationship "each BUSINESS CONCEPT ELEMENT must be *part of* one BUSINESS CONCEPT". Similarly, the relationship "each ATTRIBUTE must be *constrained by* one and only one DOMAIN" is a further sub-type of the other relationships. Similarly, the assertion that "each ATTRIBUTE must be *about* one ENTITY CLASS" is a special case of the relationship "each PROPOSITION TYPE ELEMENT must be *descriptive of* a BUSINESS CONCEPT". To eliminate the redundant representation would require explicit statement of the following business rules.

## Business Rules

1. Each CHARACTERISTIC ASSIGNMENT is a BUSINESS CONCEPT ELEMENT that must be part of one BUSINESS CONCEPT that is a CHARACTERISTIC.
2. Each ATTRIBUTE is a BUSINESS CONCEPT that must be part of one and only one FACT TYPE that is a DOMAIN.
3. Each ATTRIBUTE is a BUSINESS CONCEPT that must be descriptive of one and only one BUSINESS CONCEPT that is an ENTITY CLASS.

Attributes of ATTRIBUTE include "Default value", "Format", "Maximum length", "Average Length", and number of "Decimal places". "Default optionality" is an attribute as well, used to specify, in general, whether the ATTRIBUTE is mandatory or not. In fact, optionality is a concept that will require a more sophisticated representation than this (see Chapter Seven), but defining a "Default optionality indicator" will do for initially drawing a data model.

"Cardinality indicator" is included in this model for completeness, but it too is a constraint and is discussed more extensively in Chapter Seven. It lets you specify the maximum number of occurrences of values for this ATTRIBUTE in this ENTITY CLASS. If a normalized relational model is the object of this exercise, this must always have the value "1". Some environments are not normalized, however, and therefore if you wish to capture that fact this is where it would be recorded. (UML provides the ability to specify this.)

## Relationships and Relationship Roles

As we saw in Chapter One, a RELATIONSHIP ROLE is the fact that an ENTITY CLASS participates in a relationship with another ENTITY CLASS. Each RELATIONSHIP ROLE must be *played by* exactly one ENTITY CLASS and must be *connected to* another RELATIONSHIP ROLE being played by the same or another ENTITY CLASS. Figure 2–19 shows this.

### *Relationship Roles*

Note that each RELATIONSHIP ROLE must be *connected to* exactly one other RELATIONSHIP ROLE that in turn must be played by either the same or another ENTITY CLASS. Thus, two occurrences of ENTITY CLASSES (or two occurrences of the same ENTITY CLASS) are connected via two RELATIONSHIP ROLES. These two roles are *part of* a RELATIONSHIP, which is the entire relationship between the two ENTITY CLASSES. That is, each RELATIONSHIP must be *composed of* one or more (in this case, exactly two) RELATIONSHIP ROLES.

The RELATIONSHIP ROLE "Each RELATIONSHIP ROLE must be *played by* one and only one ENTITY CLASS" is equivalent to the statement that "each RELATIONSHIP ROLE may be *composed of* a PROPOSITION TYPE ELEMENT (actually a FACT TYPE ELEMENT) that is about a BUSINESS CONCEPT that is an ENTITY CLASS". The direct relationship is more concise and easier to understand, but it is redundant.

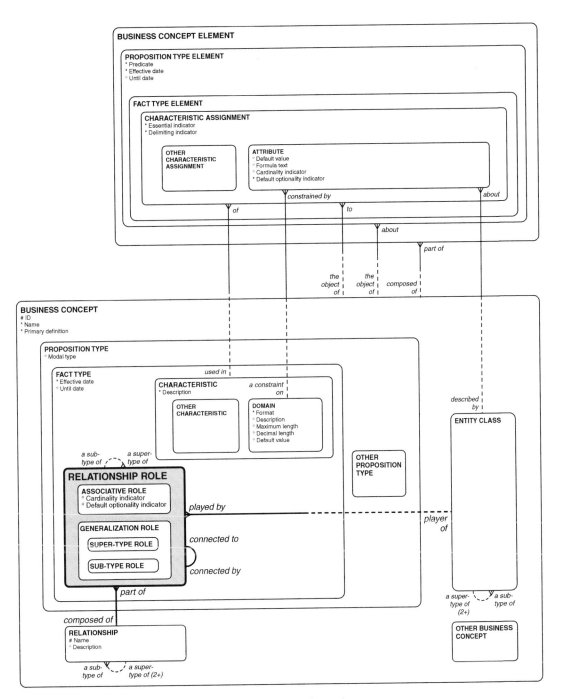

Fig. 2–19: *Relationship Roles*.

For that matter, the relationships themselves between RELATIONSHIP ROLE and ENTITY CLASS and between RELATIONSHIP ROLE and itself are similarly redundant. Each of these is an example of the fact that each BUSINESS CONCEPT (in this case, RELATIONSHIP ROLE) may be *composed of* one or more BUSINESS CONCEPT ELEMENTS (in this case, RELATIONSHIP ROLE ELEMENTS, such as *played by* and *connected to*). Each of these in turn must be *about* one or more BUSINESS CONCEPTS (in these cases, ENTITY CLASS and RELATIONSHIP ROLE, respectively). The cardinality of the relationships is conveyed by the attribute "Cardinality indicator", but the fact that the explicit relationships are required cannot be expressed directly through these more indirect relationships.

In other words, each RELATIONSHIP may be *a super-type of* two or more other RELATIONSHIPS. Rather than showing redundant relationship sub-types, the same constraints can be expressed as business rules.

**Business Rules**

1. Each BUSINESS CONCEPT that is a RELATIONSHIP ROLE must be *composed of* only one BUSINESS CONCEPT that is a PROPOSITION TYPE ELEMENT (with the Name "played by"), which must be *about* the BUSINESS CONCEPT that is ENTITY CLASS.
2. Each BUSINESS CONCEPT that is a RELATIONSHIP ROLE must be *composed of* only one BUSINESS CONCEPT ELEMENT that is a PROPOSITION TYPE ELEMENT (with the Name "connected to"), which must be *about* the BUSINESS CONCEPT that is RELATIONSHIP ROLE.
3. Each BUSINESS CONCEPT that is a RELATIONSHIP ROLE must be *composed of* only one BUSINESS CONCEPT ELEMENT that is a PROPOSITION TYPE ELEMENT (with the Name "connected from"), which must be *about* the BUSINESS CONCEPT that is RELATIONSHIP ROLE.

Note that the relationship role "each ENTITY CLASS may be *a super-type of* another ENTITY CLASS" (and its inverse) is not redundant, in that ENTITY CLASS is neither a PROPOSITION TYPE nor a PROPOSITION TYPE ELEMENT.

Figure 2–19 shows that a RELATIONSHIP ROLE is either an ASSOCIATIVE ROLE or a GENERALIZATION ROLE. An ASSOCIATIVE ROLE describes the relationship from one ENTITY CLASS to another when the ENTITY CLASSES represent fundamentally different things (or different occurrences of the same thing, as in a recursive bill of materials structure associating one product type with another). Using this model as an example of a data model, the ENTITY CLASS that is a BUSINESS CONCEPT ELEMENT is *player of* the ASSOCIATIVE ROLE *"part of"*, which is *connected to* the ASSOCIATIVE ROLE *"composed of"* that is *played by* the ENTITY CLASS that is BUSINESS CONCEPT.

A GENERALIZATION ROLE describes the fact that an instance of one ENTITY CLASS is in fact an instance of another. A GENERALIZATION ROLE must be either a SUB-TYPE ROLE or a SUPER-TYPE ROLE. If an ENTITY CLASS is a *player of* a SUB-TYPE ROLE, this must be *connected to* a SUPER-TYPE ROLE that is *played by* another ENTITY CLASS. An occurrence of the first ENTITY CLASS (in the SUB-TYPE ROLE) is then by definition also an occurrence of the second ENTITY CLASS (in the SUPER-TYPE ROLE).

Again, using this model as an example, the ENTITY CLASS that is OTHER BUSINESS CONCEPT is *player of* the SUB-TYPE ROLE that is *connected to* the SUPER-TYPE ROLE that is *played by* the ENTITY CLASS that is BUSINESS CONCEPT. The entity class ASSOCIATIVE ROLE has two attributes: "Cardinality Indicator" and "Default Optionality Indicator". Both of these are discussed in more detail in Chapter Seven.

Using Figure 2–19 itself as an example of an entity-relationship diagram, the "Cardinality indicator" of the ASSOCIATIVE ROLE from ENTITY CLASS to RELATIONSHIP ROLE that is named *player of* is "True", meaning that the role of ENTITY CLASS is to more than one occurrence of RELATIONSHIP ROLE. The "Cardinality indicator" of the ASSOCIATIVE ROLE named *"played by"* is "False", meaning that the role of RELATIONSHIP ROLE is to only one occurrence of ENTITY CLASS. Alternatively, the attribute could be called "Cardinality value" with values "1", "*", "<2", and so on. In information engineering and other similar notations, cardinality may only be "one and only one" ("False" or "1") or "one or more" ("True" or "*"); however, in UML, other values can be implied, such as ">4", "2, 4, or 6", and so on.

As with ATTRIBUTE, the attribute of ASSOCIATIVE ROLE that by all rights should be called "Optionality indicator" is in fact called "Default optionality indicator" because the optionality of an ASSOCIATIVE ROLE may be a function of either its state or the state of the affected ENTITY CLASS. (See Chapter Seven.) For the moment, however, we will assume that its default is only one "Optionality indicator" value. For the role in this model named *"player of"*, this is "true"—meaning that each occurrence of ENTITY CLASS may or may not be the *player of* at least one RELATIONSHIP ROLE. The "Default optionality indicator" of the RELATIONSHIP ROLE named *"played by"* is "False", meaning that no occurrence of RELATIONSHIP ROLE may be created that is not *played by* at least one ENTITY CLASS.

## Association Class Roles

The roles described previously are called INFORMATION ENGINEERING ROLES because they are constrained by that technique. In information engineering and related disciplines, such as the Barker/Structured Systems Analysis and Design Method (SSADM) approach used in these drawings, all relationships are assumed to be binary in that they are between only two entity classes. This provides a certain rigor to the exercise, which your author deems highly desirable. There are other notations, however, that are not as constrained.

UML, for example, primarily uses the information engineering approach, but it also has a special way of addressing many-to-many relationships. In information engineering or SSADM, when confronted with a many-to-many relationship, the response is to create a new entity class whose occurrences each represent an occurrence of one entity class being related to one occurrence of another entity class.

For example, imagine the model shown in Figure 2–20, where there is a many-to-many relationship between PROJECT and PERSON (each PROJECT may be the *work site for* one or more PEOPLE; each PERSON may be *assigned to* one or more PROJECTS). In this case, the information engineering response (using UML notation, in this case) would be to create an *intersect entity class* (as shown in Figure 2–21) as PROJECT ASSIGNMENT. Each occurrence of the intersect entity class PROJECT ASSIGNMENT is the fact that a particular PERSON was assigned to a particular PROJECT at a particular time. That is, each PROJECT ASSIGNMENT must be *of* one PERSON *to* one PROJECT at a particular time. The intersect entity class has all of the characteristics of any entity class.

UML, however, also provides the option of creating an *association class*. This is an entity class that represents the relationship itself, not simply a set of inter-actions between the base entity classes. A sample association class is shown in

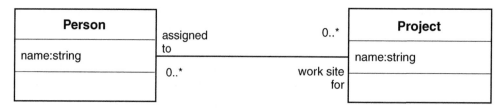

*Fig. 2–20: A many-to-many relationship.*

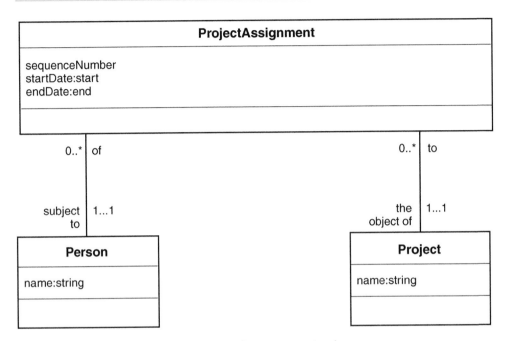

*Fig. 2–21: Sample intersect entity class.*

Figure 2–22 as ProjectAssignment. This entity class is not related to any other entity class, but only to the relationship itself.

Note that this is a very constrained device. As shown, it assumes that there will be no more than one occurrence of a particular PERSON assigned to a particular PROJECT, since, by definition, each occurrence of the association class is identified by a combination of the identities of the two base entity classes.

If Charlie works for the Brooklyn Bridge Project for a few months, goes away, and is then reassigned to that project, this cannot be recorded here. In that case, you must use the intersect entity class shown in Figure 2–21. Note that the intersect entity approach allows specification of the attribute "sequenceNumber", which can be included in the unique identifier to keep instances distinct from each other. Then there can be an unlimited number of occurrences of PROJECT ASSIGNMENT of a particular PERSON to a particular PROJECT.

In the case of multiple assignments of PROJECT to PERSON, you could use the association class if you added the attribute "Cumulative number of assignments"

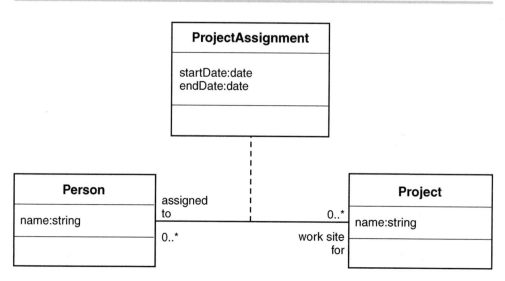

*Fig. 2–22: An association class.*

to either PERSON or PROJECT, but this would not allow you to specify the dates of each assignment.

This feature of UML calls for the definition of a new kind of RELATIONSHIP ROLE in our metamodel, the ASSOCIATION CLASS ROLE, as shown in Figure 2–23. Here again, each RELATIONSHIP must be *composed of* one or more RELATIONSHIP ROLES, but this time instead of a role being *connected to* another RELATIONSHIP ROLE, each ASSOCIATION CLASS ROLE must be *to describe* another RELATIONSHIP. A new ENTITY CLASS sub-type has also been created here—ASSOCIATION ENTITY CLASS—to describe what is at the end of an ASSOCIATION CLASS ROLE.

This is a kind of ENTITY CLASS, and as such it may be a *player of* one or more RELATIONSHIP ROLES, but in this case it is constrained to playing an ASSOCIATION CLASS ROLE. The RELATIONSHIP ROLE discussed previously is here rendered as INFORMATION ENGINEERING ROLE to distinguish it from ASSOCIATION CLASS ROLE. An INFORMATION ENGINEERING ROLE is used in entity-relationship diagrams, both in the original information engineering technique and techniques derived from that (including the Barker/SSADM notation used in this book). The ASSOCIATION CLASS ROLE occurs only in UML and IDEF1X, although both primarily use the INFORMATION ENGINEERING ROLES.

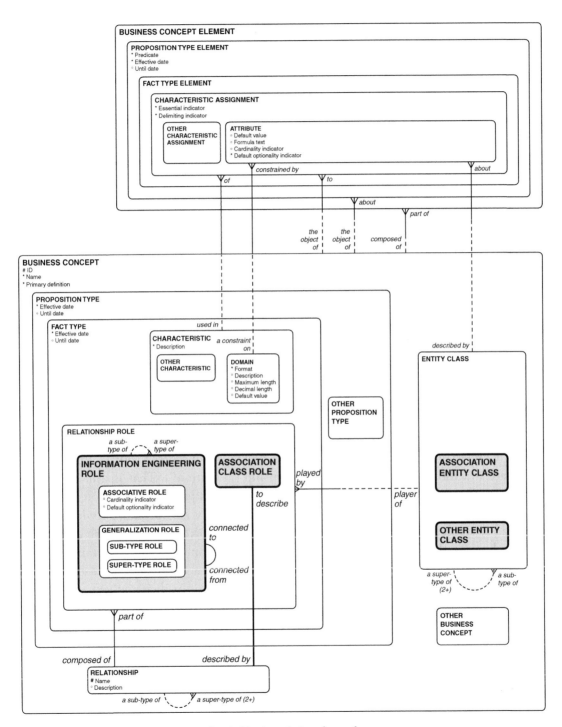

*Fig. 2–23: Association class role.*

**Business Rules**

1. An ASSOCIATION CLASS ROLE must be *played by* an ASSOCIATION ENTITY CLASS. Conversely, an ASSOCIATION ENTITY CLASS must be a *player of* one and only one ASSOCIATION CLASS ROLE.*
2. In Figure 2–23, an INFORMATION ENGINEERING ROLE may only be played by an OTHER ENTITY CLASS. (More about this later.)
3. If a relationship is composed of ASSOCIATION CLASSES, it is composed of only *one* such class.
4. If a relationship is composed of INFORMATION ENGINEERING CLASSES, it is composed of exactly *two* such classes.

## *N-ary Relationships*

Even with the addition of ASSOCIATION CLASS ROLES, UML is still primarily concerned with binary relationships. But what about notations (including UML) that permit true ternary and higher-order relationships? Predominant among those that do are *object role modeling (ORM)* and *Chen notation*. In these, multiple objects (entity classes and attributes) can be related to each other without constraint. Figure 2–24 shows, for each of the notations, an example of a Project being related to a Person, as previously discussed, but in this case there is a third participant in the relationship ("Location"). That is, this model asserts that a Person may be assigned to a Project in a particular Location.

Note that in UML, an ASSOCIATION CLASS ROLE may also be added to describe (add attributes to) the ternary relationship itself. In ORM, the lines with arrowheads mean that each Project/Person combination is unique. This constraint was implicit on the UML association class in the previous example. One PERSON can work on a PROJECT only once. In ORM, this constraint is explicit and is under the control of the modeler. Whereas a PERSON can work on a PROJECT only once, a PERSON could work at the same location multiple times, just as a PROJECT could be in a LOCATION multiple times.

This calls for a further refinement of our model. Figure 2–25 shows how a RELATIONSHIP must be *composed of* (three) or more N-ARY ROLES, without

---

*Here, a business rule is used instead of explicitly depicting that each ASSOCIATION CLASS ROLE must be *played by* one ASSOCIATION ENTITY CLASS.

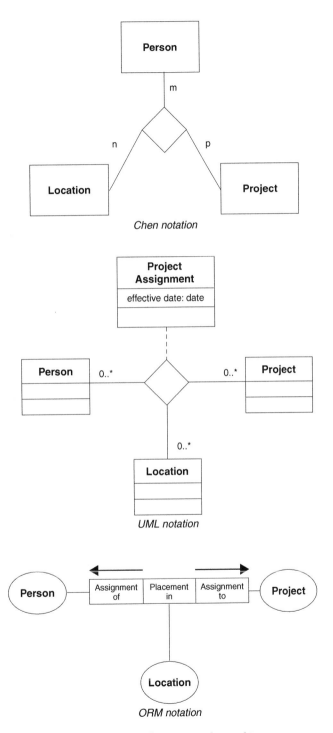

Fig. 2–24: Sample ternary relationship.

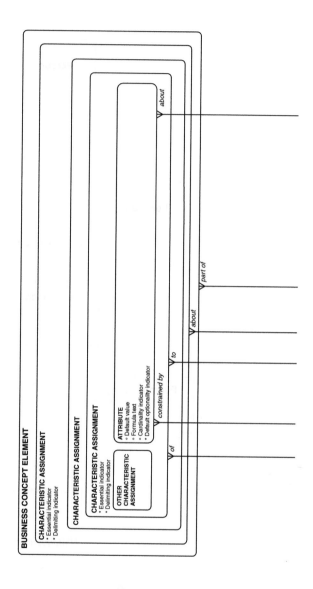

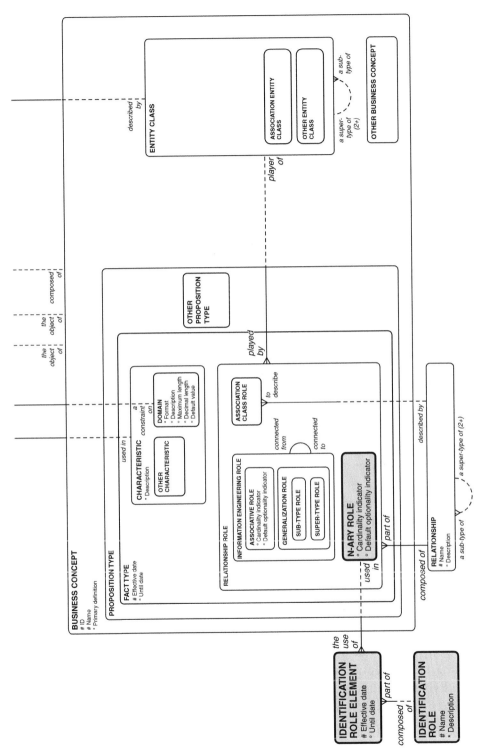

*Fig. 2–25: N-ary roles.*

restriction as to how many are involved. In the UML example, a RELATIONSHIP will be *composed of* three N-ARY ROLES and one ASSOCIATION CLASS ROLE.

> **Business Rule**
>
> An N-ARY ROLE must be *played by* one and only one OTHER ENTITY CLASS.

Note that because ORM includes the notation for uniquely identifying combinations of N-ARY ROLES, Figure 2–25 adds the concept of an IDENTIFICATION ROLE. Each N-ARY ROLE may be *used in* one or more IDENTIFICATION ROLE ELEMENTS, each of which must be *part of* one IDENTIFICATION ROLE. In the previous ORM example, an IDENTIFICATION ROLE is *composed of* the N-ARY ROLES *assignment of* and *assignment to*.

## Entity Class Views

The Row Three conceptual data model is constrained to ENTITY CLASSES that represent fundamental, often abstract, things of significance to the business. The things seen by Row Two's business owners, however, tend to be more concrete, and are usually examples, combinations, or subcategories of the ENTITY CLASSES in the conceptual model.

We have previously specified that multiple BUSINESS TERMS can be *to represent* a BUSINESS CONCEPT (ENTITY CLASS or ATTRIBUTE), but this is often not adequate to describe the detailed interactions between the two kinds of language. What we need are *virtual entity classes* that represent the business owner's language, but which can be explicitly mapped to more fundamental classes.

In the original ANSI three-schema architecture, the external schema was considered a "view" of the conceptual model, and relational database management vendors have implemented the concept of a view derived from one or more tables that in all respects behave like a table.

No modeling tool currently (as of this writing in 2005) supports this, but it is reasonable to hypothesize the similar concept of an entity view. In Figure 2–26, a VIRTUAL ENTITY CLASS is a view derived from underlying ELEMENTARY ENTITY CLASSES.

Both VIRTUAL ENTITY CLASS and ELEMENTARY ENTITY CLASS are sub-types of STANDARD ENTITY CLASS, which means that a previously cited business rule should actually read as follows.

### Business Rule

Each INFORMATION ENGINEERING ROLE must be *played by* a STANDARD ENTITY CLASS or by an OTHER ENTITY CLASS.

Each VIRTUAL ENTITY CLASS is defined in terms of the entity classes and attributes that make it up, plus the selection criteria used to select occurrences of the underlying entity classes. Specifically, each VIRTUAL ENTITY CLASS must be *defined in terms of* one or more ENTITY CLASS SELECTIONS, each of which must be *of* one and only one other (other) ENTITY CLASS. In addition, each ENTITY CLASS SELECTION must be *composed of* one or more ATTRIBUTE SELECTIONS, each of which must be *of* one and only one ATTRIBUTE.

In addition, each VIRTUAL ENTITY CLASS may be populated by rows *defined in terms of* one or more SELECTION CONDITIONS, each of which must be either in terms of an ATTRIBUTE or in terms of a RELATIONSHIP ROLE. Attributes of SELECTION CONDITION define the criteria for selecting rows to be part of the VIRTUAL ENTITY CLASS: an "Operator" evaluates the ATTRIBUTE or RELATIONSHIP ROLE involved, comparing each occurrence's value with the SELECTION CONDITION's "Value". For example, rows from the ENTITY CLASS that is "Part" could be selected if the SELECTION CONDITION is *in terms of* the ATTRIBUTE "Length" (which is also about the ENTITY CLASS "Part"), the operator is "Less than", and the value is "24". That is, the view will be populated with all parts that are less than 24 (units)* long.

As another example, in the sample model shown in Figure 2–17, suppose you wanted to define the view CUSTOMER which was the set of rows from the ENTITY CLASS PARTY (which were *buyers in* an ORDER). To do so, the VIRTUAL ENTITY CUSTOMER would be *defined in terms of* the ENTITY CLASS SELECTION that is *of* the ENTITY CLASS PARTY. This in turn would be composed of the ATTRIBUTE SELECTIONS shown in Table 2–2.

---

*This presumes that units of measure have been dealt with elsewhere.

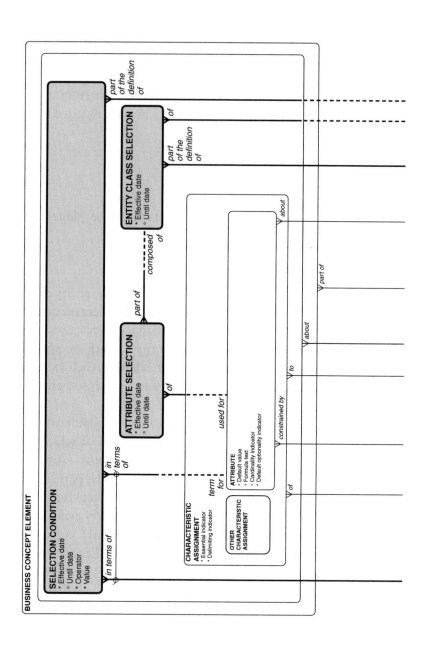

BUSINESS CONCEPT ELEMENT

SELECTION CONDITION
* Effective date
° Until date
* Operator
* Value

*in terms of*

*in terms of*

ENTITY CLASS SELECTION
* Effective date
° Until date

*part of the definition of*

*part of the definition of*

*of*

*composed of*

*part of*

ATTRIBUTE SELECTION
* Effective date
° Until date

*of*

*used for*

*term for*

CHARACTERISTIC ASSIGNMENT
* Essential indicator
* Delimiting indicator

ATTRIBUTE
° Default value
° Formula text
* Cardinality indicator
* Default optionality indicator

OTHER CHARACTERISTIC ASSIGNMENT

*about*

*part of*

*about*

*to*

*constrained by*

*of*

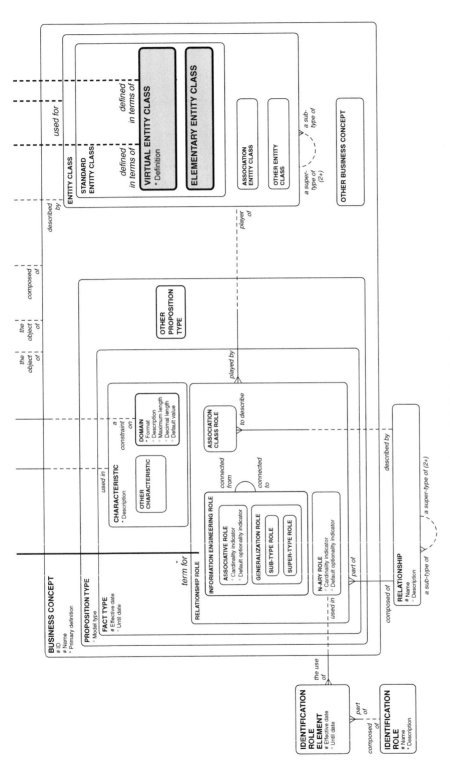

Fig. 2-26: Entity class views.

85

*Table 2–2: Virtual entity class example.*

| About | Which One | Which Implies |
|---|---|---|
| ATTRIBUTE | Party ID | ENTITY CLASS Party |
| ATTRIBUTE | Person given name | ENTITY CLASS Person |
| ATTRIBUTE | Person surname | ENTITY CLASS Person |
| ATTRIBUTE | Person middle initial | ENTITY CLASS Person |
| ATTRIBUTE | Organization name | ENTITY CLASS Organization |

In addition, the VIRTUAL ENTITY CUSTOMER would also be *defined in terms of* one SELECTION CRITERION that is *in terms of* the RELATIONSHIP ROLE *"buyer in"* (which in turn is *played by* the same PARTY). The Operator in SELECTION CRITERION would be "equal to". The process of constructing a VIRTUAL ENTITY CLASS, then, is controlled by the following business rule.

> **Business Rule**
>
> Each occurrence of ATTRIBUTE SELECTION must be *of* an ATTRIBUTE that is *about* an ENTITY CLASS. Each occurrence of ATTRIBUTE must also be *part of* an ENTITY CLASS SELECTION that is *of* an ENTITY CLASS. For each ATTRIBUTE SELECTION, the same ENTITY CLASS must be at the end of both of those navigations.

## About Reference Data

In every business data model there are some entity classes that are not dependent on other entity classes. That is, *reference data* have no mandatory relationships. Typically, these are the entity classes that contain the terms of reference used by the others. Reference data include such things as values for STATUS, CURRENCY, EVENT TYPE, LICENSE TYPE, and so forth. Usually each of these has only a few values, defined by the organization. They represent the legal values for terms used elsewhere in the model. As such, making sure that instances of these are defined correctly is appropriately the job of the people creating the system that uses them—and for this reason they are often considered part of the metadata.

These reference entity classes are not represented separately here, because they do not add anything to the structure of a model. The people managing metadata must take note of these reference data, however, and manage them along with managing the structure of any system that uses them.

In the quotation that begins this chapter, Aristotle asserts that a connection between two or more things is indeed a fact. And yes, we are concerned with whether the things involved (the business concepts) exist. We are also concerned with the nature of the business concepts (as revealed by the facts). The question of *why* the connection exists is beyond the scope of this book.

## Row Four: Data Design

Row Four of the architecture framework is the Designer's View. In the case of the Data column, this is in terms of the particular kind of data manipulation technology brought in to manage the data described in Row Three. As of 2006, the most commonly used technologies are relational databases and object-oriented program design.

Relational technology focuses on how data are stored, whereas object-oriented technology addresses how they are manipulated in programs. In principle, these should be compatible, in that stored data must be manipulated by programs somehow and manipulated data usually must be stored.

The priority in managing databases is to see that the design of them is as non-redundant as possible, and to control modifications to data structure and access to data. The relational approach to database implementation supports this approach. It makes use of database management system (DBMS) software to store and manipulate data organized as two-dimensional tables. According to E. F. Codd's *relational theory* [Codd 1970], storing data according to relational rules minimizes redundancy in storage,* but it does not in any way restrict how programs are written to use and manipulate the data so stored.

---

*A brief description of the normalization process can also be found in David C. Hay's *Requirements Analysis: From Business Views to Architecture* [Hay 2003, pp. 91–111].

Although one component of database design addresses performance issues, database administrators are indifferent as to how data are used in programs. The object-oriented approach to data, on the other hand, emphasizes the proper design and writing of programs. Data structure is embedded in programs, describing what are called classes of "objects." These may correspond to the business entity classes described previously for the Row Three conceptual model, or they may be classes of objects used by the program only. Processes (called "behaviors") are then attached to these classes.

When the objects of an object-oriented program must be made *persistent*—with values retained after the program terminates—the data involved must be stored somewhere. Here there is no single object-oriented approach, so, although it is not the only solution, its pervasiveness in the industry suggests that a relational database is a reasonable place to store such persistent data. To do so, however, requires translation of the program's object structure into the tables and columns of the database. If both the object and the database structures closely approximate the structure of the conceptual model, this should be straightforward. In both cases, the data assume a structure, and in principle both structures should come from the same Row Three model. In practice, however, the mapping is often not so easy.

Whether translating from an entity-relationship model or from an object-oriented design, relational databases' lack of facility to deal with inheritance makes translation in that direction a serious effort requiring thought.

In addition, both relational designers and object-oriented designers modify the structure to accommodate processing bottlenecks, but they view what constitutes such a bottleneck quite differently.

Data stored in a relational DBMS is subject to extensive rules to protect their integrity and control access to them. These rules do not necessarily apply to data structures as they are used in programs. The remainder of this chapter describes the metamodel of both the relational and the object-oriented approaches, revealing the similarities and differences between the two views of data.

## Relational Database Design

Codd's original relational model described data in terms of *relations, attributes,* and *tuples*. These are reflected in the conceptual model as *entity classes, attributes,*

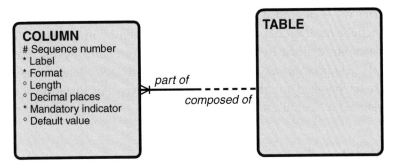

*Fig. 2–27:  Column and table views.*

and *occurrences*. In a relational database design, they are implemented as *tables*, *columns*, and *rows*, respectively.

## Tables and Columns

The entity classes TABLE and COLUMN are shown in Figure 2–27. This structure is similar to that for ENTITY CLASS and ATTRIBUTE, described previously. A TABLE is a collection of data about something, organized into a set of rows and columns. That is, the structure of a TABLE is defined by a set of COLUMNS. Thus, each TABLE may be *composed of* one or more COLUMNS, whereas each COLUMN must be *part of* a single TABLE.

A COLUMN cannot be duplicated in a table and defines one particular thing to be described by the TABLE. A ROW is an occurrence of the thing the TABLE is about. Both rows and columns be in any order. There is no meaning attributed to the sequence of either.

### Business Rules (Relational Theory Version)

1. Each COLUMN may appear only once in a TABLE.
2. Each instance of COLUMN (that is, a column's occurrence in a row) may contain only one value at a time.
3. There is no implied sequence in the way COLUMNS are presented in a TABLE.
4. There is no implied sequence in the way rows appear in a TABLE.

Each COLUMN is described by a "Label", which, among other things, may be displayed whenever the COLUMN appears on a screen or in a report. A column's characteristics are defined by its "Format", and optionally by its "Length" and (number of) "Decimal places". Its "Mandatory indicator" determines whether a value must be supplied for this column for all rows. An instance of a COLUMN may be assigned a "Default value".

## Sample Database Design

Figure 2–28 shows a diagram of a database design that could be derived from the sample entity class model of Figure 2–17. This is a generic database design diagram, produced by Oracle's Designer Modeling tool. Other tools could present the same information differently. In this diagram, each table is represented by a rectangle, with columns listed inside the rectangle. As in the entity class model, an asterisk is next to a required column. No symbol is next to an optional column. In addition, an octothorpe (#) is next to a column that is part of a *primary key* (discussed in Chapter Seven). Also next to each column is a symbol representing its data type. A capital "A" means that it is alphanumeric, whereas a diagonal "7-8-9" means it is numeric.

Thus, in this example "Parties", "Orders", "Line Items", "Product types", and "Service types" are all instances of the entity class TABLE in Figure 2–27. Note that in this design the arc notation has been preserved from the conceptual model. In this case, it means that a stored procedure or some other kind of programmed constraint must enforce the exclusivity. Either "Pdty_pdty_id" or "St_service__type_id" must be null. In addition, depending on the constraint in the conceptual model the other column may be "not null".

Much of what goes into database design involves providing for constraints: primary keys, foreign keys, domains, column constraints, arcs, and so forth. Because these are the implementation of business rules, discussion of these in detail is deferred to Chapter Seven.

## Views

SQL, the language of the relational database, provides the ability to define *views*, which are collections of data organized as though they were tables, but which are in fact derived from other tables. Figure 2–29 shows VIEW and TABLE as sub-types

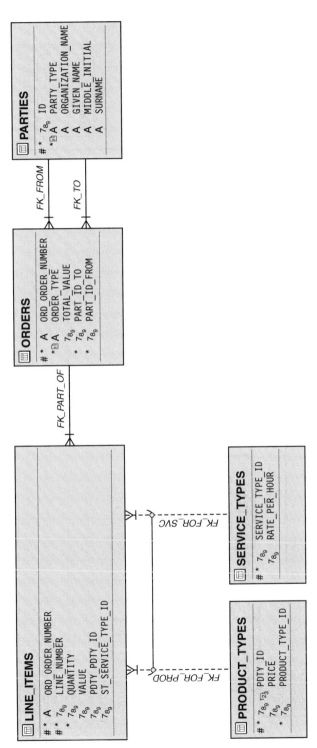

Fig. 2-28: Sample database design.

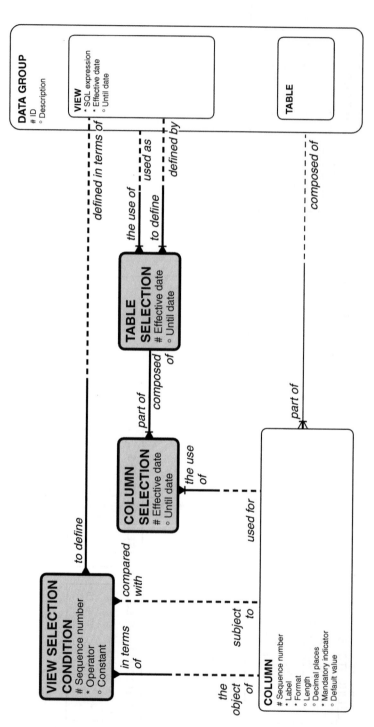

Fig. 2–29: Table views.

of the more general concept DATA GROUP. A DATA GROUP is any organized collection of data, either a TABLE, or a VIEW derived from one or more other TABLES. This is the same structure described previously for entity class model views.

A VIEW must be defined by one or more TABLE SELECTIONS, where each TABLE SELECTION is *the use of* another DATA GROUP (TABLE or VIEW). Each TABLE SELECTION, in turn, may be *composed of* one or more COLUMN SELECTIONS, each *the use of* one COLUMN from that TABLE. The view is populated from the data in component DATA GROUPS by evaluating the selected DATA GROUPS and COLUMNS in terms of one or more VIEW SELECTION CONDITIONS. Each VIEW SELECTION CRITERION compares values of a specified COLUMN with either a "Constant" or the value in another column.

### Business Rule

Any COLUMN *used for* a COLUMN SELECTION that is *part of* a TABLE SELECTION must be *part of* the DATA GROUP that is *used in* that same TABLE SELECTION.

For example, in the sample database design shown in Figure 2–28, a view could be constructed for CUSTOMER, an instance of which is defined as a PARTY that participates in an ORDER (The "Party_ID_from"), where the PARTY that is the "Party_ID_to" is us. In SQL, the view definition looks like this:

```
CREATE VIEW CUSTOMER AS
SELECT P.ID,P.PARTY_TYPE,P.ORGANIZATION_NAME,
       P.GIVEN_NAME,P.MIDDLE_INITIAL, P.SURNAME
FROM ORDERS O, PARTIES P
WHERE O.PART_ID_TO = <the 'party id' of our company>
       AND O.PART_ID_FROM = P.ID
       AND O.PART_ID_FROM <> <the 'party id' of our company>
```

In our model, this translates into a VIEW with the name "Customer" that is *defined by* the following TABLE SELECTIONS:

– *The use of* the DATA GROUP (TABLE) "Orders"

— *The use of* the DATA GROUP (TABLE) "Parties", and *composed of* the following COLUMNS that are *part of* the DATA GROUP (TABLE) "Parties"

  → ID
  → Party_type
  → Organization_name
  → Given_name
  → Middle_initial
  → Surname

— Defined in terms of the following TABLE SELECTION CONDITIONS that are *comparing* the following COLUMNS

  → *Defined in terms of* first TABLE SELECTION condition

- *In terms of* COLUMN "Party_id_from" that is *part of* TABLE "Order"
- Operator = "equal"
- *Compared with* = COLUMN "ID" that is *part of* TABLE "Party"
  <and>
- *In terms of* COLUMN "Party_id_from" that is *part of* TABLE "Order"
- Operator = "equal"
- Constant = <the *party id* of our company>

  → *Defined in terms of* second TABLE SELECTION condition

- *In terms of* COLUMN "Party_id_to" that is *part of* TABLE "Order"
- Operator = "not equal"
- Constant = <the *party id* of our company>

The SQL statement defining the view is the value of "SQL expression"—an attribute of VIEW. To the extent that design VIEWS are derived from analysis VIRTUAL ENTITY CLASSES, each TABLE SELECTION must be *based on* an ENTITY CLASS SELECTION (as shown in Figure 2–30), each COLUMN SELECTION must be *based on* one ATTRIBUTE SELECTION, and each TABLE SELECTION CONDITION must be *based on* one SELECTION CRITERION.

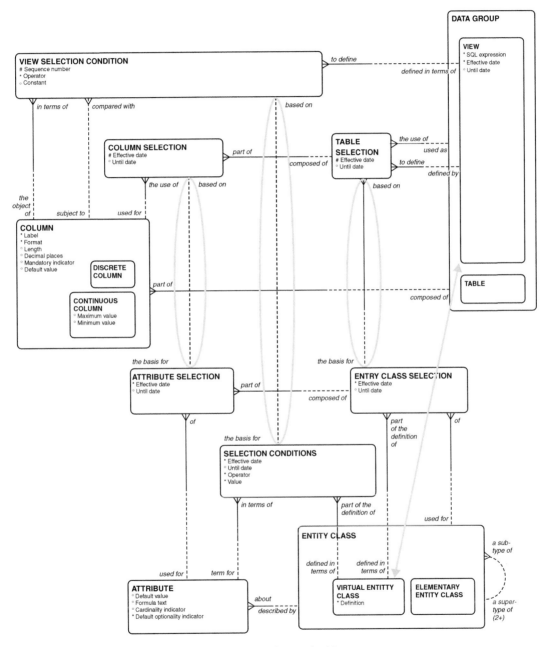

Fig. 2–30: Entity class and table views.

## *Data Group Collections and Application Systems*

Figure 2–31 shows that tables and views can be grouped for the purpose of convenience. This may have to do with the way development and implementation were organized, or it may be of functional significance. However the DATA GROUPS are organized, ultimately they should be organized by APPLICATION SYSTEM. This book presents the metamodel as though this were the case, even though it is recognized that not all actual information technology departments will do so. For our purposes, an APPLICATION SYSTEM is a grouping of data to fulfill a business function. (Programs are also part of the definition of an APPLICATION SYSTEM, and Chapter Three will go into more detail about this, as well as about how an APPLICATION SYSTEM serves a corporate function.)

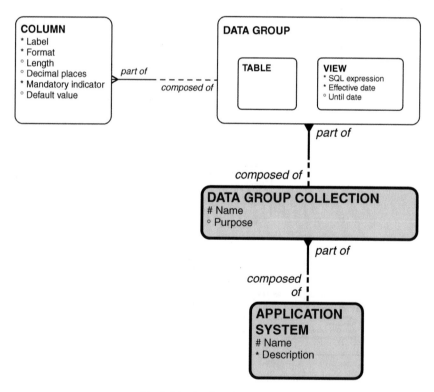

*Fig. 2–31: Application systems.*

## Object-Oriented Data Design

An alternative way of describing data is the approach taken by those using the object-oriented approach to designing programs. This is less concerned with the way data are stored than with the way they are manipulated in programs. The structures are relevant here, however, because they are derived from the conceptual model as well.

The notation most commonly used in 2005 to represent object-oriented data is the UML class diagram, which was developed by a consortium of designers in the mid 1990s [OMG 2003]. It is similar to the entity-relationship notation described previously, and in fact (as we saw in Chapter One) a subset of UML can be used to draw an entity-relationship diagram.

One of the claims made about the virtues of UML is that the same symbols used to describe business entity classes during requirements analysis can also be used to describe the classes that are program code created for a computer system. This is unfortunate, in that these *are not the same thing*, and to use the same symbol and terminology to describe both is misleading. As we shall see here, an object-oriented design model is quite different from an analysis model, whatever its notation.

### Classes

In the relational world, the distinction is made between entities that represent things of significance to the business and tables and columns that are representations of these things in the computer. It is true that many data modelers in the relational world confuse them, but at least in principle entities and tables can be treated separately. Indeed, although the database design should be *based on* the entity model it is often appropriate for the designer to *depart from* that structure for reasons of performance or other physical characteristics of the system.

Similarly, in the world of object-orientation classes of things in the world remain very different from classes that are computer artifacts. The confusion between these things can be unfortunate. Even in the object-oriented world, the bits of code that describe classes are not the same things as the entity classes the code describes.

Moreover, an object-oriented program is also concerned with things not visible to the business at all. These are objects defined strictly for the purpose of aiding in computer processing. Even so, as in the relational world, if it is to be responsive to business requirements the class structure for an object-oriented design should be derived from that of the business's entity-relationship model. Like the relational model, however, the object-oriented design model may also diverge from the entity-relationship model for good and valid design reasons.

Because of the importance of distinguishing between the real-world "class" of requirements analysis from the computerized "class" of design, the former will continue to be referred to here as ENTITY CLASS. The latter will here be called CLASS IMPLEMENTATION. Figure 2–32 shows CLASS IMPLEMENTATION, representing the piece of code that describes a class. Because it refers to a piece of program code, CLASS IMPLEMENTATION will be described in more detail in Chapter Three, and the symbols are in gray here.

Unlike in the relational world, sub-types and super-types can be implemented directly in an object-oriented design. That is, each IMPLEMENTATION may be *a generalization of* one or more other CLASSES, and each IMPLEMENTATION may be *inheriting from* one and only one other IMPLEMENTATION. (For philosophical reasons, in this book we are ruling out multiple inheritance. Although, of course, the model could be changed to accommodate it.)* Meilir Page-Jones describes a CLASS IMPLEMENTATION as being in one of four categories, represented here as sub-types of CLASS IMPLEMENTATION [Page-Jones 2000, pp. 233–240].**

– A BUSINESS CLASS represents something in the business, which may be any of the following.

> → A CLASS OF ENTITY, such as "Person" or "Contract"
> → An ATTRIBUTE CLASS, which provides a data type for INSTANCE ATTRIBUTES (described in material to follow), such as a "Balance" (of a bank account) or a "Unit cost" (of a product)
> → A ROLE CLASS such as "customer" or "patient"
> → A RELATIONSHIP CLASS, such as "AccountOwnership" or "Patient-Supervision" (analogous to an intersect entity in a Row Three entity-relationship diagram)

---

*Okay, if you insist, change the model to say that "each class may be inheriting from one or more other classes". You realize of course that this means you will have to add an intersect entity, such as CLASS STRUCTURE.

**Mr. Page-Jones calls each category a *domain*, but we are already using that word to mean something else, so here it is *category*.

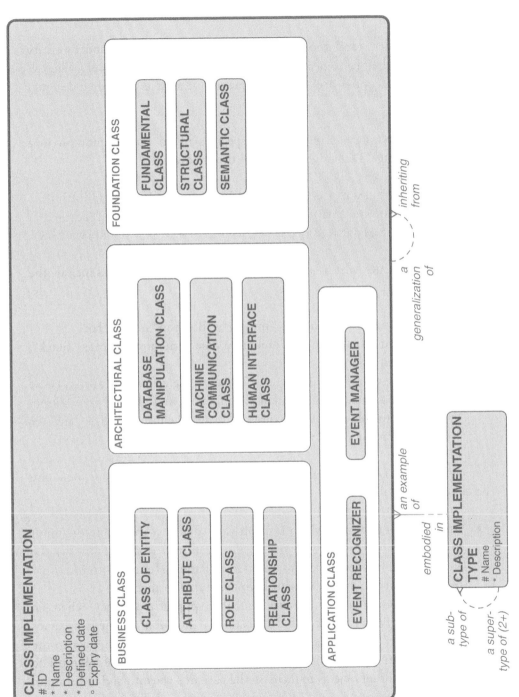

Fig. 2–32: Class implementations.

99

These correspond to (and should be based on) the conceptual model's entity classes, attributes, relationship roles, and association classes, respectively. The following remaining categories are only the concern of the object-oriented designer and programmer.

– An ARCHITECTURAL CLASS concerns the specifics of an implementation in a particular computer. This might be one of the following.

  → A HUMAN INTERFACE CLASS such as a "Window" or "CommandButton"
  → A DATABASE MANIPULATION CLASS such as a "Transaction" or "Backup"
  → A MACHINE-COMMUNICATION CLASS, such as "Port" or "RemoteMachine"

– A FOUNDATION CLASS, which is usable widely. FOUNDATION CLASSES include the following.

  → A FUNDAMENTAL CLASS, such as "Integer", "Boolean", and "Char".
  → A STRUCTURAL CLASS that implements a data structure, such as "Stack", "Queue", and so on.
  → A SEMANTIC CLASS, such as "Date", "Time", "Angle", and so forth. (These classes have richer meaning than the fundamental classes. In addition, their attribute values may be expressed in specific units, such as "feet" or "seconds" [Page-Jones 2000, pp. 233–240].)

– An APPLICATION CLASS represents something specific to an application, and may be either of the following.

  → An EVENT-RECOGNIZER, which is a software construct that monitors input to check for the occurrence of specific events in (messages from) the environment. For example, this might be a "Patient-TemperatureMonitor" that looks for the event "Patient becomes hypothermic".
  → An EVENT-MANAGER that carries out the appropriate policy when an event of a given type occurs. For example, the event "Patient becomes hypothermic" is a message from the appropriate event-recognizer to the class "WarmHypothermicPatient", which in turn sends the appropriate messages to other objects to increase the patient's warmth and to summon medical attention.

To provide for a bit more flexibility, the model redundantly also asserts that each CLASS IMPLEMENTATION must be an example of one and only one CLASS IMPLEMENTATION TYPE. These are the same categories represented previously as sub-types. That is, "Business class", "Application class", "Architectural class", and "Foundation class" are all CLASS IMPLEMENTATION TYPES. In addition, each CLASS TYPE may be a *super-type of* two or more other CLASS IMPLEMENTATION TYPES. The CLASS IMPLEMENTATION TYPE structure allows for further specification of the subcategories listed, which may not be shown on the model as sub-types.

### Business Rule

The first instances of CLASS IMPLEMENTATION TYPE must be "Business class", "Architectural class", "Foundation class", and "Application class". "Business class" must be listed as a *super-type of* a "Class of entity", "Attribute class", "Role class", and a "Relationship class". Similarly, other instances of CLASS TYPE must include the other sub-types shown in Figure 2–32.

The attributes shown in Figure 2–32 for CLASS IMPLEMENTATION ("Name" and "ID") are discussed in detail in Chapter Three in conjunction with program modules. Figure 2–33 shows that each CLASS IMPLEMENTATION can be *described by* one or more CLASS ELEMENTS. A CLASS ELEMENT is *an attribute of* one and only one CLASS IMPLEMENTATION describing it. This is analogous to ATTRIBUTE, which was *about* an ENTITY CLASS in the Row Three model shown previously. In object-oriented design, however, there are two kinds of CLASS ELEMENTS. An INSTANCE ATTRIBUTE takes on a different value for every occurrence of the CLASS. The INSTANCE ATTRIBUTE "Name", for example, for the CLASS IMPLEMENTATION "Person" is uniquely assigned to each person.

You can also have CLASS ATTRIBUTES. In entity-relationship modeling these are usually handled by creating a parent entity, but in object-oriented design they can be dealt with more directly and more intimately within the entity being described. A CLASS ATTRIBUTE for CONTRACT, for example, could be "Next Contract Number".

Note that CLASS ELEMENT also has the attribute "Visibility". This indicates the extent to which this CLASS ELEMENT (this INSTANCE ATTRIBUTE, for example) is

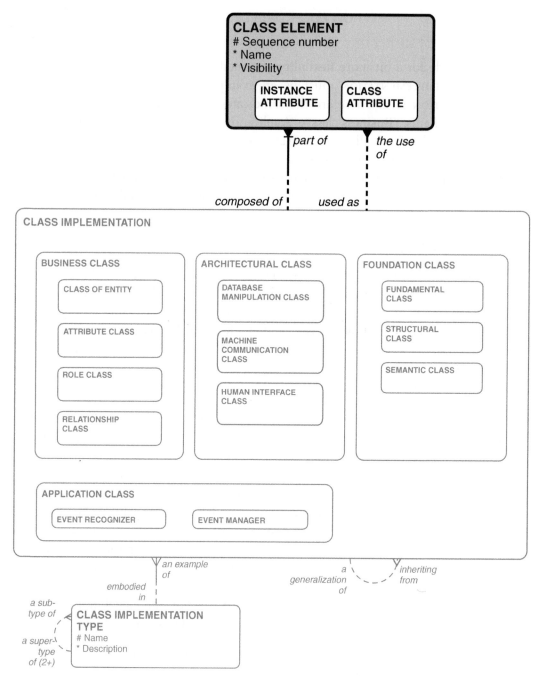

Fig. 2–33: Class elements.

available to any part of a system outside the CLASS it is *part of*. Visibility is of at least three kinds:

- *Public:* The CLASS ELEMENT may be seen and used by any other CLASS IMPLEMENTATION or OPERATION.
- *Protected:* The CLASS ELEMENT may be seen and used only within its CLASS IMPLEMENTATION and by classes that are inheriting from that class.
- *Private:* The CLASS ELEMENT may only be seen within the context of its CLASS IMPLEMENTATION.

Other kinds of visibility are implemented by specific object-oriented languages, but these three are the most commonly used. Note that a CLASS ELEMENT may itself be *the use of* another CLASS IMPLEMENTATION—specifically, a FOUNDATION CLASS or an ARCHITECTURE CLASS. For example, the INSTANCE ATTRIBUTE "Name" could itself be an ATTRIBUTE CLASS. Note also that although CLASS IMPLEMENTATION is grayed out—because as program code it is really owned by the Activities column (Chapter Three)—CLASS ELEMENT is not. It only appears here in the Data column.

## Objects

Figure 2–34 shows that a CLASS may be *embodied in* one or more actual OBJECTS; that is, an OBJECT is *an instance of* one and only one CLASS.*

## The Conceptual Model to Relational Database Design

Figure 2–35 shows how the COLUMN and TABLE definitions may be based on ATTRIBUTE and ENTITY CLASS definitions—via COLUMN ATTRIBUTE MAPPINGS and TABLE ENTITY CLASS MAPPINGS. In principle, an initial database design should be directly derived from the entity-relationship model structure. In most cases, a TABLE should be *based on* a single ENTITY CLASS. Things are not always as tidy as that, of course, because, among other things, the super-type/sub-type structures in an entity-relationship model cannot be directly implemented in a purely relational database.

---

*This, strictly speaking, is not part of the metamodel, but of the business model itself. OBJECTS contain the actual data values of an application. It is useful to show it here, though, because some important metamodel concepts can only be described in terms of actual OBJECTS.

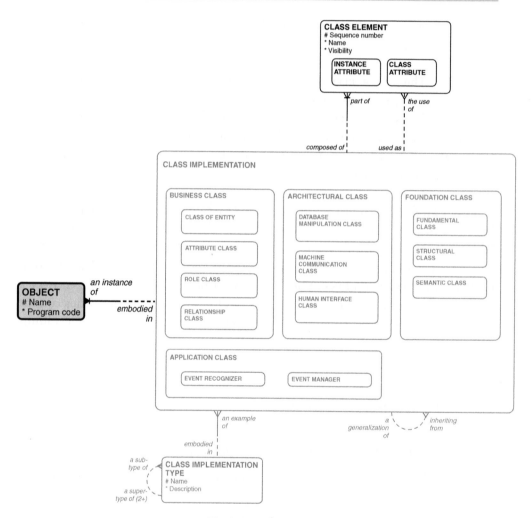

*Fig. 2–34: Objects.*

There are fundamentally three different approaches to mapping super-type/ sub-type structures to flat relational tables. Each has advantages and disadvantages, so the selection of an approach must be made with some care:

– A table can be defined for each super-type, encompassing all of its sub-types. Columns are then defined both for the super-type attributes and for those in

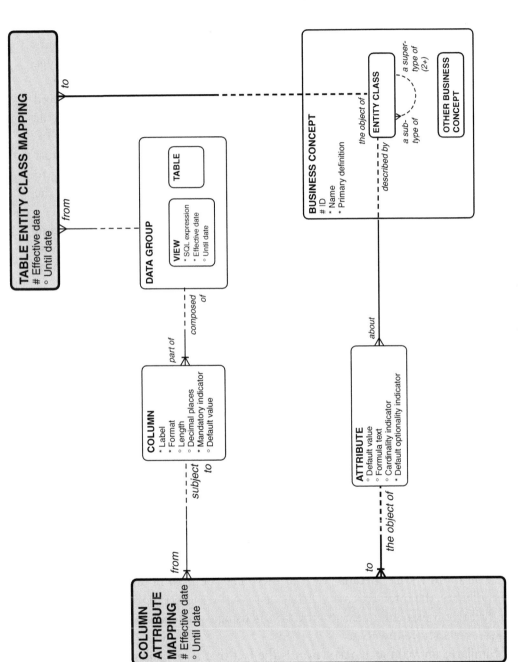

Fig. 2–35: Tables and entity classes.

each sub-type. This has the advantage of simplicity, but it means that many columns will have null values. Moreover, it will not be possible to require values for any of the sub-type columns. A column that describes a sub-type will only have values for rows that represent occurrences of that sub-type.

—  One table can be defined for each sub-type, to include both columns derived from its attributes and columns for all inherited super-type attributes. This allows for requiring a value for each row of a column, but it adds complexity to the structure. Any relationship pointing to the super-type, for example, must now be implemented (via an exclusionary arc) with foreign keys pointing to each of the corresponding sub-type tables. In addition, the columns for the super-type must be defined redundantly for each sub-type.

—  One table can be defined for the super-type and for each sub-type, with foreign keys pointing from the super-type to each sub-type. This approach is the most elegant, with the least redundancy and best control, but it is also the most complex to implement.

In principle, it should not be necessary to connect ENTITY CLASS and TABLE, since that relationship is implied by the mapping entity class, COLUMN ATTRIBUTE MAPPING, between ATTRIBUTE and COLUMN. Frequently, though, in the design process the relationships between entity classes and tables are identified before the individual columns and attributes are mapped. The configuration shown here provides the ability to make such provisional design decisions. Again, this is provisional. Once the COLUMN ATTRIBUTE MAPPINGS are complete, the TABLE ENTITY CLASS MAPPING entity class is redundant.

### The Conceptual Model to Object-Oriented Design

As implied by the definition given previously, a BUSINESS CLASS may be derived directly from the conceptual model created during requirements analysis. Specifically, as shown in Figure 2–36 a BUSINESS CLASS may be *based on* one or more CLASS DEFINITIONS, each of which is in turn *the use of* an ATTRIBUTE, ENTITY CLASS, or RELATIONSHIP ROLE. Because each of these may be *used in* one or more BUSINESS CLASSES, the intersect entity class CLASS DEFINITION ELEMENT is defined to be the fact that a particular CLASS DEFINITION is using a particular ATTRIBUTE, ENTITY CLASS, or RELATIONSHIP ROLE.

Similarly, an ATTRIBUTE DEFINITION is the fact that a particular ATTRIBUTE from the entity-relationship model is implemented as an INSTANCE ATTRIBUTE. That is,

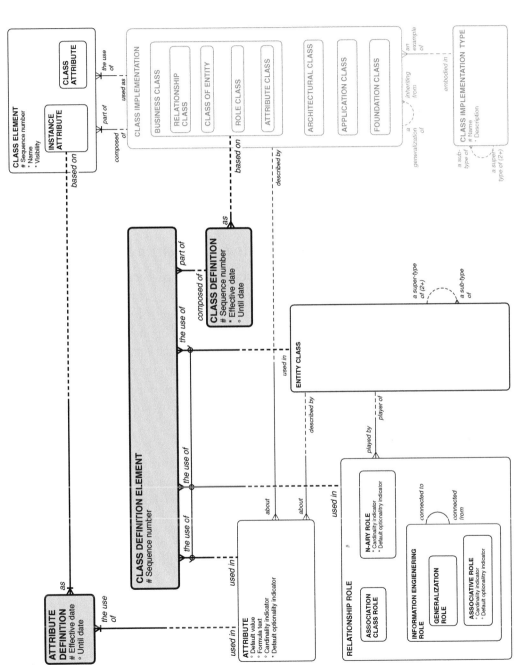

Fig. 2-36: Class definitions.

an ATTRIBUTE DEFINITION is *the use of* an ATTRIBUTE *as* an INSTANCE ATTRIBUTE. (As pointed out previously, the INSTANCE ATTRIBUTE may itself be *the use of* another CLASS.)

Among other things, this means that an ATTRIBUTE in a Row Three entity-relationship model may be either *used in* the definition of an INSTANCE ATTRIBUTE or *used in* the definition of a BUSINESS CLASS. Note that although the validation logic of the conceptual model can be drawn also for the object-oriented model the logic behind derived attributes does not apply here. This is because in the object-oriented world all attributes are considered derived, even if the derivation is "simply retrieve a value for the attribute". This derivation is more appropriately covered in the discussion of activities in Chapter Three.

### Object-Oriented Model to Relational Model: Persistence

Object-oriented programming may not have to be concerned with a physical database at all. Object-oriented design originated in the world of real-time systems, where it is perfectly common to define objects that only survive for the period the program defining them is running. In business applications, however, it is usually necessary to preserve an object's identity and data beyond the life of the program. That is, it is necessary to maintain *persistent objects*. A persistent object is an object whose existence continues after the program involved stops running. Given current technology, this is typically done by storing the objects as data in relational tables and columns.

Figure 2–37 shows that each CLASS IMPLEMENTATION may be *made persistent in* one or more PERSISTENCE MECHANISMS. Currently, the most common PERSISTENCE MECHANISMS are TABLES and COLUMNS in a *relational database management system*. CLASS IMPLEMENTATIONS are typically *made persistent in* TABLES, and INSTANCE ATTRIBUTES are typically *made persistent in* COLUMNS. This does not mean, however, that an OTHER PERSISTENCE MECHANISM might not also be used. Historically, they have been such things as ISAM files, network databases, or even simple files.

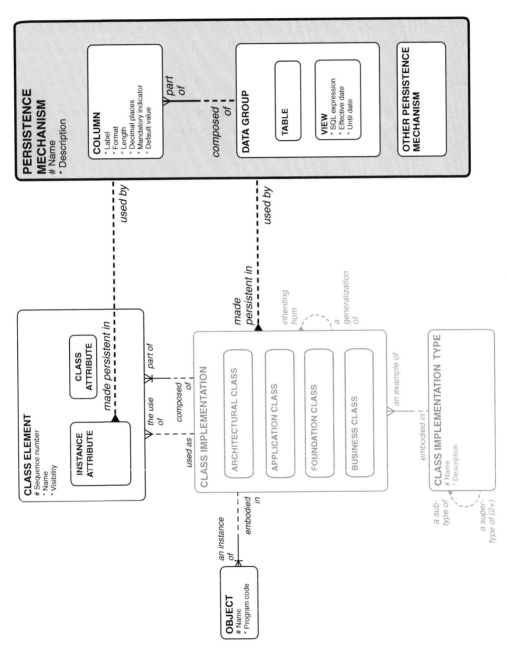

Fig. 2–37: Persistence class implementation.

Note that CLASS IMPLEMENTATIONS can made persistent in VIEWS. It is, after all, common for an object-oriented CLASS IMPLEMENTATION to be derived from someone's view of a collection of TABLES.

> **Business Rule**
>
> In a relational environment, an INSTANCE ATTRIBUTE may be *made persistent* only *in* a COLUMN. A CLASS IMPLEMENTATION may be *made persistent* only *in* a DATA GROUP.

## Extensible Markup Language

The *Extensible Markup Language (XML)* is a language for describing and giving structure to text and numeric data so that they can be transmitted from one place to another. It makes use of *tags* (like HTML tags) that identify data and the data's relationship to other data. It is analogous to data modeling in that it gives structure to data, but rather than being a graphic notation it is a means of labeling data with text. The following is an example of XML used to describe a data record that might be presented in a document.

```
<?XML version="1.0"?>
<!-    **** Basket ****    ->
<PRODUCT>
   <product_id>98756</product_id>
   <product_name>basket</product_name>
   <unit_of_measure>each</unit_of_measure>
   <specification>
         <variable>color</variable>
         <value>blue</value>
   </specification>
   <specification>
         <variable>size</variable>
         <value>large</value>
   </specification>
   <specification></specification>
   </specification>
</PRODUCT>
```

Most of what you see is descriptive of structure. The only data elements are the values shown in boldface. Around each data element are tags describing it. Each tag is enclosed in <angle brackets>. Each tag is paired. The first is a word or phrase (for example, <PRODUCT>); the second, further down, has the same word or phrase preceded by a right slash (for example, </PRODUCT>). According to the rules of XML, an end tag is always required in order to specify a set of data, although there may be no data between the beginning tag and end tag (e.g., <specification></specification>). A single tag can represent this, with the right slash simply following the initial tag phrase (such as <specification/>).

Tags can be nested. In the previous example, the tag <PRODUCT> contains (among others) the tag for <specification>, which in turn contains tags for <variable> and <value>. The data model in Figure 2–38 shows that an XML DOCUMENT may be *composed of* one or more XML TAGS, each of which in turn may also be *composed of* yet more XML TAGS. Note the attribute "Tag" for XML TAGS, which contains the word or phrase that is the tag for the element.

Note that the previous XML example, like all XML files, began with a standard header that revealed the version of XML the document uses. That is, each XML DOCUMENT is defined in terms of the rules appropriate to the XML VERSION it is *an example of*.

You may have noticed that in the example <PRODUCT> was described by one each of <product_id>, <product_name>, and <unit_of_measure>, but multiple occurrences of <specification>. There is nothing in XML by itself to determine which tags should be used where, but this nesting structure can be controlled by a specialized XML document called a *document type declaration (DTD)*. The DTD for the example looks as follows.

```
<!DOCTYPE PRODUCT [
  <!ELEMENT PRODUCT (product_id, product_name,
                     unit_of_measure?, specification*)>
  <!ELEMENT product_id (#PCDATA)>
  <!ELEMENT product_name (#PCDATA)>
  <!ELEMENT unit_of_measure (#PCDATA)>
  <!ELEMENT specification (variable, value)>
  <!ELEMENT variable (#PCDATA)>
  <!ELEMENT value (#PCDATA)>
]
```

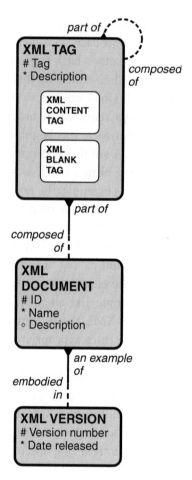

*Fig. 2–38: XML documents and elements.*

Because the subject of the DOCUMENT is products, the DOCTYPE is called PRODUCT. The first ELEMENT of this specification identifies the first tag (also PRODUCT), followed by a list of the tags contained with in it (product_id, product_name, unit of measure, and specification).

The question mark (?) following unit_of_measure means that whenever a <PRODUCT> is specified there may be one <unit_of_measure> tag, but there may be no more than one group following it. The asterisk (*) following specification means there may be one or more <specification> tag groups following <PRODUCT>, or there may not. If there had been a plus sign (+) after any tag, that would mean must be one or more. That is, the tag must appear after the parent tag, but it could appear multiple times. Absence of an asterisk or a question mark (as in "<product id>" and "<product name>") means that there must be one and only one value for each occurrence of <PRODUCT>.

After the list of tags within PRODUCT, each tag gets its own ELEMENT line. In most cases the argument with each is (#PCDATA), meaning simply that this tag will describe data. Specification, on the other hand, has its own list of arguments, "variable" and "value", just as PRODUCT did. Its tags are then listed as their own ELEMENTS.

Figure 2–39 shows that each XML DOCUMENT must be *constrained by* exactly one DOCUMENT TYPE DECLARATION. (Actually, you can create an XML DOCUMENT

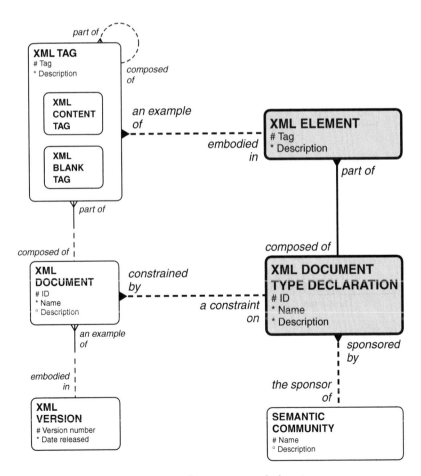

*Fig. 2–39: XML document type declaration.*

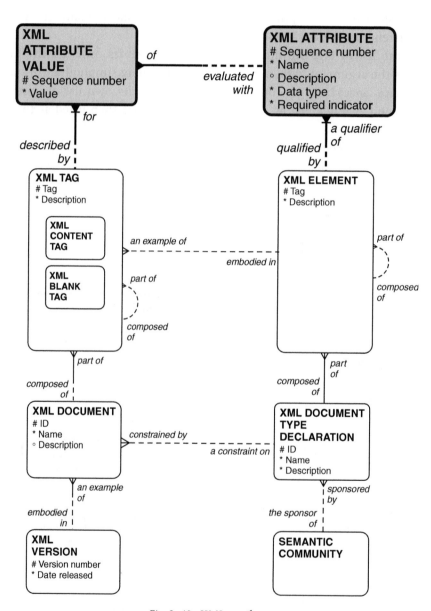

*Fig. 2–40: XML attributes.*

without a DTD, but it is not recommended.) Each DOCUMENT TYPE DECLARATION, then, must be *composed of* one or more XML ELEMENTS, where each XML ELEMENT may be *embodied in* one or more XML TAGS on real XML DOCUMENTS.

In addition to specifying data between beginning and ending tags, you can specify values for *XML attributes* in the beginning tag. For example, an alternative to the previous example might be the following.

```
<PRODUCT product_id=98756><\PRODUCT>
```

This would effectively "hard code" the document to be about product 98756. The DTD specification for that would look like this:

```
<!ELEMENT PRODUCT (#PCDATA)>
<!ATTLIST PRODUCT
        product_id CDATA #REQUIRED>
```

In Figure 2–40, XML ATTRIBUTE is *a qualifier of* an XML ELEMENT. It is *evaluated with* an XML ATTRIBUTE VALUE *for* a TAG that is *part of* an XML DOCUMENT.

XML is clearly a Row Four designer's way of representing data. Its strength is its ability to provide definitions for formats so that different organizations can communicate with each other. But it is hierarchical, so it is limited in its ability to express concepts. If it is only used to send batches of data, this is not a problem, but use of XML has to take into account this fundamental limitation.*

What is reasonable to do is to map the tags to elements in a conceptual data model, so that the implications of their relationships can be fully understood. Figure 2–41 shows how one or more XML TAG DEFINITIONS define either an XML ELEMENT (from a DTD) or an XML TAG using an ATTRIBUTE or an ENTITY CLASS. Similarly, an XML CONTENT TAG may be *the container of* one or more BUSINESS TERMS via an XML ELEMENT CONTENT.

## ROW SIX: THE PRODUCTION SYSTEM

To model Row Five, the builder's view, would require intricate metamodels describing the inner workings of Oracle, DB2, SQL Server, Sybase, and the rest. That is beyond the scope of this book.

---

*Some people are indeed creating databases using XML. This is very worrisome.

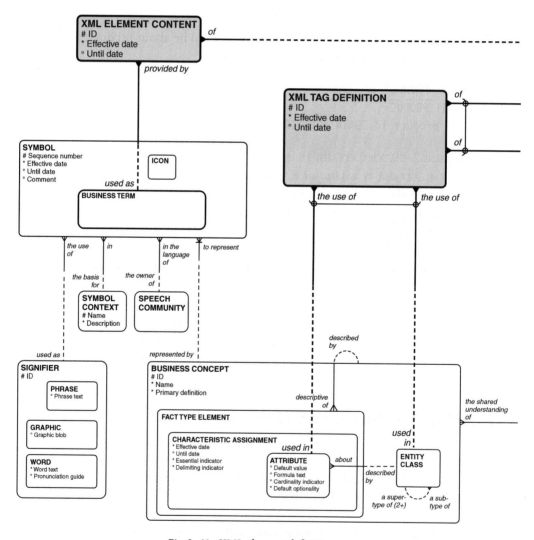

*Fig. 2–41: XML element definitions.*

116

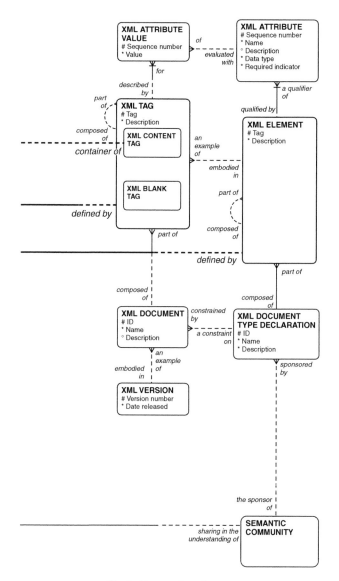

**XML ATTRIBUTE VALUE**
\# Sequence number
\* Value

*of*

*evaluated with*

**XML ATTRIBUTE**
\# Sequence number
\* Name
° Description
\* Data type
\* Required indicator

*for*

*described by*

*part of*

*a qualifier of*

*qualified by*

**XML TAG**
\# Tag
\* Description

*composed of*

*container of*

**XML CONTENT TAG**

*an example of*

**XML ELEMENT**
\# Tag
\* Description

*embodied in*

*part of*

**XML BLANK TAG**

*composed of*

*defined by*

*defined by*

*part of*

*part of*

*composed of*

*composed of*

**XML DOCUMENT**
\# ID
\* Name
° Description

*constrained by*

*a constraint on*

**XML DOCUMENT TYPE DECLARATION**
\# ID
\* Name
\* Description

*embodied in*

*an example of*

*sponsored by*

**XML VERSION**
\# Version number
\* Date released

*the sponsor of*

*sharing in the understanding of*

**SEMANTIC COMMUNITY**

*Fig. 2–41: continued.*

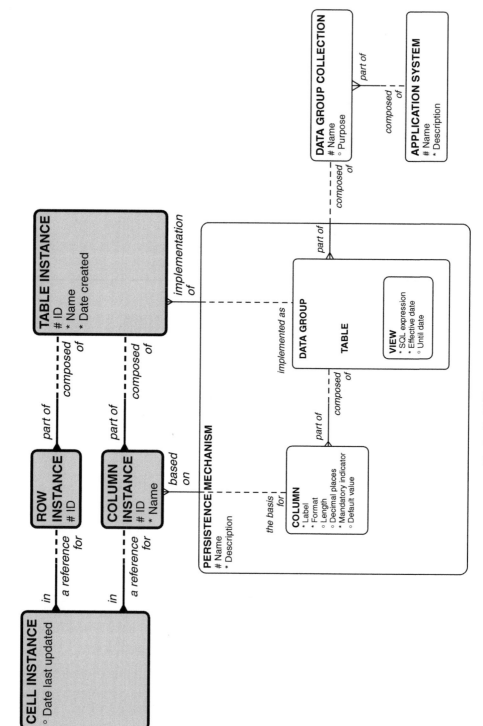

Fig. 2–42: Table instances.

What is useful, however, is to take a moment to look at the model of a built, existing database. This is shown in Figure 2–42. Each DATA GROUP is implemented in one or more TABLE INSTANCES, which by definition must each be *composed of* ROW INSTANCES and COLUMN INSTANCES. The intersection of one row and one column is a CELL INSTANCE. Each datum in the database corresponds to one CELL INSTANCE.

As shown in Figure 2–43, the collections of CELLS that constitute TABLE INSTANCES must reside somewhere. In fact, they are *kept in* a DATABASE INSTANCE, which is a kind of VIRTUAL SITE (described further in Chapter Four). Each DATABASE INSTANCE and TABLE INSTANCE must in turn be *created on* a PROGRAM COPY *of* a DATABASE MANAGEMENT SYSTEM (DBMS).

A database management system is *created by* a COMPANY, such as Oracle, Microsoft, IBM, Sybase, or the like. Note that DATABASE MANAGEMENT SYSTEMS change over time, and when a PROGRAM COPY (DBMS version) of a new one is installed this brings with it a new set of DATABASE INSTANCES and TABLE INSTANCES. The new set of TABLE INSTANCES can still be *an implementation of* the older DATA GROUP, just as the new set of COLUMNS can still be *based on* the older COLUMN designs.

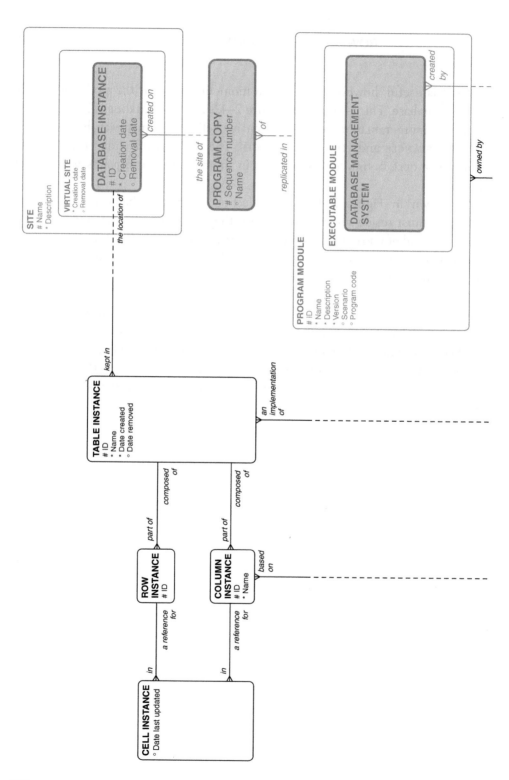

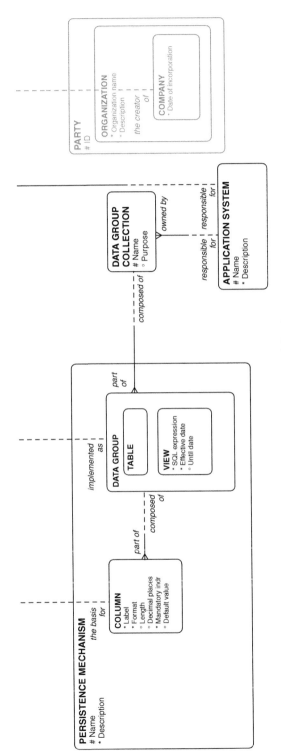

Fig. 2–43: The physical database.

121

# 3

# ACTIVITIES, FUNCTIONS, AND PROCESSES

*The test of a first-rate intelligence is the ability to hold two opposed ideas in the mind at the same time, and still retain the ability to function.*

—F. SCOTT FITZGERALD

*Home computers are being called upon to perform many new functions, including the consumption of homework formerly eaten by the dog.*

—DOUG LARSON

*Cats are intended to teach us that not everything in nature has a function.*

—UNKNOWN

## ACTIVITIES AND THE ARCHITECTURE FRAMEWORK

The Activities column (see Figure 3–1) of the architecture framework is concerned with *how* the enterprise carries out its work.

— The *planner* looks at the vision and mission of the enterprise and lays out an approach to how the organization will function.
— The *business owner* sees the overall functions of the business, as well as the actual processes that occupy its daily life, in terms of the mechanisms used to carry them out, the people involved, and the way the two communicate.
— The *architect* sees processes as expressions of business function, without regard to the systems and other mechanisms required to carry them out. The architect then organizes them in terms of responses to external events.
— The *designer* is concerned with the structure of the programs to be created to assist in carrying out the processes.
— The *builder* is deeply involved in the intricacies of programming languages and the other technologies required to create the systems.
— The *functioning system* is the inventory of programs and other technologies and the processes for keeping track of their use.

123

| | Data (What) | Activities (How) | Locations (Where) | People (Who) | Time (When) | Motivation (Why) |
|---|---|---|---|---|---|---|
| Objectives/ Scope (Planner's View) | List of things important to the enterprise | List of functions the enterprise performs | List of enterprise locations | Organization approaches | Business master schedule | Business vision and mission |
| Enterprise Model (Business Owner's View) | Language, divergent data model | Business process model | Logistics network | Organization chart | State / transition diagram | Business strategies, tactics, policies, rules |
| Model of Fundamental Concepts (Architect's View) | Convergent e/r model | Essential data flow diagram | Locations of roles | The viable system, use cases | Entity Life History | Business rule model |
| Technology Model (Designer's View) | Database design | System design, program structure | Hardware, software distribution | User interface, security design | Event processing | Business rule design |
| Detailed Representation (Builder's View) | Physical storage design | Detailed program design | Network architecture, protocols | Screens, security coding | Timing definitions | Rule specification program logic |
| Functioning System | _(Working System)_ | | | | | |
| | Databases | Program inventory, logs | Communications facilities | Trained people | Business events | Enforced rules |

_Fig. 3–1: Activities column._

Figure 3–1 shows the framework with the cells to be addressed by this chapter highlighted. These cells represent the views of the business owner, the architect, the designer, and the functioning system.

## DEFINITIONS

In his original framework, John Zachman labeled Column Two *Function*. In both the original data flow diagram notations and later in business process re-engineering, what a company does was called a *process*. In common conversation, we talk of *activities*. Indeed, in common conversation all three terms are bandied about as though they were synonymous. For our purposes, however, it is important to make distinctions among these terms.

— An *activity:* the most general super-type that encompasses all the following terms.
— A *function* is a type of activity to carry out an objective of the enterprise. It is described solely in terms of what it is intended to accomplish, and without regard to the technology used to carry it out or who is to perform it.* This is also described without reference to time. Functions represent a conceptual version of the Business Owner's View in Row Two. They begin from a global perspective (What is the mission of the enterprise?) and may be broken down to reveal a considerable amount of detail.
— A *process* is a type of activity performed by the enterprise to produce a specific output or to achieve a goal. It may or may not be described in terms of the mechanisms used or the parties performing it. A set of processes is usually described in sequence.

A *business process* describes an activity as carried out by business people, including the mechanisms involved. This is in the domain of Row Two, the Business Owner's View. Alternatively, the Architect in Row Three sees a *system process* that is about the data transformations involved in carrying out

---

*Note that this is different from the colloquial reference to system *functions*.

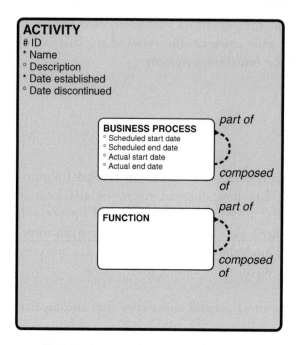

*Fig. 3–2: Activities, functions, and processes.*

a business process.* In either case, processes can be viewed at a high level or in atomic detail.

Figure 3–2 shows the Row Two (Business Owner's View) of ACTIVITY, with FUNCTION and BUSINESS PROCESS as sub-types. More about this later.

The terms are compared in Table 3–1. For this book, the term *activity* will be used as the title of the Architecture Framework column, in that it encompasses all of these concepts, although in this model ACTIVITY will be distinguished from SYSTEM PROCESS, which is described in the Row Three section (see pages 142 through 157).

---

*Note that in spite of the use of the word *system* to distinguish what are Row Three activities from the *business processes* of the Business Owner's View this is still not describing any particular computer system technology. It is only concerned with what processing of data might be carried out, and remains completely independent of any particular technology that might be used.

*Table 3–1: Activity types.*

| Term | Framework row | With mechanisms and parties? | In sequence? |
|------|---------------|------------------------------|--------------|
| Function | 2 | No | No |
| Business Process | 2 | Yes | Yes |
| System Process | 3 | No | Yes |
| Activity | 2, 3 | Yes/no | Yes/no |

This book primarily discusses functions and business processes (see Figure 3–2) when talking about the Business Owner's View and system processes when talking about the Architect's View.

## TYPES OF PROCESS MODELS

One difficulty in trying to describe activity modeling is that there are so many different ways to do it! To be sure, the underlying concepts are pretty universal, but you would never know it to look at the variety of techniques available.

The first type of process model in general use was introduced almost simultaneously by Tom DeMarco [DeMarco 1978] and by Chris Gane and Trish Sarson [Gane and Sarson 1979]. This was the *data flow diagram*, which provided a means of representing the flows of data among processes, external entities (the ultimate sources and destinations of data), and *data stores* (where data could reside temporarily between processes). It included the ability to decompose processes into more detail. In addition, the authors made a distinction between the *physical data flow diagram* and the *logical data flow diagram*. Mr. DeMarco extended these ideas to describe the process of moving from a current physical data flow diagram to a logical data flow diagram to a new physical data flow diagram.

Mr. DeMarco was a little fuzzy, however, as to how one distinguished a physical data flow diagram from a logical one. It was not until James McMenamin and John Palmer published *Essential Systems Analysis* [McMenamin and Palmer 1984] that this process was formalized. Messrs. McMenamin and Palmer came up with the idea of the *essential data flow diagram*. Its characteristic is that it consists of *essential processes*, which are defined to be the complete responses to an external event. Essential processes, in turn, are subdivided into *fundamental processes*, which carry out the work of the enterprise, and *custodial processes*, which maintain the data required by fundamental processes.

In the early 1990s the subject of *business process re-engineering* became popular and resulted in the rise of something Geary Rummler and Alan Brache called a *process map* [Rummler and Brache 1995]. These are similar to physical data flow diagrams, but they organize processes according to the departments or people who perform them. They focus less on the data being communicated than on the sequence of tasks expressed in common language, and instead of being concerned with physical and logical data flows they simply reflect the structure of tasks that currently exist ("as is") and that are planned as the result of the analysis ("to be").

Shortly after this, *use cases* became popular in the object-oriented world. This technique was originally described by Ivar Jacobson [Jacobson 1992] and then elaborated on by, among others, Alistair Cockburn [Cockburn 2000]. These are also similar to data flow diagrams, in that they have communications between external entities (here called "actors") and processes, but the assumption is that the processes involved represent computer systems (typically shown only as a single process representing the entire system). The content of data flows are not documented, and rather than being decomposed into lower-level detail, these details are simply described in text as "steps". There is no notion of storing data in intermediate data stores.

Meanwhile, back when Ms. Sarson and Messrs. DeMarco and Gane were inventing data flow diagrams, the federal government was embarking on its Integrated Computer Aided Manufacturing (ICAM) project. This was an approach to designing and building aircraft. Out of this work came some modeling techniques that were later codified by ITT as a Structured Analysis and Design Technique (SADT). In 1981, the Air Force recognized the value of SADT and requested a version for the Air Force. This was the source of the *IDEF* series of modeling techniques.*

"The full IDEF set (IDEF0, IDEF1, and IDEF3—later expanded to include IDEF1X, IDEF4 and IDEF5)** was designed to support systems analysis, where a 'system' may be a computer system, a non-computerized process, or an entire enterprise" [Feldmann 1998, p. 7]. *IDEF1* is a general approach to modeling data,

---

*IDEF stands for ICAM Definition.

**For a very good summary of all IDEF techniques, see the web site sponsored by Knowledge Based Systems at *http://www.idef.com* [Knowledge Based Systems 2005].

whereas *IDEF1X* specifically addresses the design of relational databases. IDEF4 is a way of looking at object-oriented design. IDEF5 provides a method that assists in the creation, modification, and maintenance of *ontologies*.

*IDEF3* is an approach to describing flows in terms of decisions made, whereas *IDEF0* is for simply laying out an enterprise's functions. According to the IDEF web site, "IDEF0 is a method designed to model the decisions, actions, and activities of an organization or system" [KBSI 2005]. In this sense, the idea is that it is modeling functions rather than processes. The same site describes *IDEF3* as providing "a mechanism for collecting and documenting processes. IDEF3 captures precedence and causality relations between situations and events in a form natural to domain experts by providing a structured method for expressing knowledge about how a system, process, or organization works" [KBSI 2005].

In 1998, Clarence Feldmann published *The Practical Guide to Business Process Re-engineering Using IDEF0* [Feldmann 1998], which is a very clear description of IDEF0. It discusses "actions", however, which leaves the subtler distinctions between function and process unresolved.

IDEF0 is very similar to data flow diagramming in its discipline, although it does not explicitly document the external entities or data stores involved. It models the logical structure of each process, but it includes the ability in each case to add an arrow describing the mechanism used for the process. In addition, unlike any other technique it distinguishes between data used by the process and controls that affect it and trigger it.

One of the model types provided with UML is a process model [Rumbaugh et al. 1999]. This is organized like a BPR process model, in terms of who is doing the processing, and it does have data stores in the form of "objects". It also has an explicit symbol for representing processes occurring in parallel.

Table 3–2 shows the techniques just described and their primary characteristics. It is the objective of the metamodel in this book to encompass nearly all concepts revealed by all of these techniques. By necessity, each entity class can have only one name (and many of them come from data flow diagramming), but the intention is to provide a structure that can accommodate all approaches.

## ROW TWO: FUNCTIONS AND BUSINESS PROCESSES

The sections that follow explore functions and business processes.

*Table 3–2: Comparison of techniques.*

| Technique | Framework row | Mechanisms? | External entities? | Identify controls? | Swim lanes? | Decompose processes? |
|---|---|---|---|---|---|---|
| Physical DFD | 2, 4 | Yes | Yes | No | No | Yes |
| Logical/essential DFD | 3 | No | Yes | No | No | Yes |
| Process Map | 2 | Yes | Yes | No | Yes | Yes |
| UML Process Model | 3, 4 | No | No | (Use state chart instead) | Yes | No |
| Use Case | 3, 4 | No | Yes | Yes | No | No |
| IDEF0 | 2, 3, 4 | Yes | No | Yes | No | Yes |

## Functions

A *function* is an activity performed by the business, described without regard to any mechanisms, sequence, or actors involved with doing it. Each function is intended to carry out the *mission* of the business, which is why they are usually presented in hierarchical form, with the mission at the top. That is, underneath the mission are typically presented between five and nine functions to carry it out. Each of these, then, is further decomposed into another five to nine functions. The process is repeated until one arrives at a set of elementary business functions that constitute the bottom of the hierarchy.

An *elementary business function* is defined as a function at the lowest level of detail. This is a function that once started cannot be stopped without changing the nature of the function [Barker and Longman 1992, p. 40]. A sample function hierarchy diagram for a public library is shown in Figure 3–3.*

The MISSION of an organization differs from its FUNCTIONS, in that the former sets the tone for everything the company does. More than describing just a thing to be done, it is a statement of the overall method for the ongoing operation of the organization. Where FUNCTIONS tend to be terse verb-object combinations ("Hire employees"), the mission tends to be a complex sentence not only describing what the organization is out to do ("Provide donuts to the community") but including

---

*This example is taken from the author's *Requirements Analysis: From Business Views to Architecture* [Hay 2003].

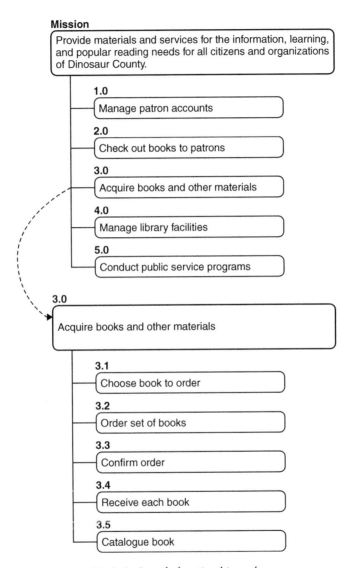

*Fig. 3–3: Sample function hierarchy.*

descriptions of why it wants to do that. It includes value statements such as "…thereby increasing that community's joy and pleasure".

In the case of the library whose function hierarchy is shown in Figure 3–3, its mission is to "Provide materials and services for the information, learning,

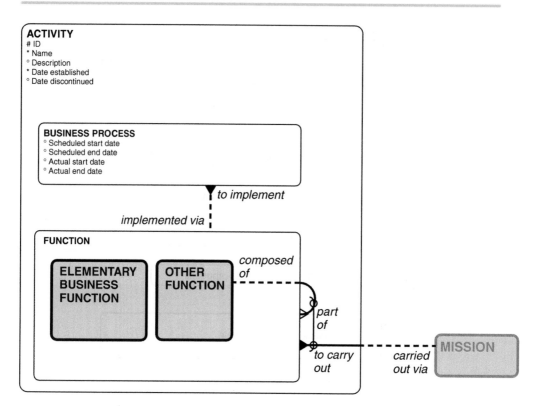

*Fig. 3–4: Functions.*

and popular reading needs for all citizens and organizations of Dinosaur County." More succinctly, functions include "Manage patron accounts", "Check out books to patrons", and so forth. Note that "Acquire books and other materials" is further broken down into five sub-functions.

Figure 3–4 shows the metamodel of FUNCTION as a hierarchy, starting with the MISSION of the organization at the top, and numerous BUSINESS FUNCTIONS underneath it, culminating with a set of ELEMENTARY BUSINESS FUNCTIONS at the bottom. That is, a MISSION may be *carried out via* one or more FUNCTIONS. Each OTHER FUNCTION (that is, each function that is not an ELEMENTARY BUSINESS FUNCTION) may then be *composed of* one or more OTHER FUNCTIONS or ELEMENTARY BUSINESS FUNCTIONS.

Each FUNCTION, then, must be *to carry out* either one MISSION or one OTHER FUNCTION. Note that MISSION is gray. It is here borrowed from Chapter Seven.

Previously, it was stated that "between five and nine" functions are to appear at each level. These numbers are not arrived at by accident: In a fascinating 1956 study, "The Magical Number Seven, Plus or Minus Two: Some Limits on Our Capacity for Processing Information" [Miller 1956], G. A. Miller postulated that the human brain can only hold seven (plus or minus two) "things" in active memory.

This is why we used to be able to remember seven-digit phone numbers, but now that area codes are meaningless we have a terrible time learning our friends' new 10-digit numbers. When confronted with a display of two or three points in a presentation, we see it as trivial.* When confronted with 10 or more points, it looks complex. In short, to make a function hierarchy understandable each row in the hierarchy should have only seven plus or minus two functions.

It is possible to establish a hierarchy of FUNCTIONS, where every function meets the standards described previously (no mechanisms or actors, and no sequence) all the way to ELEMENTARY BUSINESS FUNCTIONS. As you get further down, however, the temptation is to describe the actual BUSINESS PROCESSES being carried out *to implement* each of these FUNCTIONS. This is also shown in Figure 3–4.

## Business Processes

A *business process* is an activity that transforms either physical materials or data from one state into another. As the output of one process is typically used by the next, a sequence is implied. It is possible also to describe the particular mechanisms (forms, equipment, computer systems, and so on) used to carry out each process.

Figure 3–5 again shows that a FUNCTION may be *implemented via* one or more BUSINESS PROCESSES. As with FUNCTIONS, each OTHER BUSINESS PROCESS may be *composed of* one or more OTHER BUSINESS PROCESSES or ELEMENTARY BUSINESS PROCESSES.

By definition, an ELEMENTARY BUSINESS PROCESS is at the bottom of the tree, so it may not be *composed of* any other BUSINESS PROCESSES. Note that although each FUNCTION *must* be *to carry out* either a MISSION or an OTHER FUNCTION a BUSINESS PROCESS may exist by itself.

Figure 3–5 shows that a BUSINESS PROCESS differs from a FUNCTION in that it may be *the user of* one or more MECHANISM TYPES, where a MECHANISM TYPE is

---

*After all, *trivial* comes from the Latin words for "three" and "way".

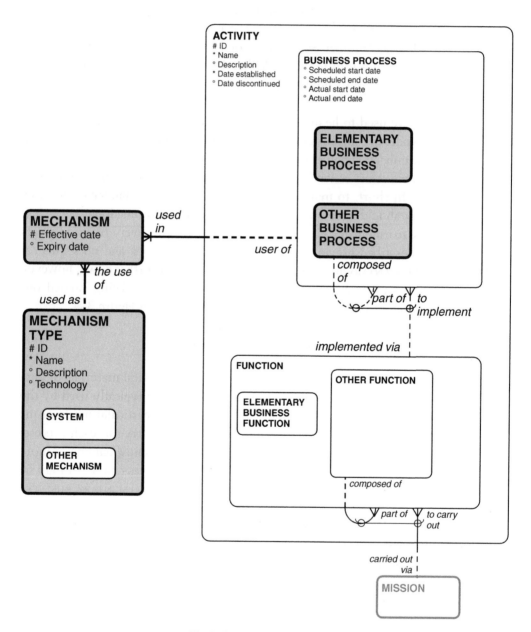

*Fig. 3–5: Business processes.*

the definition of a system, form, or some other tangible tool required to carry out the BUSINESS PROCESS. Because of the many-to-many nature of that relationship, MECHANISM is inserted to represent the fact that a particular BUSINESS PROCESS (such as "take order") is *the user of* a particular MECHANISM TYPE (such as the "Terminal attached to the Framis System").

BUSINESS PROCESS also differs from FUNCTION in that a BUSINESS PROCESS may be *the source of* one or more INTERNAL BUSINESS EVENT TYPES (shown in Figure 3–6),

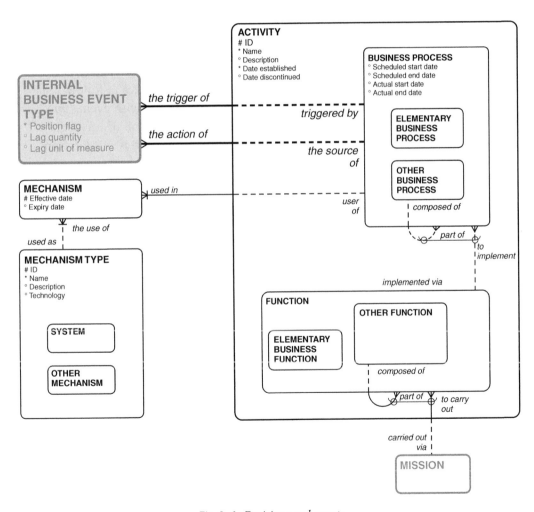

*Fig. 3–6: Decisions and events.*

each of which must then be *the trigger of* another BUSINESS PROCESS. (BUSINESS EVENT TYPES are defined and discussed in detail in Chapter Six.)

Note that although some process modeling techniques have a separate symbol (usually a diamond shape) to represent the decision point this is unnecessary in the metamodel. As long as we can represent one or more INTERNAL BUSINESS EVENT TYPES as *the action of* a BUSINESS PROCESS, the alternative decision values are implicit in the definition of the BUSINESS PROCESS itself. For example, an instance of the BUSINESS PROCESS ("Evaluate credit rating") may be the cause of either the INTERNAL BUSINESS EVENT TYPE "loan granted" or the INTERNAL BUSINESS EVENT TYPE "loan refused". "Loan granted" will then be *the trigger of* the BUSINESS PROCESS to process the loan, and "loan refused" will be *the trigger of* the BUSINESS PROCESS to "close the application".

Because events are going to be an important concept in the pages to follow, it is important to realize that in a metamodel we are only concerned with event *types*, not actual events. That is, a BUSINESS EVENT TYPE is the *definition of* a *category* of events: "Receive order from a customer on a date", not "Receive order from Smith Co. on July 18, 2005." Actual events are the subject of the business model, not the metamodel.

By definition, both a BUSINESS EVENT TYPE and a business event represent an instant in time, whereas a BUSINESS PROCESS takes place over a period in time. For this reason, when a BUSINESS PROCESS is *the decision to trigger* a BUSINESS EVENT TYPE only a specified point in the BUSINESS PROCESS is involved. This is identified by the "Position flag", an attribute of BUSINESS EVENT TYPE. It can have the values "Start", "End", or "Lag", meaning the event takes place at the start of the BUSINESS PROCESS, the end of it, or at some specified point during it. If the value of "Position flag" is "Lag", then the attribute "Lag quantity" tells how far into the process constitutes the event. "Lag unit of measure" defines whether the Lag quantity is in "days", "weeks", or even "hours".

Figure 3–7 introduces the ESSENTIAL BUSINESS PROCESS, which is defined as the collection of ELEMENTARY BUSINESS PROCESSES that constitutes a complete response to an EXTERNAL BUSINESS EVENT TYPE. As discussed in more detail in Chapter Six, an EXTERNAL BUSINESS EVENT TYPE is something that occurs in the world, outside the control of the enterprise. This may not only be something that happens, such as the receipt of an order; it may simply be the passage of time, as in "the end of the quarter" or "the first day of the month". In this case, the "Temporal indicator" attribute of EXTERNAL BUSINESS EVENT TYPE **must be set** to "True". This is distinct

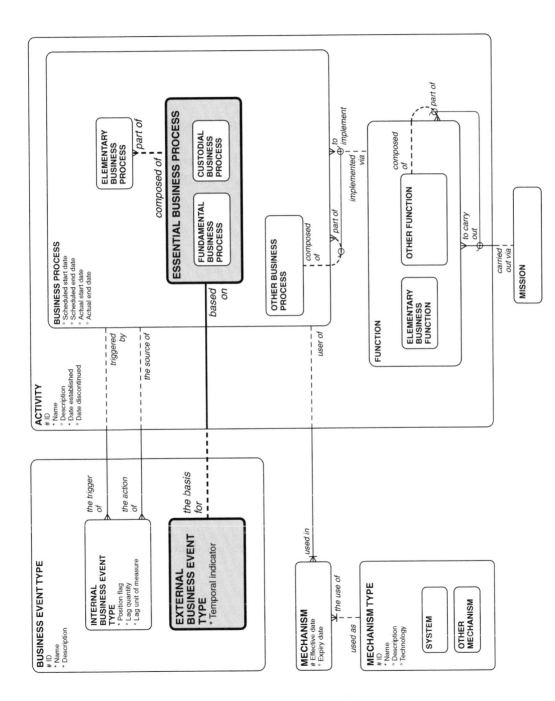

Fig. 3–7: Essential business processes.

from an INTERNAL BUSINESS EVENT TYPE, which is *the action of* another BUSINESS PROCESS within the enterprise itself.

An ESSENTIAL BUSINESS PROCESS must be either a FUNDAMENTAL BUSINESS PROCESS (which is directly *to implement* a BUSINESS FUNCTION) or a CUSTODIAL BUSINESS PROCESS, which provides data required for a FUNDAMENTAL BUSINESS PROCESS. For example, the process to "Maintain product definitions" is a CUSTODIAL BUSINESS FUNCTION required to support the FUNDAMENTAL BUSINESS PROCESS, "Sell products". An INTERNAL EVENT TYPE must be *the trigger of* any type of BUSINESS PROCESS, but an EXTERNAL EVENT TYPE must specifically be *the basis for* (defining) an ESSENTIAL BUSINESS PROCESS.

## Sample Process Model

Figure 3–8 shows a detailed process model for functions 3.4 and 3.5 of the library described in the function hierarchy model shown previously. It is organized in terms of "swim lanes" so that all processes carried out by the same department are in the same swim lane. In this example, the Receiving Department work begins with the event "Receipt of book". The department then confirms that the shipment is correct, based on comparison with the "blue" copy of a purchase order on file. (Presumably, when the books were ordered the blue copy of the purchase order was sent to the Receiving department for this purpose.) The book is handed off to the Cataloguing department, which in turn assigns a Dewey Decimal number to it, thereby identifying its classification—and from that its proper location in the library. The book is then added to the shelves, and a catalogue card is prepared, describing the book and recording its Dewey number.*

The Receiving department also marks the blue purchase order copy "Received" and sends it to the Accounts Payable department. (This is equivalent to sending a message "Book received".) When that department subsequently receives an invoice from the vendor, it pays for the book. Figure 3–8 shows three ELEMENTARY BUSINESS PROCESSES.

- Confirm title, quantity
- Classify book
- Pay invoice

---

*Yes, this is an old library, with paper purchase orders and a card catalogue. It seems ripe for some systems updating, yes?

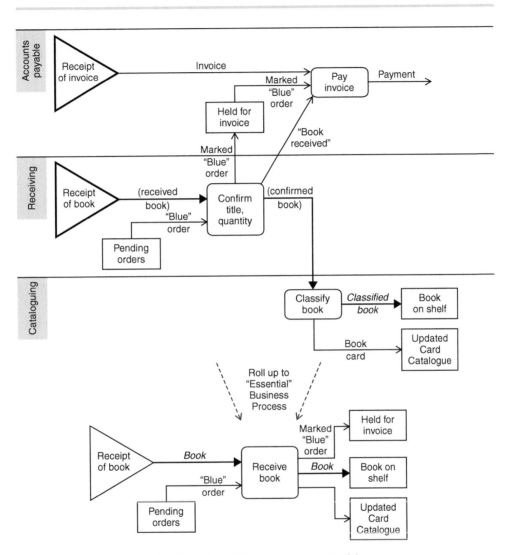

Fig. 3–8: Sample Business Process Model.

In addition, four *data stores* are shown:

– Pending orders
– Held for invoice
– Book on shelf
– Updated Card Catalogue

All of these elements, except for the two concerning invoices, can be rolled up into the ESSENTIAL BUSINESS PROCESS "Receive each book". The controlling EXTERNAL BUSINESS EVENT TYPE in this case is "Receipt of book". "Pay invoice" is not part of this ESSENTIAL BUSINESS PROCESS, because it is not triggered by the "Receipt of book" event. Instead, it is triggered by a combination of the EXTERNAL EVENT TYPE "Receipt of invoice" and the INTERNAL EVENT TYPE "Book received".

In addition to *external* EVENT TYPES, OTHER BUSINESS PROCESSES within the organization often trigger ELEMENTARY BUSINESS PROCESSES and OTHER BUSINESS PROCESSES. These triggerings (like the message "Book received", described previously) are examples of INTERNAL BUSINESS EVENT TYPES. That is, these describe events internal to the enterprise and under its control.

## Motivating Business Processes

In Chapter Seven, we will learn about the means and ends that are the foundation of a company's motivation. It is useful to understand these concepts here, however, at least to some extent. In that chapter you will learn that the *means* by which an enterprise can achieve its objectives can be either a *mission* or a *course of action*. In this case, a course of action must be either a *strategy* or a *tactic*.

As shown in Figure 3–9, it is important to note that these MEANS have an effect on BUSINESS PROCESSES. Predominant among the possible effects is an EFFORT *invoked by* a COURSE OF ACTION *through the use of* a BUSINESS PROCESS *to achieve* a DESIRED RESULT.

For example, the library's objective of increasing circulation by 10% this year may be *achieved via* an EFFORT that is *invoked by* the TACTIC of "increasing the advertising budget" *through the use of* the BUSINESS PROCESS of "Place advertisements in the local newspaper". The most significant type of EFFORT is the PROJECT, which in most companies is a unit of work and accomplishments. Often, these are grouped into an overall PROGRAM, which encapsulates the effort of a year or so.

## Access Roles

Chapter Five describes the effect of PEOPLE and ORGANIZATIONS have on (as well as the roles they play within) various parts of the metamodel. There, you will see a more complex model showing how PEOPLE are assigned to POSITIONS, along with the responsibilities that accompany those POSITIONS, but a couple of the definitions should suffice for our purposes here. Chapter Two introduced PARTY,

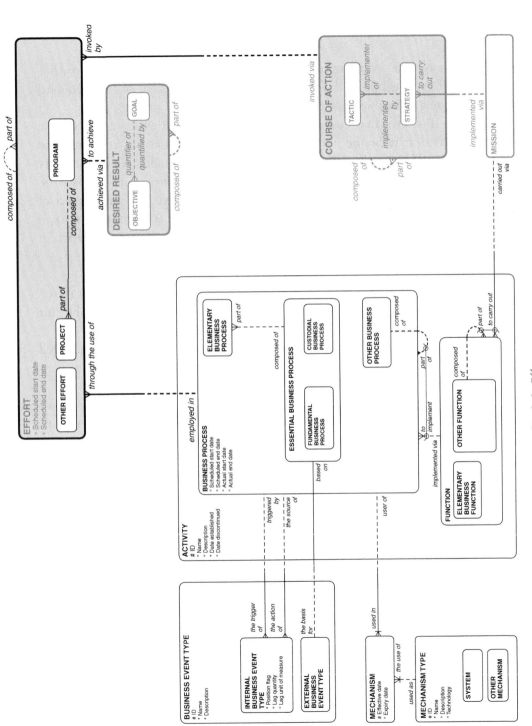

Fig. 3–9: Efforts.

which is a PERSON or ORGANIZATION of interest to the enterprise. POSITION is a specific set of responsibilities *defined by* an ORGANIZATION (such as a department) for carrying out its business.

Figure 3–10 shows that either a PARTY (a PERSON or an ORGANIZATION) or a defined POSITION may be the *player of* one or more ACCESS ROLES *for* a BUSINESS PROCESS. This addresses the "swim lanes" of the process model. An ACCESS ROLE is simply the fact that a PARTY or a POSITION (or other dimensions of POSITION, but more on that in Chapter Five*) is in some way involved in some aspect of the enterprise. In this context, an ACCESS ROLE must be a MANAGEMENT ROLE, a SPECIFICATION ROLE, or a PERMISSION ROLE, or it may be on OTHER ACCESS ROLE. Specifically:

— A MANAGEMENT ROLE is about the PARTY or POSITION that *manages* an ACTIVITY.
— A SPECIFICATION ROLE describes how a PARTY or POSTION is responsible for *specifying* exactly what the ACTIVITY, the EFFORT, or the MEANS is.
— A PERMISSION ROLE asserts that a PARTY or POSITION is *permitted or prohibited* from participating in the BUSINESS PROCESS.

In the previous example, the POSITION "Cataloguer" (that is, *the responsibility of* the ORGANIZATION "Catalogue Department") is the *player of* a MANAGEMENT ROLE *for* the ELEMENTARY BUSINESS PROCESS "Book classified".

## ROW THREE: PROCESSING DATA

If BUSINESS PROCESSES describe what the business does, how do we describe the corresponding data processes that support those activities? These "data processes" (herein called *system processes*) are described in detail in this section. Again, remember that by "system" is meant only that it is defined with the rigor that will be necessary to automate it. This makes its definitions more rigorous than the "business processes" described for the business owner's perspective. A system process is *not* concerned with any technology that might be employed.

---

*Chapter Five will show that ACCESS ROLE is granted to (*for*) a wide variety of elements throughout the model, not just BUSINESS PROCESS. It is also *played by* a wide variety of actors, not just PARTY and POSITION.

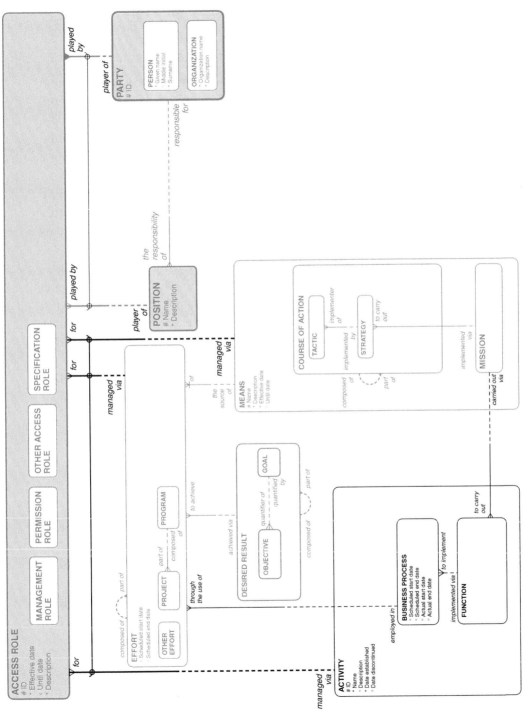

Fig. 3–10: Access roles.

## A Data Flow Diagram

A venerable and still commonly used model for describing the structure of system processes and their communications with each other is the *data flow diagram*. Figure 3–11 displays a data flow diagram.* This diagram differs from the Row Two process model described previously (Figure 3–8) in several ways. First, it has more data details, specifically describing the content of each data flow and including a process for "Record arrival of shipment".

Second, it is not represented in terms of the forms and mechanisms involved. For example, the Card catalogue from the process model is described here simply as a "Book archive". This helps free people from assuming that in future systems it has to be in the form of 3-inch by 5-inch paper cards.

Third, *data stores*—places where data rest while awaiting another process— are shown explicitly as open-sided rectangles. Finally, the system process model is different from the business process model because it is not organized into swim lanes. Indeed, although in this example each SYSTEM PROCESS is identified as to what department is doing it, even this is often not done in order not to prejudice any future implementation.

Note that this notation can also be used to produce Row Two process models. The "Physical" data flow diagram describes both processes and flows in terms of the mechanisms used, just as the Process Model described before did. Indeed, it is a good way to do that because it does provide for more detail in describing the data flows and stores.

To get to the Row Three "Logical" (or "Essential") data flow diagram, it is necessary to:

- Remove all references to physical mechanisms, changing the terms to describe the actual data involved.
- Remove any data stores that are only "buffers", accounting for differences in processing speed between the two processes.
- Remove any processes that are simply validating the results of the previous process. (Instead, fix the previous process.)

---

*This example is taken from the author's *Requirements Analysis: From Business Views to Architecture* [Hay 2003].

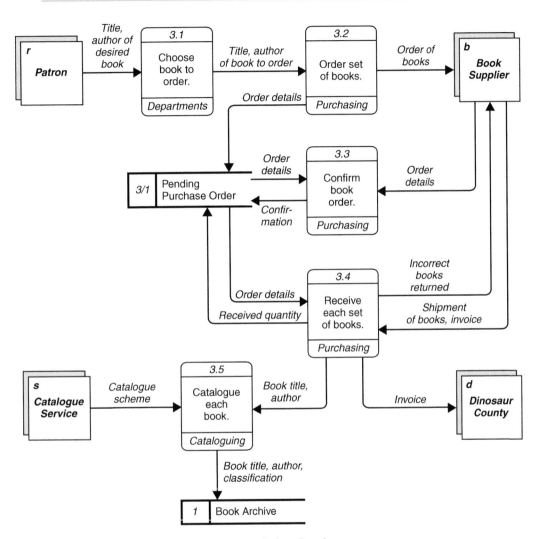

*Fig. 3–11: Sample data flow diagram.*

Figure 3–12 crosses the boundary between Row Two and Row Three of the framework. It shows that each BUSINESS PROCESS may be *carried out via* one or more BUSINESS PROCESS DESIGNS, where each BUSINESS PROCESS DESIGN is *described in terms of* one SYSTEM PROCESS. Thus, the BUSINESS PROCESS of receiving a shipment is *carried out via* the system (data) processes of: "Record receipt",

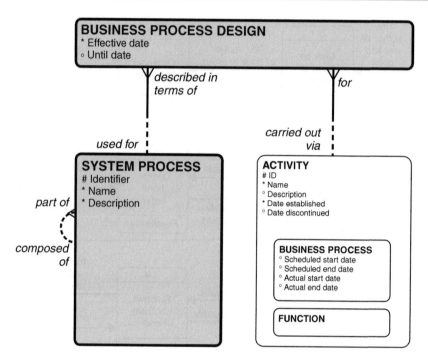

*Fig. 3–12: Business processes and system processes.*

"Record discrepancy", "Send message to Accounts Payable that goods are received", and so on.

Note that as with FUNCTIONS and BUSINESS PROCESSES each SYSTEM PROCESS may be *composed of* one or more other SYSTEM PROCESSES. This relationship is actually more complex than this, as will be shown below, but as shown here, the concept is valid. This supports the idea of taking one of the processes cited previously (such as "Receive each book") and creating another data flow diagram from it, revealing its component processes.

## System Processes and Data Flows

The data flow diagram of Figure 3–11 shows round-cornered boxes representing *system processes*, where data are transformed from one structure to another. *Data flows* (such as "Title, author of desired book", "Order details", and so forth) are represented by labeled arrows. By definition, all data originate and ultimately arrive at the square-cornered boxes, called *external entities*, such as "Patron", "Book Supplier", and so forth. In terms of our metamodel, these external entities nearly always correspond to our PARTIES—either PEOPLE or ORGANIZATIONS.

In the diagram, examples of system processes include "Choose book to order", "Order a set of books", and so forth. The rectangles that are open on the right represent *data stores*, where data may sit for a period of time before being further processed. The diagram shows two data stores: "Pending purchase order" (a list of orders awaiting the arrival of books) and "Book archive" (a modern word for what used to be called the card catalogue). As stated above, the arrows represent data flows from one system process, external entity, or data store to another.

The data flow arrows and the data stores are labeled with the content of the flows and stores in normal English. Each of these represents a *view* of a set of the data entity classes, relationships, and attributes of the sort discussed in Chapter Two. That is, each represents a VIRTUAL ENTITY CLASS that contains a reformulated collection of basic ENTITY CLASSES, RELATIONSHIP ROLES, and ATTRIBUTES (as described in Chapter Two).

Figure 3–13 shows the beginning of the metamodel for a data flow diagram. Here, a DATA FLOW defines how data (a VIRTUAL ENTITY CLASS) can be moved *from* one SYSTEM PROCESS *to* another. That is, a SYSTEM PROCESS may be the *source of* one or more DATA FLOWS, each *to* another SYSTEM PROCESS. In the library example cited previously, the VIRTUAL ENTITY CLASS "Title, author of book to order" is a DATA FLOW *from* the SYSTEM PROCESS "Choose book to order" *to* the SYSTEM PROCESS "Order set of books".

Processing is often not continuous over time. It may be necessary for data to be queued before it can be processed. In a Row Three model, this can only be because the system process is awaiting another piece of data. In a Row Two model, it could be a "buffer", which exists only because a process simply does not operate at the same speed as business processes that feed it. Such data stores must be removed for a Row Three model. Figure 3–14 shows that a DATA STORE is also *the use of* a VIRTUAL ENTITY CLASS, and that it may also be *the source of* and/or *the destination of* a DATA FLOW. That is, a DATA FLOW may either be *from* a SYSTEM PROCESS or *from a* DATA STORE, and it may also either be *to* a SYSTEM PROCESS or *to a* DATA STORE.

In the example, "Pending purchase order" is a DATA STORE that is *the use of* a VIRTUAL ENTITY CLASS probably of the same name. That VIRTUAL ENTITY CLASS is assembled from entity classes for "Patron", "Order", "Line Item", and "Book".

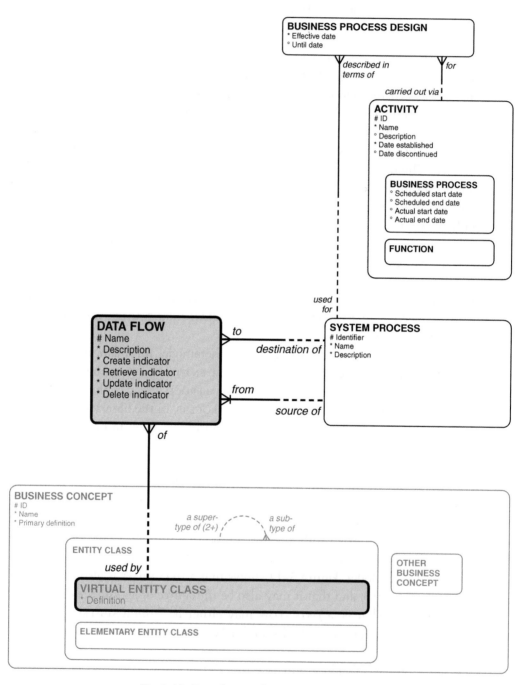

Fig. 3–13: *Data flows and system processes.*

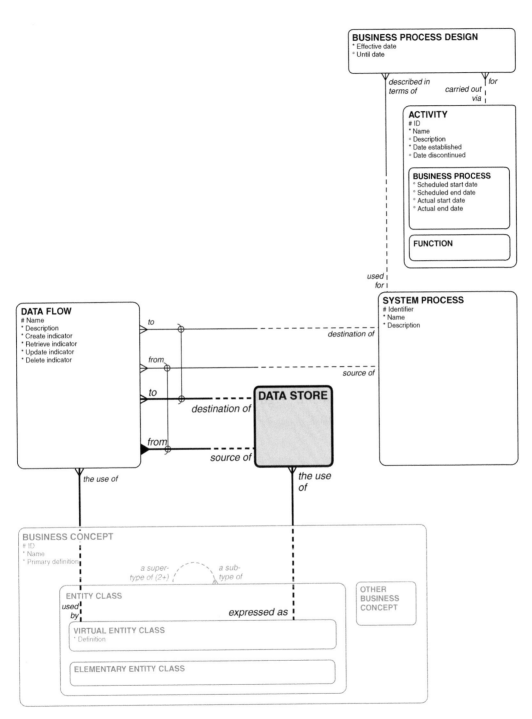

*Fig. 3–14: Data stores.*

"Order detail" is a flow of this VIRTUAL ENTITY CLASS *from* the DATA STORE "Pending purchase order" to the system process "Receive each book".

As perceived by business owners, processes are rarely seen separate from the mechanisms and the people who perform them. By the time a Row Three data flow diagram is created, however, mechanisms should no longer be represented. It is necessary in a Row Three data flow, though, to show the sources and destinations of *all* data, so Figure 3–15 again introduces PARTY and POSITION entity classes from column 3.

Here you can see that in addition to what has been seen so far, a DATA FLOW may be *from* or *to* a specified PARTY (such as "Sarah Jones" or "The Accounting Department") or simply defined as being *from* or *to* a POSITION, such as "Chief Bookkeeper". These are examples of EXTERNAL ENTITY. In the example, the EXTERNAL ENTITIES "Catalogue service" and "Book supplier" would be COMPANIES (a type of ORGANIZATION); "Dinosaur County" (Government) is a GOVERNMENT AGENCY; and "Patron" can be treated as a PARTY TYPE.

Note that in Row Three it is actually rare to see a data flow identified as *to* or *from* an individual person. The PARTY involved is usually an ORGANIZATION, such as a vendor company or a department.* Figure 3–15, then, shows that a DATA FLOW must be *from* one of the following.

- — PARTY
- — PARTY TYPE
- — POSITION
- — SYSTEM PROCESS
- — DATA STORE

Moreover, it also must be *to* one of the same entity classes.

## Access Roles and System Events

In the previous sample diagram, the data flow line from the external entity "Book Supplier" to the process "Receive each book" is labeled "Shipment of books". This flow need not actually contain any information, other than the fact that the

---

*On rare occasions, it may seem reasonable for a computer system to take on the role of external entity, but this is invariably when the system is being a mechanism used by a PARTY (specifically, an ORGANIZATION) to process data. Although that is okay in a Row Two model, it should be vigorously resisted in the architect's model.

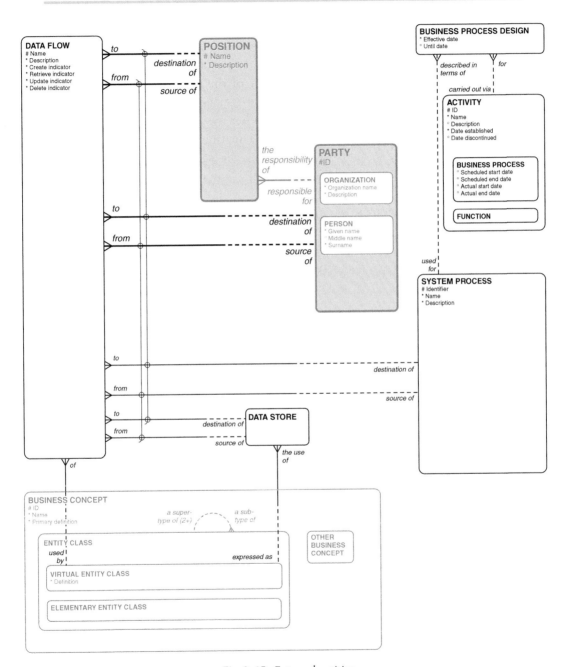

*Fig. 3–15: External entities.*

books were received. For this reason, it is not so much a DATA FLOW as a SYSTEM EVENT TYPE, as shown in Figure 3–16. That is, a SYSTEM EVENT TYPE is a message to a process that causes something to happen. It may not contain any of the data to be processed. Rather, it is simply a trigger of the process. The SYSTEM EVENT TYPE must have come *from* either another SYSTEM PROCESS or from a PARTY or a POSITION, or it must be *the action of* another SYSTEM PROCESS. In the latter case, since a SYSTEM EVENT TYPE is a moment in time, while a SYSTEM PROCESS takes place over time, SYSTEM EVENT TYPE has the same attributes as BUSINESS EVENT TYPE—described previously as "Position", "Lag quantity", and "Lag unit of measure".

As mentioned previously, we are here only concerned with event types, the definition of types of events. The example is about the idea of receiving books, not an actual receipt on July 18. Note that the MANAGEMENT ROLE that applied to BUSINESS PROCESS also applies to SYSTEM PROCESS.

## Essential System Processes

In speaking of FUNCTIONS and BUSINESS PROCESSES previously, much was made of the fact that at the lowest level one could find ELEMENTARY FUNCTIONS and ELEMENTARY BUSINESS PROCESSES. As shown in Figure 3–17, something similar may be found in analyzing the hierarchy of SYSTEM PROCESSES—the ELEMENTARY SYSTEM PROCESS. As with ELEMENTARY FUNCTIONS and ELEMENTARY BUSINESS PROCESSES, an ELEMENTARY SYSTEM PROCESS is the smallest unit of work that retains its identity. You can identify this most atomic process by realizing that once started it is not meaningful to say that it can be stopped before it is completed. Thus, each OTHER SYSTEM PROCESS may be *composed of* either one or more OTHER SYSTEM PROCESSES, ESSENTIAL SYSTEM PROCESSES, and/or ELEMENTARY SYSTEM PROCESSES.

EXTERNAL BUSINESS EVENT TYPES group ELEMENTARY BUSINESS PROCESSES together into ESSENTIAL BUSINESS PROCESSES. Similarly, ELEMENTARY SYSTEM PROCESSES may be grouped by SYSTEM EVENT TYPES to create an ESSENTIAL SYSTEM PROCESS [McMenamin and Palmer 1984].

Previously we asserted that a SYSTEM PROCESS can be *triggered by* a SYSTEM EVENT TYPE. Again, we are looking for the level of process that represents *a complete response* to an external event. For example, when a customer order is received (a SYSTEM EVENT TYPE) there might be numerous steps required for first filling out the order, and then for filling it. Each of these steps could reasonably be called

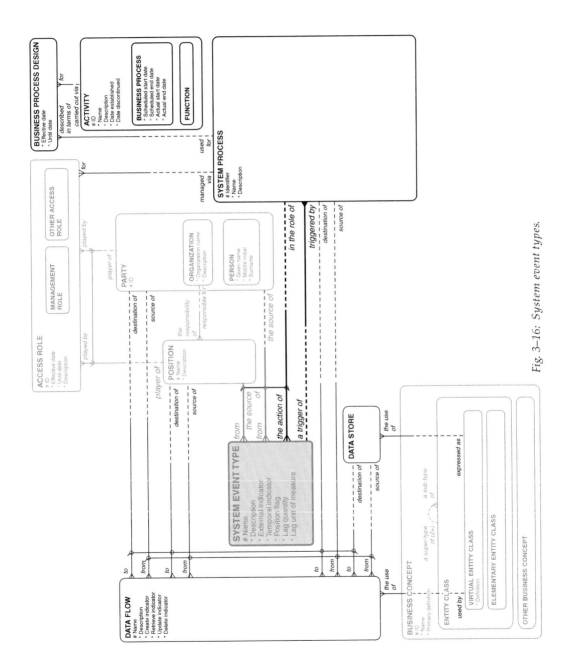

Fig. 3–16: System event types.

153

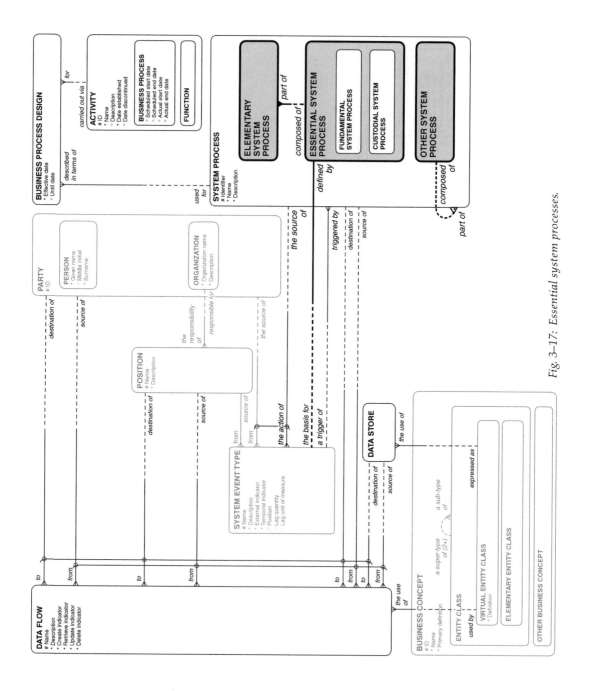

Fig. 3–17: Essential system processes.

a SYSTEM PROCESS (specifically, an ELEMENTARY SYSTEM PROCESS). But the objective of the entire effort is to complete the order.

The SYSTEM PROCESS that encompasses all of those ELEMENTARY SYSTEM PROCESSES is here called an ESSENTIAL SYSTEM PROCESS. That is, by definition an ESSENTIAL SYSTEM PROCESS must be the complete response to (*defined by*) a particular EVENT TYPE. Note that although each ESSENTIAL SYSTEM PROCESS must be *defined by* exactly one SYSTEM EVENT TYPE it may be *composed of* one or more ELEMENTARY SYSTEM PROCESSES.

As with ESSENTIAL BUSINESS PROCESSES, it is important to recognize that only *external* SYSTEM EVENTS can be *the basis for* defining an ESSENTIAL SYSTEM PROCESS. Where in the case of BUSINESS EVENT TYPE this distinction is depicted in the sub-types EXTERNAL BUSINESS EVENT and INTERNAL BUSINESS EVENT, it is here shown by the attribute "External indicator". If the SYSTEM EVENT TYPE is external, this attribute has the value "True". Otherwise, it is "False".*

### Business Rule

If a SYSTEM EVENT TYPE is *the basis for* an ESSENTIAL SYSTEM PROCESS, the value of the attribute "External indicator" must be "True".

Figure 3–17 also shows that as was the case with ESSENTIAL BUSINESS PROCESS there are two types of ESSENTIAL SYSTEM PROCESS. A FUNDAMENTAL SYSTEM PROCESS is one that contributes directly to the business objective implied by the external event that triggered it. To carry out this FUNDAMENTAL SYSTEM PROCESS, however, some data are required that may not have come directly from the process. So, a CUSTODIAL SYSTEM PROCESS is defined as one responsible for compiling data to be used by a FUNDAMENTAL PROCESS. CUSTODIAL SYSTEM PROCESSES typically maintain reference data. These are not *defined by* SYSTEM EVENT TYPES.

Figure 3–18 shows the collection of ELEMENTARY SYSTEM PROCESSES that were assembled to constitute the ESSENTIAL SYSTEM PROCESS "Receive each set of books". This is also a good example of decomposition. Note that at the lower level there

---

*Sub-types will not work here because, as you shall soon see, there are other ways to categorize SYSTEM EVENT TYPE.

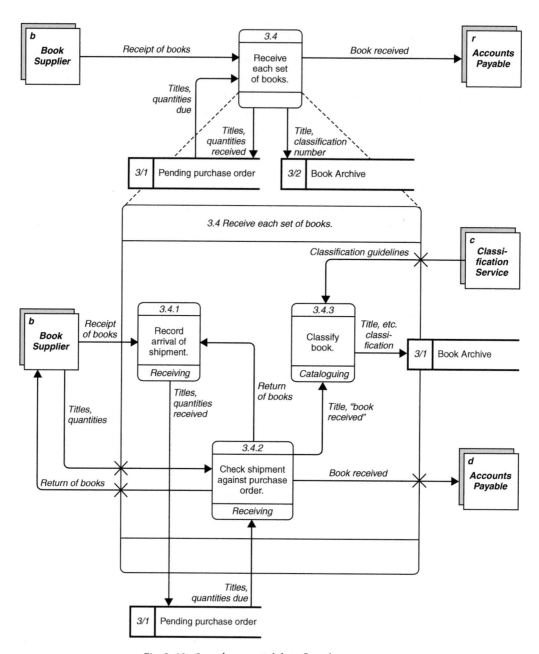

Fig. 3–18: Sample essential data flow diagram.

are external entities (ORGANIZATIONS) that are removed for simplicity's sake at the higher level.

The DATA FLOWS to these external entities in the detailed diagram have an X across them at the boundary of the upper-level process. It is the remaining external entity "Book Supplier" that provided the external SYSTEM EVENT that defined the ESSENTIAL SYSTEM PROCESS. In addition to that event, however, there were other communications that were not carried to the summary level. These are also marked with an X at the boundary.

**Business Rules**

1. External entities, data flows, and data stores recognized in a decomposed process need not appear in higher-level processes.
2. *Every* data store, external entity, and data flow portrayed in a higher-level process must appear in its decomposition.

## ROW FOUR: PROGRAM MODULES

Once activities—processes and functions—have been mapped, it is then possible to ask which of these should be automated. In addition, when the business rules (described in Chapter Seven) have been fully documented it is appropriate to ask how they will be implemented. This implementation will be via *program modules*. Row Four is concerned with the design of these modules. So, the Activities column of the designer's row is all about programs.

### Basic Module Structure

A PROGRAM MODULE* is a piece of program code that performs a task for the business. This may be the processing of input data, the creation of a report, or some internal processing or calculation. Each PROGRAM MODULE must be *written*

---

*I am told that *program module* is passé (actually, *dated* was the term used). More appropriate apparently would be *component*, *binary*, *service*, *executable*, or *interface*. Because the first two words do not add any information, and the last three are explicit *types* of programs, *program module* still seems the best term for any piece of program code, regardless of its purpose.

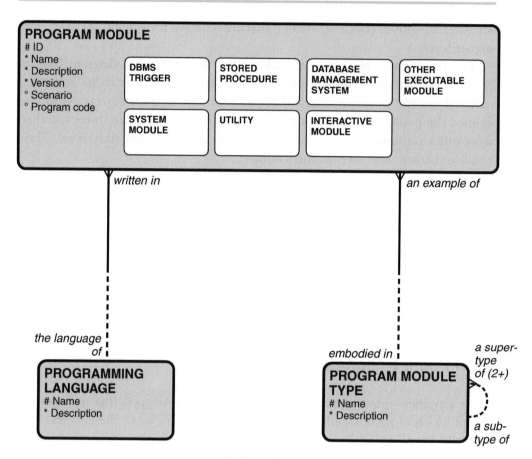

*Fig. 3–19: Modules.*

*in* a PROGRAMMING LANGUAGE, such as Java, C++, COBOL, or even FORTRAN. This is shown in Figure 3–19. In the figure, seven types of PROGRAM MODULES are shown. More will be added later, when we discuss object-orientation, but these will do for now.

- DBMS TRIGGER: A piece of code linked to a database TABLE or COLUMN, to be activated when a specified action takes place, such as updating the COLUMN
- STORED PROCEDURE: Program code stored in a database management system to control the updating and retrieval of data

- DATABASE MANAGEMENT SYSTEM: A complex piece of software that performs many useful functions related to the storage and retrieval of data and that plays a key role in protecting the integrity of data
- SYSTEM MODULE: An operating system or a portion of an operating system (including server software and services)
- UTILITY: A program that performs a support function, providing a service to the user of other software
- INTERACTIVE MODULE: Program code that controls the elements of a screen (its windows, cursors, and so on)
- OTHER EXECUTABLE MODULE: Everything else

The model also shows that each PROGRAM MODULE must be *an example of* exactly one PROGRAM MODULE TYPE. The first of these are the same types shown as sub-types of the PROGRAM MODULE itself. Each PROGRAM MODULE TYPE may be a *super-type of* two or more other PROGRAM MODULE TYPES. This structure, as we have seen before, allows the user of a system based on it to define types in more detail than is shown in the model.

### Business Rule

The first instances of PROGRAM MODULE TYPE must be "DBMS Trigger", "Stored procedure", and so on to correspond to the sub-types shown previously.

It is possible to describe a scenario that represents the processing of the module. This, plus the program code itself, are attributes of PROGRAM MODULE. PROGRAM MODULES can be linked in at least three different ways.

First, PROGRAM MODULE may be *composed of* one or more other PROGRAM MODULES. Figure 3–20, then, shows that each PROGRAM MODULE COMPOSITION must be *the use of* a PROGRAM MODULE ...*in another* PROGRAM MODULE.

Second, the figure shows that each PROGRAM MODULE may be *dependent on* another PROGRAM MODULE. That is, each PROGRAM MODULE may be *called by* another PROGRAM MODULE, shown here as the fact that each PROGRAM MODULE may be *subject to* one or more PROGRAM MODULE DEPENDENCIES, each of which must be *on* another PROGRAM MODULE.

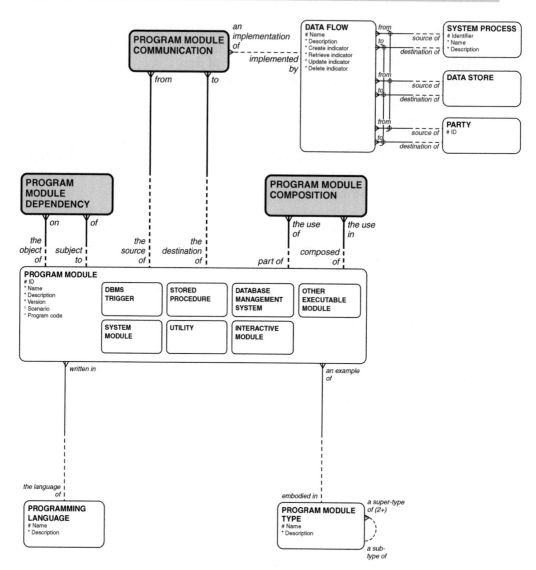

*Fig. 3–20: Program module links.*

Third, each PROGRAM MODULE may be *the source of* one or more PROGRAM MODULE COMMUNICATIONS *to* other PROGRAM MODULES. Note that each of these Row Four PROGRAM MODULE COMMUNICATIONS may be *an implementation of* a Row Three DATA FLOW described previously.

Before the advent of database management systems and object-oriented design, pretty much all programs were in the category of OTHER EXECUTABLE MODULE. In recent years, however, these distinctions have become more important, as will be seen in the remainder of this chapter.

Figure 3–21 summarizes the links from Figure 3–20. PROGRAM MODULE STRUCTURE is a super-type encompassing PROGRAM MODULE DEPENDENCY, PROGRAM MODULE COMMUNICATION, and PROGRAM MODULE COMPOSITION, while adding the possibility of an OTHER PROGRAM MODULE STRUCTURE. Thus, each PROGRAM MODULE STRUCTURE must be *from* one PROGRAM MODULE and *to* another PROGRAM MODULE.

Just as entity types have super-types, so too can relationships have super-types. Unfortunately, this is *not* something that can be easily shown in an entity-relationship diagram. In this case, the relationship "Each PROGRAM MODULE STRUCTURE must be *from* one and only one PROGRAM MODULE" has the following sub-types.

— Each PROGRAM MODULE DEPENDENCY must be *of* one and only one PROGRAM MODULE. This includes subroutine calls.
— Each PROGRAM MODULE COMMUNICATION must be *from* one and only one PROGRAM MODULE, including message types sent from one PROGRAM MODULE to another. Messages are discussed in the section on object modules (see page 171).
— Each PROGRAM MODULE DECOMPOSITION must be *the use of* one and only one PROGRAM MODULE. A large PROGRAM MODULE (actually a program module group) may be *composed of* one or more other PROGRAM MODULES.

Of course, the reverse relationship roles also have a corresponding sub-type structure. This is significant because, to explain the concepts presented here clearly, it is sometimes necessary to present the relationship between two sub-types before presenting the more general super-type relationships. Unfortunately, the language used at the sub-type level does not always correspond to that at the super-type level.

In this book, your author has tried both approaches. In this case, the sub-type relationship names seen in Figure 3–20 do not appear in Figure 3–21, although they continue to exist in the underlying model.* In other cases, the

---

*Note to anyone trying to implement this: Make sure you have reduced the number of relationships in the conceptual model before trying to generate a trial database design. If you don't, you will wind up with extra foreign keys.

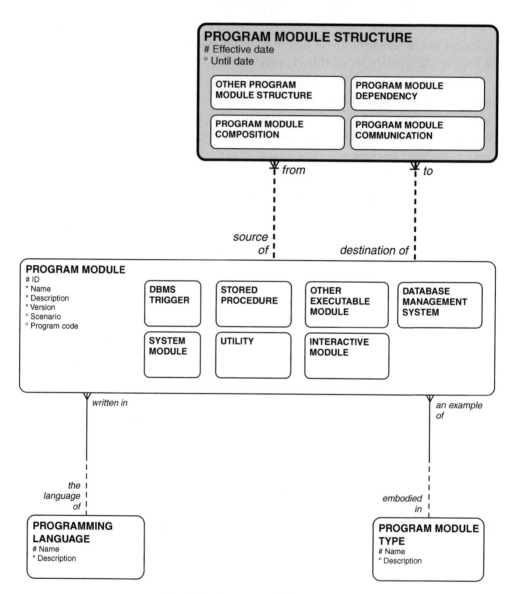

*Fig. 3–21: Program module structure.*

super-type names have been used exclusively in describing the details—at the cost of readability. In those cases, business rules must be added to describe the sub-type constraints.

Figure 3–22 shows that each PROGRAM MODULE must be *part of* a single APPLICATION SYSTEM. This expands Chapter Two's definition—a collection of DATA GROUPS

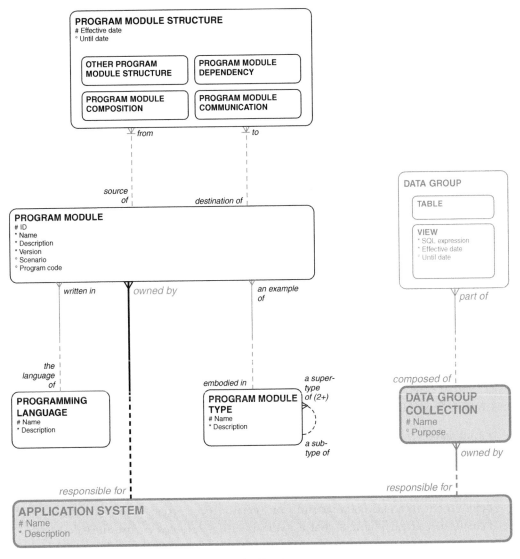

*Fig. 3–22: Application systems.*

assembled—to now include PROGRAM MODULES. That is, an APPLICATION SYSTEM is a collection of DATA GROUPS and PROGRAM MODULES to carry out a business function.

Remember that a PROGRAM MODULE COMMUNICATION *from* one PROGRAM MODULE *to* another is the fact that one is designed to communicate in some way with another. Figure 3–23 shows that although one APPLICATION SYSTEM may *be responsible for* a PROGRAM MODULE and a DATA GROUP COLLECTION there is nothing to prevent a PROGRAM MODULE from being the *source of* or *destination of* a PROGRAM MODULE COMMUNICATION *of* TABLE, VIEW, or COLUMN in any application.

Remember that a DATA FLOW and a DATA STORE are *the use of* VIRTUAL ENTITY CLASSES—views of other ENTITY CLASSES and ATTRIBUTES. Similarly, the PROGRAM MODULE COMMUNICATION that is *an implementation of* a DATA FLOW will usually be *of* a VIEW of other TABLES and COLUMNS.

While the MODULE COMMUNICATION describes how programs communicate with each other, it does not really describe the effect of the communication on the data. Figure 3–24 shows MODULE DATA USAGE—the fact that a particular PROGRAM MODULE specifically *creates, retrieves, updates* or *deletes* instances of either a DATA GROUP as a whole or a particular COLUMN. Each attribute of MODULE DATA USAGE ("Create indicator", "Retrieve indicator", etc.) identifies the action.

## Program Roles

Different people and organizations play different roles in the creation of PROGRAM MODULES, be they individual PROGRAM MODULES or more complex APPLICATION SYSTEMS. These roles might include programmers, managers, or administrators of various types. Figure 3–25 borrows from Chapter Five to show PARTY, ACCESS ROLE, and ACCESS ROLE TYPE. ACCESS ROLE is a complex topic, discussed at length in Chapter Five, but here three sub-types of ACCESS ROLE are shown:

- PROGRAMMING ROLE: Simply the fact that a PARTY (or POSITION, and so on) has something to do with some aspect of *creating* a PROGRAM MODULE or APPLICATION SYSTEM.
- MANAGEMENT ROLE: The fact that a PARTY *is responsible for* the development or deployment of a PROGRAM MODULE or APPLICATION SYSTEM.
- PERMISSION ROLE: The fact that a PARTY is either *allowed* or *prohibited* access to the PROGRAM MODULE or the APPLICATION SYSTEM as a whole. The attribute

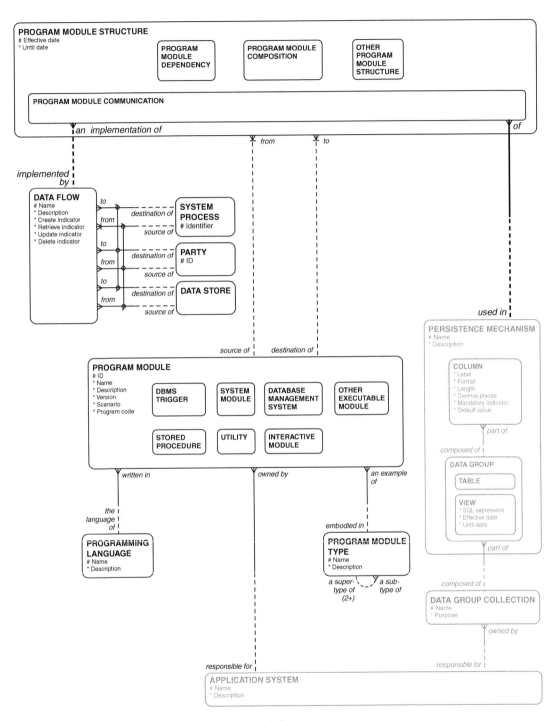

*Fig. 3–23: Module communication.*

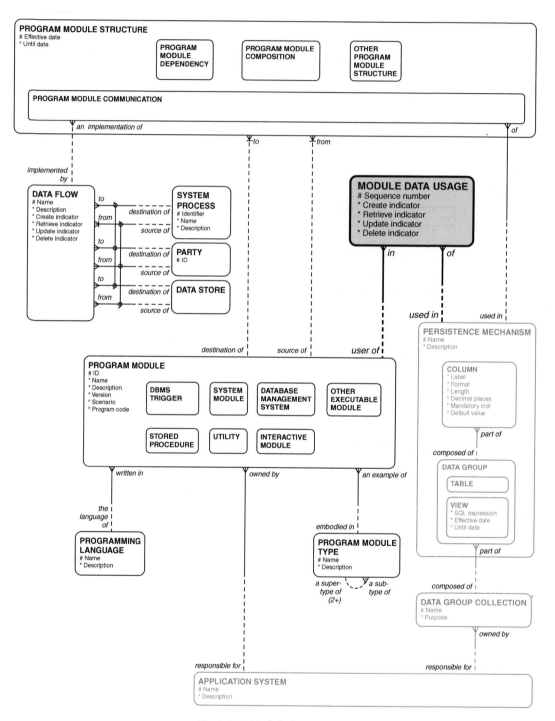

Fig. 3–24: Module data usage.

166

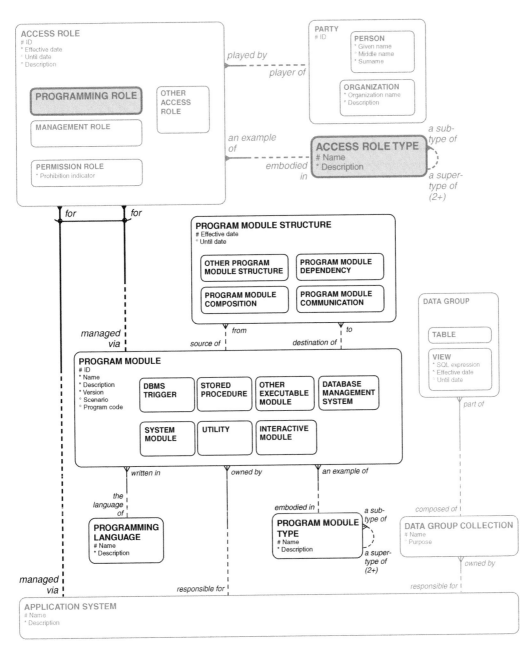

*Fig. 3–25: Access roles.*

"Prohibition indicator" is "True" if the role indicates that the PARTY is prohibited from access to the PROGRAM MODULE or APPLICATION SYSTEM, and is "False" if the role indicates permission.

Here we introduce the assertion that each ACCESS ROLE must be *an example of* one ACCESS ROLE TYPE. These, of course, must include "Programming role", "Management role", and "Permission role". Each ACCESS ROLE TYPE may be *a super-type of* two or more other ACCESS ROLE TYPES, so "Program module role" may be *a super-type of*, for example, "Programmer" and "Programming manager".

Alternatively, if no further detail is required "Programmer" and "Programming manager" could simply be instances of PROGRAM MODULE ROLE.

**Business Rules**

1. One instance of ACCESS ROLE TYPE must be "Programming role".

Common usage of the words APPLICATION SYSTEM is often much less disciplined than is described here. Often companies imagine that a program module or a table is owned by multiple application systems. But if they are to be managed successfully, responsibility for each element of a system must be designated in terms of the particular project (APPLICATION SYSTEM) responsible for its creation in the first place.

Given that responsibility, permission for access can be widely spread. Once APPLICATION SYSTEMS have been carefully defined, as often as not, ACCESS ROLES can be defined entirely in terms of them, with minimal requirement to give access to specific PROGRAM MODULES or TABLES.

Sometimes PROGRAM MODULES can be written for the purpose of generating other PROGRAM MODULES. Figure 3–26 shows that a GENERATION SPECIFICATION can be *for* a PROGRAM MODULE and is *according to* a DATA GROUP, which contains the actual specifications for the PROGRAM MODULE. Once the PROGRAM MODULE that is *the generator in* the GENERATION SPECIFICATION has been created, when it is run (on a "Generation date") it will be *the basis for* one or more GENERATIONS *of* other PROGRAM MODULES.

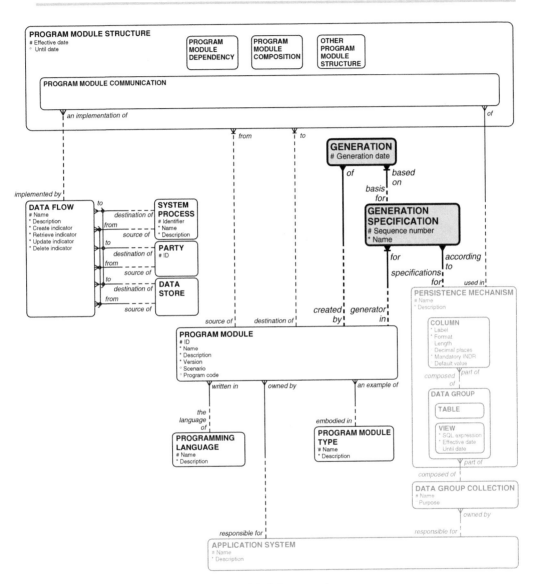

*Fig. 3–26: Module generation.*

Figure 3–27 shows that the Row Four artifact PROGRAM MODULE is also *based on* one or more Row Three SYSTEM PROCESSES. Specifically, it may be *based on* one or more PROCESS IMPLEMENTATIONS, each of which must be *of* one and only one SYSTEM PROCESS. Note that a SYSTEM PROCESS, however, may be *the source of*

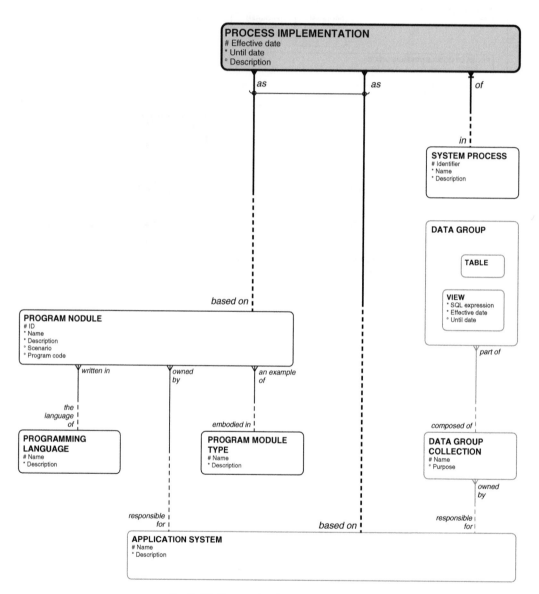

Fig. 3–27: Process implementations.

either an individual PROGRAM MODULE or an entire APPLICATION SYSTEM. That is, a SYSTEM PROCESS may not only be *in* one or more implementations *as* individual PROGRAM MODULES but *in* one or more IMPLEMENTATIONS *as* complete APPLICATION SYSTEMS.

## Object Modules

Figure 3–28 shows two new types of PROGRAM MODULE. First, a CLASS IMPLEMENTATION (as described in Chapter Two) plays the role of a Row Four data thing, but it is in fact a piece of code. So, it is shown in that chapter and highlighted here. CLASS IMPLEMENTATION was described in Chapter Two as a piece of code that describes a category of ("class" of) objects. This can refer to a BUSINESS ENTITY CLASS, or it can categorize "objects" that are part of a computer system, such as window cursors, screen windows, and other elements.

The second type of PROGRAM MODULE is an EXECUTABLE MODULE. This is the code that old-timers will remember simply as what was once called a "computer program". That is, it is any program (or program component) that does something. Note that (as shown in Figure 3–28) EXECUTABLE MODULE includes the seven sub-types previously presented, plus two new ones, specifically for object orientation:

- METHOD: Program code to carry out an OPERATION, as described next
- PACKAGE: A collection of CLASS IMPLEMENTATIONS. That is, a PACKAGE may be *composed of* one or more CLASS IMPLEMENTATIONS.

Figure 3–29 includes CLASS ELEMENT (described in Chapter Two), and adds what object-oriented design calls OPERATION to the model. An OPERATION is a function *performed by objects in* a CLASS IMPLEMENTATION and *implemented by* an EXECUTABLE MODULE that is a METHOD.

Typically, an OPERATION is *on* one or more INSTANCE ATTRIBUTES, although it might not be. "Visibility" is also an attribute of OPERATION. That is, as with CLASS ELEMENTS an OPERATION may be seen throughout the system, within its own CLASS, or only within its CLASS and its sub-types.

Note that what relational programmers would consider an attribute may in fact be implemented as a *call to* an OPERATION that returns the requested value. In object-oriented land, it does not matter whether the value was stored in a table or derived in some other way.

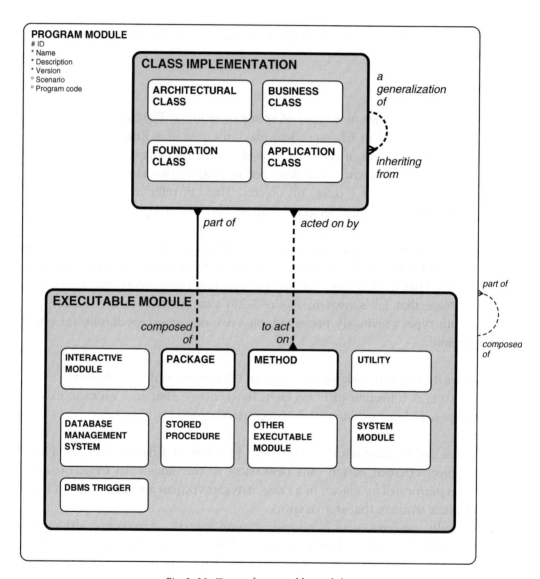

*Fig. 3–28: Types of executable module.*

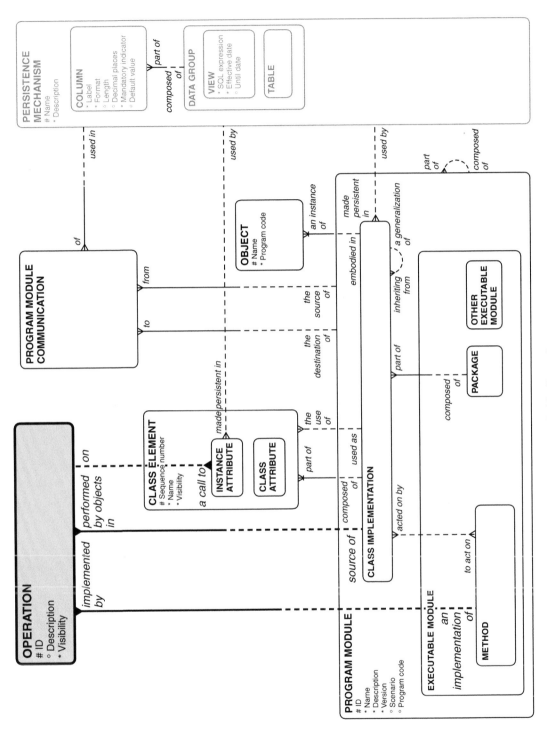

Fig. 3–29: Operations.

173

> **Business Rule**
>
> An INSTANCE ATTRIBUTE may be either *a call to* an OPERATION that is *performed by objects in* a CLASS IMPLEMENTATION or *the use of* a CLASS IMPLEMENTATION directly, but not both.

Meilir Page-Jones uses an example in his book, written in his version of a generic object-oriented language [Page-Jones 2000, p. 6]. His class Hominoid is a video game character that turns right or left and goes forward. It can also detect if it is facing a wall and must turn. It is described as follows.

```
Hominoid
     New: Hominoid
          // creates and returns a new instance of Hominoid
     (Operations)
     turnLeft
          // turns the hominoid counterclockwise by 90°
     turnRight
          // turns the hominoid clockwise by 90°
     advance (noOfSquares: Integer, out advanceOK: Boolean)
          // moves the hominoid a certain number of squares
          // along the direction that it's facing and
          // returns whether successful
     display
          // shows the hominoid as an icon on the screen
     (Instance attributes that are really operations)
     location: Square
          // returns the current square that the
          // hominoid is on
     facingWall: Boolean
          // returns whether or not the hominoid is at a
          // wall of the grid
```

Essentially, the definition of the CLASS hominoid is in terms of its OPERATIONS. These include New, which creates an instance of hominoid at runtime, plus turnLeft, turnRight, advance, and display. It does have two INSTANCE ATTRIBUTES (location and facingWall), but as noted previously these are each *a call to* an OPERATION that will return a value. So, even the INSTANCE ATTRIBUTES refer to OPERATIONS.

An OPERATION must be *implemented by* a METHOD, a piece of program code that carries it out. Like other types of program code, this is a type of PROGRAM MODULE; specifically, an EXECUTABLE MODULE. Another type of EXECUTABLE MODULE is a PACKAGE, which is a collection of CLASS IMPLEMENTATIONS. Actually, because a PROGRAM MODULE may be *composed of* other PROGRAM MODULES so a METHOD may be composed of other METHODS, and a PACKAGE may be composed of other PACKAGES.

When a program is run, an OBJECT behaves by having its OPERATIONS send messages to other OBJECTS. As shown in Figure 3–30, a MESSAGE is *from* one OBJECT *to* another OBJECT. A MESSAGE is also *sent by* one OPERATION *to invoke* another OPERATION.

If the messages are asynchronous, there may be a MESSAGE QUEUE in front of the receiving OBJECT to store messages until they can be processed. That is, messages that are concurrent or asynchronous must be stored until the receiving OBJECT can process them. Hence, each MESSAGE must be either *to* an OBJECT or *to* a MESSAGE QUEUE *for* an OBJECT.

A MESSAGE, being between objects, is an actual communication that occurs when a PROGRAM MODULE is running. Each MESSAGE, then, must be *an example of* a MESSAGE TYPE, where a MESSAGE TYPE is designed as part of PROGRAM MODULE. Specifically, each MESSAGE TYPE must be *sent by* an OPERATION, and may be *to invoke* an other OPERATION. Each MESSAGE TYPE must also be *via* a PROGRAM MODULE COMMUNICATION, a link between two PROGRAM MODULES. A MESSAGE TYPE must be one of the following.

— INFORMATIVE MESSAGE TYPE, which provides an object with information to update itself
— INTERROGATIVE MESSAGE TYPE, which requests an object to reveal something of itself
— IMPERATIVE MESSAGE TYPE, which requests an object to take some action upon itself

Each MESSAGE may include one or more input or output MESSAGE ARGUMENTS, as shown in Figure 3–31. Each MESSAGE ARGUMENT must be *for* a particular MESSAGE

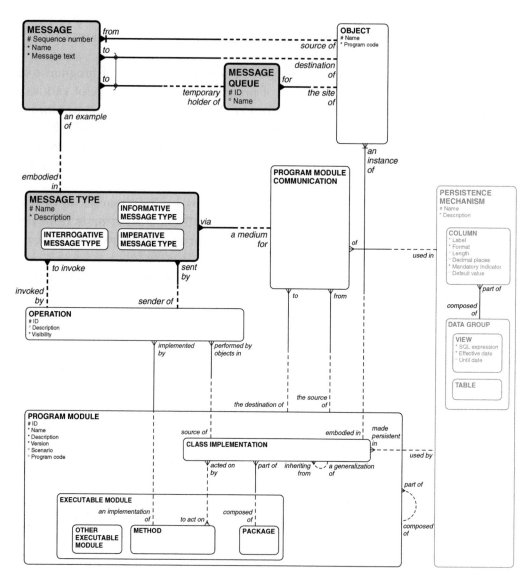

*Fig. 3–30: Messages.*

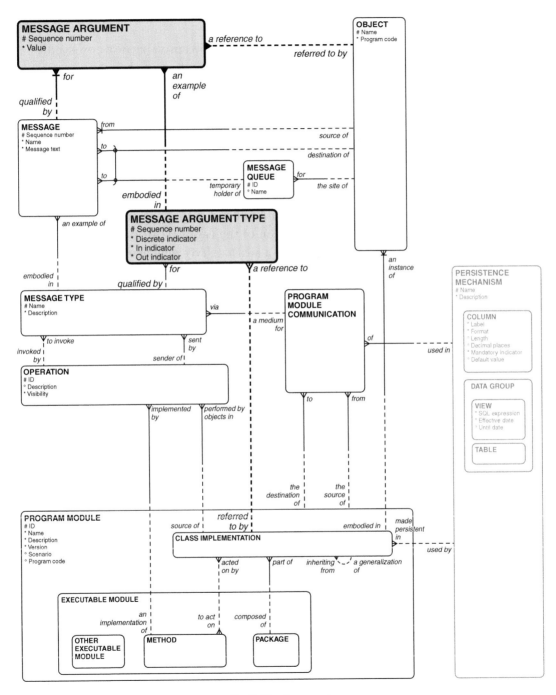

Fig. 3–31: Arguments.

177

and may be *a reference to* another OBJECT. Again, because MESSAGES exist only at runtime so do their MESSAGE ARGUMENTS. The definition of the MESSAGE TYPE therefore also includes MESSAGE ARGUMENT TYPE.

MESSAGE arguments may be either input arguments or output arguments, as determined by the value of each MESSAGE ARGUMENT TYPE's "In indicator" and "Out indicator". Both indicators are present, since the same MESSAGE ARGUMENT TYPE could be both an input and an output argument. In a program, these arguments are shown with input arguments first (optionally preceded by the word "in"), followed by the word "out" and the output arguments, optionally followed by "inout" and any arguments that are both input and output arguments.

In Mr. Page-Jones' example, if execution of the PROGRAM MODULE (a PACKAGE) `hom1` creates an OBJECT of class `Hominoid` a MESSAGE TYPE `advance` would be specified as `hom1.advance(noOfSquares, out advanceOK)`. Here, `noOfSquares` is an input parameter (the number of squares to advance) and `advanceOK` is an output parameter ("True" or "False", depending on whether the advance was successful) [Page-Jones 2000, p. 22]. Again, a runtime occurrence of `advance` would have an object ID and would in fact advance a particular number of squares (such as "5").

Each MESSAGE ARGUMENT is itself typically *a reference to* an OBJECT, mirroring the fact that each MESSAGE ARGUMENT TYPE may be *a reference to* a CLASS IMPLEMENTATION. This can be a reference to an object in a "Foundation Class"—for example, a type of integer, character, or some such. In the previous example, the MESSAGE ARGUMENT TYPE "noOfSquares" could refer to objects in the IMPLEMENTATION CLASS "Integer".

## ROW SIX: PROGRAM INVENTORY*

Row Six is concerned with the inventory of systems that *exist*. This includes not only systems developed in-house but commercial off-the-shelf packages. In Row Four we designed programs, determined their structures, and defined how they would use data. Row Five would be concerned with the coding involved. Row Six is where we catalogue the actual program copies that have been produced, along with the data produced and used by them (described in Chapter Two).

---

*I am told that the chic word for this is now *application portfolio*. Because we are talking about a collection of programs stored somewhere, the word *inventory* strikes me as more appropriate and less pretentious.

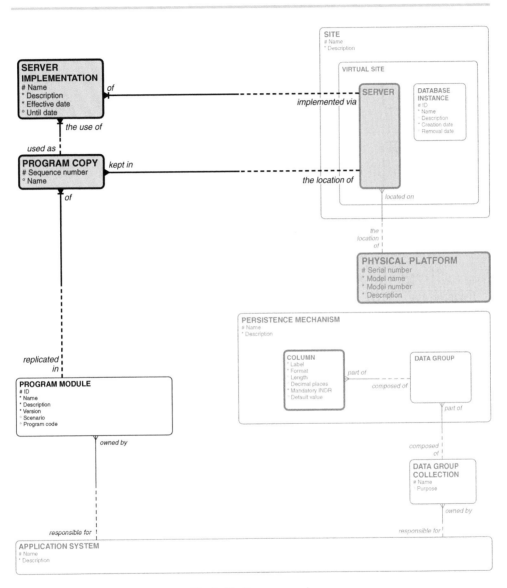

*Fig. 3–32: Program copies.*

Figure 3–32 shows the PROGRAM COPIES *of* each PROGRAM MODULE designed at Row Four. Each PROGRAM COPY, then, must be *of* a PROGRAM MODULE, and must be *kept in* a VIRTUAL SITE that is a SERVER. SERVER, defined in more detail in Chapter Four, is a piece of an operating system that supports the continuous

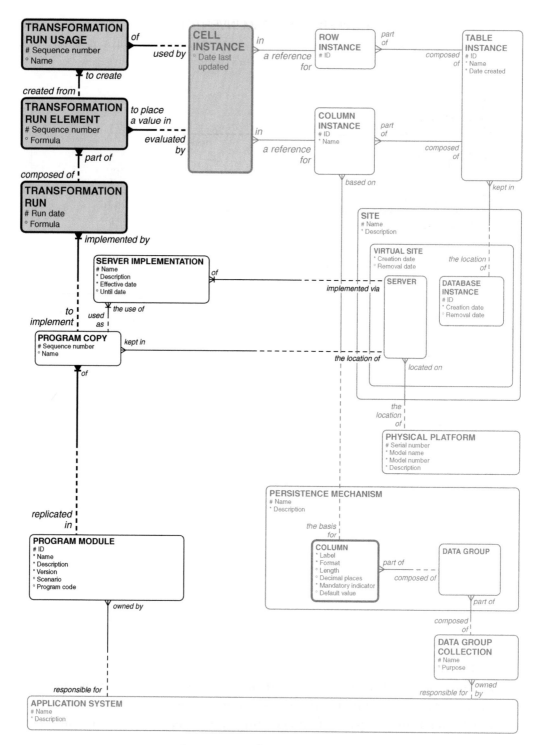

*Fig. 3–33: Transformation runs.*

running of a program, so that the PROGRAM MODULE can interact asynchronously with other programs. That is, a SERVER is itself *implemented via* one or more SERVER IMPLEMENTATIONS, each of which must be *the use of* another PROGRAM COPY.

This is to say that a PROGRAM COPY of, for example, the Oracle database management system may be *used as* one or more SERVER IMPLEMENTATIONS *of* separate SERVERS. This is also referred to as a database management system having multiple instances.

Figure 3–33 describes the running of a PROGRAM COPY, the data it produced, and the data it used to produce them. Specifically, a TRANSFORMATION RUN must be *an implementation of* a PROGRAM COPY, executed on a particular "Run date". Each TRANSFORMATION RUN may then be *composed of* one or more TRANSFORMATION RUN ELEMENTS, each of which must be *to place a value in* a CELL INSTANCE.

A cell instance is a particular COLUMN INSTANCE of a particular ROW INSTANCE in a TABLE INSTANCE. The TRANSFORMATION RUN ELEMENT may then be *composed of* one or more TRANSFORMATION RUN USAGES, each *of* a (presumably different) CELL INSTANCE. That is, a TRANSFORMATION RUN may read and operate on one or more CELL INSTANCES in order to place a value in another CELL INSTANCE.

# 4

# LOCATIONS

*Network—Any thing reticulated, or decussated, at equal distances, with interstices between the intersections.*

—SAMUEL JOHNSON [1755]

## ABOUT LOCATIONS

The Locations column of the architecture framework is concerned with *where* the enterprise does business.

- The *planner* sees a simple set of enterprise locations, typically by city.
- The *business owner* sees a set of offices, factories, and warehouses that constitute the enterprise's logistics network.
- The *architect* sees the roles played by each location in the processing of information and communications.
- The *designer* sees the potential distribution of hardware and software and the design of communications networks.
- The *builder* is concerned with the details of communications nodes and protocols.
- The *functioning system* consists of the facilities where communications take place.

Figure 4–1 shows the architecture framework with the cells that will be the concern of this chapter highlighted. Specifically, these are the views of the business owner, the architect, the designer, and the functioning system.

The Locations column is both about where things are and the networks by which they are connected to each other. Where is the business and how do its components talk to each other? How are data communicated from place to place?

| | Data (What) | Activities (How) | Locations (Where) | People (Who) | Time (When) | Motivation (Why) |
|---|---|---|---|---|---|---|
| Objectives/ Scope (Planner's View) | List of things important to the enterprise | List of functions the enterprise performs | List of enterprise locations | Organization approaches | Business master schedule | Business vision and mission |
| Enterprise Model (Business Owner's View) | Language, divergent data model | Business process model | Logistics network | Organization chart | State / transition diagram | Business strategies, tactics, policies, rules |
| Model of Fundamental Concepts (Architect's View) | Convergent e/r model | Essential data flow diagram | Locations of roles | The viable system, use cases | Entity Life History | Business rule model |
| Technology Model (Designer's View) | Database design | System design, program structure | Hardware, software distribution | User interface, security design | Event processing | Business rule design |
| Detailed Representation (Builder's View) | Physical storage design | Detailed program design | Network architecture, protocols | Screens, security coding | Timing definitions | Rule specification program logic |
| Functioning System | (Working System) | | | | | |
| | Databases | Program inventory, logs | Communications facilities | Trained people | Business events | Enforced rules |

*Fig. 4–1: Locations column.*

How will we wire technologies together? The answers to these questions are the domain of the Locations column.

To model the *structure* of data entity classes or activities is not the same thing as modeling the entity classes or the activities *themselves* in the business. In our metamodel of data, we have been concerned with the concepts of, for example, "entity class" and "attribute". In our model of activities, we were concerned with the concepts of "process" and "function." The actual entity classes (e.g., PRODUCT) and processes (e.g., "Accept order") that describe a particular company would themselves be modeled in the course of developing systems for that company. But for the most part, the realms of business data and metadata are quite different.

Locations, on the other hand, are basically modeled the same way at the business level and meta level. As with the People and Organizations column, described in Chapter Five, the central entity classes for the Locations column is actually taken from the generic business model. In both the business model and the metamodel, we must model the locations we are concerned with, whether we are conducting business there or operating a system there. For this reason, as with Chapter Five, the core of the model in this chapter makes extensive use of the business model for locations presented in *Data Model Patterns: Conventions of Thought* [Hay 1996].

The Locations and People column share another characteristic: the Locations column and the People and Organizations column are primarily about the location of and management of the *other* columns. Specifically, the location part of the model shows the location of *activities*, *business rules*, *tables*, and so forth.

## Site

All perspectives in the Locations column make use of the same core entity class, SITE, shown in Figure 4–2. A SITE which also could be called ADDRESS, is a means for locating people, organizations, or other resources. There are two primary types of SITES.

— A PHYSICAL SITE is a tangible place on Earth that has a purpose, such as an office building, a home, or an oil well. An alternative name is FACILITY. This must be one of the following:

→ STREET ADDRESS: This includes a reference to one or more streets, plus the city, state or province, and country where the site is located.

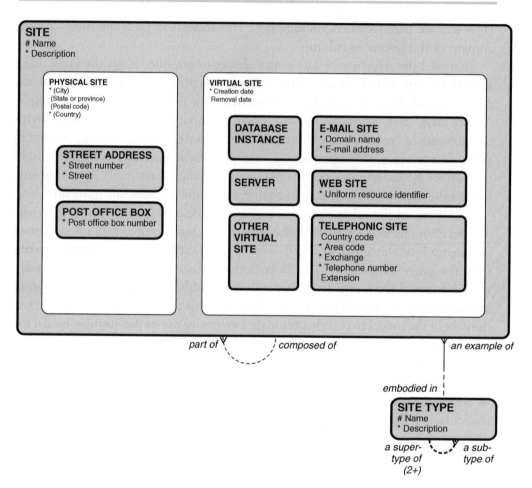

*Fig. 4–2: Sites.*

→   POST OFFICE BOX: Because a post office box has a single physical location as well, PHYSICAL SITE also includes those.

–   A VIRTUAL SITE does not have a physical reality beyond bits in a computer somewhere. It is identified by an address that is meaningful only in an electronic environment. This includes:

→   E-MAIL SITE, identified by an e-mail address (contained in the attributes "Domain name" and "E-mail address").

→ WEB SITE, identified by a "Uniform resource locator (URL)", "the generic term for all types of names and addresses that refer to objects on the World Wide Web".*

→ TELEPHONIC SITE, identified by a telephone number (contained in the attributes "Country code", "Area code", "Exchange", "Telephone number" and "Extension").

→ DATABASE INSTANCE, which is where data may be located.

→ SERVER, a portion of the operating system that controls the running of a system to which access is gained asynchronously.

→ OTHER VIRTUAL SITE, a VIRTUAL SITE that is not one of the preceding.

As was done elsewhere in the metamodel, the entity class SITE TYPE redundantly represents the *sub-types* shown for SITE. This structure allows us to show the displayed *sub-types* as fundamental to the nature of the entity class SITE, while providing flexibility in the more detailed *sub-types* as necessary. Each SITE TYPE may be *a super-type of* two or more other SITE TYPES. For example, *sub-types of* "Physical site" could be added, such as "Office building", "Home", "Warehouse", and so forth.

### Business Rule

The first instances of SITE TYPE must include "Physical site", "Virtual site", "E-mail site" (a *sub-type of* "Virtual site"), "Telephonic site" (also a *sub-type of* "Virtual site"), and so forth.

Figure 4–3 introduces the concept of SITE STRUCTURE, which must be a PHYSICAL COMMUNICATION LINK (the fact that it is possible to send messages from one SITE to another), a SITE COMPOSITION (the fact that one SITE contains another), or an OTHER SITE STRUCTURE. The attribute of SITE COMPOSITION, "Overlap indicator",

---

*There are copious of references on both sides arguing definitively that it should be either a "uniform" resource locator or a "universal" one. Tim Berners-Lee uses *uniform* though so that is good enough for your author [Berners-Lee 1988].

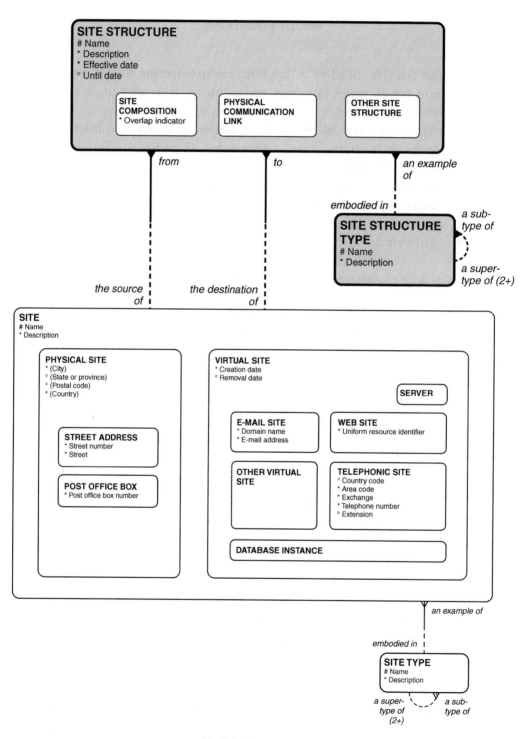

*Fig. 4–3: Site structures.*

188

determines whether the two SITES overlap (True) or one is contained entirely within the other (False).

Each SITE STRUCTURE must be *an example of* one and only one SITE STRUCTURE TYPE. Each SITE STRUCTURE TYPE may be *a super-type of* at least two other SITE STRUCTURE TYPES.

### Business Rule

By definition, the first instances of SITE STRUCTURE TYPE must be "Site composition", "Physical communication link", and "Other site structure".

## Geographic Location

If a PHYSICAL SITE is a place with a purpose, where is it? Figure 4–4 shows a GEOGRAPHIC LOCATION to be simply any identified place on the Earth. This may be either a GEOGRAPHIC AREA or a GEOGRAPHIC POINT.* A GEOGRAPHIC AREA is either a GEOPOLITICAL AREA or a MANAGEMENT AREA. A GEOPOLITICAL AREA, such as a state or country, has boundaries defined by law or treaty. A MANAGEMENT AREA, such as the "Southeastern sales region", has boundaries defined by the company itself.

A GEOGRAPHIC POINT is simply a point in one dimension. In this model the attributes are shown as the components of latitude and longitude, plus elevation. Schemes of reference can be much more complex than this, but this is sufficient for metadata purposes. As with other entity classes in this model, each GEOGRAPHIC LOCATION must be *an example of* exactly one GEOGRAPHIC LOCATION TYPE, where the first instances of GEOGRAPHIC LOCATION TYPE correspond to the *sub-types* explicitly shown for GEOGRAPHIC LOCATION. *Sub-types of* Geopolitical area can then be "State", "Country", "County", "City", and so forth. A *sub-type of* ADMINISTRATIVE AREA can be "Postal area".

---

*In the oil industry, it is necessary to also have a GEOGRAPHIC SOLID to describe oil reservoirs, but that is beyond the scope of this book.

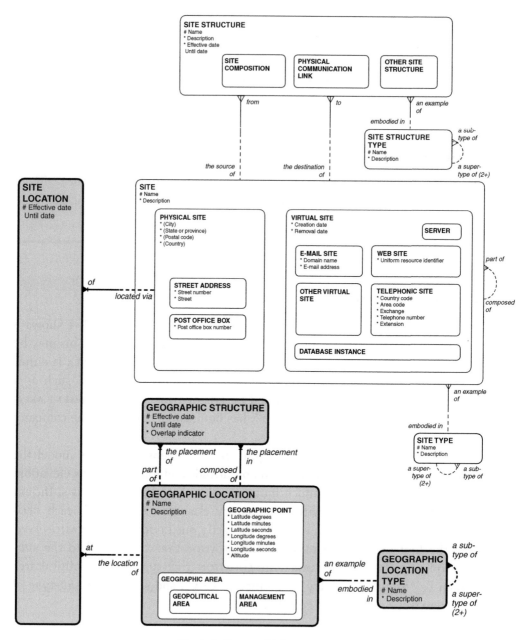

*Fig. 4–4: Geographic locations.*

### Business Rule

The first two instances of GEOGRAPHIC LOCATION TYPE must be "Geographic area", "Geographic point", "Geopolitical area", and "Management area", where "Geopolitical area" and "Management area" are both *sub-types of* "Geographic area".

Since the same PHYSICAL SITE can be in more than one GEOGRAPHIC LOCATION and vice versa, the intersect entity class SITE LOCATION represents the fact of a single PHYSICAL SITE being located in a particular GEOGRAPHIC LOCATION. Note that the "(City)", "(State)", "(Country)", and "(Postal area)" as attributes of PHYSICAL SITE are shown with parentheses to denote that they are really derived attributes. They are derived from the GEOGRAPHIC LOCATION entity class via the SITE LOCATION entity class, where SITE LOCATION is the fact that a particular SITE is located in a particular GEOGRAPHIC LOCATION. For example, the value of (City) in PHYSICAL SITE is actually the "Name" of the GEOGRAPHIC LOCATION that is *an example of* the GEOGRAPHIC LOCATION TYPE "City", and that is *the location of* the SITE LOCATION that is *of* the PHYSICAL SITE involved.

### Business Rule

Although a PHYSICAL SITE may be associated with multiple GEOGRAPHIC LOCATIONS, it may only be associated with one each of "City", "State", "Country", and "Postal area".

A GEOGRAPHIC LOCATION can be complex. For example, it is possible for one U.S. "Postal area" to be in two (or more?) cities. Thus, it is necessary to add the entity class GEOGRAPHIC STRUCTURE, which allows any GEOGRAPHIC LOCATION to be *part of* one or more (GEOGRAPHIC STRUCTURES, each of which must be *the placement in* one and only one) other GEOGRAPHIC LOCATION. The attribute "Overlap indicator" describes whether one GEOGRAPHIC LOCATION is entirely contained within the other ("False") or if they simply overlap ("True").

Note that among other things this permits each GEOGRAPHIC AREA to be defined in terms of the set of GEOGRAPHIC POINTS that demark its boundary. Because each

PHYSICAL SITE may be *located via* one or more GEOGRAPHIC LOCATION and each GEOGRAPHIC LOCATION may be *the location of* one or more PHYSICAL SITES, each instance of the entity class SITE LOCATION is the fact that one PHYSICAL SITE is located in one GEOGRAPHIC LOCATION.

## ROW TWO: PLACING PARTIES, BUSINESS PROCESSES, AND MOTIVATION

### Business Locations

In addition to the relationship between PARTY and SITE (from the People and Organizations column, discussed in Chapter Five on pages 218 and 219), two other columns have a strong association with SITE. Figure 4–5 shows the relationships among SITE and BUSINESS PROCESS (from the Activity column, which is discussed in Chapter Three). Specifically, BUSINESS LOCATION is defined to be the fact that one SITE is associated with (*for*) one BUSINESS PROCESS at a particular time. The timing of the location is constrained by the attributes "Effective date" and "Until date". The nature of the association is defined by BUSINESS LOCATION TYPE, which may be "Conducted in", "Managed via", and so forth.

### Means, End, and Effort

Figure 4–6 reproduces a part of the model from Chapter Seven about the Motivation column. In particular, this is from the Row Two view of the model, showing END, MEANS, and EFFORT. An END for an organization is simply something it sets out to accomplish. Primary among these, of course, is the company's VISION—its overall view of what it wants to be. Other ENDS include various types of DESIRED RESULT, each of which is a state or target the enterprise intends to achieve or maintain.

A MEANS is any capability that may be called on, activated, or enforced in order to achieve one or more ENDS. This entity class describes the nature of the ongoing operational activities of the enterprise—what the business is or will be doing on a day-to-day basis. The principal types of MEANS are COURSE OF ACTION and DIRECTIVE. A COURSE OF ACTION is an approach or plan for configuring some

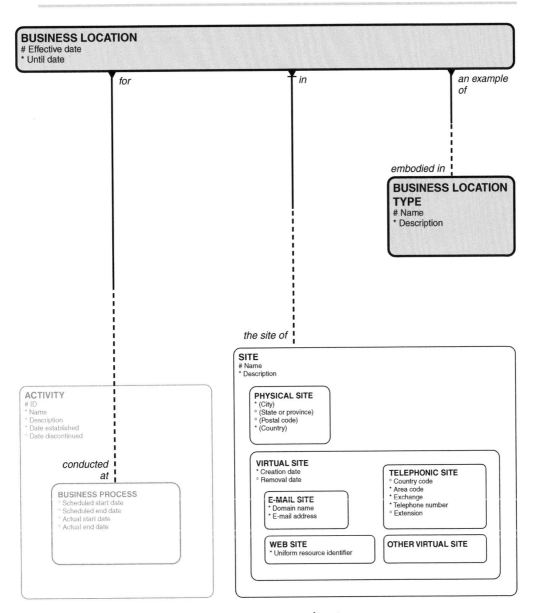

*Fig. 4–5: Business process locations.*

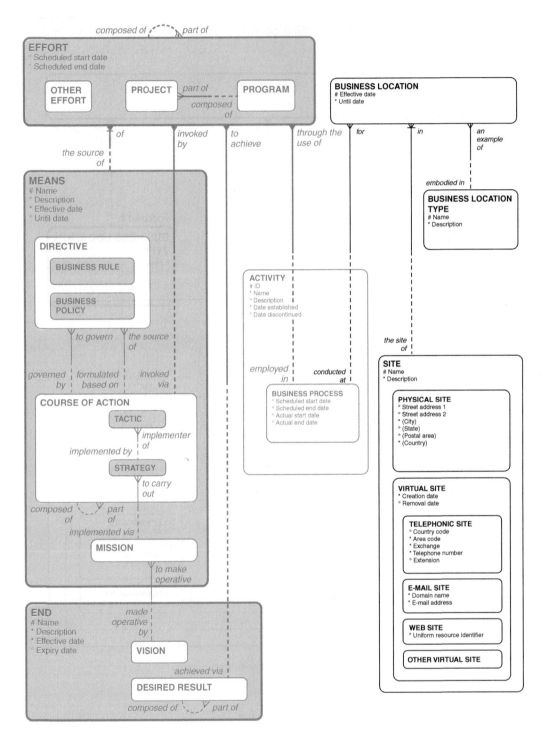

*Fig. 4–6: Efforts.*

aspect of the enterprise, whereas a DIRECTIVE is a specification—such as a BUSINESS POLICY or a BUSINESS RULE—that constrains COURSE OF ACTION.

As shown in Figure 4–6, EFFORT is the application of a BUSINESS PROCESS to carry out a COURSE OF ACTION. Specifically, an EFFORT is either a PROJECT or a PROGRAM that is a group of steps. Each EFFORT, then, must be *invoked by* a COURSE OF ACTION *to achieve* a DESIRED RESULT *through the use of* a BUSINESS PROCESS.

MEANS, END, and EFFORT are shown in Figure 4–6 to prepare the way for locating them at a SITE. Figure 4–7 introduces (again, borrowed from Chapter Seven) an INFLUENCER. An INFLUENCER is anything that can produce an effect on the enterprise without apparent exertion of tangible force or direct exercise of command. An INFLUENCER often acts without deliberate effort or intent.

INFLUENCERS are either INTERNAL INFLUENCERS (internal to the company, that is)—such as "limitations on available technology"—or external influencers, such as "competition" or "supply problems". See Chapter Seven for more on INFLUENCERS. The point of all this is that (as shown in Figure 4–7) a MOTIVATION LOCATION *at* a SITE must be the location *of* an EFFORT, DIRECTIVE, or INFLUENCER.

## ROW THREE: DATA FLOW DIAGRAMS

For the most part, Row Three is a conceptual model, describing processes and data flows without respect to where these are going to happen. It is for Row Two (where things happen in the business), Row Four (where things are intended to happen), and Row Six (where systems are installed) to accommodate the Locations column. It is possible to define that a SYSTEM PROCESS in Row Three might be *done at* a SITE, but this is only if the SITE is somehow central to the meaning of the SYSTEM PROCESS. Normally, this would not be specified in an essential data flow diagram.

The concept of network, however, will be important to a system's design, and it does apply here, primarily in the form of DATA FLOWS. Figure 4–8 is derived from the Chapter Three (activities) view of the metamodel, showing DATA FLOWS and the SYSTEM PROCESSES, DATA STORES, PARTIES, and POSITIONS they link. As just stated, this is a conceptual network, without regard to mechanisms, identified people, or offices. It is possible, however, to identify that this data flow may be

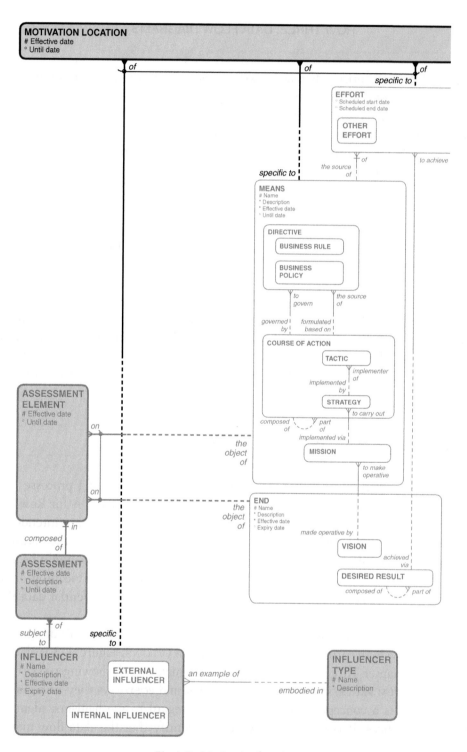

*Fig. 4–7: Motivation locations.*

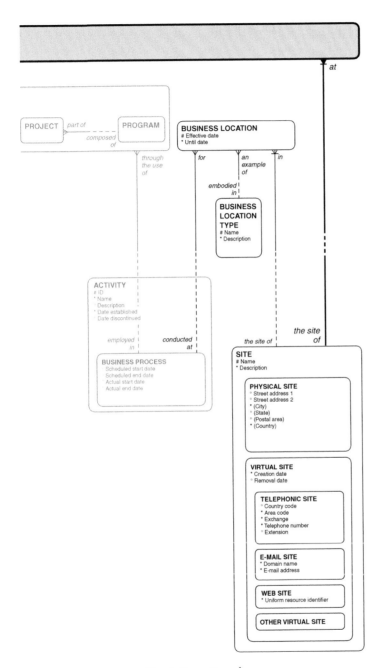

Fig. 4–7: continued.

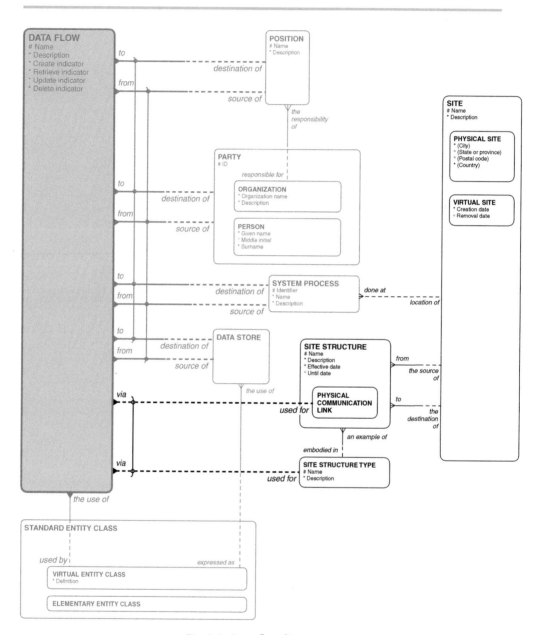

*Fig. 4–8: Data flow diagrams.*

*via* a PHYSICAL COMMUNICATION LINK between two SITES (described previously), as a way of documenting what is meant in the Row Three model. Again, this would not be done in an essential data flow diagram.

## ROW FOUR: PLACING DATA AND PROGRAMS

Row Four is concerned with the design of systems, and that design must take into account where programs and data will be placed and how the programs will communicate with each other. Figure 4–9 shows part of the designer's Row Four model as discussed in Chapters Two and Three. In it we see the entity classes of CLASS IMPLEMENTATION, CLASS ELEMENT, and PERSISTENCE MECHANISM (particularly TABLE, VIEW, and COLUMN). To that we add SITE, and link it to the tables and columns with PERSISTENCE MECHANISM LOCATION. That is, a PERSISTENCE MECHANISM LOCATION is the fact that a particular TABLE, VIEW, or COLUMN is expected to be kept in a particular SITE.

Note that this allows us to place a TABLE not only in the Cleveland data center (for example) but in a particular database. That is, a PERSISTENCE MECHANISM may be *specific to* a PERSISTENCE MECHANISM LOCATION *at* a SITE TYPE. From the designer's point of view, it is probably premature to specify a particular SITE. Instead, by making a PERSISTENCE MECHANISM LOCATION *at* a SITE TYPE the designer simply specifies whether the location will be a PHYSICAL SITE (such as the aforementioned Cleveland data center) or a VIRTUAL SITE (such as the WHIMSY* DATABASE INSTANCE).

This is an opportunity to expand on the list of SITE TYPES through the *super-type of* relationship. Naturally, SITE STRUCTURE also allows you to specify that the WHIMSY DATABASE INSTANCE is *part of* the Cleveland data center PHYSICAL SITE, so it is not necessary to specify a PERSISTENCE MECHANISM LOCATION for both of them.

Figure 4–10 borrows from the object-oriented part of the model in Chapter Three, and shows that a MODULE LOCATION can link a SITE TYPE with either a PROGRAM MODULE or a particular OPERATION.

---

*The "Warehouse Information System," of course…

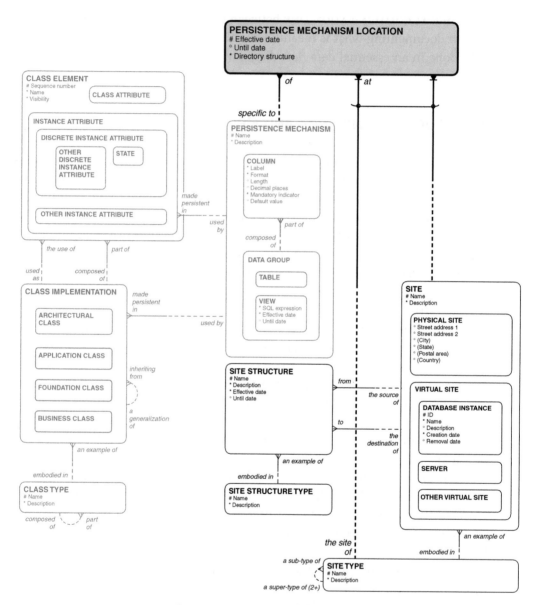

*Fig. 4–9: Persistence mechanisms.*

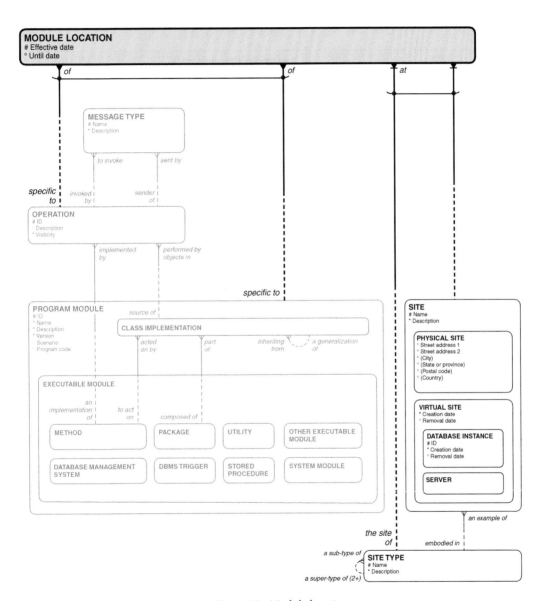

*Fig. 4–10: Module locations.*

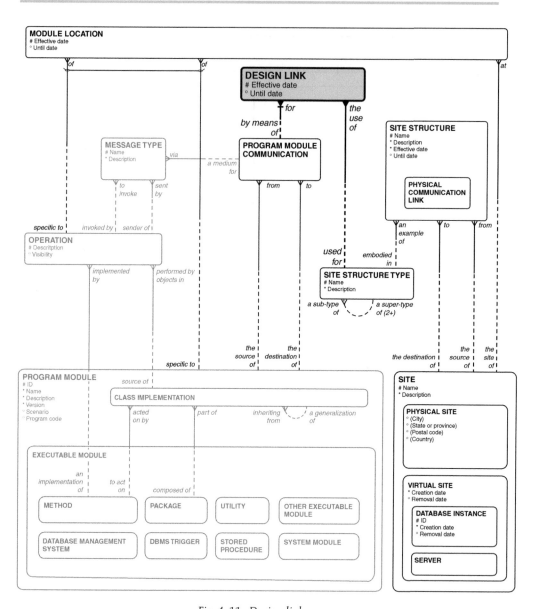

*Fig. 4–11: Design links.*

Figure 4–11 shows a second way a network can be designed. First, "Physical communication link" is a SITE STRUCTURE TYPE that can be *a super-type of* one or more other SITE STRUCTURE TYPES. Thus, we have a way of cataloguing the types of "Physical communication links" that are possible.

As described in Chapter Three, a PROGRAM MODULE COMMUNICATION is the fact that as part of its operation one PROGRAM MODULE will send messages to another. In Figure 4–11 DESIGN LINK is the fact that a PROGRAM MODULE COMMU-NICATION makes use of a particular SITE STRUCTURE TYPE. Specifically, a DESIGN LINK must be *for* a PROGRAM MODULE COMMUNICATION, and must be *the use of* a particular SITE STRUCTURE TYPE, specifically one that is *a sub-type of* the SITE STRUCTURE TYPE "Physical communication link". For example, a PROGRAM MODULE COMMUNICATION might describe PROGRAM MODULE A invoking PROGRAM MODULE B. A SITE STRUCTURE TYPE might describe the fact that a headquarters data center communicates with Field office data centers. A DESIGN LINK, then would assert that the MODULE A/B connection can make use of the Headquarters/Field office link.

### Business Rule

Each DESIGN LINK must be *the use of* a SITE STRUCTURE TYPE that is *a sub-type of* "Physical communication link".

## Row Six: System Inventory

### Database Instances

DATABASE INSTANCE is a specialized VIRTUAL SITE that is solely the home of the TABLE INSTANCES that were described for Row Six in Chapter Two. This is shown in Figure 4–12. TABLE INSTANCE is defined as the fact that a particular DATA GROUP (TABLE or VIEW) is installed into a particular DATABASE INSTANCE. Over the life of a system, a DATA GROUP may be *kept in* one or more DATABASE INSTANCES, and thus the entity class TABLE INSTANCE has "Date created" and "Date removed" as attributes.

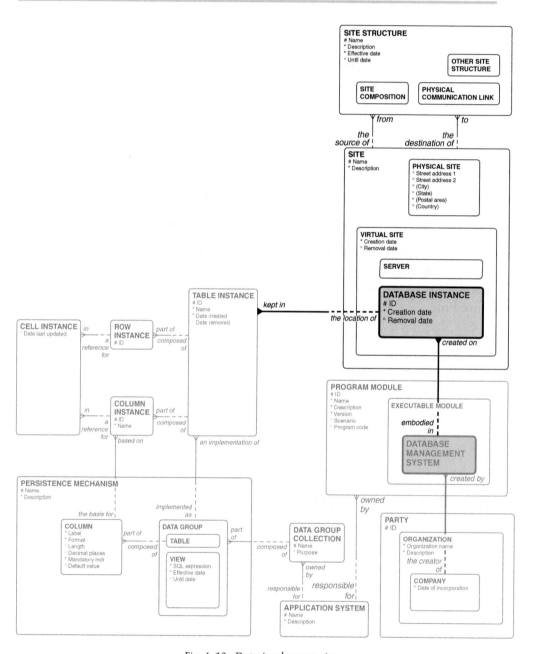

*Fig. 4–12: Data implementation.*

Note that the fact that a SITE may be *part of* another SITE (via SITE COMPOSITION—a kind of SITE STRUCTURE) allows representation of the fact that a particular DATABASE INSTANCE may be located in a particular physical data center.

Also note that, each DATABASE INSTANCE must be *created on* a particular DATABASE MANAGEMENT SYSTEM, which must be *created by* a (vendor) COMPANY.

## Servers

Figure 4–13 shows PROGRAM COPY as it is *kept in* a SERVER. A SERVER, a VIRTUAL SITE, is a piece of an operating system that controls the running of an asynchronous program. That is, the program runs continuously, and responds to inputs as they happen.

The SERVER is itself *implemented via* a PROGRAM COPY *of* a PROGRAM MODULE; specifically, an EXECUTABLE MODULE that is a SYSTEM MODULE. Because a PROGRAM COPY may be *used as* more than one SERVER, SERVER IMPLEMENTATION is the fact that one PROGRAM COPY is being *used as* one SERVER.

In Figure 4–14, we see that a SERVER must be *located on* a PHYSICAL PLATFORM— that is, a computer. A PHYSICAL PLATFORM, of course, must be currently located at a PHYSICAL SITE, and this is shown in the figure by its having been *located via* a MOVEMENT *from* one PHYSICAL SITE *to* another PHYSICAL SITE. The PHYSICAL SITE that is the *destination of* the MOVEMENT with the latest "Movement date" is, of course, the current location.

The physical implementation of a network is through a series of PHYSICAL COMMUNICATION LINKS from one SITE to another, as shown in Figure 4–15. Each PROGRAM COPY, then, is the *user of* one or more PHYSICAL COMMUNICATION LINKS. Because each PHYSICAL COMMUNICATION LINK may be *used in* one or more PRO-GRAM COPIES, the entity class PHYSICAL UNIT IMPLEMENTATION is the fact that one PROGRAM COPY is the *user of* one PHYSICAL COMMUNICATION LINK. That is, each PHYSICAL LINK IMPLEMENTATION must be *of* one PROGRAM COPY and *in* one PHYSICAL COMMUNICATION LINK.

Each PHYSICAL LINK IMPLEMENTATION must be *of* one and only one DESIGN LINK. The attribute "Input indicator" in PHYSICAL LINK IMPLEMENTATION describes whether the link is input to the PHYSICAL COMMUNICATION LINK ("True") or output from it ("False").

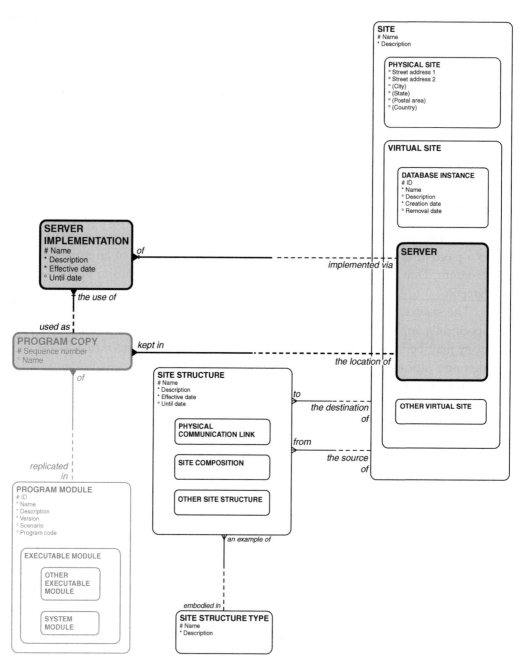

*Fig. 4–13: Program locations.*

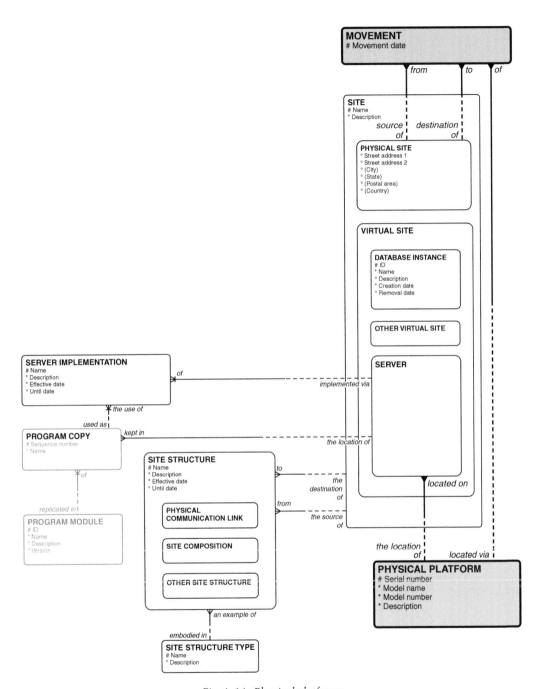

Fig. 4–14: Physical platforms.

207

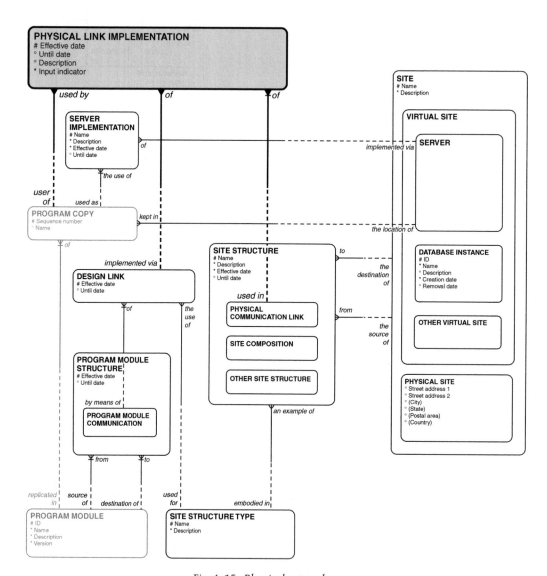

*Fig. 4–15: Physical networks.*

# PEOPLE AND ORGANIZATIONS

*One of the many reasons for the bewildering and tragic character of human existence is the fact that social organization is at once necessary and fatal. Men are forever creating such organizations for their own convenience and forever finding themselves the victims of their home-made monsters.*

—ALDOUS HUXLEY [1950]

## THE PEOPLE AND ORGANIZATIONS COLUMN

The People and Organizations view encompasses the following.

- The *planner* is responsible for a statement of the organization's philosophy and approach to managing human resources. Is this an authoritarian organization, such as the Army or more informal, such as a commune?
- The *business owner* sees the organization chart. How is the enterprise organized in terms of reporting structures and overall responsibilities?
- The *architect* captures and describes roles and responsibilities. In terms of roles and positions: what is each person responsible for in the operation of the company?
- The *designer* specifies user interfaces and security requirements. First, how will people interact with any prospective system? Second, what elements are involved in providing security for access to data?
- The *builder* is responsible for the actual construction of user interfaces and security schemes.
- The *functioning system* consists of the actual mechanisms for controlling access to systems and databases.

Figure 5–1 shows the architecture framework with the cells highlighted that we will cover in this chapter. Specifically, these include the views of the business owner, the architect, the designer, and the functioning system.

## ABOUT PEOPLE AND ORGANIZATIONS

As with locations, described in Chapter Four, people and organizations are modeled the same way at the business level and the meta levels. We must model the people and organizations we are concerned with, whether they are conducting business or managing a data warehouse. For this reason, the models in this chapter are going to look much like the business models for people and organizations in *Data Model Patterns: Conventions of Thought* [Hay 1996]. The difference is that the primary entity classes from the business will be related not to other business entity classes but to the metamodel entity classes we have been discussing. Moreover, the business entity classes borrowed by the metamodel will be used in all rows.

Figure 5–2 shows the primary entity classes in this topic. Just as PERSON is an important entity class in any business model, it is also essential for our metamodel. Included here are records of all people of interest to a particular effort. In the business, these are employees, customers, vendors, agents, and so forth. In the metamodel world, people also play many roles (database administrator, programmer, data steward, etc.), but these are for producing systems and maintaining the quality (accuracy, currency, and so on) of each datum* used by an enterprise.

Groups of PEOPLE are ORGANIZATIONS. ORGANIZATIONS of interest both to the business and to the data manager might include COMPANY, GOVERNMENT AGENCY, and INTERNAL ORGANIZATION. A COMPANY is organized to conduct business. In the United States, a COMPANY is a corporation, a sole proprietorship, or a partnership.

A GOVERNMENT AGENCY is an ORGANIZATION in a national, state or provincial, or local government. This also includes nation states as well as international organizations, such as the European Union and the United Nations. An INTERNAL ORGANIZATION is any permanent or temporary department, section, branch, or other group within either a COMPANY or a GOVERNMENT AGENCY. This includes

---

*If data are plural, you have to use datum for the singular, right?

| | Data (What) | Activities (How) | Locations (Where) | People (Who) | Time (When) | Motivation (Why) |
|---|---|---|---|---|---|---|
| **Objectives/ Scope** (Planner's View) | List of things important to the enterprise | List of functions the enterprise performs | List of enterprise locations | Organization approaches | Business master schedule | Business vision and mission |
| **Enterprise Model** (Business Owner's View) | Language, divergent data model | Business process model | Logistics network | Organization chart | State/ transition diagram | Business strategies, tactics, policies, rule |
| **Model of Fundamental Concepts** (Architect's View) | Convergent e/r model | Essential data flow diagram | Locations of roles | The viable system, use cases | Entity life history | Business rule model |
| **Technology Model** (Designer's View) | Database design | System design, program structure | Hardware, software distribution | User interface, security design | Event processing | Business rule design |
| **Detailed Representation** (Builder's View) | Physical storage design | Detailed program design | Network architecture, protocols | Screens, security coding | Timing definitions | Rule specification program logic |
| **Functioning System** | *(Working system)* | | | | | |
| | Databases | Program inventory, logs | Communications facilities | Trained people | Business events | Enforced rules |

*Fig. 5–1: People and Organizations column.*

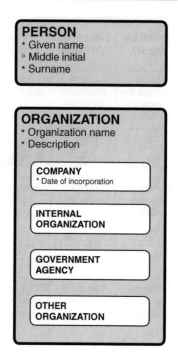

*Fig. 5–2: People and organizations.*

temporary organizations, such as project teams and task forces. In addition, there are OTHER ORGANIZATIONS that do not fall into these categories. These might be labor unions, professional societies, or households.

Of greatest interest in the metadata world are the organizations that are the source of business rules, data quality standards, and the like. These will largely be INTERNAL ORGANIZATIONS, although in many industries GOVERNMENT AGENCIES will be a factor as well.

There are numerous examples of relationships that apply to *either* a PERSON or an ORGANIZATION. For this reason, it is convenient to invent the concept of PARTY, which is either a PERSON or an ORGANIZATION of interest to us. This is shown in Figure 5–3.

As it happens, PARTIES are often related to each other. "Corporate structure" refers to an INTERNAL ORGANIZATION's being part of another INTERNAL ORGANIZATION or of a COMPANY; "Employment" describes a PERSON's being employed by

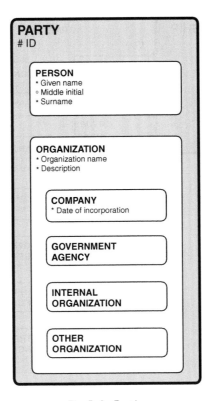

*Fig. 5–3: Parties.*

a COMPANY or by a GOVERNMENT AGENCY; and so forth. A PERSON is married to another PERSON.* Figure 5–4 shows that a PARTY RELATIONSHIP is the fact that one PARTY is related to another PARTY. That is, each PARTY RELATIONSHIP must be *from* one PARTY and *to* another PARTY.

In Figure 5–5, each PARTY RELATIONSHIP is seen to be *an example of* one and only one PARTY RELATIONSHIP TYPE. Examples of PARTY RELATIONSHIP TYPES are as just presented. "Corporate structure" refers to an INTERNAL ORGANIZATION's being part of another INTERNAL ORGANIZATION or of a COMPANY, "Employment" describes a PERSON's being employed by a COMPANY or by a GOVERNMENT AGENCY, and so forth.

---

*I know, this has nothing to do with metadata, but it is a good example of a PARTY RELATIONSHIP.

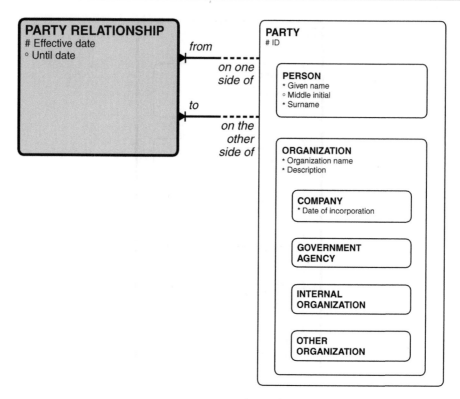

*Fig. 5–4: Party relationships.*

An EMPLOYMENT is a special type of PARTY RELATIONSHIP that is always *of* a PERSON and *with* an ORGANIZATION.* Note that this is an alternative to having EMPLOYEE as an entity class. If you think about it, a PERSON is not *inherently* an employee. He or she only becomes one by virtue of maintaining an EMPLOYMENT relationship with an ORGANIZATION.

This is another case where the ···TYPE entity class reproduces the sub-type structure of the parent entity class. In this case, the first two instances of PARTY RELATIONSHIP TYPE must be "Employment" and "Other party relationship".

---

*Note that in a business setting it is reasonable to assert that each EMPLOYMENT must always be *with* an ORGANIZATION, but in a more general case, an individual can hire a maid or a chauffer and thus the purer version of this model would have PARTY rather than ORGANIZATION be the *sponser of* an EMPLOYMENT. In our metadata environment, however, the version presented seems suitable.

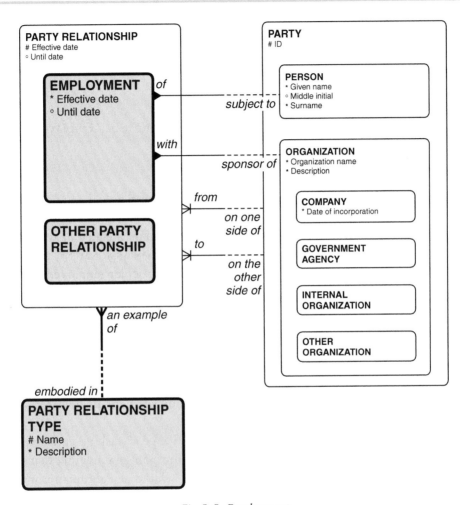

*Fig. 5–5: Employment.*

Each PARTY RELATIONSHIP TYPE, however, may be *a super-type of* two or more other PARTY RELATIONSHIP TYPES so it would be possible to specify other sub-types of OTHER PARTY RELATIONSHIP as instances of this entity class. These might include the aforementioned "Corporate structure", "Corporate ownership", and so forth. CONTRACT EMPLOYMENT is not shown explicitly as a sub-type on this diagram, but it could be included as another instance of PARTY RELATIONSHIP TYPE. Depending on company policy, "Contractor" could be considered a *sub-type of* "Employment", or it could simply be *a sub-type of* "Other party relationship".

---

**Business Rule**

The first instances of PARTY RELATIONSHIP TYPE must be "Employment" and "Other party relationship".

---

An EMPLOYMENT (and by extension, a PARTY) may be a *holder of* one or more POSITION ASSIGNMENTS, and each POSITION ASSIGNMENT must be *to* one and only one POSITION. A POSITION is the definition of a particular category of work to be done by someone with a specific set of skills. A POSITION ASSIGNMENT, therefore, is the fact that a particular EMPLOYMENT (that is, a particular employed PERSON) is *holder of* a particular POSITION. Figure 5–6 shows this, with each POSITION *the responsibility of* one and only one ORGANIZATION.

Note that a PERSON'S EMPLOYMENT can involve multiple POSITION ASSIGNMENTS to POSITIONS over time. This also includes being seconded* to a different department temporarily. This also means that at any point in time the number of persons *employed by* a department (via an EMPLOYMENT) is not necessarily the same as the number of persons actually working for the department in POSITIONS it is *responsible for*.

A POSITION RESPONSIBILITY (see Figure 5–7) is a type of task given to either a PERSON in a POSITION ASSIGNMENT (*to* a POSITION) or to anyone holding that POSITION. For example, anyone holding the POSITION "Database Administrator" has, among others, the POSITION RESPONSIBILITY "Install new DBMS versions". Because a POSITION ASSIGNMENT may be *holder of* multiple POSITION RESPONSIBILITIES and each POSITION RESPONSIBILITY may be *held in* one or more POSTION ASSIGNMENTS or one or more POSITIONS, the entity class POSITION RESPONSIBILITY HOLDING is the fact that a particular POSITION or POSITION ASSIGNMENT holds a particular POSITION RESPONSIBILITY. That is, each POSITION RESPONSIBILITY HOLDING must be *by* either a POSITION or a POSITION ASSIGNMENT (that is, a position assigned to an individual), and it must be *of* a particular POSITION RESPONSIBILITY.

---

*To my American readers: "Seconded" is a Britishism for being temporarily assigned elsewhere. A wonderful word!

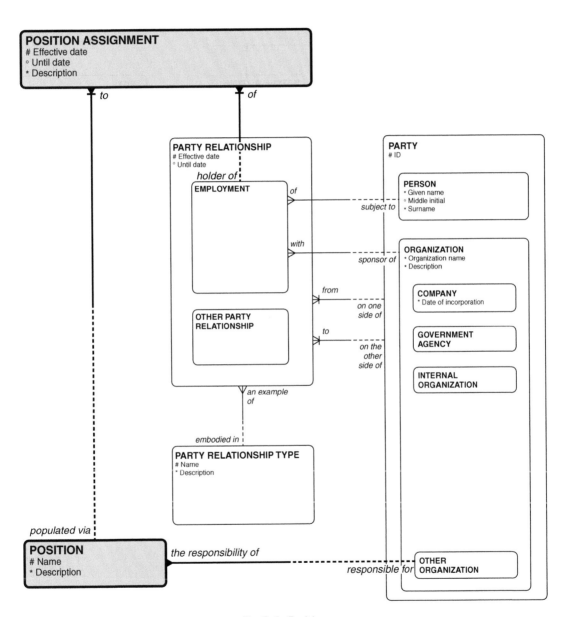

*Fig. 5–6: Positions.*

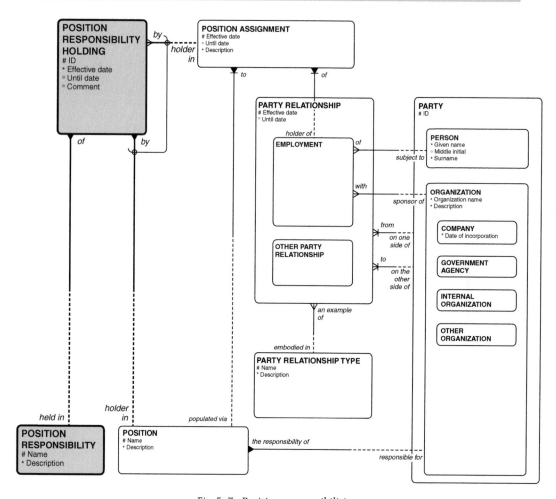

*Fig. 5–7: Position responsibilities.*

## ROW TWO: THE BUSINESS OWNER'S VIEW

### Access Roles

Now that we have described the business environment for metadata—people and their jobs with organizations—we can start to see how the business entity classes are related to the metadata entity classes that have concerned us so far. The figures that follow, starting with Figure 5–8, show that an ACCESS ROLE is the fact that

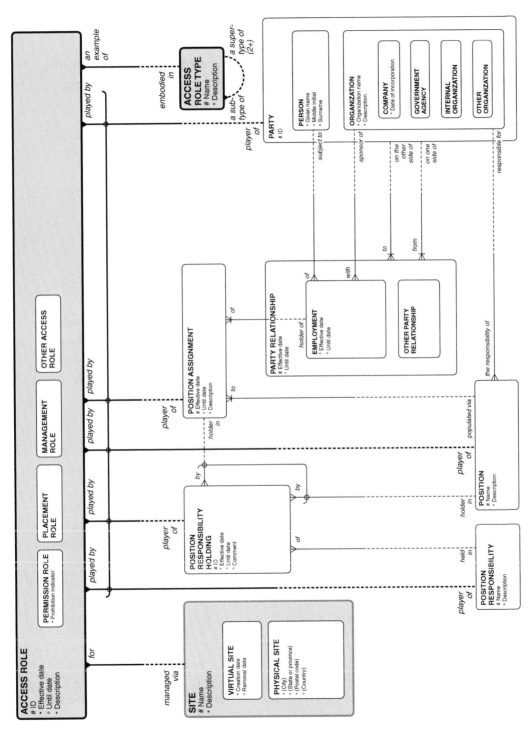

Fig. 5–8: Access roles and sites.

someone plays a role in the management of some aspect of (in this case) enterprise systems. Specifically, an ACCESS ROLE must be played by one of the following:

—  A particular PARTY (PERSON or ORGANIZATION)
—  A POSITION ASSIGNMENT *of* a PERSON employed with an ORGANIZATION *to* a POSITION
—  Anyone in a specified POSITION
—  A POSITION RESPONSIBILITY HOLDING *of* a POSTION RESPONSIBLITY by anyone
—  Anyone holding a particular POSITION RESPONSIBLITY

Initially, we can say that an ACCESS ROLE must be one of the following:

—  A PLACEMENT ROLE, which places the PERSON, POSITION, and so on, physically in a particular SITE.
—  A PERMISSION ROLE, granting the PERSON, POSITION, and so on permission to have access to a SITE. (The attribute "Prohibition indicator", if "True", indicates that the role is in fact a prohibition of the PARTY, and so on, from having access.)
—  A MANAGEMENT ROLE, asserting that the PERSON, POSITION, and so on, has management responsibility over the SITE involving the ACCESS ROLE
—  An OTHER ACCESS ROLE, which covers any role other than the previous ones

Each ACCESS ROLE must be *an example of* an ACCESS ROLE TYPE. Again, note that this entity class redundantly represents the same facts as are shown in the sub-type structure of ACCESS ROLE.

As this chapter progresses, we will see that an ACCESS ROLE can be for many other things in the metamodel—not just SITE, as shown in Figure 5–8.* Here, a SITE is a place for locating PEOPLE, ORGANIZATIONS, or other resources as was defined in the previous chapter. A particular PERSON, for example, might be a *player of* an ACCESS ROLE—a PLACEMENT ROLE—that asserts that he or she is located at a particular (PHYSICAL or VIRTUAL) SITE. A PERMISSION ROLE, on the other hand, is the fact that this PERSON has permission to get into the SITE. Or, most common

---

*The relationship says *must be* because, as you will soon see, this is part of an extensive arc, and it is true that each ACCESS ROLE must be *for* one of the alternatives. As we discuss each alternative, however, that alternative is clearly optional.

of all, the PARTY may simply be responsible (*player of* a MANAGEMENT ROLE) *for* the SITE.

> **Business Rule**
>
> The first instances of ACCESS ROLE TYPE must be "Enforcement Role", "Placement Role", and so on.

## Concepts, Symbols, and Signifiers

In Chapter Two, we saw that a SYMBOL was a SIGNIFIER (a WORD, PHRASE, or GRAPHIC) that represented a BUSINESS CONCEPT or a BUSINESS CONCEPT ELEMENT. A BUSINESS CONCEPT is simply something we understand to exist or to be the case. The set of BUSINESS TERMS and the BUSINESS CONCEPTS that they represent constitute the organization's vocabulary or ONTOLOGY.

Figure 5–9 shows that PARTIES and the like have roles to play—that is, ACCESS ROLES—*for* SYMBOLS, BUSINESS CONCEPTS, and BUSINESS CONCEPT ELEMENTS. Of the ACCESS ROLE sub-types listed before, only MANAGEMENT ROLE (and of course, OTHER ACCESS ROLE) apply here. But the following two new sub-types have been added.

—  ENFORCEMENT ROLE: To be played by a *data steward*, ensuring that consistent definitions of WORDS and PHRASES are used throughout the organization*
—  SPECIFICATION ROLE: To be played by appropriate people *for* the original definition of BUSINESS CONCEPTS and SYMBOLS and their ongoing maintenance

Note the arc, by the way. By implication, it is also across the relationship we saw previously *for* one and only one SITE. That is, each ACCESS ROLE must be *for* one SITE, or *for* one SYMBOL, or *for* one BUSINESS CONCEPT, and so forth. As other elements of this model are added, by implication the arc will extend to them as well.

---

*Yes, the model says that a particular SIGNIFIER can represent more than one BUSINESS CONCEPT, and it often does, but the objective of data management is to reduce the occurrences of that as much as possible. And, of course, someone also must be responsible for MANAGEMENT of the definition of the BUSINESS CONCEPT in the first place.

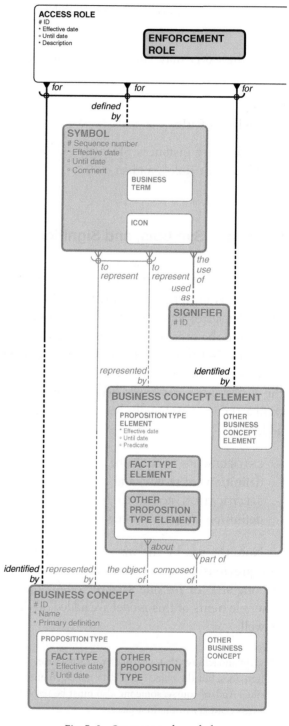

*Fig. 5–9: Concepts and symbols.*

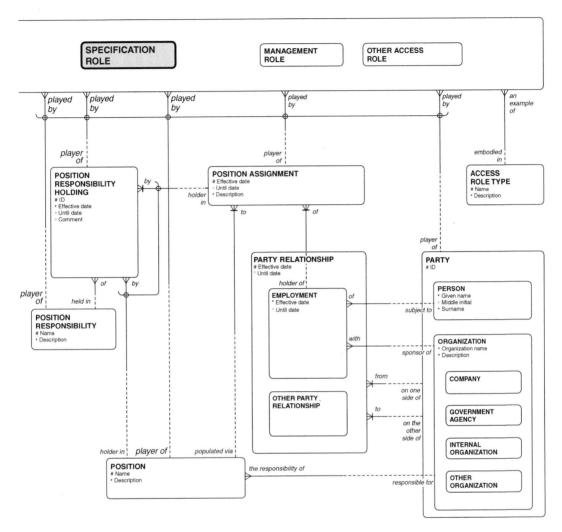

Fig. 5–9: continued.

223

In addition to the BUSINESS CONCEPTS and BUSINESS CONCEPT ELEMENTS (and the SYMBOLS and SIGNIFIERS that represent them), ACCESS ROLES can be defined for either the RESOURCES that supply and record them or for physical COPIES of those RESOURCES. (RESOURCES and COPIES are described in Chapter Two.) This is shown in Figure 5–10. In addition to the MANAGEMENT ROLE and PERMISSION ROLE described previously, the figure introduces the following:

– AUTHORSHIP ROLE: This applies to a RESOURCE only (all COPIES) and describes the creators of the resource. ACCESS ROLE TYPES that are *sub-types* of "Authorship role" could be "author", "publisher", "editor", and so on.

### Business Rule

Each AUTHORSHIP ROLE must specifically be *for* one and only one RESOURCE. (This is typically a DOCUMENT, but possibly *for* an OTHER RESOURCE.)

Recall from Chapter Two that according to the Dublin Core the types of authorship role (and thus the sub-types of the ACCESS ROLE TYPE that is "Authorship role") are (among others):

– Author
– Contributor
– Publisher
– Rights holder [ISO 2003]

## Activities, Decisions, and Events

An ACCESS ROLE may be *for* an ACTIVITY. (ACTIVITY was defined in Chapter Three.) This is shown in Figure 5–11 (see pages 226 and 227) . Thus, a PARTY (or a PARTY in a POSITION or with a POSITION RESPONSIBILITY) may be *player of* an ACCESS ROLE *for* an ACTIVITY. This may apply to either a FUNCTION or a BUSINESS PROCESS.

In particular, the ACCESS ROLES that are *for* an ACTIVITY include SPECIFICATION ROLE (defining the nature of the ACTIVITY); ENFORCEMENT ROLE (requiring that the ACTIVITY be carried out under appropriate circumstances); PERMISSION

ROLE (permitting or prohibiting participation in the ACTIVITY); MANAGEMENT ROLE (in charge of the overall conduct of the ACTIVITY); and, as always, OTHER ACCESS ROLE. Again, note that the relationship *for* one ACTIVITY is "arced" with the ACCESS ROLES *for* the other relationships we have seen.

## Means and Ends

Chapter Seven describes the Motivation column in the Architecture Framework more extensively than can be done here. To summarize, though, in the Business Owner's Row Two view in the Motivation column the cell describes the organization's goals and objectives, strategies and tactics, and directives (business policies and business rules) that make it all work. Specifically, the model centers on the following.

— END: Something the organization is trying to achieve, such as:

→ A VISION
→ A GOAL
→ An OBJECTIVE

— MEANS: A capability the organization uses to accomplish it, through:

→ A MISSION
→ A COURSE OF ACTION, such as a strategy or a tactic
→ A DIRECTIVE, such as a business policy or a business rule

— ASSESSMENT *of* an INFLUENCER, such as "Competition" *on* either a MEANS or an END

These entity classes are relevant here, of course, because it is possible to specify the PARTIES who play an ACCESS ROLE *in* either a MEANS, an END, an INFLUENCER, or an ASSESSMENT (see Figure 5–12). The ACCESS ROLE might be *played by* the PARTY (or POSITION, and so on) responsible *for* ENFORCEMENT of a DIRECTIVE, the PARTY responsible *for* MANAGEMENT *of* an ASSESSMENT, or the PARTY responsible *for* the MANAGEMENT *of* an INFLUENCER, an END, or a MEANS. Note that in general in Row Two, and especially here, if an ACCESS ROLE is played by a PARTY, it is probably being *played by* an INTERNAL ORGANIZATION, although it could be *played by* a COMPANY or a GOVERNMENT AGENCY.

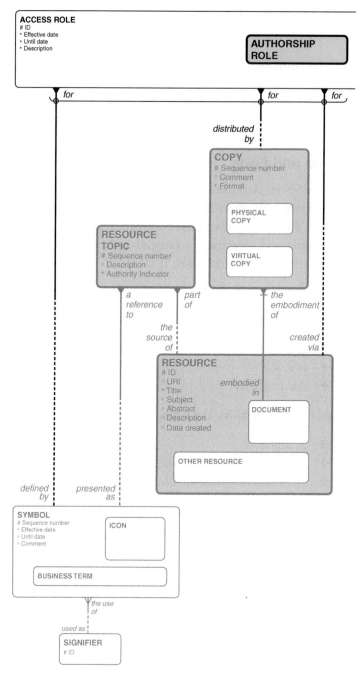

**ACCESS ROLE**
# ID
* Effective date
◦ Until date
* Description

**AUTHORSHIP ROLE**

*for*        *for*        *for*

*distributed by*

**COPY**
# Sequence number
◦ Comment
* Format

PHYSICAL COPY

VIRTUAL COPY

**RESOURCE TOPIC**
# Sequence number
◦ Description
* Authority Indicator

*a reference to*        *part of*        *the embodiment of*

*the source of*        *created via*

**RESOURCE**
# ID
◦ URI
* Title
◦ Subject
◦ Abstract
◦ Description
◦ Date created

*embodied in*

DOCUMENT

OTHER RESOURCE

*defined by*        *presented as*

**SYMBOL**
# Sequence number
* Effective date
◦ Until date
◦ Comment

ICON

BUSINESS TERM

*the use of*

*used as*

**SIGNIFIER**
# ID

*Fig. 5–10: Resources.*

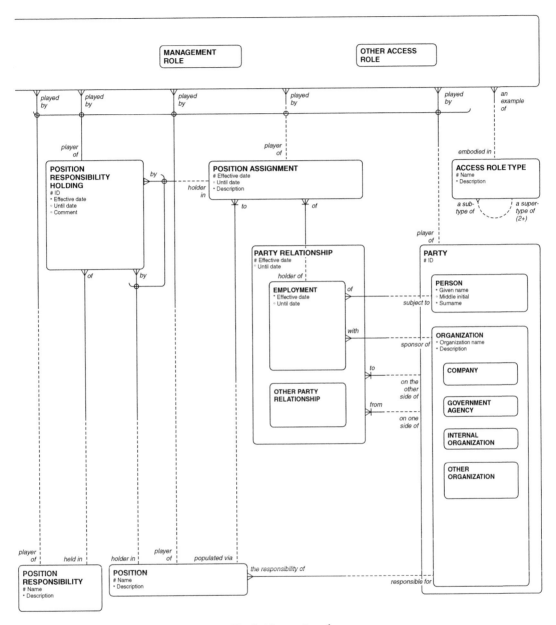

*Fig. 5–10: continued.*

227

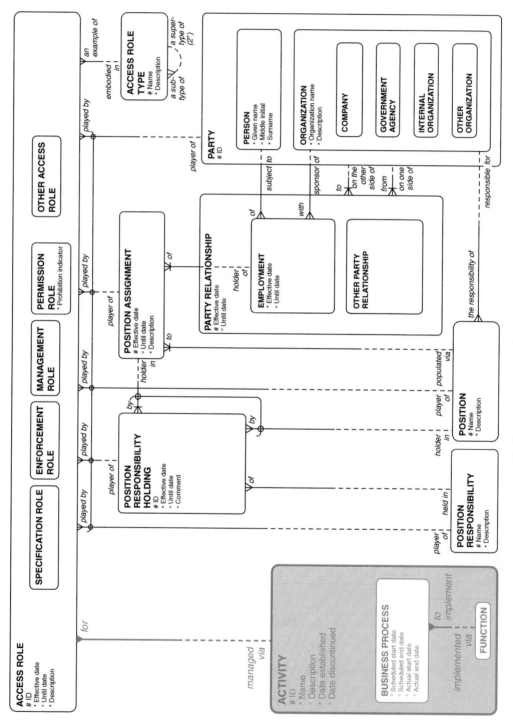

Fig. 5–11: Activities and events.

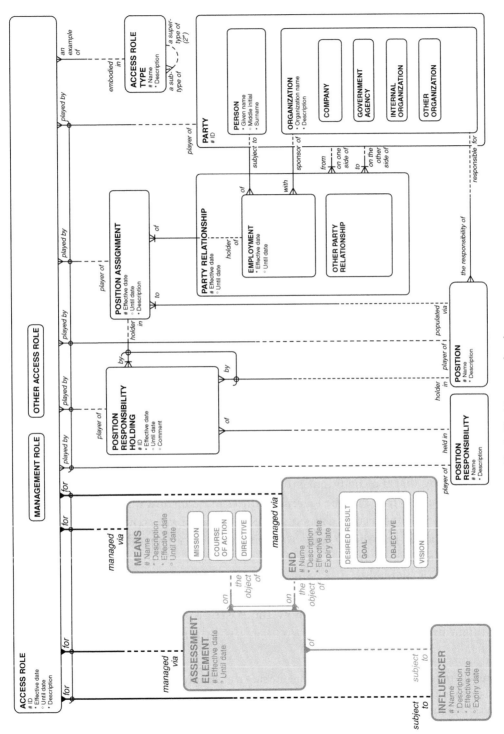

Fig. 5–12: Means and ends.

229

In addition, the Motivation column describes an EFFORT (see Figure 5–13), such as a project or a program, *to achieve* a DESIRED RESULT *through the use of* a BUSINESS PROCESS. This EFFORT may also be *managed via* a MANAGEMENT ROLE.

## ROW THREE: THE ARCHITECT'S VIEW

Just as ACCESS ROLE determines how PARTIES and the like relate to Row Two things, such as BUSINESS CONCEPTS and ACTIVITIES, so too can it be used to represent people's responsibilities for such Row Three artifacts as SYSTEM PROCESSES and DATA FLOWS. One of these is shown in Figure 5–14. Here, an ACCESS ROLE, *played by* any of the various entity classes shown, must be *for* one SYSTEM PROCESS.*

Note that in a Row Three data flow diagram typically we do not identify who is performing the process. In describing a MANAGEMENT ROLE—being in charge of the SYSTEM PROCESS—this model allows for more than would typically be shown.

Still, it is useful to be able to say that one of the entity classes that is a *player of* an ACCESS ROLE may be playing a SPECIFICATION ROLE defining just who is responsible for defining the nature of the process in the first place. The *player of* an ACCESS ROLE may be playing a PERMISSION ROLE, controlling who is allowed to carry out the SYSTEM PROCESS. Alternatively, it may be playing an ENFORCEMENT ROLE, ensuring that the conditions around the SYSTEM PROCESS are met.

In addition, it is true that the *external entities* in a data flow diagram do usually refer to individual PEOPLE or ORGANIZATIONS. Hence, DATA FLOW in Figure 5–14 has added that it may be *to* and *from* either a PARTY (typically, an INTERNAL ORGANIZATION) or a POSITION.

Figure 5–15 highlights that some of the ACCESS ROLES that are *for* a BUSINESS CONCEPT, or *for* a BUSINESS CONCEPT ELEMENT, really are *for* an ENTITY CLASS or an ATTRIBUTE. This is to show how the POSITION RESPONSIBILITY *data steward* might be the *player of* a SPECIFICATION ROLE or a MANAGEMENT ROLE *for* the

---

*Naturally, this relationship is under the same arc shown previously to designate all possible things an ACCESS ROLE can be *for*. For example, an ACCESS ROLE must be *for* either a Row Two BUSINESS CONCEPT or a Row Three ACTIVITY or SYSTEM PROCESS.

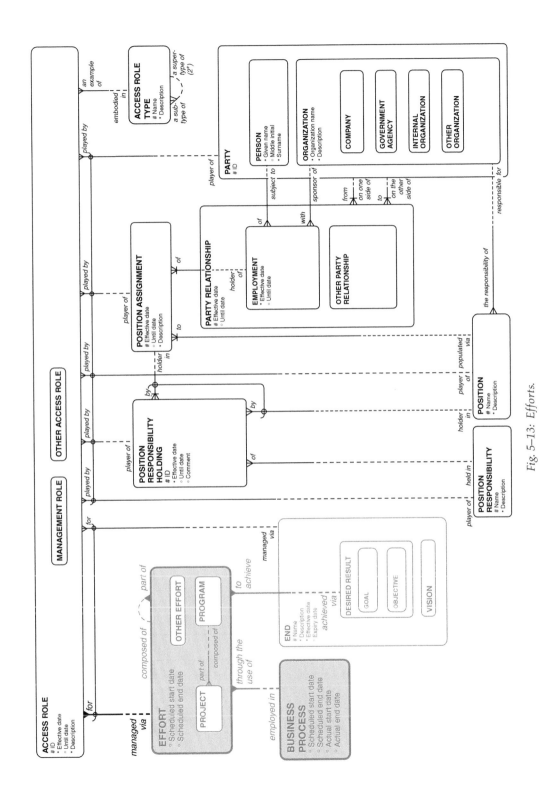

Fig. 5–13: Efforts.

231

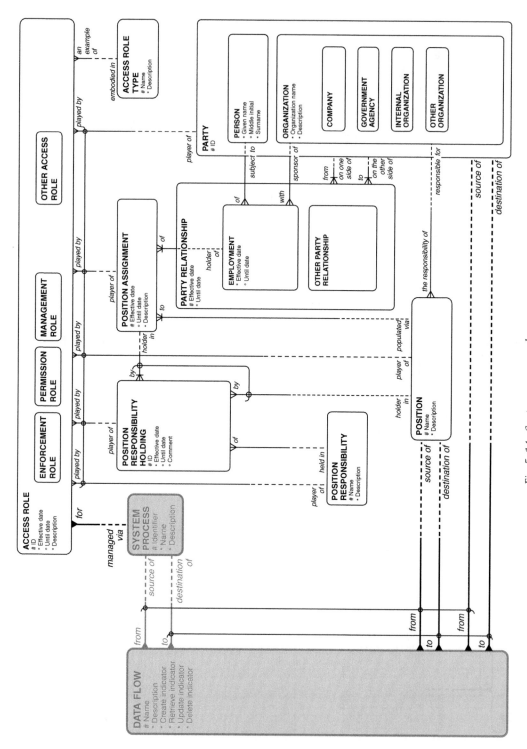

Fig. 5-14: System process roles.

232

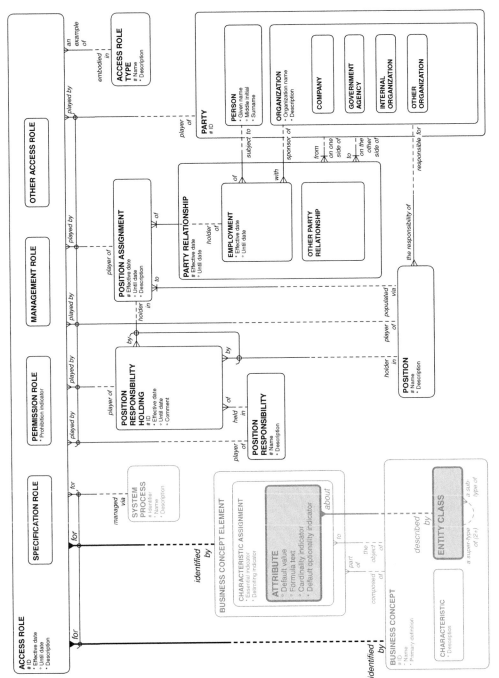

*Fig. 5–15: Entity Classes and Attributes.*

233

definitions of each ENTITY CLASS and ATTRIBUTE. This includes evaluating the sensitivity of data or assigning a security classification level. In addition, the data steward plays an ENFORCEMENT ROLE in making sure the definitions are uniformly published.

Figure 5–16 shows that people also play a role in enforcing business rules (SYSTEM CONSTRAINTS in the figure). The full nature of SYSTEM CONSTRAINTS will be revealed in Chapter Seven, but here we can see that each SYSTEM CONSTRAINT must be *to constrain* either an ATTRIBUTE, an ENTITY CLASS, or an ASSOCIATIVE ROLE.

## ROW FOUR: THE DESIGNER'S VIEW

In Row Four, as shown in Figure 5–17, each ACCESS ROLE may be *for* a PROGRAM MODULE. Most significant, as we saw in Chapter Three, is PROGRAMMING ROLE. This is the person who is the programmer or tester of the PROGRAM MODULE. In addition, the SPECIFICATION ROLE describes the responsibility for designing the module. Additional categories of ACCESS ROLES in play are typically concerned with MANAGEMENT, although PERMISSION ROLES (determining who is allowed to work on or operate the PROGRAM MODULE) may also apply.

Among the tasks a PROGRAM MODULE must perform is to be for a DATABASE CONSTRAINT, as is shown in Figure 5–18. DATABASE CONSTRAINT and DATABASE CONSTRAINT ELEMENT are discussed in detail in Chapter Seven, but here it is sufficient to say that a DATABASE CONSTRAINT places a restriction on a database table: the constraint may be a FOREIGN KEY, a UNIQUENESS CONSTRAINT, or the fact that a column in the table is derived from a COMPUTATION. A DATABASE CONSTRAINT ELEMENT is a reference to another table or column that is a component of the constraint. A PROGRAMMING ROLE, a SPECIFICATION ROLE, or a MANAGEMENT ROLE may be *for* either a DATABASE CONSTRAINT or a DATABASE CONSTRAINT ELEMENT.

Figure 5–19 shows that someone may play a MANAGEMENT ROLE for each PERSISTENCE MECHANISM (TABLE, VIEW, or COLUMN). In addition, one type of PROGRAMMING ROLE would be the database designer who is responsible for determining the structure of the tables and columns. Other ACCESS ROLES include PERMISSION ROLE (having permission to see and/or manipulate the tables and columns) and ENFORCEMENT ROLE (to ensure that proper design standards are followed).

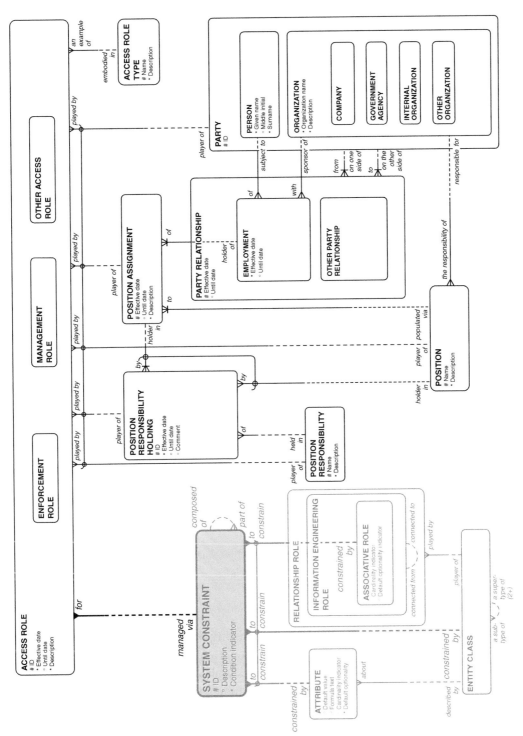

Fig. 5–16: System constraint roles.

235

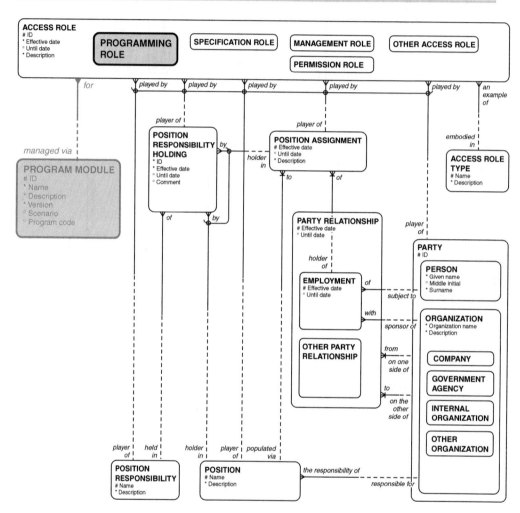

*Fig. 5–17: Program modules.*

## Interactive Modules

As we have seen, the basic metamodel for addressing people and organizations is the same as the business model for addressing people and organizations. The difference is that the metamodel describes the roles they play in managing information and systems, rather than the roles they play in managing the business.

A large amount of the software written for modern computer systems concerns the display and input of information on screens. Your author entered the computer

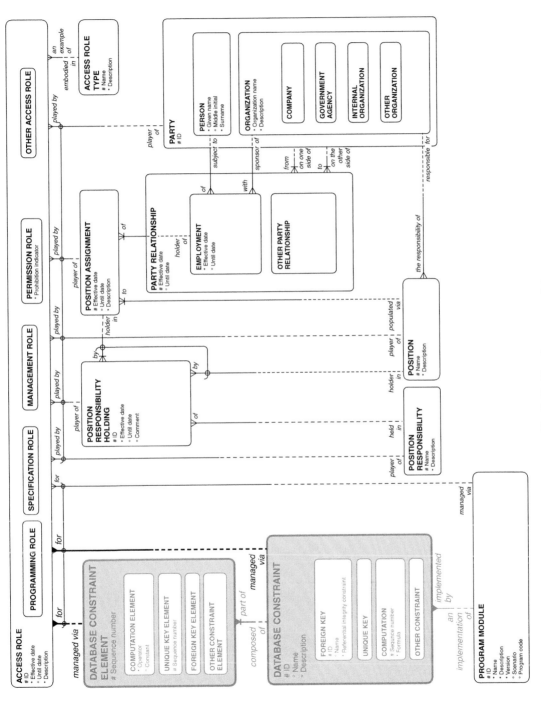

Fig. 5–18: Database constraints.

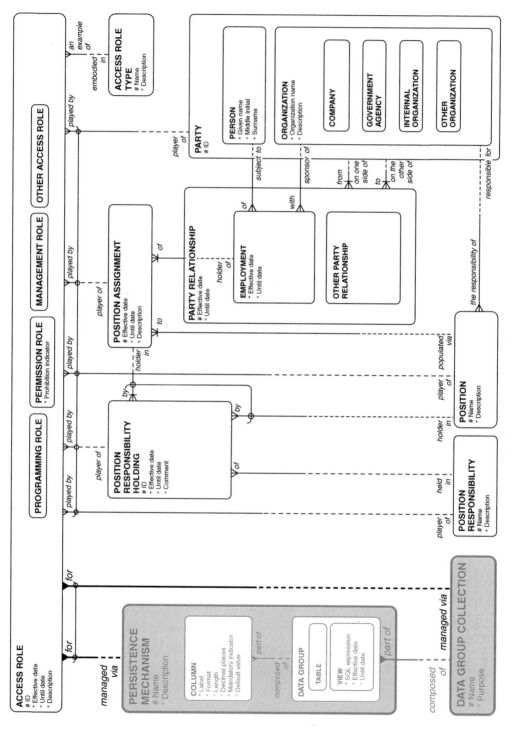

Fig. 5–19: Persistence mechanisms.

238

business in the late 1960s through a fluke that had him working with a new technology called *computer time-sharing*. At that time, most computers dealt with punched cards, and limited processing power meant that the entire focus of the programming effort was on carrying out the calculations and other tasks that constituted the work of the program.

With computer time-sharing, however, it was now possible to sit at a teletype machine, type something in, and have the computer type something back. It was a revolutionary idea! Among other things, in developing systems in this environment, it very quickly became apparent that attention must be paid to the nature of the dialogue between human and computer. In particular, the teletype was very slow (only 10 characters per second, or 100 Baud*), so it mattered if the prompt for information was very long. No one had the patience to wait for the computer to ask a very long question. But new users needed more help. So early on, computer dialogues were designed for two modes: beginner and expert.

The point is that the code required to support the interaction was in addition to the code required to do the work. More significantly, it had to be designed with skill. For many years, the time-sharing world was on the outside of mainstream computing. People who talked about user interfaces were clearly speaking in tongues to the rank-and-file COBOL group.

Then personal computers happened. Suddenly software was being developed that was to be used by people unfamiliar with computers. Suddenly the characteristics of human interaction with computers became important. At the same time, the economics of computing was changing so that cycles could be spent on the niceties of user interfaces.

In the twenty-first century, the biggest part of most programs' code is devoted to that user interface, either directly or through calls to program libraries for that purpose. To produce even a generic model of a user interface sets this book up as vulnerable to future obsolescence, but the structure is so fundamental in 2005 that it is worth looking at.

Figure 5–20 shows a new sub-type of EXECUTABLE MODULE, the INTERACTIVE MODULE. Like a PACKAGE, an INTERACTIVE MODULE may be *composed of* one or more CLASS IMPLEMENTATIONS, specifically ARCHITECTURAL CLASSES that are HUMAN INTERFACE CLASSES. Indeed, we observe here two specific types of HUMAN INTERFACE

---

*Compare with the 52,000,000 Baud of today's DSL lines!

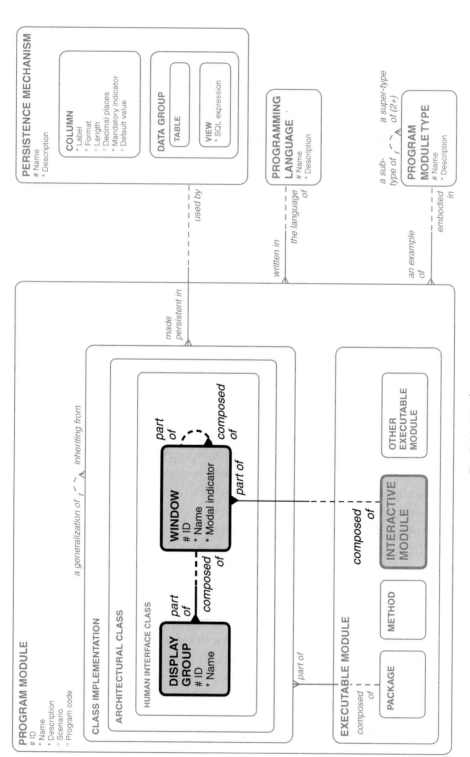

Fig. 5–20: Windows.

CLASSES: a WINDOW and a DISPLAY GROUP. A WINDOW is a defined area on the screen that can be implemented as an object in its own right. This may then be *composed of* one or more DISPLAY GROUPS, where a DISPLAY GROUP is a set of fields or other objects to be treated as a logical unit.

Each DISPLAY GROUP must be *an example of* one PROGRAM MODULE TYPE that is a *sub-type of* "Display group type". A WINDOW may be "modal" in that no other WINDOW can be acted on if it is open, or it may be "non-modal," meaning that other windows can be moved to the front and manipulated. The "Modal indicator" attribute determines this.

These are examples of CLASS IMPLEMENTATION that are computer objects, not analogues to something in the business world. They would not appear in an entity-relationship diagram, even if it were drawn in UML. Note also that these are not *made persistent in* a PERSISTENCE MECHANISM.

Figure 5–21 shows that both a WINDOW and a DISPLAY GROUP may be *composed of* one or more other HUMAN INTERFACE CLASSES, this time INTERFACE ELEMENTS. An INTERFACE ELEMENT must be one of the following.

— A FIELD, which displays a column from the database or accepts a typed-in value to be added to the database. That is, a FIELD must be *the use or display of* one and only one PERSISTENCE MECHANISM (that is, usually a COLUMN in a database). A FIELD may also be a *trigger of* an EXECUTABLE MODULE when the Enter key is pressed.
— A DISPLAY ELEMENT, which simply displays specific text or graphic elements.
— An ICONIC TRIGGER, which if touched by a cursor will cause another program action (an ICONIC TRIGGER must be *of* one and only one EXECUTABLE MODULE).
— An OTHER INTERFACE ELEMENT, which may be anything else (graphic or text) displayed in a window.

Each INTERFACE ELEMENT must be *an example of* exactly one "Interface element type".

### Business Rule

The first instances of the PROGRAM MODULE TYPE "Interface element type" must be "Field", "Display element", "Interface trigger", and "Other interface element". Each of these may then be *a super-type of* other PROGRAM MODULE TYPES.

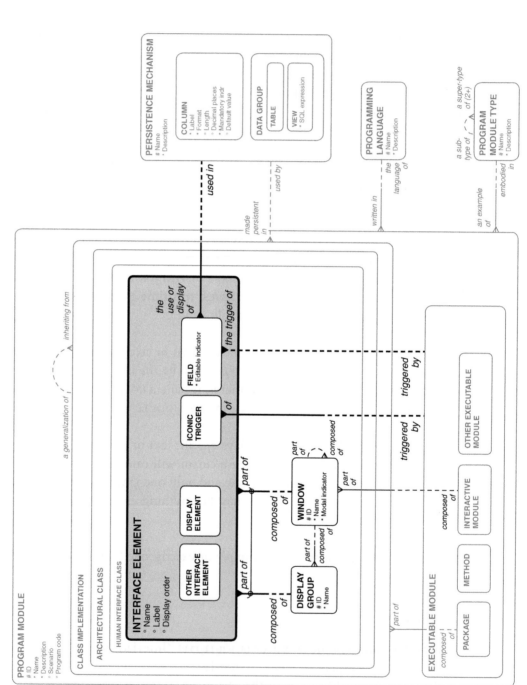

Fig. 5–21: Interface elements.

## Row Six: Security and Governance

The Functioning System view of the Framework is concerned with the actual databases and programs of an APPLICATION SYSTEM. This means that in the People and Organizations column we are concerned with the ACCESS ROLES that are *for:*

— PROGRAM COPIES
— DATABASE INSTANCES
— TABLE INSTANCES

Figure 5–22 shows this, again along with, the ACCESS ROLE *for* PROGRAM MODULE (specifically when it is a DATABASE MANAGEMENT SYSTEM). Note that in this case we are only granting ACCESS ROLES to named PARTIES. In particular, these are the ENFORCEMENT ROLE and PERMISSION ROLE. PERMISSION ROLE, of course, is simply the fact that a PARTY has permission to enter a DATABASE INSTANCE or a particular TABLE INSTANCE. It also provides overall permission to make use of the PROGRAM COPY of a DATABASE MANAGEMENT SYSTEM. The ENFORCEMENT ROLE is the ability to establish the rules (and PERMISSION ROLES) for any of those three. A MANAGEMENT ROLE or a PROGRAMMING ROLE is responsible for taking care of PROGRAM COPIES.

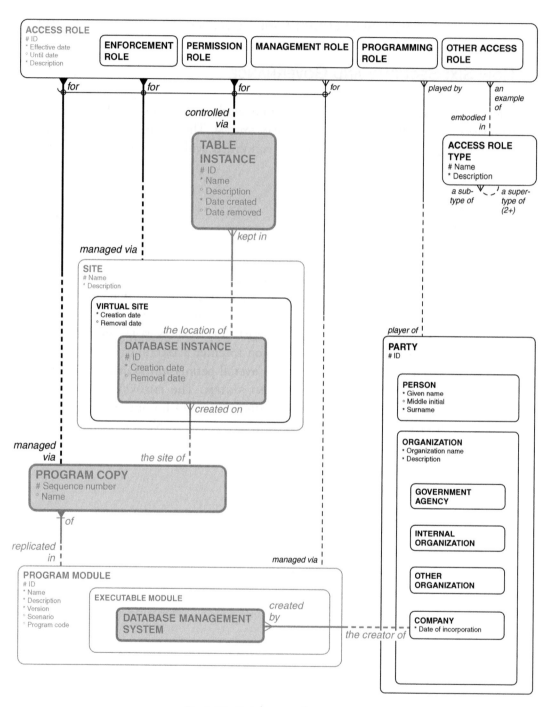

*Fig. 5–22: Databases and programs.*

244

# EVENTS AND TIMING

*Time is that quality of nature which keeps events from happening all at once. Lately it doesn't seem to be working.*

—Unknown

*When I can't handle events, I let them handle themselves.*

—Henry Ford

## The Events and Timing Column

The Activities column of the architecture framework is concerned with *when* the enterprise carries out its work.

- The *planner* lays out annual and longer-term plans and schedules.
- The *business owner* sees the business event types that control what a business does.
- The *architect* sees the system event types that control the processing of data.
- The *designer* defines program event types to cause specific program activities.
- The *builder* is concerned with the detailed programming required to respond to system events.
- The *functioning system* is the system responding to events as they happen.

Figure 6–1 shows the architecture framework with this chapter's cells highlighted. In particular, we will be looking at event types from three perspectives: the business owner, the architect, and the designer.

| | Data (What) | Activities (How) | Locations (Where) | People (Who) | Time (When) | Motivation (Why) |
|---|---|---|---|---|---|---|
| **Objectives/ Scope** (Planner's View) | List of things important to the enterprise | List of functions the enterprise performs | List of enterprise locations | Organization approaches | Business master schedule | Business vision and mission |
| **Enterprise Model** (Business Owner's View) | Language, divergent data model | Business process model | Logistics network | Organization chart | State/ transition diagram | Business strategies, tactics, policies, rule |
| **Model of Fundamental Concepts** (Architect's View) | Convergent e/r model | Essential data flow diagram | Locations of roles | The viable system, use cases | Entity life history | Business rule model |
| **Technology Model** (Designer's View) | Database design | System design, program structure | Hardware, software distribution | User interface, security design | Event processing | Business rule design |
| **Detailed Representation** (Builder's View) | Physical storage design | Detailed program design | Network architecture, protocols | Screens, security coding | Timing definitions | Rule specification program logic |
| **Functioning System** | *(Working system)* | | | | | |
| | Databases | Program inventory, logs | Communications facilities | Trained people | Business events | Enforced rules |

*Fig. 6–1: Timing column.*

## Row Two: Business Event Types

Modeling the timing of business and system activities is really about modeling types of *events*. An event is something happening that causes something else to happen. This can be a business event that triggers an activity in the enterprise or a technological event that causes something to happen in a computer system. An *event type* is the definition of a category of events. Because we are concerned here with metadata and not the data of the business, this model will cover event types, not the actual events that occur on particular days.

Note that this includes the *temporal event* concept, which is simply the fact that the clock (including the calendar) passed a certain point. For example, the end of a month may be a temporal event triggering the closing of a company's accounts. A schedule, such as a manufacturing master schedule, is simply a collection of temporal events.

The metamodel for the Timing column overlaps significantly with the metamodel for activities, described in detail in Chapter Three. Here, in Row Two, a *business event type* is something that causes an occurrence of a *business process* to be carried out.

### External Business Event Types

In Chapter Three, we saw that an ESSENTIAL BUSINESS PROCESS is defined as the collection of ELEMENTARY BUSINESS PROCESSES into a complete response to an external event type. Figure 6–2 shows the part of the metamodel that covers this. Specifically, we are defining as part of the nature of an ESSENTIAL BUSINESS PROCESS that it must be *based on* an EXTERNAL BUSINESS EVENT TYPE. An EXTERNAL BUSINESS EVENT TYPE defines something that happens in the world outside of the enterprise's control. This includes such things as "Receipt of a payment", "Arrival of a candidate for a job", and so forth. Note that this could also include something happening within the organization's facilities, such as "a fire in the refinery", as long as it is *not* in the enterprise's control. This is as opposed to an INTERNAL BUSINESS EVENT TYPE that defines something happening under the control of the enterprise, such as completion of a manufacturing step. (INTERNAL BUSINESS EVENT TYPES are discussed further in the material following.)

Note that an attribute of EXTERNAL BUSINESS EVENT TYPE is a "Temporal indicator", which indicates whether events of this event type are temporal events. As stated previously, a temporal event is one that is triggered by the passage of time, such as "the first of the month", "December 25", and so forth.

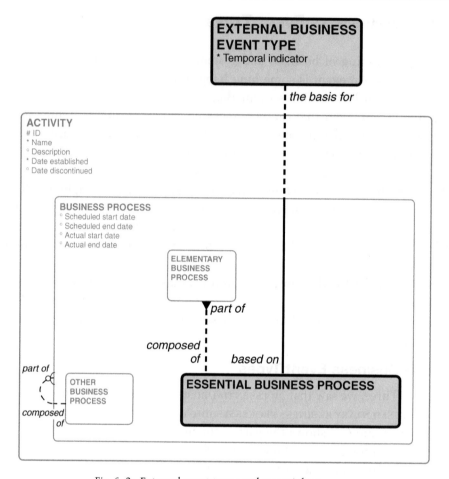

*Fig. 6–2: External event types and essential processes.*

Figure 6–3 shows the detailed business process model for the library procurement department originally described in Chapter Three. Note that two EXTERNAL BUSINESS EVENT TYPES drive the model: "Receipt of invoice" and "Receipt of book". "Receipt of book" triggers two ELEMENTARY BUSINESS PROCESSES, which can then be rolled up into the ESSENTIAL BUSINESS PROCESS "Book received". It also sends the message "Marked 'Blue' order" to the BUSINESS PROCESS "Pay invoice". Note that "Pay invoice" cannot happen until an event that is an example of the EXTERNAL BUSINESS EVENT TYPE, "Receipt of invoice", occurs.

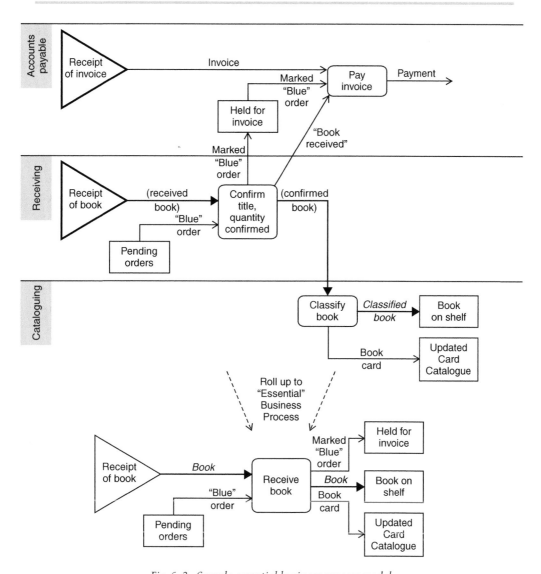

*Fig. 6–3: Sample essential business process model.*

## Internal Business Event Types

In addition to EXTERNAL BUSINESS EVENT TYPES, ELEMENTARY BUSINESS PROCESSES, and OTHER BUSINESS PROCESSES within the organization are also often *triggered by* BUSINESS PROCESSES. These triggerings (like the message "Book received", described previously) are examples of INTERNAL BUSINESS EVENT TYPES. That is, they describe events that are internal to the enterprise and under its control.

In Figure 6–3 we saw ELEMENTARY BUSINESS PROCESSES that affect each other. There are two types of flows in this model. The thick lines are the movements of the physical book itself. The thinner lines are movements of the set of mechanisms (color-coded copies of purchase orders and the like) required to pass information from one process to the next. Each of these latter flows is, in effect, an INTERNAL BUSINESS EVENT TYPE (shown in Figure 6–4).

An INTERNAL BUSINESS EVENT TYPE represents the fact that one BUSINESS PROCESS may trigger another. The INTERNAL BUSINESS EVENT TYPE that is *the trigger of* a BUSINESS PROCESS may be *the action of* another BUSINESS PROCESS. That is, a BUSINESS PROCESS may be *the decision to trigger* one or more INTERNAL BUSINESS EVENT TYPES, each of which must then be *the trigger of* another BUSINESS PROCESS.

Note that decisions themselves are not explicitly represented in this model. The *decision to trigger* one INTERNAL BUSINESS EVENT TYPE/BUSINESS PROCESS instead of another is contained in the logic of the triggering BUSINESS PROCESS.

In Figure 6–3, the PROCESS FRAGMENT (a type of BUSINESS PROCESS) "Classify book" is *initiated by* an INTERNAL BUSINESS EVENT TYPE, completion of the PROCESS FRAGMENT "Title, quantity confirmed". An EXTERNAL BUSINESS EVENT TYPE is something that happens outside the control of the enterprise. It may be something that happens in the marketplace, an act of God, or simply the passage of time (defined by the "Temporal indicator" attribute's being "True"). Temporal events, by definition, cannot be internal events.

Note, by the way, that although a BUSINESS PROCESS may be *in the role of* an INTERNAL BUSINESS EVENT TYPE, an event type is very different from a process. A process, by definition, takes place over time, whereas an event type is instantaneous. If a BUSINESS PROCESS is *the decision to trigger* a BUSINESS EVENT TYPE, it is not the entire process doing so. It is rather the point of time at the completion of, at the beginning of, or somewhere else during the duration of the BUSINESS PROCESS that is acting as a BUSINESS EVENT.

The INTERNAL BUSINESS EVENT TYPE attribute "Position flag" takes the value "Beginning" if the event type is at the beginning of the BUSINESS PROCESS. It takes the value "End" if the event type is at the end of the BUSINESS PROCESS; or it takes the value "Lag" if it is at a predefined point after the start of the BUSINESS PROCESS. If it is "Lag", the attribute "Lag quantity" is the length of time after the beginning of the BUSINESS PROCESS that constitutes the event. The "Lag quantity" must have

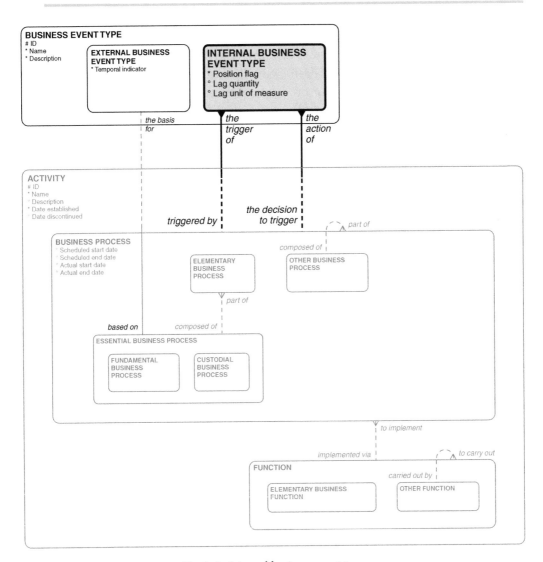

*Fig. 6–4: Internal business event types.*

a "Unit of measure", such as "Weeks" or "Days", and this is stored in the attribute "Lag unit of measure".

Figure 6–4 also shows that both INTERNAL BUSINESS EVENT TYPE and EXTERNAL BUSINESS EVENT TYPE are sub-types of BUSINESS EVENT TYPE. Again, remember that these are event *types* we are discussing here. The date and time of actual events is not a subject of this model.

## Motivation

Note that in the model so far a BUSINESS EVENT TYPE defines a direct effect on a BUSINESS PROCESS. In Chapter Seven, we will encounter INFLUENCERS, where an influencer is "anything that can produce an effect on the enterprise *without apparent exertion of tangible force or direct exercise of command*" [Business Rules Group 2005, p. 21]. That is, whereas a BUSINESS EVENT TYPE directly causes a BUSINESS PROCESS to occur, an INFLUENCER's effect is more indirect. It first must be judged to be important.

As described in Chapter Seven, an INFLUENCER works by affecting the ENDS (specifically, DESIRED RESULTS) that describe what the enterprise is in the business to accomplish (see Figure 6–5). It also affects the MEANS (specifically, the COURSES OF ACTION) that define any capability that may be called on, activated, or enforced to achieve an organization's objectives. The MEANS available, then, constrain the actual BUSINESS PROCESSES that are possible.

Specifically, each INFLUENCER may be *subject to* one or more ASSESSMENTS, each of which may be *composed of* one or more ASSESSMENT ELEMENTS. Each of these in turn is an assessment of an influencer's effect *on* a MEANS or an END. In response to such an ASSESSMENT, a MEANS may be *used to* a MEANS EFFECT *on* a BUSINESS PROCESS. A MEANS EFFECT can offer GUIDANCE or impose GOVERNANCE on the BUSINESS PROCESS, but more typically it is an EFFORT using the BUSINESS PROCESS *to achieve* a DESIRED RESULT.

## ROW THREE: SYSTEM EVENTS

Whereas Row Two (the Business Owner's View) was concerned with the BUSINESS EVENTS that trigger the work of the enterprise, Row Three (the Architect's View) is concerned with the SYSTEM EVENTS* that deal with the enterprise's data. Three types of models are described in this chapter to recount event types.

-   The *state-transition diagram*, which represents the sequence of states an entity class (or system) may go through, as triggered by defined types of events

*Again, it should be noted that the word *system* is used here to denote that we are looking at events that could be automated, not that any particular technology is expected to be used.

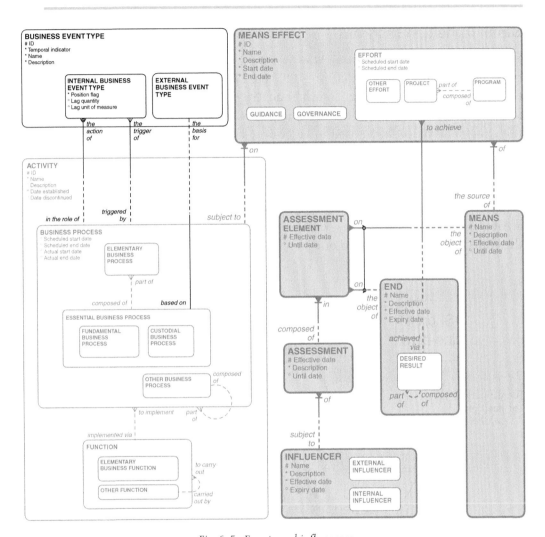

*Fig. 6–5: Events and influencers.*

- The *entity life history*, which also represents the sequence of states an entity class may go through, but whose focus is more on the event types triggering these state changes than on the states themselves
- The *essential system process diagram*, which like the essential *business* process diagram reduces processes to those required to carry out a company's response to a type of system event

## State-Transition Diagram

Figure 6–6 shows a sample of a *state-transition diagram*. This is a relatively old technique [e.g., Martin and McClure 1985, pp. 219–230], but is included as one of those supported by UML [e.g., Booch et al. 1999, pp. 286–307]. The diagram as a whole represents the life cycle of an entity class, although as a Row Two diagram the same notation could be used to describe a sequence of states for a portion of the company.

This figure is a modified UML version of a state-transition diagram. In it, each round-cornered rectangle represents the *state* of an entity class. A state is a condition the entity class is in, represented by a specific set of values for its attributes and relationship roles. Each arrow represents an event type that causes the entity class to change from one state to another.

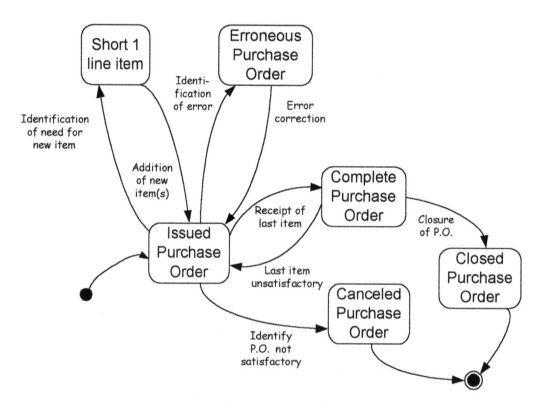

*Fig. 6–6: Sample state-transition diagram.*

In this example, the entity class is ORDER, from the sample entity relationship model described in Chapter Two. Specifically, it is PURCHASE ORDER. Once it has become an "Issued Purchase Order", the following transitions can take place as shown in this model.

—  The need for a new line item is identified. This changes the state from "Issued" to "Short 1 line item". Subsequent to that, the event type "Addition of new item(s)" changes the state back to "Issued".
—  An error in the purchase order is identified. This changes the state from "Issued" to "Erroneous". Subsequently, the correction of the error changes the state back to "Issued". (Receipt of most items against the purchase order does not change its state.)
—  "Receipt of the last item" against the purchase order changes its state to "Complete".
—  After the purchase order has been deemed complete, determination that one of the received products is faulty causes it to be returned and the state of the purchase order goes back to "Issued".
—  When the last item has again been received, the state can again return to "Complete".
—  Once the decision is made to close the purchase order, its state is changed to "Closed".
—  Alternatively, at any point during its life, the purchase order can be found to be unsatisfactory, which changes its state to "Canceled".

The metamodel for all of this is shown in Figure 6–7. A SYSTEM EVENT TYPE is the definition of something that happens in the world that produces data affecting the business. It is represented by a line on the state-transition diagram. It may be *triggered by* a BUSINESS EVENT TYPE.* Ultimately, every SYSTEM EVENT TYPE must be a *changer from* one ENTITY CLASS STATE ... *to* another ENTITY CLASS STATE. And of course an ENTITY CLASS STATE must be *of* an ENTITY CLASS—either an ELEMENTARY ENTITY CLASS or an assembly of those embodied in a VIRTUAL ENTITY CLASS.

Like a BUSINESS EVENT TYPE, a SYSTEM EVENT TYPE is either a *temporal system event type* (which is triggered by the passage of time) or another kind of event

---

*Later we will see how it must be *triggered by* either a BUSINESS EVENT TYPE or a BUSINESS PROCESS. This is why the relationship line is a mandatory solid in the figure even though the text says "may".

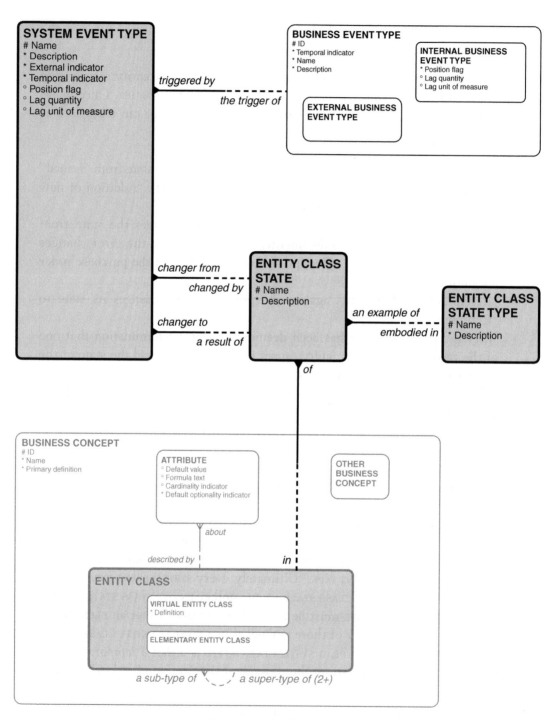

Fig. 6–7: Entity class states.

type, triggered by something in the world. This is represented by the attribute "Temporal indicator", which is "True" if an event is temporal. Also, like BUSINESS EVENT TYPE occurrences of SYSTEM EVENT TYPE are either internal to the company or external. Rather than representing this with sub-types, the SYSTEM EVENT TYPE entity class has the attribute "External indicator", which is "True" if the event is outside the enterprise's control.

Note that similar to the case discussed for the Row Two model we are interested in *event types* here, not in *system processes*. An event is something in the world that happens, causing something else to happen. This means that there is no *elapsed* time in an event—only a *point* in time. Even where a business or system process is triggered by another process, what is triggering it is *completion of* (or *beginning of*, and so on) the previous process, not its duration.

Specifically, whereas a SYSTEM EVENT TYPE is *caused by* a SYSTEM PROCESS, the attribute "Position flag" tells whether the SYSTEM EVENT TYPE was the "Beginning" of the BUSINESS PROCESS, the "End" of the BUSINESS process, or "Lagged" a specified "Lag time" from the beginning of the BUSINESS PROCESS. The attribute "Lag time" is expressed in terms of the attribute "Lag unit of measure", such as "weeks" or "days".

## Entity Life History

The object-oriented community claims that the advantage of object modeling over entity-relationship modeling is object models' representation of *object class behavior*. That is, what happens to an object in that class over the course of its existence. In that object models are fundamentally about program design, this is not that remarkable. This is especially true because behavior is not actually represented in a model by program logic but only by the name of a program. This makes it very easy to do.

In principle, the entity boxes in an entity-relationship model could also be expanded to include references to behavior. The problem is that in the real world represented by such models behavior cannot be identified simply by named packages. It is possible to model the behavior of entity classes, of course, but this results in a model that is much more complex than can be squeezed into an entity class box on a model.

One type of model that specifically addresses this task is called the *entity life history* [Jackson 1983; Eva 1994]. The idea here is that an entity class is described

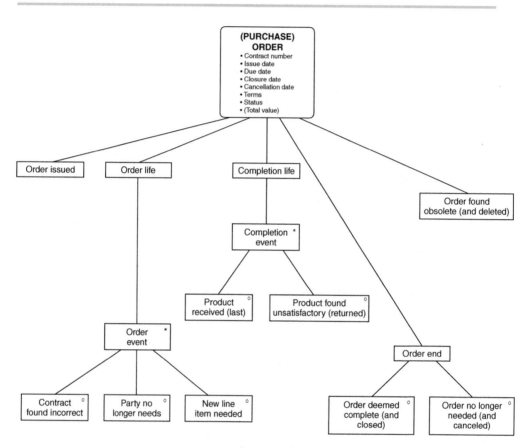

*Fig. 6–8: Sample entity life history.*

in terms of the *system events* that affect a typical instance of the entity class throughout its life.

Figure 6–8 shows an example. In it, the entity class (PURCHASE) ORDER is shown at the top, with a collection of rectangles representing events hanging down from it in a hierarchical formation. In this case, a (PURCHASE) ORDER is for the purpose of acquiring products. There are three types of events.

- *Sequence:* Each of these is expected to take place in the order shown.
- *Iteration:* Each of these can happen more than once.
- *Alternative:* Only one of a set of these can happen within an occurrence of a parent event.

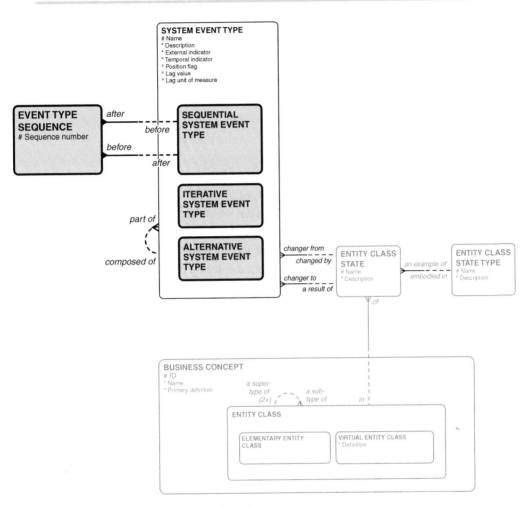

*Fig. 6–9: System event types.*

In the metamodel of this in Figure 6–9, an instance of the entity class SYSTEM EVENT TYPE is now shown to be a SEQUENTIAL SYSTEM EVENT TYPE, an ITERATIVE SYSTEM EVENT TYPE, or an ALTERNATIVE SYSTEM EVENT TYPE. This corresponds to the three event types just described.* The entity class SEQUENTIAL SYSTEM EVENT TYPE

---

*These sub-types are the reason I chose earlier not to represent INTERNAL EVENT TYPE and EXTERNAL EVENT TYPE as sub-types of EVENT TYPE, but used the attribute "External indicator" to show that distinction.

is shown to be *after* an EVENT TYPE SEQUENCE that is *after* another SEQUENTIAL SYSTEM EVENT TYPE. The figure also shows that each SYSTEM EVENT TYPE may be *composed of* one or more other SYSTEM EVENT TYPES. In Figure 6–8, the primary *sequence* of events (to be carried out in this order) is:

- *Order issued:* Creating each instance of order
- *Order life:* Consisting of the events that might take place during its life
- *Completion life:* Meeting the terms of the order
- *Order end:* Triggering the official closure of an order
- *Obsolescence:* Causing the physical deletion of an order

In this example, three of the SEQUENTIAL EVENT TYPES are indeed *composed of* other SYSTEM EVENT TYPES. "Order life", for example, is *composed of* one ITERATIVE SYSTEM EVENT TYPE, "Order event". "Order event" in turn is *composed of* three ALTERNATIVE SYSTEM EVENT TYPES.

- Order found incorrect
- Party no longer needs
- New line item needed

Each "Order event" must be the fact of one (and only one) of the following:

- The order was found to be incorrect (and therefore had to be corrected).
- One of the parties participating in it left (and therefore had to be removed from the order).
- A new line item (referring to a new ordered physical asset type) was required (and therefore must be added).

Note that the overall configuration of this branch says that during the life of the order one or more of these things may happen. Similarly, the SEQUENTIAL SYSTEM EVENT TYPE "Completion life" consists of one or more instances of the iterative SYSTEM EVENT TYPE, "Completion event". Each instance of "Completion event", then, consists of either of the alternative SYSTEM EVENT TYPES "Product received (last)" or "Product found unsatisfactory (returned)". If the latter happens, there subsequently may be another occurrence of "Completion event", this time implemented as "Product received (last)".

In this particular example, it is company policy that an order is not considered "Closed" until someone reviews all deliveries and says it is so (hence the event type "Order end", which may be either a person's saying it is "Closed" or someone's canceling it).

In the logical model, this is the end of the order. In deference to the physical maintenance of the data, however, it is possible to add the event type "Order found obsolete (and deleted)". That is, the order would remain on file with the status "Deleted" until the event "Order found obsolete" caused it to be physically deleted.

As with BUSINESS EVENT TYPES, it is possible to talk about a SYSTEM EVENT TYPE that is *the trigger of* one or more SYSTEM PROCESSES. The fact that an event can trigger a SYSTEM PROCESS is shown in the example in Figure 6–10. Each numbered box in the diagram represents an *operation* (ELH-speak for "process") that responds to the event. For example, in this figure the event type "Order issued" would be implemented by eight SYSTEM PROCESSES:

1. Create ORDER.

2. Tie ORDER to *from* PARTY.

3. Tie ORDER to *to* PARTY.

4. Create one or more LINE ITEMS, and tie them to an ORDER.

5. Set ORDER (Issue date).

6. Set ORDER (Due date).

7. Set ORDER (State) to "open".

8. Set ORDER (Terms).

Note that the entity life history does not describe the source of the events. The part of the metamodel shown in that is Figure 6–11 does, however, allow us to specify that a SYSTEM EVENT TYPE must be *triggered by* either a BUSINESS EVENT TYPE (as was described previously) or that it must be *the action of* a SYSTEM PROCESS.

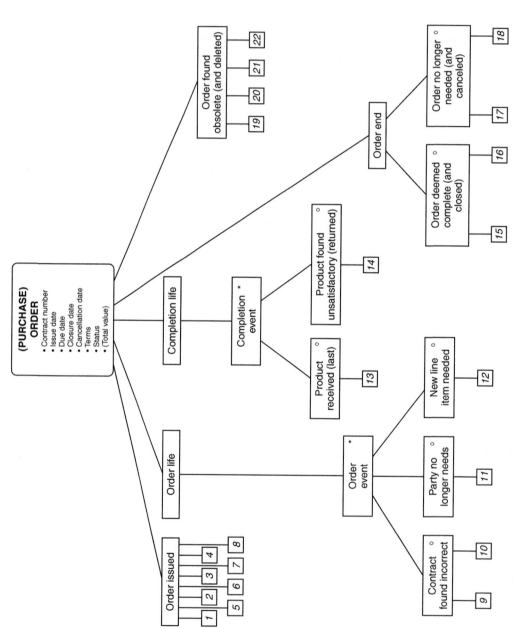

Fig. 6–10: Operations in an entity life history.

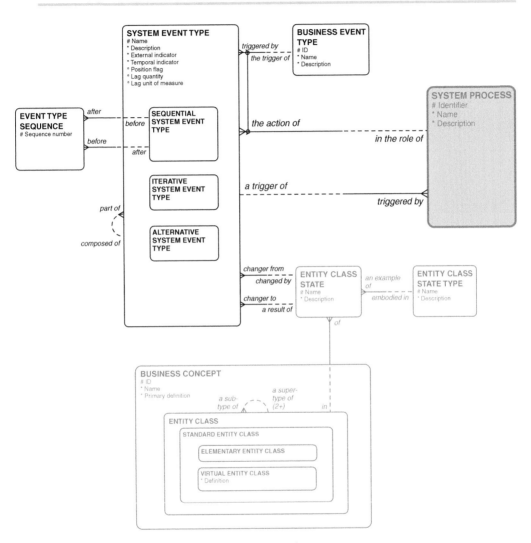

*Fig. 6–11: Events and processes.*

## Essential System Processes

Chapter Three discussed the process of developing an *essential system process model* [McMenamin and Palmer 1984]. Figure 6–12 reproduces the sample data flow diagram from Chapter Three, showing the derivation of an essential data flow diagram from a set of process fragments. Here we examine it from the point of

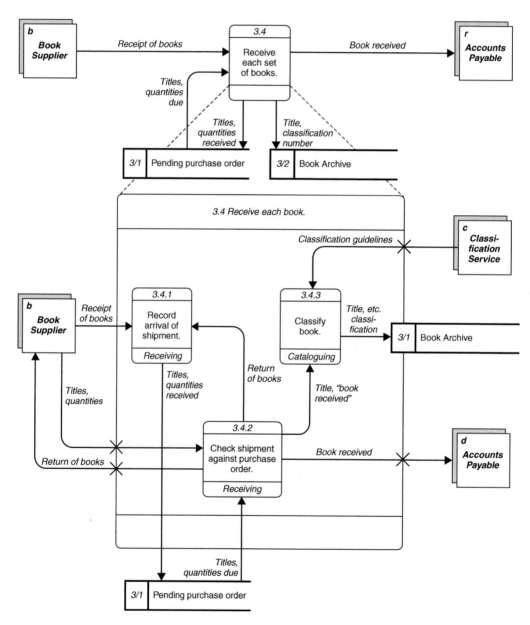

*Fig. 6–12: Sample essential data flow diagram.*

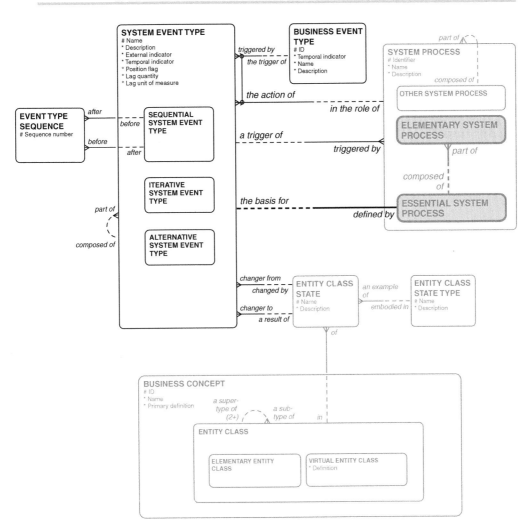

*Fig. 6–13: Essential system processes.*

view of the EXTERNAL SYSTEM EVENT "Receipt of books", and the INTERNAL SYSTEM EVENTS connecting "Book received" from SYSTEM PROCESS "Check shipment against purchase order" to SYSTEM PROCESS "Classify book".

The metamodel for this is shown in Figure 6–13. This includes entity classes we have seen before, but adds a specialized relationship showing that each ESSENTIAL SYSTEM PROCESS must be *defined by* exactly one SYSTEM EVENT TYPE. That is, although it is true that a SYSTEM EVENT TYPE may be *a trigger of* any type of SYSTEM PROCESS, it can only be *the basis for* an ESSENTIAL SYSTEM PROCESS. And similar to ESSENTIAL BUSINESS PROCESS, each ESSENTIAL SYSTEM PROCESS may be *composed of* one or more ELEMENTARY SYSTEM PROCESSES.

### Business Rule

A SYSTEM EVENT TYPE may only be *the basis for* an ESSENTIAL SYSTEM PROCESS if its "External indicator" is "True".

## The Feedback Loop

The great insight from the field of *cybernetics* in the twentieth century was its representation of the structure of control. The premise is that any process must be managed via some sort of controller. The controller sends commands to the process and receives information back about its performance. The returning information is evaluated in terms of specified *set points* that are values against which to compare the information. (See Figure 6–14.)

The best-known example of this is the household thermostat. A target temperature is set (the "Set point"), and the actual temperature of the room is

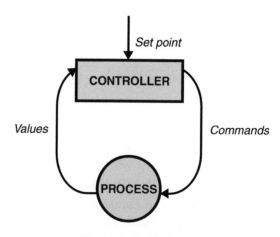

*Fig. 6–14: Feedback loop.*

continuously monitored ("Values" coming back). If the temperature goes above the set point, a command is sent to the air conditioner to turn it on.*

This structure came out of engineering and process control during World War II. Once it was articulated clearly [Ashby 1956], it became clear that it also applies in the "softer" disciplines of enterprise management. Fundamentally, all management data processing activities (data warehouses and the like) are concerned with feeding back the appropriate information to management so that it can make appropriate decisions to control and guide the organization. Indeed, Stafford Beer wrote *The Heart of Enterprise* to document his specific cybernetic model for describing a business [Beer 1979]. Your author has summarized these principles in *Requirements Analysis: From Business Views to Architecture* [Hay 2003, pp. 210–235].

Figure 6–15 shows PROCESS OBJECTIVE and SUCCESS CRITERION, which are the basis for cybernetic control. (SUCCESS CRITERION here is the "Set point".) Each SYSTEM PROCESS may be *directed towards* one or more PROCESS OBJECTIVES. Each of these in turn is *controlled by* one or more SUCCESS CRITERIA (set points). A SUCCESS CRITERION is defined by either a "Maximum value" or a "Minimum value".

Figure 6–16 shows the feedback part of the loop. It adds the entity class PROCESS MEASUREMENT, which is *of* the ATTRIBUTE the SUCCESS CRITERION is *in terms of*. This PROCESS MEASUREMENT can then be the *source of* a SYSTEM EVENT TYPE, which is in turn the trigger of another SYSTEM PROCESS.

## ROW FOUR: PROGRAM EVENTS

In traditional computer programming, events did not originally play a significant part. The implicit event was the launching of a program, and as a result, steps were carried out in sequence. Two trends have changed that: object-orientation and the movement to systems based on direct user interaction with the computer.

---

*For those of you in more northern climates, if the temperature goes below the set point a command is sent to the furnace to turn it on. Same idea.

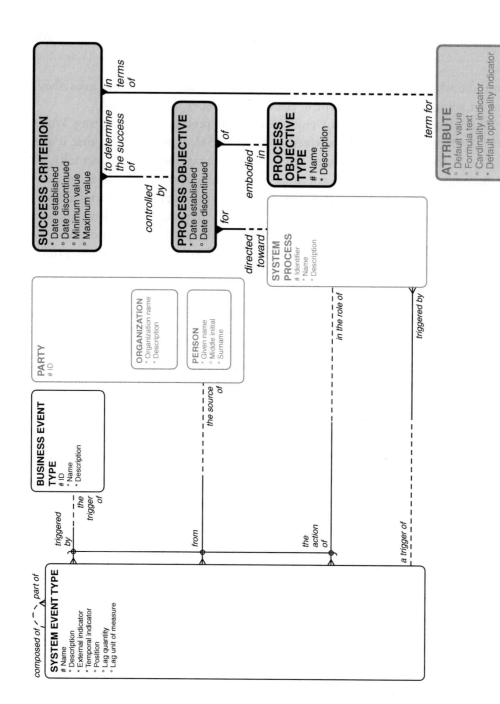

Fig. 6–15: Commands.

268

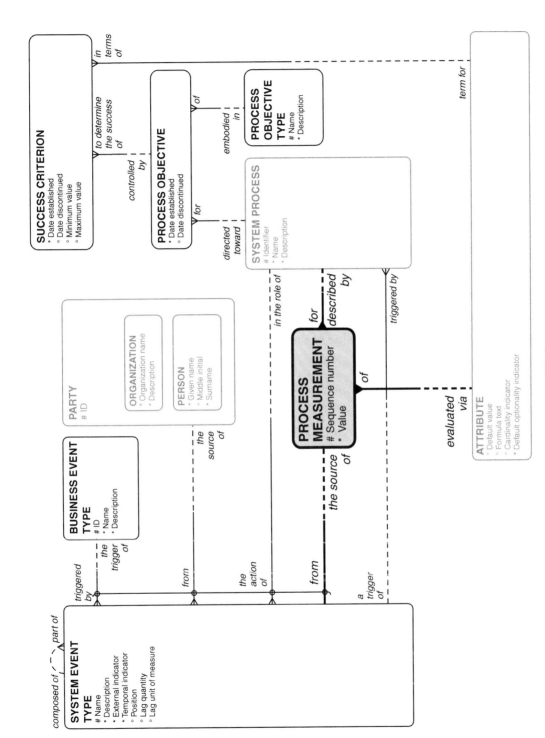

Fig. 6-16: Feedback.

269

## Object Orientation

Figure 6–17 shows an expansion of the object-oriented metamodel from Chapter Three. Note the addition of DISCRETE INSTANCE ATTRIBUTE and OTHER INSTANCE ATTRIBUTE as sub-types of INSTANCE ATTRIBUTE. An OTHER INSTANCE ATTRIBUTE can take as a value any real number or piece of text. A DISCRETE INSTANCE ATTRIBUTE can only take one of a list of values, represented in the model by the entity class DISCRETE INSTANCE VALID VALUE. A particularly significant DISCRETE INSTANCE ATTRIBUTE is STATE. If a DISCRETE INSTANCE ATTRIBUTE is a STATE, its VALID ATTRIBUTE VALUES describe the states of the CLASS IMPLEMENTATION that the DISCRETE INSTANCE ATTRIBUTE is *part of*. This is the value of the state the CLASS IMPLEMENTATION is in at any point in time.

An INSTANCE ATTRIBUTE may be a STATE that describes a condition for each OBJECT that is *an instance of* a class. A STATE is an INSTANCE ATTRIBUTE controlled by business rules (LEGAL TRANSFORMATIONS), which in turn constrain how an OBJECT can move from one value of STATE to another. (See Figure 6–17.)*

### Business Rules

1. As stated previously, any DISCRETE INSTANCE ATTRIBUTE may be *given* one or more LEGAL VALUES. In the case of STATE, however, it must be *given* one or more LEGAL VALUES.

2. In the model, a LEGAL TRANSFORMATION appears to be a rule for changing the value of any DISCRETE INSTANCE ATTRIBUTE *from* one DISCRETE INSTANCE LEGAL VALUE to another. In fact, a STATE LEGAL TRANSFORMATION specifically applies to the conversion of one DISCRETE INSTANCE LEGAL VALUE to another for a STATE, not for any other type of DISCRETE ATTRIBUTE INSTANCE. Similarly, an OTHER LEGAL TRANSFORMATION applies only to a DISCRETE INSTANCE LEGAL VALUE that is *of* an OTHER DISCRETE INSTANCE ATTRIBUTE.

---

*In practice, STATE is not usually recognized as an explicit attribute, but is a composite of the values of other attributes. That is, the complete "state" of a CLASS is the sum of the values of all of its STATE attributes. For the sake of this model, however, it is easier to represent it this way.

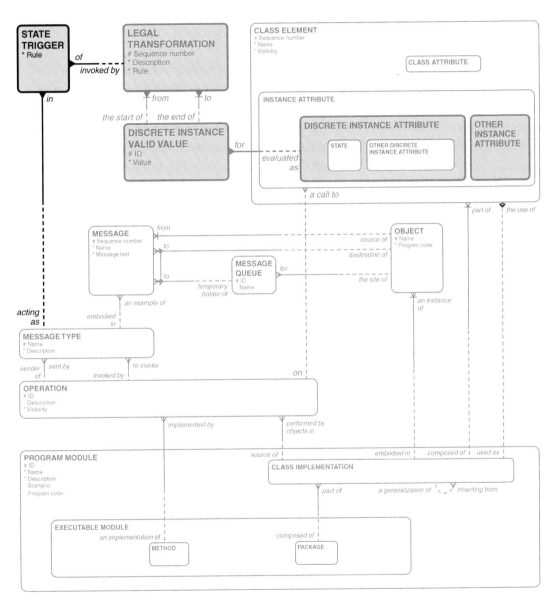

*Fig. 6–17: State triggers.*

Note, by the way, that this concept of state can also be implemented in a corresponding way in a relational design. Because object-oriented models began in the real-time systems world, however, the concept is more central to this approach.

Also shown in Figure 6–17 is the fact that a MESSAGE TYPE may be *acting as* one or more STATE TRIGGERS *of* LEGAL TRANSFORMATIONS *from* one VALID ATTRIBUTE VALUE *to* another. That is, a STATE may move from one . . . VALUE to another via a LEGAL TRANSFORMATION *invoked by* a STATE TRIGGER *in* a MESSAGE.

For example, assuming the previous examples are implemented by object-oriented applications, a CLASS IMPLEMENTATION of ORDER might have LEGAL TRANSFORMATIONS *from* the VALID ATTRIBUTE VALUE (*for* a STATE) of "Issued" to "Complete", and *from* "Complete" *to* "Closed", but there may not be a LEGAL TRANSFORMATION *from* "Issued" *to* "Closed". A MESSAGE *sent by* the OPERATION "Receive shipment" to the OPERATION "Catalogue book" could be *acting as* the STATE TRIGGER that is *of* the LEGAL TRANSFORMATION *from* "Issued" *to* "Complete".

In the program code example describing hominoid in Chapter Three, the INSTANCE ATTRIBUTE facingWall is an example of a STATE. In this model, the business rule governing the TRANSFORMATION is simply presented as a text attribute of STATE TRIGGER. Perhaps a more sophisticated model could represent the structure of such a rule more explicitly. This is left as an exercise for the reader.

# MOTIVATION

*Hell, there are no rules here—we're trying to accomplish something.*

—Thomas A. Edison

*There are two rules for success:*
*1. Never tell everything you know.*

—Roger H. Lincoln

## The Motivation Column

The Motivation column is concerned with *why* the enterprise does what it does.

- The *planner* lays out the vision and mission of the enterprise, along with approaches for defining business policies and rules.
- The *business owner* is concerned with all factors that motivate business activities in an enterprise, from vision and mission bestowed by the planner's view to the goals and objectives and the strategies and tactics that make up the business plan. Also included are the business policies and business rules that constrain the operation of the business.
- The *architect* is the one responsible for translating business rules into constraints on the structure of the data in the architectural data model.
- The *designer* is responsible for implementing constraints—both those that reside directly inside a database management system and those that must be programmed externally from the database itself.
- The *builder* is responsible for constructing the systems and system components that will monitor and enforce business rules.
- The *functioning system* implements and enforces the business rules and policies of an enterprise.

## About Motivation

Figure 7–1 shows the architecture framework with the cells highlighted that will be the subject of this chapter. In 2000, the Business Rules Group published a paper describing the Motivation column from the perspective of the Business Owner's View. The paper, updated and republished in 2005, is the basis for the first section of this chapter [BRG 2005]. In that paper, the Group set out to describe both the ends and means of business plans and the influencers that shape the elements of those plans. Along with this, the paper describes the assessments of the impacts of those influencers, as well as the directives that initiate and constrain the carrying out of the plans.

The elements of business planning are considered metadata because they describe the structures (and motivation) within which the actual business processes take place. The concepts and facts needed to support the business are described here, appropriately part of the metadata for the Business Owner's View.

The enterprise as a whole is constrained by competition, the laws of physics, and governments. Its goals and objectives and its strategies and tactics, like it or not, are influenced by these constraints. Moreover, in expressing its goals and objectives, management is imposing further constraints on its employees. For these reasons, business rules from all perspectives are very important components of the Motivation column.

## Mission and Vision

According to the Business Rules Group (BRG), "if an enterprise prescribes a certain approach for its business activity, it ought to be able to say *why*; that is, what result(s) the approach is meant to achieve... The BRG realized early on that a cornerstone of any work addressing motivation had to be the enterprise's aspirations (its Vision) and its action plans for how to realize them (its Mission)" [BRG 2005, p. 3].

Rather than Row Two, an enterprise's mission and vision represent the planner's Row One perspective on the company's motivation. They do, however, provide the context for understanding the Row Two elements, so we will take a moment to address them. Figure 7–2 shows MISSION and VISION as entity classes. As stated, these really are the domain of Row One, the Planner's View. Here, a

| | Data (What) | Activities (How) | Locations (Where) | People (Who) | Time (When) | Motivation (Why) |
|---|---|---|---|---|---|---|
| **Objectives/ Scope** **(Planner's View)** | List of things important to the enterprise | List of functions the enterprise performs | List of enterprise locations | Organization approaches | Business master schedule | Business vision and mission |
| **Enterprise Model** **(Business Owner's View)** | Language, divergent data model | Business process model | Logistics network | Organization chart | State/ transition diagram | Business strategies, tactics, policies, rule |
| **Model of Fundamental Concepts** **(Architect's View)** | Convergent e/r model | Essential data flow diagram | Locations of roles | The viable system, use cases | Entity life history | Business rule model |
| **Technology Model** **(Designer's View)** | Database design | System design, program structure | Hardware, software distribution | User interface, security design | Event processing | Business rule design |
| **Detailed Representation** **(Builder's View)** | Physical storage design | Detailed program design | Network architecture, protocols | Screens, security coding | Timing definitions | Rule specification program logic |
| **Functioning System** | *(Working system)* | | | | | |
| | Databases | Program inventory, logs | Communi- cations facilities | Trained people | Business events | Enforced rules |

*Fig. 7–1: The Motivation column.*

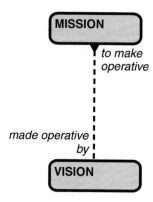

*Fig. 7–2: Mission and vision.*

VISION is a description of a desired future state of the enterprise, without regard to how it is to be achieved.*

A particularly famous vision statement was developed by the pharmaceutical giant Johnson & Johnson, as its "Credo" in 1943. Covering four paragraphs, one paragraph is devoted to the company's responsibilities to each of its partners: doctors, nurses, and patients; its employees; the community; and its stockholders [Johnson & Johnson 1943].

A MISSION, on the other hand, is the overall method for the ongoing operation of the enterprise—what the business is or will be doing on a day-to-day basis. Note that the model asserts that each VISION may be *made operative by* more than one MISSION, but that each MISSION may be *to make operative* one and only one VISION. Neither this cardinality nor this optionality may be true in your company. In the original Business Rules Group model, no assertions were made about the cardinality and optionality of relationships.**

---

*The definitions used in this section are paraphrased from "The Business Motivation Model" paper [BRG 2005], but for simplicity they will not be individually footnoted. I assume responsibility for any misinterpretations that may result from my paraphrasing.

**The imposition of such assertions in this book is my responsibility, not that of the Business Rules Group.

## Ends

Figure 7–3 shows that a VISION is but one type of END. An END for an organization is simply something it sets out to accomplish. Whereas the company's VISION is the primary END, others include various types of DESIRED RESULT. A DESIRED RESULT is an END that is a state or target the enterprise intends to maintain.

There are two types of DESIRED RESULTS: GOALS and OBJECTIVES. A GOAL is a DESIRED RESULT that is a specific statement about a state or condition of the enterprise to be brought about or sustained through appropriate MEANS. (More about MEANS in a moment.) A GOAL is *an amplifier* of a VISION. That is, where a VISION describes a future state of the enterprise in general, a GOAL is one of the steps to be taken to accomplish that VISION. A GOAL, by definition, is more narrow than a VISION.

An OBJECTIVE is a statement of an attainable time-targeted and measurable DESIRED RESULT the enterprise seeks to meet in order to achieve its GOALS. Note

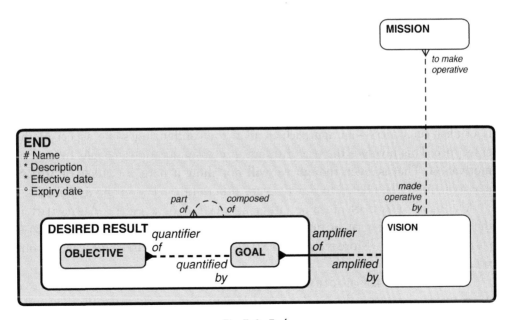

*Fig. 7–3: Ends.*

that a GOAL is narrower than a VISION, but is more general than an OBJECTIVE. Unlike a GOAL, an OBJECTIVE is:

- *Attainable:* You can tell when it has been achieved.
- *Time-targeted:* There is either a specific date (such as "December 31, 2007") or a relative date (such as "within two years").
- *Measurable:* An OBJECTIVE must contain in its expression one or more specific criteria that can be measured to determine when the objective has been achieved, such as "Increase sales by 10%".

Whereas a GOAL is a general statement about a desirable future state, an OBJECTIVE is a similar expression, but in specific, quantifiable terms. A GOAL may be to "Increase revenue every year", but an OBJECTIVE would be to "Increase revenue by 10% next year". In addition to the explicit relationship that an OBJECTIVE may be a *quantifier* of a GOAL, a DESIRED RESULT may also be *composed of* one or more other DESIRED RESULTS. In general, this applies only within GOALS or OBJECTIVES (a GOAL may be *composed of* other GOALS, and an OBJECTIVE may be composed of other OBJECTIVES), but not always.

## Means

Just as a VISION is a type of END, so a MISSION is a type of MEANS, as shown in Figure 7–4. A MEANS is any capability that can be called on, activated, or enforced to achieve ENDS. Here, in addition to MISSION, the other principal type of MEANS is COURSE OF ACTION—an approach or plan for configuring some aspect of the enterprise. This involves the use of things, processes, locations, people, timing, or motivation. That is, even though we will not show it here, a COURSE OF ACTION may potentially be related to nearly every other entity class in the metamodel.

A COURSE OF ACTION must be either a STRATEGY or a TACTIC. A STRATEGY is the essential COURSE OF ACTION attempted to achieve an enterprise's ENDS—particularly GOALS. Moreover, a STRATEGY must be *to carry out* exactly one MISSION.

A TACTIC is a COURSE OF ACTION that represents one or more details of a STRATEGY. A STRATEGY, then, may be *implemented by* one or more TACTICS. For example, whereas a library's VISION is to "Provide reading and other intellectual materials to the county", its STRATEGY is to "Operate the County Library"; and one of

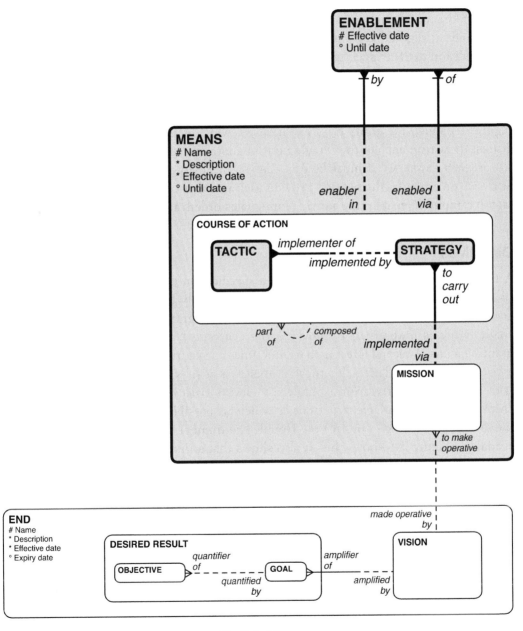

*Fig. 7–4: Means.*

its TACTICS is to "Obtain current books on a wide variety of subjects". Note that although the model does not impose this constraint, in general STRATEGIES address GOALS and TACTICS address OBJECTIVES.

In addition to the explicit relationship that each STRATEGY may be *implemented by* one or more TACTICS, in general any COURSE OF ACTION may be *composed of* one or more other COURSES OF ACTION. Also, one COURSE OF ACTION may *enable* another COURSE OF ACTION. That is, one makes the other COURSE OF ACTION possible. Figure 7–4 shows the entity class ENABLEMENT, which is the fact that a particular COURSE OF ACTION enables the carrying out of another COURSE OF ACTION. In other words, each ENABLEMENT must be *of* a COURSE OF ACTION *by* another COURSE OF ACTION. For example, the TACTIC "Provide each member of the sales force with a laptop computer" enables the TACTIC "Input sales orders at the source".

## Directives

A third type of MEANS is the DIRECTIVE—a specification that constrains COURSES OF ACTION. It does this in two ways. First, it may simply be designed *to govern* a COURSE OF ACTION. For example, "A loan is not to be granted to someone whose credit rating is lower than B" governs the COURSE OF ACTION concerned with granting loans. A second effect is that sometimes a DIRECTIVE is itself *the source of* a COURSE OF ACTION. This is for those COURSES OF ACTIONS whose whole purpose is to enforce a DIRECTIVE. For example, a BUSINESS POLICY for a library might be "Make computers available to patrons as widely as possible", and this is *source of* the COURSE OF ACTION (a TACTIC) to "Double the number of computers currently available"; Figure 7–5 shows this. It also shows that a DIRECTIVE must be either a BUSINESS POLICY or a BUSINESS RULE.

A BUSINESS POLICY is a nonactionable DIRECTIVE that guides the activities of the business or governs them in a general way. Note that it "governs", it does not control or shape COURSES OF ACTION. For example, to say that "We will not permit on-site visits" constrains the TACTICS available for meeting the STRATEGY to "Increase market share". It does not specify what those TACTICS should be.

A BUSINESS RULE is a more specific and actionable *constraint on* the enterprise. In particular, *based on* a BUSINESS POLICY, it imposes a *constraint on* a FACT or FACT TYPE. A FACT TYPE could, for example, be the assertion that "A customer is charged for damage to a rental car". The business rule may add obligation to this statement thus: "A customer *must be* charged for damage to a rental car". Or the

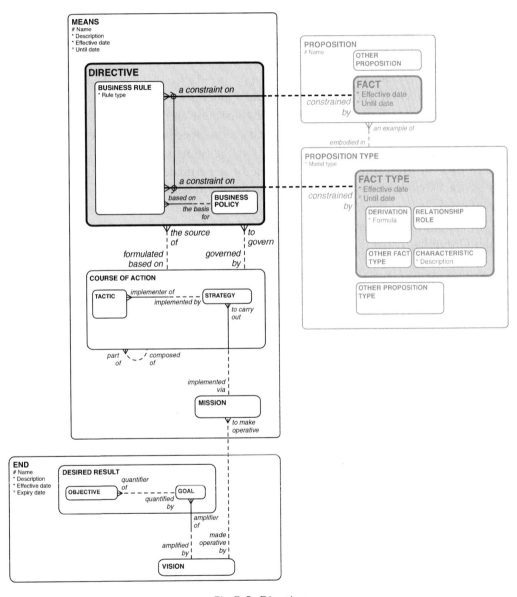

*Fig. 7–5: Directives.*

rule may add permission to the FACT TYPE: "A customer *need not* be charged for damage to a rental car".

In its submission to the Object Management Group, "The Semantics of Business Vocabulary and Business Rules", the Business Rules Group defines a business rule as "an element of guidance that introduces an obligation or necessity, that is under business jurisdiction" [BRT 2005, pp. 167–169]. In general, a BUSINESS POLICY sets direction and provides general guidelines for COURSES OF ACTION, whereas a BUSINESS RULE is a more specific constraint on them.

Figure 7–6 shows more details about DIRECTIVES. Specifically, it shows that each DIRECTIVE may be *subject to* one or more ENFORCEMENT LEVEL IMPLEMENTATIONS, where each of these must be *an example of* a particular ENFORCEMENT LEVEL. An ENFORCEMENT LEVEL is a measure of the extent to which a BUSINESS RULE is to be enforced.

Although an ENFORCEMENT LEVEL could be defined in various ways, the Business Rules Group has listed the following [BRG 2005, pp. 14–15]:

- *Strictly enforced:* If the rule is violated, the penalty is always applied.
- *Pre-authorized override:* Enforced, but exceptions are allowed with prior approval.
- *Post-justified override:* If not approved after the fact, there may be sanctions or other consequences.
- *Override with explanation:* When the violation occurs, there must be a comment justifying it.
- *Guideline:* A suggested rule, but not enforced.

An ENFORCEMENT LEVEL IMPLEMENTATION is the fact that a particular BUSINESS RULE will be enforced at a specified ENFORCEMENT LEVEL. It is this ENFORCEMENT LEVEL IMPLEMENTATION that is *the source of* one or more CONSEQUENCE INVOCATIONS. Each CONSEQUENCE INVOCATION, in turn, must be *an example of* a particular CONSEQUENCE, such as "Termination", "Salary deduction", and so on.

Thus, for example, the BUSINESS RULE that a "company car may not be used for personal business" may be *subject to* an ENFORCEMENT LEVEL IMPLEMENTATION that is *of* the ENFORCEMENT LEVEL "Pre-authorized override" (you can borrow it with prior approval), whereas the rule that "Material may not be withdrawn from inventory without a signed pick ticket" may be *the object of* an ENFORCEMENT LEVEL IMPLEMENTATION that is *of* the ENFORCEMENT LEVEL

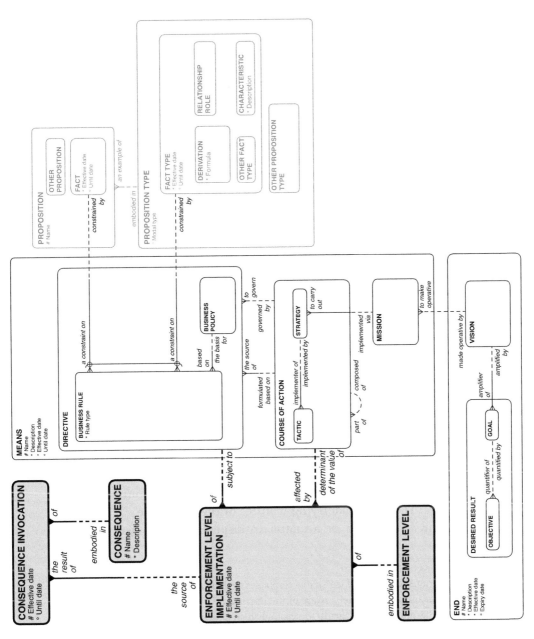

Fig. 7–6: Enforcement levels.

"Strictly enforced". This ENFORCEMENT LEVEL IMPLEMENTATION may in turn be *the source of* the CONSEQUENCE INVOCATION *of* the CONSEQUENCE "loss of pay".

Note that the ENFORCEMENT LEVEL IMPLEMENTATION *of* a DIRECTIVE may be *affected by* the TACTIC being *governed by* (or *formulated based on*) the DIRECTIVE. That is, under one TACTIC the DIRECTIVE may be "Strictly enforced" but under another the same DIRECTIVE might be a "Post-justified override".* For example, the assignment of the ENFORCEMENT LEVEL "Strictly enforced" to the BUSINESS RULE "Material may not be withdrawn from inventory without a signed pick ticket" may be *affected by* (a response to) a TACTIC to "improve inventory accuracy".

## Influencers and Assessments

To fully understand the motivation of an organization, it is necessary to deal with the environment within which it operates. In this model, the environment is characterized as a set of INFLUENCERS, where an INFLUENCER is anything that can produce an effect on the enterprise without apparent exertion of tangible force or direct exercise of command. An INFLUENCER often acts without deliberate effort or intent.

An INFLUENCER must be either an INTERNAL INFLUENCER, originating within the organization, or an EXTERNAL INFLUENCER, coming from the outside world in some form. Each INFLUENCER must be *an example of* exactly one INFLUENCER TYPE. This redundant representation means that the first two INFLUENCER TYPES are "Internal Influencer" and "External Influencer".

According to the Business Rules Group, INTERNAL INFLUENCERS include the following.

- *Habit:* A customary practice or use.
- *Assumption:* An assertion that is taken for granted or is without proof.
- *Infrastructure:* The basic underlying features of the enterprise.
- *Issue:* A point in question or a matter in dispute between two contending parties.

---

*In recent years, various scandals and legislative responses to them (specifically the Sarbanes–Oxley Act) have made companies more acutely aware of the importance of governance to their operations. Although this can be immensely difficult to accomplish in practice, the elements—as shown in this model—are simplicity itself. BUSINESS POLICIES translate into BUSINESS RULES, with a clear ENFORCEMENT POLICY.

- *Prerogative:* A right or privilege exercised by right of ownership or position in the enterprise.
- *Resource:* The resources available for carrying out the business of an enterprise, especially their quality.
- *Corporate value:* An ideal, custom, or institution the enterprise promotes or agrees with. Each of these in turn must be an:

  → *Explicit corporate value:* A corporate value stated as a written policy
  → *Implicit corporate value:* A corporate value that is understood by some or all in the enterprise, but that is not explicitly stated

- *Other internal influencer:* An internal influencer not itemized here [BRG 2005, p. 29].

Also according to the Business Rules Group, each EXTERNAL INFLUENCER of an enterprise must be one of the following.

- *Environment:* The aggregate of surrounding conditions that affect the existence or the development of the enterprise.
- *Technology:* The development and limitations of the technical processes, methods, or knowledge applied to the enterprise.
- *Supplier:* An individual or enterprise that can furnish or provide products or services to the enterprise.
- *Customer:* An individual or enterprise that has investigated, ordered, received, or paid for products or services from the enterprise.
- *Competitor:* A rival enterprise.
- *Partner:* An enterprise that shares risks and profits with the subject enterprise because it is mutually beneficial.
- *Regulation:* An order prescribed by an authority such as a government body or the management of the enterprise.
- *Other external influencer:* An external influencer not itemized here [BRG 2005, p. 26].

Figure 7–7 shows that the effect of INFLUENCERS on MEANS and ENDS is determined by one or more ASSESSMENTS, whereas an ASSESSMENT is a judgment about the implications of the INFLUENCER either *with respect to* one or more MEANS (such as a particular COURSE OF ACTION) or *with respect to* one or more ENDS (such as a particular DESIRED RESULT) because an ASSESSMENT can have multiple implications.

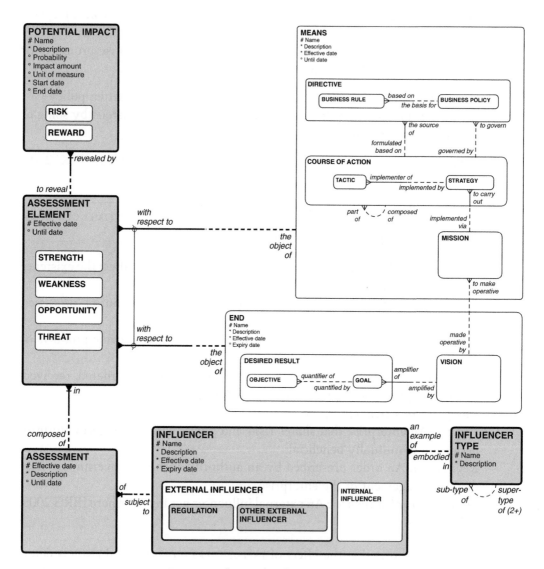

Fig. 7–7: Influencers and assessments.

Thus, the model also shows that each ASSESSMENT must be *composed of* one or more ASSESSMENT ELEMENTS. It is then each of these that must be either *with respect to* one MEANS or one END.

In addition, Figure 7–7 shows four sub-types for ASSESSMENT ELEMENT, based on a particular approach to assessments called the "SWOT" method. This approach asserts that the INFLUENCER can be assessed to constitute one of the following *with respect to* an END or a MEANS.

- — STRENGTH: An advantage of area of excellence within the enterprise
- — WEAKNESS: An area of inadequacy within the enterprise
- — OPPORTUNITY: A favorable impact
- — THREAT: An unfavorable impact

Other schemes for evaluating an INFLUENCER are possible. For example, a "Corporate Value" could represent a STRENGTH *with respect to* a particular COURSE OF ACTION, if it is compatible with a new trend, or it could represent a WEAKNESS *with respect to* a specific OBJECTIVE if it causes behavior that hurts sales. Problems with a competitor's marketing campaign could be an OPPORTUNITY, whereas problems with a PARTNER could be a THREAT.

The net effect of an ASSESSMENT ELEMENT is the identification of a measured POTENTIAL IMPACT, which may be either a potential RISK or potential REWARD. POTENTIAL IMPACT can be expressed in terms of the "Probability" of the RISK or REWARD, and its "Impact value". The value is in terms of a "Unit of measure". For example, the POTENTIAL IMPACT of a "Corporate Value" could be an 80% probability that there would be a reward for that STRENGTH.

## Directive Motivation

As indicated by the original Business Rules Group Motivation Paper definition, an ASSESSMENT can trigger creation of one or more BUSINESS RULES or BUSINESS POLICIES. That is, as shown in Figure 7–8, each ASSESSMENT ELEMENT may be *the source of* one or more DIRECTIVE MOTIVATIONS, each of which must be *to create* a DIRECTIVE (either a general BUSINESS POLICY or a specific BUSINESS RULE). In other words, each DIRECTIVE may be *initiated by* one or more DIRECTIVE MOTIVATIONS, each of which is *by* an ASSESSMENT ELEMENT—a THREAT, an OPPORTUNITY, a WEAKNESS, or a STRENGTH.

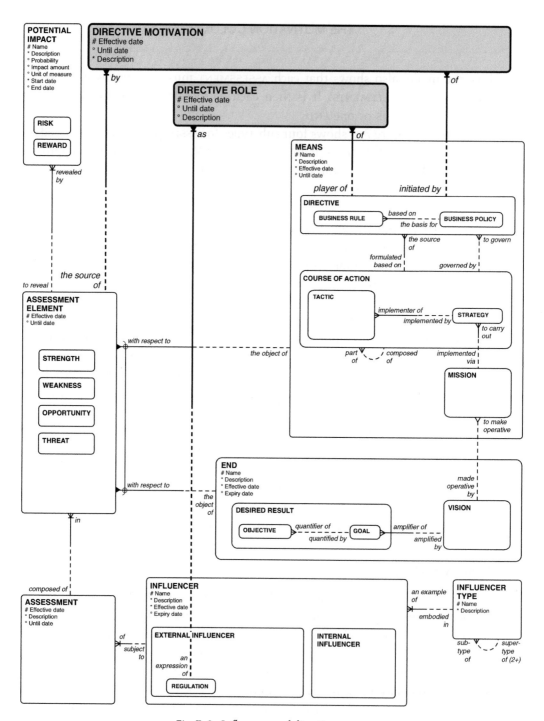

Fig. 7–8: Influences and directives.

Note that a parent company's BUSINESS RULE can be a subsidiary company's (or a department's) REGULATION. That is, each DIRECTIVE by a parent organization may be a *player of* one or more DIRECTIVE ROLES for subordinate organizations *as* an INFLUENCER of INFLUENCER TYPE "Regulation".

## Activities

Figure 7–9 brings back the ACTIVITIES entity class from Chapter Three. Recall from Chapter Three that a BUSINESS FUNCTION (that is not part of another BUSINESS FUNCTION) must be *to carry out* one of the enterprise's MISSIONS.

The previous section described how a COURSE OF ACTION is an approach or plan for configuring some aspect of the enterprise. This is to achieve its goals and objectives in order to carry out its mission. Although that describes what the enterprise is setting out to do, it does not describe how it will be done. It is Figure 7–9 that shows how each COURSE OF ACTION may be *invoked via* one or more EFFORTS.

Specifically, in the model an EFFORT must be *invoked by* a COURSE OF ACTION *to support* a DESIRED RESULT *through the use of* a BUSINESS PROCESS. If more than one BUSINESS PROCESS is involved, multiple EFFORTS can be specified. An EFFORT is usually a PROJECT (to implement a technology, for example) or a PROGRAM that may be *composed of* many PROJECTS.

As it happens, EFFORT is but one of the MEANS EFFECTS a MEANS can have *on* a BUSINESS PROCESS. (See Figure 7–10.) Among other things, each BUSINESS PROCESS may be *subject to* one or more instances of DIRECTION *from* a DIRECTIVE (either a BUSINESS POLICY or a BUSINESS RULE). That is, each DIRECTIVE may be *the source of* either GUIDANCE (overall supervision) or GOVERNANCE (setting boundaries and direction) *through the use of* a BUSINESS PROCESS.

For example, the library BUSINESS RULE that "Overdue books shall be promptly retrieved" provides GOVERNANCE *through the use of* the BUSINESS PROCESS "Call patron who has an overdue book". The BUSINESS POLICY that "The Library will always provide an attractive and clean appearance" provides GUIDANCE *through the use of* all BUSINESS PROCESSES concerned with cleaning and maintenance.

Note that in general each MEANS EFFECT must be *of* one MEANS and *through the use of* one BUSINESS PROCESS *to support* one DESIRED RESULT. But what you have here is another example of relationships having sub-types. Clearly, an instance of an EFFORT being *invoked by* a COURSE OF ACTION and an instance of a DIRECTION being *from* a DIRECTIVE are also both sub-types of a MEANS EFFECT being *of* a MEANS.

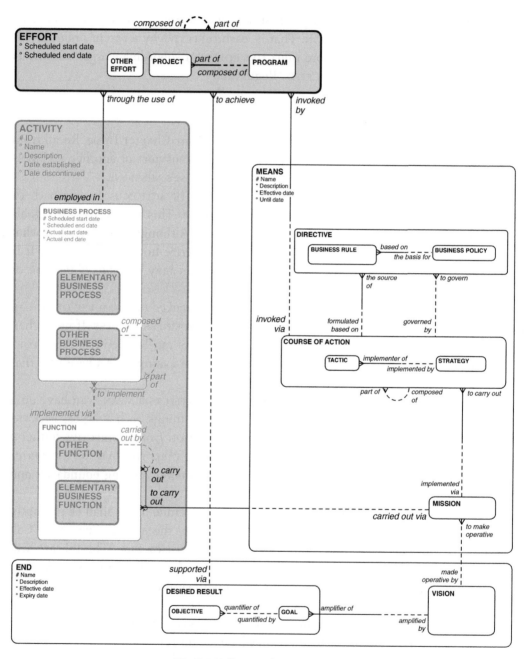

Fig. 7–9: Efforts and activities.

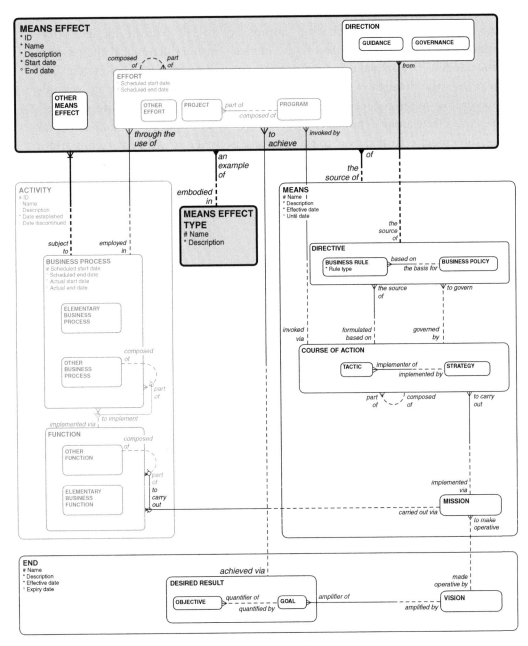

*Fig. 7–10: Means effects.*

Unfortunately, as we have seen before, this concept of a relationship being a sub-type of another relationship cannot be directly shown in an entity-relationship diagram. This confronts the modeler with a dilemma. If the purpose of the model is to explain concepts, the approach used here is suitable. The viewer sees the detailed relationship first, and then sees how it is an example of something more general. This, after all, is how entity classes are unveiled. It has the disadvantage, however, of creating what could be a significant task when the model is turned over to the database designer. It will be very important to remove such redundancy before generating a database design.

Alternatively, only the general relationships may be shown, but business rules must be added to assert, for example, that an EFFORT may only be *of* a COURSE OF ACTION.

## ROW THREE: THE ARCHITECT'S VIEW

In addressing the topic of motivation, the architect is concerned with *business rules* and sees them as *system constraints*. As stated at the beginning of this chapter, the enterprise as a whole is constrained by competition, by the laws of physics, logistics, and governments. Its goals and objectives as well as its strategies and tactics are influenced by these constraints. Moreover, in expressing its goals and objectives, management is imposing further constraints on its employees. For these reasons, business rules from all perspectives are very important components of the Motivation column. The Architect's View of these constraints is specifically concerned with how rules are interpreted in data.

### About Business Rules

The Row Two model set out the parameters for describing a company's motivation. When you get to the Architect's View in Row Three, it is necessary to be more specific in describing the business rules that constrain and direct an enterprise's actions. Specifically, the architect is concerned with how business rules constrain *data*.

In 1994, Ron Ross specified a syntax for describing business rules. At the same time, he recognized that in the information processing context business rules apply to data more than they do to processes [Ross 1994, 1997]. Nearly every rule is a constraint on what data can be updated, deleted, or accessed—and when.

In 1995 (updated in 2000), the Business Rules Group laid out the concept of a business rule from the information system (Row Three) perspective. Although they called it "a statement that defines or constrains some aspect of the business" [BRG 2000], their intention was to describe the effects of business rules on data. For this reason, here Row Three business rules will be referred to as *system constraints*.* In the "Defining Business Rules" paper, the Business Rules Group divided business rules into the following categories.

– Structural assertions, including:

  → Terms (and the concepts behind them)
  → Facts (based on combinations of terms)
  → Derivations

– Action assertions, which can be further categorized as:

  → Uniqueness constraints
  → Optionality and functionality
  → Referential integrity constraints
  → All other constraints on data [BRG 2000, p. 6]

Of these, only terms and facts can be readily described in entity-relationship models, because they are about the structure of data. Action assertions, on the other hand, are about the processing of data and are thus generally not represented in an entity-relationship diagram. For this reason, the notions of terms and facts are not part of the business rules discussion and are instead described in Chapter Two as being column 1 (data) topics. This is also why the Business Rules Team has more recently excluded terms and facts from the category "business rules". Instead they assert that business rules are built on fact types [BRT 2005].

One thing Mr. Ross's efforts highlighted was that for the most part a data model cannot describe action assertions. For this, a different model is required.

---

*Again, this is the Architect's View, so the word *system* does not imply any particular technology. It only means that the constraints have to be represented rigorously enough to allow implementation by an automated system.

This is related to data modeling's connection with relational theory. Although it is possible to imagine a database management system enforcing referential integrity, uniqueness, cardinality, and optionality constraints, for all others it would be necessary to write a program to produce the constraint.*

There are some structural constraints that are typically shown in data models (cardinality, optionality, identifiers, and domains), but they are in fact constraints, so they are properly discussed here in the context of business rules. The same is true of derivations, even though derived *attributes* (like all other attributes) can be shown in an entity-relationship model.

It is the action assertions that are the most difficult constraints to address. Not the least of it is to come up with a language for expressing them. Mr. Ross created a notation that is the basis for *The Business Rules Book* [Ross 1997], and the Object Role Modeling technique has some syntax for describing certain rules, but neither of these have been widely accepted. The need for such a language was part of the motivation for the Business Rules Team to take up semantics as its target in the work described in Chapter Two [BRT 2005].

We can use a metamodel, however, to dissect the meaning of Row Three constraints on data. The model here describes just what it is such a language *should* express. It will begin by addressing the constraints typically addressed by data models (unique identifiers, optionality and cardinality, domains, and derivations). It will then address action assertions, here called *system constraints*.

## Sample Model

To illustrate the topics in this and the following sections, Figure 7–11 shows the same sample entity-relationship model first shown in Chapter Two. In it, an ORDER must be *from* one PARTY (the *buyer*) *to* another PARTY (the *seller*). It may also be *composed of* one or more LINE ITEMS, each of which must be either *for* one PRODUCT TYPE or one SERVICE TYPE. This the following diagram illustrates the constraints that can be represented in such a model.

---

*I consider the constraint language that is now part of many database management systems to be a programming language. Yes, implementation of constraints thus become intimate parts of the database but they are not fundamentally part of the data's structure.

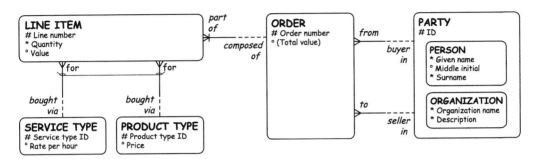

*Fig. 7–11: Sample entity-relationship model.*

— Any ATTRIBUTE participating in a *unique identifier* is annotated with an octothorpe (#), and any RELATIONSHIP ROLE participating is shown with a short line across the relationship line, near the identified entity class. Other notations represent this differently, but the meaning is the same.

Thus, occurrences of PURCHASE ORDER are uniquely identified by values of the ATTRIBUTE "Order number", just as occurrences of PARTY are identified by its "Id". The UNIQUE IDENTIFIER of an occurrence of LINE ITEM, on the other hand, is a combination of the ATTRIBUTE "Line number" and the RELATIONSHIP ROLE *"part of* one and only one ORDER". That is, to uniquely identify a line item, you must know both the "Line number" and the ORDER it is related to.

— Each solid half-line for a relationship means that each occurrence of the entity class it is next to *must be* related to at least one instance of the opposite entity class (*optionality constraint*).

— If an end of a relationship line is not marked by a "crow's-foot", an occurrence of the entity class opposite *may not* be associated with more than one occurrence of the adjacent entity class (*cardinality constraint*).

— Attributes shown in parentheses are *derived*. "(Value)" in LINE ITEM, for example, is derived by inferring the "Price" or the "Rate per hour" from PRODUCT TYPE or SERVICE TYPE, and multiplying that by "Quantity" in LINE ITEM. "(Total value)" in ORDER is computed by summing "(Value)" across all the LINE ITEMS that are *part of* an instance of ORDER. (The algorithms for doing these calculations must be described behind the scenes in most CASE tools.)

— The arc across the two *for* relationships from LINE ITEM means that each LINE ITEM must be either *for* one SERVICE TYPE or *for* one PRODUCT TYPE (*exclusivity constraint*).

These are described more fully and modeled in the sections that follow.

## Unique Identifiers

The first constraint that applies in a relational environment is that by definition each occurrence of an entity class must be uniquely identified. That is you must be able to distinguish one occurrence of an ENTITY CLASS from another. This is done through the value of one or more ATTRIBUTES or RELATIONSHIP ROLES. The combination of ATTRIBUTES and ASSOCIATIVE ROLES that can be used to uniquely identify an occurrence of an ENTITY CLASS is the *unique identifier* of that ENTITY CLASS.

The model in Figure 7–12 shows that each UNIQUE IDENTIFIER *of* an ENTITY CLASS (as a FACT TYPE) must be *composed of* one or more UNIQUE IDENTIFIER ELEMENTS (as FACT TYPE ELEMENTS). Each UNIQUE IDENTIFIER ELEMENT, in turn, must be *the use of* either an ATTRIBUTE or an ASSOCIATIVE ROLE.

### Business Rules

1. Each UNIQUE IDENTIFIER ELEMENT must be *part of* only a UNIQUE IDENTIFIER.
2. Each UNIQUE IDENTIFIER must be *composed of* at least one and possibly more UNIQUE IDENTIFIER ELEMENTS.

## Optionality Constraint

In a data model, one of the arguments for a relationship role is whether there *must be* an occurrence of the second entity class for each occurrence of the first class. In other words, is the role *mandatory* or *optional*? Similarly, for each occurrence of an entity class is each attribute *mandatory* or *optional*?

Most notations have symbols to represent this. In the notation used in this book, a role is optional if the half of the line closest to the first entity class is

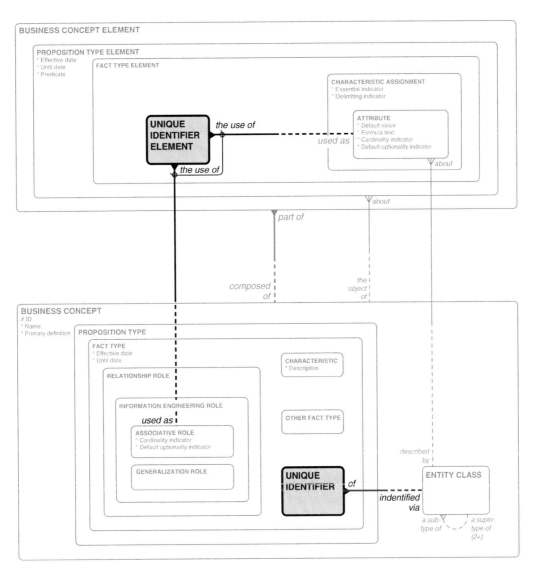

*Fig. 7–12: Unique identifiers.*

dashed; it is mandatory if that line half is solid. An attribute is optional if its name on the diagram is preceded by a circle (o), and mandatory if it is preceded by an asterisk (*) or an octothorpe (#).

In the metadata model displayed so far (see Figure 7–13), ASSOCIATIVE ROLE does have the attribute "Default optionality indicator", as does ATTRIBUTE. This is misleading, however. In the real world, things are rarely that simple. At the very least, it would be useful to be able to say "initially may be, but eventually must be". For example, sometimes an attribute is ultimately required, but when data are being entered, it is permissible to create the record even if that value is not available. Clive Finklestein's version of information engineering has just such a symbol [Finklestein 1989, pp. 57–63]. But "initially may be, but eventually must be" is not really sufficient either.

What is needed is the ability to specify how optionality might change, depending on the state of the entity class involved. Perhaps the value is optional when something is "pending", but required before it can be "in force", but optional again when it becomes "obsolete".*

For example, in the model shown in Figure 7–14, an ASSET ACCOUNT is an account in the company's general ledger, whereas an ASSET is a physical item held by the organization. It is easy to assert that each ASSET ACCOUNT must be *an accounting of* one or more physical ASSETS,** and it is reasonable to expect that eventually every ASSET acquired will be recorded. But it is also reasonable to expect that this may not happen right away. What is needed is a way of expressing the fact that each ASSET must be *accounted for in* an ASSET ACCOUNT within a specified time limit.

Entity-relationship modeling notations and the CASE tools that support them cannot show this, but we can put this in the metamodel. The OPTIONALITY CONSTRAINT entity class is shown in Figure 7–15. This determines whether a particular RELATIONSHIP ROLE or ATTRIBUTE is optional. An instance of the ATTRIBUTE "Optionality indicator" (of the entity class OPTIONALITY CONSTRAINT) is either "True" or "False" for a particular ATTRIBUTE or ASSOCIATIVE ROLE. This is *based on* the ENTITY CLASS STATE TYPE. Whether a particular ATTRIBUTE or RELATIONSHIP ROLE is optional

---

*Your author is indebted to Larry English for conversations with him that helped clarify this point.

**The Corporate Controller and the IRS frown on having assets on the books that don't correspond to real stuff.

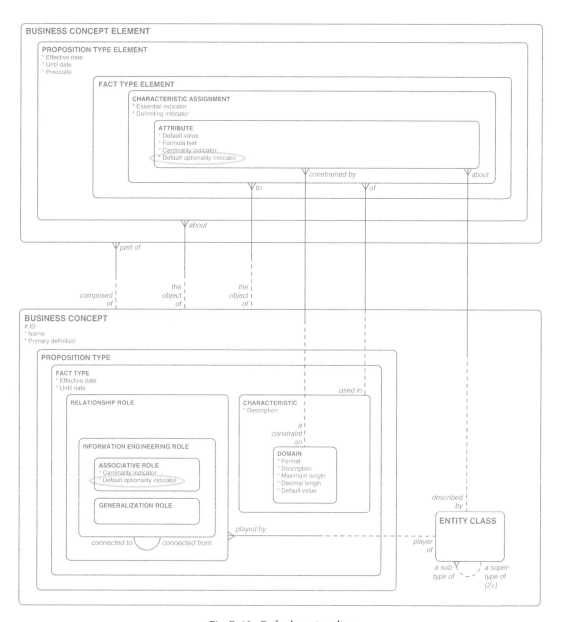

*Fig. 7–13: Default optionality.*

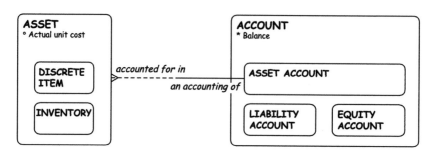

*Fig. 7–14: Optionality rule.*

or not is based on the ENTITY CLASS the ATTRIBUTE is *about* or the ENTITY CLASS the RELATIONSHIP ROLE is *played by*.

---

**Business Rules**

1.  An ATTRIBUTE is OPTIONAL if the ENTITY CLASS it is *about* is *in* an ENTITY CLASS STATE that is *an example of* an ENTITY CLASS STATE TYPE that is *the basis for* the OPTIONALITY CONSTRAINT the ATTRIBUTE is *constrained by*.
2.  An ASSOCIATIVE ROLE is OPTIONAL if the ENTITY CLASS it is *played by* is in an ENTITY CLASS STATE that is *an example of* an ENTITY CLASS STATE TYPE that is *the basis for* the OPTIONALITY CONSTRAINT the ATTRIBUTE is *constrained by*.
3.  An OPTIONALITY CONSTRAINT may only be to constrain an ATTRIBUTE, an N-ARY ROLE, or an ASSOCIATIVE ROLE.

---

In the example, an OPTIONALITY CONSTRAINT can be defined *to constrain* the RELATIONSHIP ROLE "accounted for in" such that when ENTITY CLASS "Asset" is *in* the ENTITY CLASS STATE "Received" then "accounted for in" is optional (the value of Optionality indicator is "True"). On the other hand, if the ENTITY CLASS STATE is "Installed", another OPTIONALITY CONSTRAINT establishes that "accounted for in" is now mandatory (Optionality indicator is "False").

## *Cardinality Constraint*

A second constraint directly represented in an entity-relationship model is *cardinality*. In the case of relationships, this is the issue of whether an instance of an

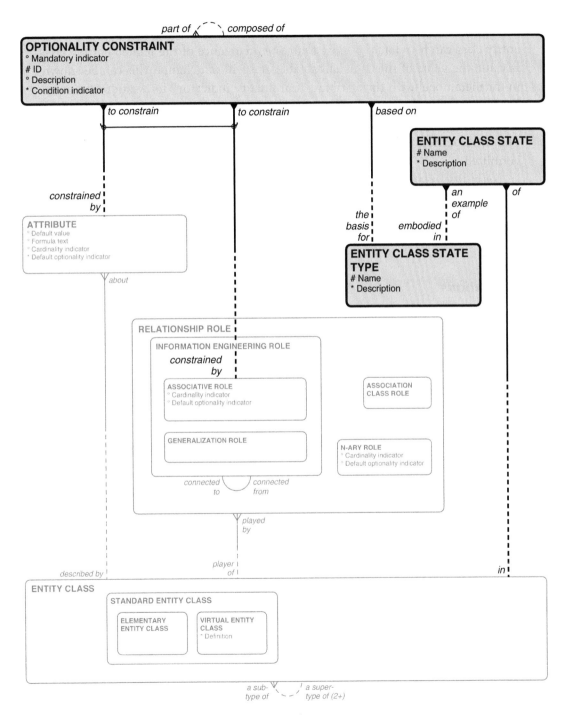

*part of*   *composed of*

**OPTIONALITY CONSTRAINT**
° Mandatory indicator
# ID
° Description
* Condition indicator

*to constrain*     *to constrain*     *based on*

**ENTITY CLASS STATE**
# Name
* Description

*constrained by*

**ATTRIBUTE**
° Default value
° Formula text
° Cardinality indicator
° Default optionality indicator

*about*

*the basis for*    *embodied in*    *an example of*

**ENTITY CLASS STATE TYPE**
# Name
* Description

**RELATIONSHIP ROLE**

**INFORMATION ENGINEERING ROLE**

*constrained by*

**ASSOCIATIVE ROLE**
° Cardinality indicator
° Default optionality indicator

**ASSOCIATION CLASS ROLE**

**GENERALIZATION ROLE**

**N-ARY ROLE**
° Cardinality indicator
° Default optionality indicator

*connected to*    *connected from*

*played by*

*player of*

*described by*

*in*

**ENTITY CLASS**

**STANDARD ENTITY CLASS**

**ELEMENTARY ENTITY CLASS**

**VIRTUAL ENTITY CLASS**
° Definition

*a sub-type of*    *a super-type of (2+)*

Fig. 7–15: *Optionality constraint.*

entity class can be related to *more than one* occurrence of the related entity class. Because the value of this is usually stable and will not change, this can be shown in the metamodel with the attribute "Cardinality indicator" for ASSOCIATIVE ROLE. This is shown in Figure 7–16. The concept also applies to ATTRIBUTES, in that you could specify whether it is permitted for an attribute to have more than one value. The UML permits this, but in the relational world multi-valued attributes are not permitted.

For entity/relationship notations, the value of "Cardinality indicator" must be either "True" (only one instance of the attribute or relationship is possible) or "False" (more than one are permitted). For UML, the "Cardinality indicator" can take a value ("1", "*", "2–3", etc.).

## Derivations

A *derivation* is a statement of knowledge derived from other knowledge in the business. In gathering Row Two information from business owners, it may be appropriate to capture and record the most important derivations as FACT TYPES. To add derivations to our Row Three metamodel, however, it is necessary to express them in terms of the Row Three ENTITY CLASSES, ATTRIBUTES, and RELATIONSHIP ROLES. This is shown in Figure 7–17.

---

**Business Rules**

1. As a FACT TYPE, a DERIVATION must be *composed of (a constraint on)* one or more FACT TYPES ELEMENTS that are ATTRIBUTES and *composed of* one or more FACT TYPES ELEMENTS that are DERIVATION ELEMENTS.
2. Each DERIVATION ELEMENT must be *part of* one and only one DERIVATION.

---

A DERIVATION ELEMENT may also be *via* ("SUM-THROUGH" or "INFER-THROUGH") an ASSOCIATIVE ROLE (see page 306 for examples of this).

The calculation of the formula can be expressed using Reverse Polish Notation: each variable in a formula is separated and assigned an "Operator". Each DERIVATION ELEMENT, then, may be *the use of* a variable, which is another ATTRIBUTE, a SYSTEM VARIABLE, or a "Constant". In addition to a variable, each DERIVATION

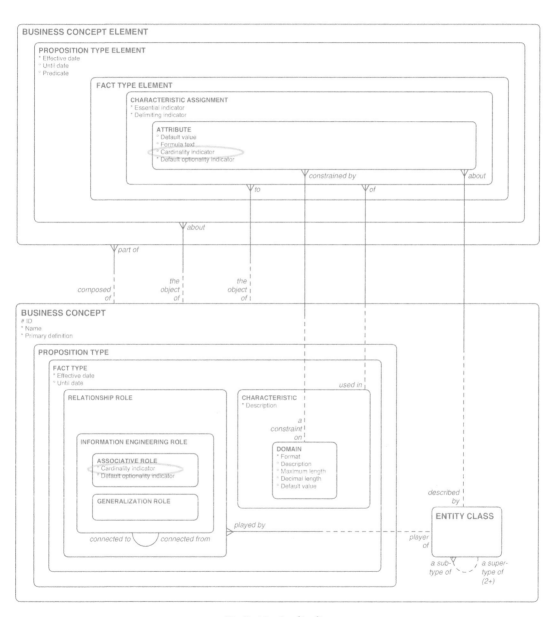

*Fig. 7–16: Cardinality.*

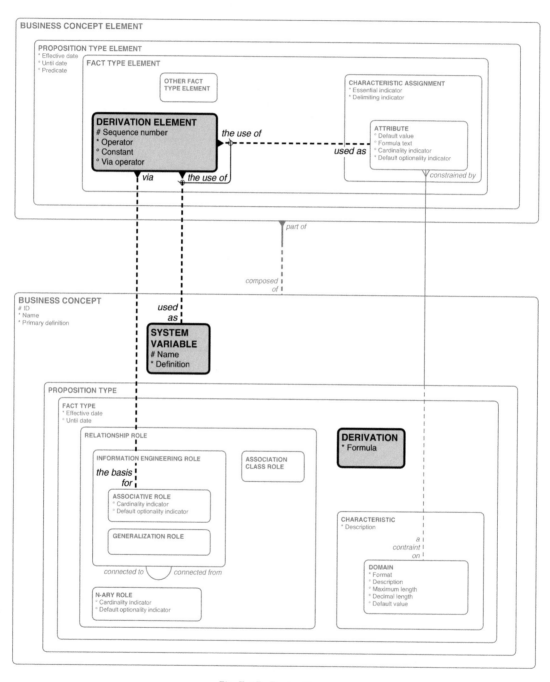

*Fig. 7–17: Derivations.*

ELEMENT includes the attribute "Operator" to define the variable's role in the formula. For example, attribute "A" may be derived from attributes "B", "C", and "D" according to the formula "(A = ((B + C)*D) + 15". This would be represented as shown in Table 7–1. Note that sequence of calculation is from the inner most parenthesis out.

In three cases, the DERIVATION ELEMENT is *the use of* other ATTRIBUTES as variables. In one case, it uses an attribute of DERIVATION ELEMENT itself: "Constant". Thus, first the ATTRIBUTE "B" is added (to nothing), resulting in "B". Then "C" is added, resulting in "B + C". Then "D" is multiplied by the result to this point, resulting in turn in "(B + C) * D".

Finally, the Constant "15" is added to come up with the final result. As a more realistic example, "Age last week" can be defined as "<system date> – Birthdate – 7 days", where <system date> is an example of a SYSTEM VARIABLE. The DERIVATION ELEMENTS for this formula are shown in Table 7–2.

Note that this description is for the Architect's View of the framework, not the designer's view. Nothing is said here about whether the calculation will be done when data are entered (and then stored), or whether it will be done dynamically when the result is requested. That is a design decision, based on the relative expected frequency of updates and retrievals.

*Table 7–1: Derivation elements.*

| Attribute | Constant | Operator |
|-----------|----------|----------|
| B         |          | +        |
| C         |          | +        |
| D         |          | *        |
|           | 15       | +        |

*Table 7–2: System variable.*

| Attribute | Constant | System Variable | Operator |
|-----------|----------|-----------------|----------|
| Birthdate |          |                 | –        |
|           |          | <system date>   | +        |
|           | "7" (days) |               | –        |

Note also that calculations can be across relationships between entity classes. For example, in Figure 7–11 the "Price" of a PRODUCT may be inferred across the relationship between LINE ITEM and PRODUCT. Because each LINE ITEM must be *for* one and only one PRODUCT, after all, "Price" is then available to LINE ITEM. Thus, the "(Value)" of a LINE ITEM then might be expressed something like "Quantity* Price INFER-THROUGH (*for* PRODUCT TYPE)", as shown in Table 7–3.

Similarly, the "(Total value)" of a PURCHASE ORDER might be the sum of "(Value)" in all LINE ITEMS the PURCHASE ORDER is *composed of*. This case might be expressed as Value SUM-THROUGH (*composed of* LINE ITEM), as shown in Table 7–4.

This all is recognized in Figure 7–17 by the relationships asserting that each DERIVATION ELEMENT may be *the use of* an ATTRIBUTE, *via* one and only one ASSOCIATIVE ROLE. (Although this example illustrates the point, the actual solution in this case is made more complicated by the fact that the sample model actually asserts that each LINE ITEM must be either *for* one PRODUCT TYPE or *for* one SERVICE TYPE. The navigation would have to be sophisticated enough to choose which relationship to navigate. This is not adequately represented in the metamodel, and its solution is left as an exercise for the reader.)

Derived attributes can be shown in an entity/relationship diagram, but of course the derivation logic itself must be documented separately.* (In the UML

*Table 7–3: Navigation 1 (Value).*

| Attribute | Navigation | Constant | System Variable | Operator |
|---|---|---|---|---|
| Quantity | | | | + |
| Price | INFER-THROUGH (*for* PRODUCT TYPE) | | | * |

*Table 7–4: Navigation 2 (Total value).*

| | | |
|---|---|---|
| Value | SUM-THROUGH (*composed of* LINE ITEM) | + |

---

*Note that by your author's convention derived attributes are represented in parentheses. This makes for effective graphics, but it does not work if the entity-relationship model is used to generate a database design. In that environment, simply precede each derived attribute name with a letter, such as d_.

and ORM, the derivation formulae can be shown on the diagram, next to the model.) Interestingly enough, in an object model *all* attributes are considered to be derived, even if the derivation is simply "retrieve this from persistent memory".

### *Exclusivity Constraint*

The sample entity-relationship diagram shown in Figure 7–11 contains a particular constraint worth discussing. Specifically, each LINE ITEM must be **either** *for* one PRODUCT TYPE **or** *for* one SERVICE TYPE. This is an example of an EXCLUSIVITY CONSTRAINT.

The arc in the sample model constrained the entity class LINE ITEM to being related to one or the other ASSOCIATIVE ROLES. If there was a PRODUCT TYPE instance, there could not be a SERVICE TYPE instance, and vice versa. Figure 7–18 shows the metamodel for this.

An EXCLUSIVITY CONSTRAINT *to constrain* one or more ENTITY CLASSES must be *composed of* two or more (2+) EXCLUSIVITY CONSTRAINT ELEMENTS, each of which is *constrained by* an ASSOCIATIVE ROLE.

> ### Business Rule
>
> When two or more ASSOCIATIVE ROLES are *constraints on* EXCLUSIVITY CONSTRAINT ELEMENTS that are part of a single EXCLUSIVITY CONSTRAINT *to constrain* an ENTITY CLASS, both ASSOCIATIVE ROLES must be *played by* the same ENTITY CLASS.

If unique identifiers, optionality, cardinality, and exclusivity are constraints that can be shown in an entity-relationship model, what then remains? Two types of constraints remain: domains and other system constraints.

## Domains

Figure 7–19 shows that an ATTRIBUTE must be a CONTINUOUS ATTRIBUTE, a DISCRETE ATTRIBUTE, or an OTHER ATTRIBUTE. The value of an occurrence of a CONTINUOUS ATTRIBUTE may be any real number or date. It may be subject to the limits "Maximum value" and "Minimum value". The value of an occurrence of a DISCRETE ATTRIBUTE, on the other hand, must be equal to the value *of* a PERMITTED ATTRIBUTE

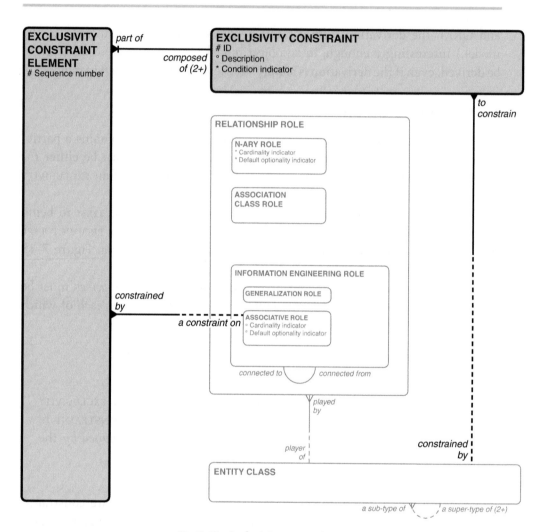

*Fig. 7–18: Exclusivity constraints.*

VALUE that is *for* the DISCRETE ATTRIBUTE in question. That is, each DISCRETE ATTRIBUTE may be *constrained to* one or more PERMITTED ATTRIBUTE VALUES. OTHER ATTRIBUTES include dates and Boolean expressions.

This validation of ATTRIBUTE values can be specified for each ATTRIBUTE, as shown. Note that the model, however, requires that each ATTRIBUTE be *constrained by* one DOMAIN. In practice, this requirement is often ignored, implying that

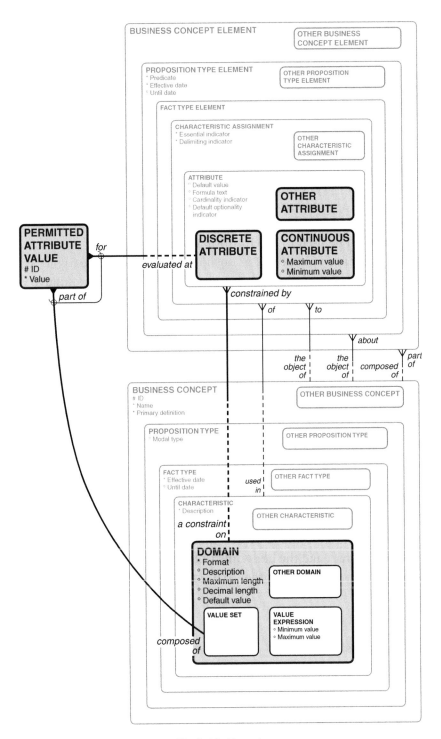

*Fig. 7–19: Domains.*

the conditions described by the DOMAIN are identical to those of the ATTRIBUTE. Alternatively, a DOMAIN can be specified to apply to numerous ATTRIBUTES. Each DOMAIN, after all, may be *a constraint on* one or more ATTRIBUTES.

Similar to the sub-types of ATTRIBUTE, each DOMAIN must be a VALUE SET, a VALUE EXPRESSION, or an OTHER DOMAIN. A VALUE SET is used to validate DISCRETE ATTRIBUTES, and is similarly *composed of* one or more PERMITTED ATTRIBUTE VALUES. A VALUE EXPRESSION applies mathematics to constrain ATTRIBUTES. Among other things, this can be a DERIVATION for arriving at an ATTRIBUTE "Value", or a "Maximum value" and/or a "Minimum value" for a set of CONTINUOUS ATTRIBUTES. An OTHER DOMAIN can be used to specify formats or patterns.

Note that nothing is indicated as to how DOMAIN and PERMITTED ATTRIBUTE VALUE will be expressed. Rather, given a particular PERMITTED ATTRIBUTE VALUE, it must be *represented by* one or more VALID CODE (see Figure 7–20). (Note that this is a sub-type of the more generic relationship between BUSINESS CONCEPT and SYMBOL.)

The difference between a VALUE SET and a CODE SET is that a PERMITTED ATTRIBUTE VALUE is the *concept* of the value. The PERMITTED ATTRIBUTE VALUE is *represented by* a VALUE CODE that in turn is *the use of* a SIGNIFIER, such as a WORD or ABBREVIATION. For example, the VALUE SET of "Canadian Provinces" consists of PERMITTED ATTRIBUTE VALUES of the concepts "Quebec", "Alberta", "Ontario", and so on. Each of these may be *represented by* one or more VALID CODES. For example, British Columbia might be represented by "British Columbia", "BC", "02", and so on.

Each VALID CODE in turn must be *part of* a CODE SET that is, in this case, *a representation of* a VALUE SET. In the provincial Canadian example, the VALUE SET of "Canadian Provinces" could be represented by the CODE SETS "Official names", "Postal abbreviations", and the like with "Official names" being the CODE SET that is *the standard representation of* the VALUE SET "Canadian Provinces".

### Business Rules

1. A VALUE SET may be *a constraint on* only a DISCRETE ATTRIBUTE.
2. An OTHER DOMAIN may be *a constraint on* only a CONTINUOUS ATTRIBUTE.

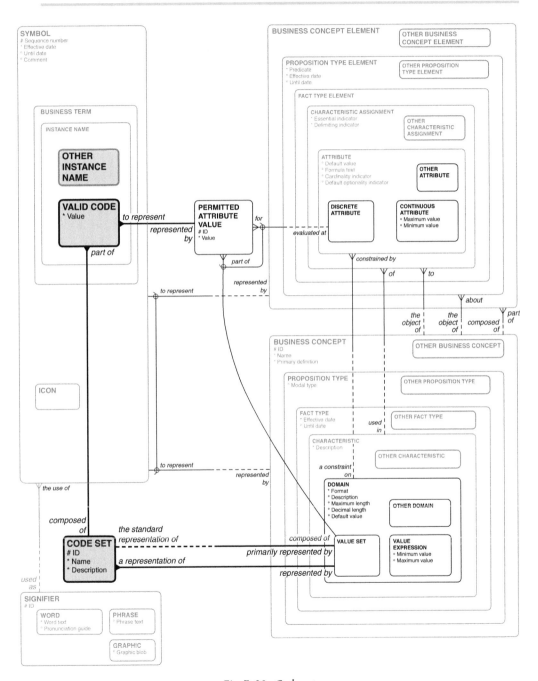

*Fig. 7–20: Code sets.*

3. A PERMITTED ATTRIBUTE VALUE may be *represented by* only one VALID
   CODE that is *part of* the CODE SET that is *the standard representation of*
   the VALUE SET the PERMITTED ATTIBUTE VALUE is *part of.*

## System Constraints

Because a data model can represent cardinality and optionality, unique identifiers, and derived attributes, the metamodel for these constraints (as well as
the metamodel for domains) is closely connected to that for the data model
described in Chapter Two. There are many other constraints, however, that the
entity-relationship model cannot represent. Consequently, the metadata for data
modeling is not adequate to represent them either. But where notations are limited, this metamodel is not. The model can easily be extended, as shown in
Figure 7–21.*

This figure introduces the concept of a SYSTEM CONSTRAINT, which must be
*to constrain* an ATTRIBUTE, an ASSOCIATIVE ROLE, or an ENTITY CLASS. That is, a
SYSTEM CONSTRAINT is an assertion limiting what data can be created or updated.
Presumably, this is a reflection of a BUSINESS RULE that asserts what can or cannot be done in the business. This link to BUSINESS RULES is discussed further in
material to follow.

Each SYSTEM CONSTRAINT may be *part of* a more complex SYSTEM CONSTRAINT.
Note that SYSTEM CONSTRAINT is but a generalization of the OPTIONALITY CON-
STRAINT and the EXCLUSIVITY CONSTRIANT we have already seen. Those were special
cases, though, and this is a far more extensive model.

The attribute "Condition indicator" determines whether the SYSTEM CON-
STRAINT is an *integrity constraint* (the indicator's value is "False")—meaning that
it is asserting that something *must be* the case—or whether it is a *condition* (the
indicator's value is "True"), meaning that *if* a situation exists *then* some other
specified action must take place. (Note that both the OPTIONALITY CONSTRAINT and
the EXCLUSIVITY CONSTRAINT are by definition integrity constraints.)

---

*This section is largely derived from Ron Ross's previously cited book [Ross 1997].

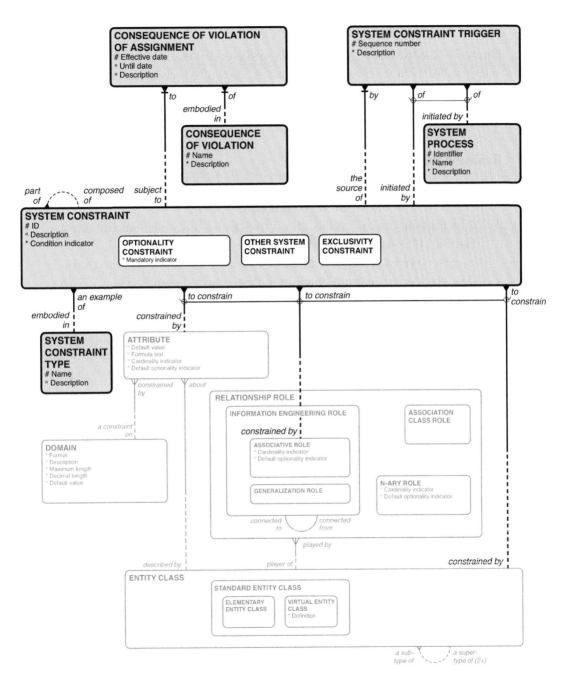

Fig. 7–21: System constraints.

Figure 7–21 also shows the fact that a SYSTEM CONSTRAINT may be *the source of* one or more SYSTEM CONSTRAINT TRIGGERS, each of which must be *of* either a SYSTEM PROCESS or *of* another SYSTEM CONSTRAINT. Note that this is only possible if the SYSTEM CONSTRAINT attribute "Condition indicator" is "True".

**Business Rules**

1. Only SYSTEM CONSTRAINTS whose "Condition indicator" is "True" may be *the source of* one or more SYSTEM CONSTRAINT TRIGGERS.
2. By definition, each EXCLUSIVITY CONSTRAINT must be an integrity constraint ("Condition indicator" is "False").
3. An OPTIONALITY CONSTRAINT must be *based on* one and only one ENTITY CLASS STATE. (This is not shown here, but it was shown in Figure 7–15 on page 301.)

Also shown in Figure 7–21, each SYSTEM CONSTRAINT must be *subject to* one or more CONSEQUENCE OF VIOLATION ASSIGNMENTS *of* a CONSEQUENCE OF VIOLATION. A CONSEQUENCE OF VIOLATION ASSIGNMENT, then, might assert that if a particular SYSTEM CONSTRAINT is violated the CONSEQUENCE OF VIOLATION would be "Flag for subsequent correction".

In addition to OPTIONALITY CONSTRAINT and EXCLUSIVITY CONSTRAINT there are many OTHER (types of) SYSTEM CONSTRAINT. Each SYSTEM CONSTRAINT must be *an example of* exactly one SYSTEM CONSTRAINT TYPE, repeating the structure shown in the sub-types. As before, when the ... TYPE entity class reproduces the sub-type structure, the first three instances of SYSTEM CONSTRAINT TYPE here must be "Optionality Constraint", "Exclusivity Constraint", and "Other System Constraint".

### System Constraint Elements and Arguments

If the SYSTEM CONSTRAINT is *to constrain* something, what is doing the constraining? EXCLUSIVITY CONSTRAINT, for example, constrained ENTITY CLASSES with the value of ASSOCIATIVE ROLES (as was shown in Figure 7–18 on p. 308). That is, the EXCLUSIVITY CONSTRAINT is *constrained by* two or more EXCLUSIVITY CONSTRAINT ELEMENTS, each of which must be *constrained by* exactly one ASSOCIATIVE ROLE.

Most SYSTEM CONSTRAINTS are not limited to having a single thing doing the constraining, so we need an additional entity class, SYSTEM CONSTRAINT ELEMENT. This, a generalization of EXCLUSIVITY CONSTRAINT ELEMENT, is the fact that a particular ATTRIBUTE, RELATIONSHIP ROLE, or ENTITY CLASS participates in a SYSTEM CONSTRAINT.

Figure 7–22 shows that each SYSTEM CONSTRAINT is *composed of* one or more SYSTEM CONSTRAINT ELEMENTS, each of which is *a constraint by* another ENTITY CLASS, ATTRIBUTE, or RELATIONSHIP ROLE. Or, it could be *a constraint by* another SYSTEM CONSTRAINT. The figure also shows how either a SYSTEM CONSTRAINT or a SYSTEM CONSTRAINT ELEMENT may be *qualified by* one or more SYSTEM CONSTRAINT ARGUMENTS.

Mr. Ross, in his book [Ross 1997], has itemized forty SYSTEM CONSTRAINT TYPES, grouped into seven categories.

— *Instance verifiers:* The integrity constraint requires an instance of the constrained object to exist. This includes the optionality constraint described previously. The condition tests to see whether it exists.
— *Type verifiers:* The integrity constraint requires an instance of the constrained object to be related to objects in a specified relationship (mutually exclusive, mutually inclusive, and so on). This includes the mutually exclusive arc shown in Figure 7–11. In that example, the notation asserts that "Each LINE ITEM must be for *either* one PRODUCT TYPE *or* one SERVICE TYPE". The condition tests to see whether this is so.
— *Position verifiers:* The integrity constraint requires a specific ranking of the constrained object relative to other objects (lowest, highest, oldest, newest, or a specified ranking, such as fifth). The condition tests to see whether this is so.
— *Functional verifiers:* The integrity constraint requires an object to assume a function relative to the constrained object. For example, the value of an attribute may be required to be unique within an entity class. The condition tests to see whether this is so.
— *Comparative evaluators:* Usually applying to attributes, the integrity constraint requires that an object be greater than, less than, or equal to the constrained object. The condition tests to see whether this is so.
— *Mathematical evaluators:* This is an alternative way to specify derived attributes as presented previously. In this case, an integrity constraint specifies that an attribute be calculated according to a formula (or a function, such as SUM) for a constrained entity class. A condition tests to see whether this is so.

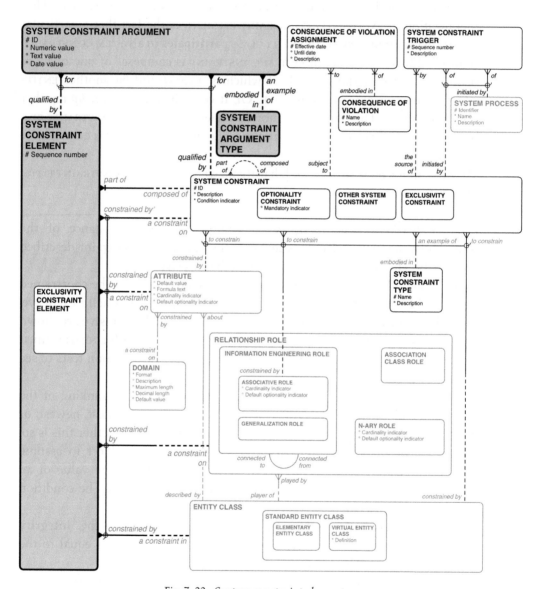

*Fig. 7–22: System constraint elements.*

— *Projection controllers:* Where other types of constraints prevent things from happening, a projection controller asserts that under specified circumstances something *must* happen. A state is enabled, something is copied, or an action is executed.

In addition, there are a number of rule types derived from these. Figure 7–23 shows the Ross notation for a different way of dealing with the optionality problem we see in Figure 7–14. The notation shows one SYSTEM CONSTRAINT (Timing) represented by the bicycle seat-shaped symbol with a "TI", and another SYSTEM CONSTRAINT (Optionality) represented by the arrowhead with an "X" in it. The bicycle seat symbol shows that the timing constraint is a Condition, and the arrowhead symbol shows that the optionality constraint is an integrity constraint.

TI and X are examples of the SYSTEM CONSTRAINT TYPES discussed previously. TI is a derived SYSTEM CONSTRAINT TYPE that means that if something happens within a specified time period something else should happen. In this case, the "something else" is an "X" SYSTEM CONSTRAINT (an "Instance Verifier" from the previous list), which means that the thing it is pointing to (in this case, the *accounted for in* RELATIONSHIP ROLE) *must* happen. In other words, after the timing interval shown for the TI constraint, the *accounted for in* relationship must be populated.

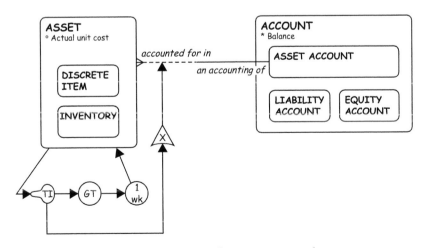

*Fig. 7–23: Business rule argument example.*

In each case, the thing being constrained is at the other end of the line pointing *into* the constraint, and the things doing the constraining are at the end of lines pointing *away from* the constraint. That is, TI is constraining the ENTITY CLASS "Asset", and X is constraining the constraint TI. An alternative way of understanding the "constrained by" / "a constraint on" syntax is to imagine each rule as an *if/then* statement: (1) If an ASSET exists for greater than 1 week, then invoke the mandatory ("X") constraint; (2) if the timing ("TI") constraint fires, then the *accounted for in* relationship role must exist.

Note that the circles showing "GT" (representing "greater than") and "1 wk" (for "one week") are examples of SYSTEM CONSTRAINT ARGUMENTS to the constraint, in this case meaning "If a time period of greater than one week transpires" then... "In Figure 7–22, SYSTEM CONSTRAINT ARGUMENT is shown to be either for one SYSTEM CONSTRAINT ELEMENT or *for* one SYSTEM CONSTRAINT, and it must be *an example of* one SYSTEM CONSTRAINT ARGUMENT TYPE, such as "operator" or "duration".

## Business Rule Mapping

Note the assumption that all system constraints described in this section are derived from BUSINESS RULES, as specified for Row Two in the previous section. Figure 7–24 shows specifically how a BUSINESS RULE from Row Two can be mapped to any of the constraints described here for Row Three.

- Unique Identifiers
- Domains
- System Constraints

Specifically, each BUSINESS RULE may be *subject to* one or more BUSINESS RULE MAPPINGS, where each of these in turn must be *composed of* one or more BUSINESS RULE MAPPING ELEMENTS. Each BUSINESS RULE MAPPING ELEMENT, then, must be a mapping *to* a DOMAIN, UNIQUE IDENTIFIER, or SYSTEM CONSTRAINT.

## Parties

Figure 7–25 shows how the PARTY and ACCESS ROLES described in Chapter Four come into play here. Note that either a MANAGEMENT ROLE or an ENFORCEMENT

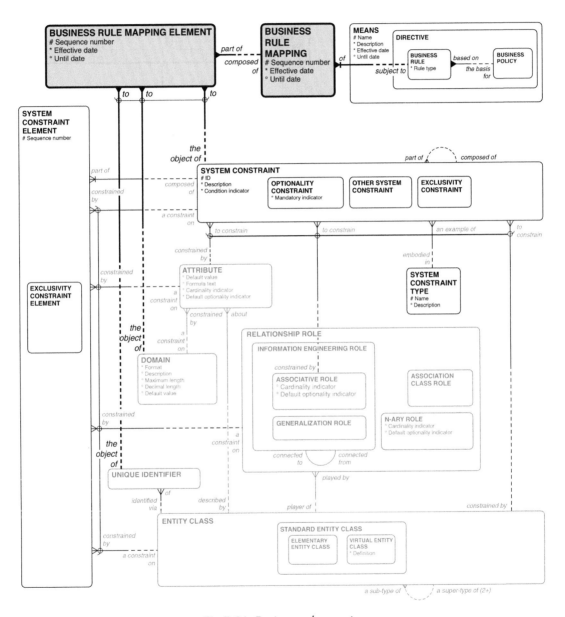

*Fig. 7–24: Business rule mapping.*

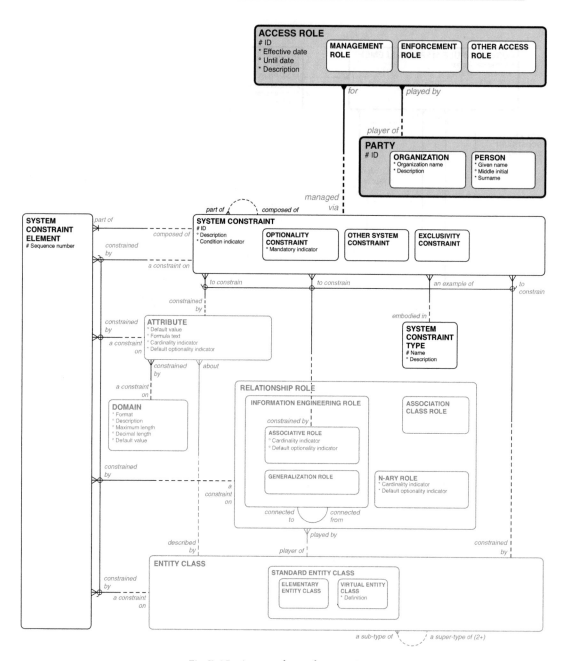

*Fig. 7–25: Access roles and constraints.*

ROLE *played by* a PARTY (or, by extension, *by* a POSITION, POSITION RESPONSIBILITY, or any of the other entity classes described in Chapter Four) can be specified *for* a SYSTEM CONSTRAINT.

## Data Quality

The quality of the data that constitute the ATTRIBUTES and RELATIONSHIP ROLES of our system is usually measured in terms of one or more QUALITY CHARACTERISTICS. According to Larry English, these include two major categories [English 1999, pp. 147–153]. First, there are measures of the *inherent* quality of the data.

—  *Definition conformance:* The consistency of the meaning of the actual data values with its data definition.
—  *Completeness (of values):* A measure of the extent to which an attribute has values for all instances of an entity class.
—  *Validity or business rule conformance:* A measure of the degree of conformance of data to its domain values and business rules.
—  *Accuracy (to surrogate source):* A measure of the degree to which data agrees with an original source of data, such as a form, document, or unaltered electronic data received from outside the control of the organization that is acknowledged to be an authoritative source.
—  *Accuracy (to reality):* The degree to which data accurately reflects the real-world object or event being described. Accuracy is the highest degree of inherent information quality possible.
—  *Precision:* The characteristic of having the right level of granularity in the data values.
—  *Nonduplication:* The degree to which there is a one-to-one correlation between records and the real-world object or events being represented.
—  *Equivalence of redundant or distributed data:* The degree to which data in one data collection or database is semantically equivalent to data about the same object or event in another data collection or database.
—  *Concurrency of redundant or distributed data:* The information float or lag time between when data is knowable (created or changed) in one database and is also knowable in a redundant or distributed database.
—  *Accessibility:* The characteristic of being able to access data when it is required.

Second, there are measures of the *pragmatic* quality, including intuitiveness of presentation and value to knowledge workers.

- *Timeliness:* A measure of the relative availability of data to support a given process within the timetable required to perform the process.
- *Contextual clarity:* A measure of the relative degree to which data presentation enables the knowledge worker to understand the meaning of the data and avoid misinterpretation.
- *Derivation integrity:* A measure of the correctness with which derived or calculated data are calculated from its base data.
- *Usability:* A measure of the degree to which the information presentation is directly and efficiently usable for its purpose.
- *"Rightness" or fact completeness:* A measure of having the right type of data with the right quality to support a given process or a decision.

Figure 7–26 shows QUALITY CHARACTERISTIC as an entity class, where each QUALITY CHARACTERISTIC may be *defined in terms of* one or more VALID QUALITY CHARACTERISTIC VALUES. For example, the QUALITY CHARACTERISTIC "Accuracy (to surrogate source)" may be rated on a scale with five VALID QUALITY CHARACTERISTIC VALUES: "Not at all", "Approximate", "Moderately accurate", "Very accurate", and "Perfectly accurate".

The data captured to describe an ATTRIBUTE or a RELATIONSHIP ROLE may then be *evaluated via* one or more QUALITY STANDARDS, where each QUALITY STANDARD must be *the use of* a single VALID QUALITY CHARACTERISTIC VALUE. Thus, a business policy for the model shown in Figure 7–11 in Chapter Two might dictate that a PERSON "Last Name" must be "Very accurate" and that the identity of the PARTY identified in the *from* role from ORDER must be "Perfectly accurate".

## Row Four: The Designer's View

Whereas in Row Two we looked at the overall motivation and constraints on the operation of the business and in Row Three at the specific structure of business rules in terms of data (system constraints), Row Four is concerned with how

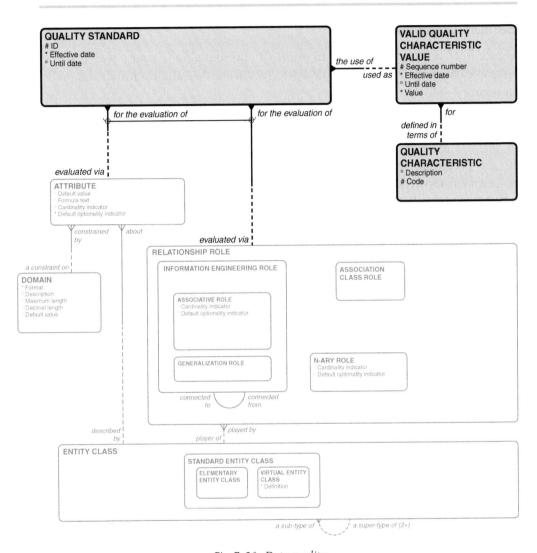

*Fig. 7–26: Data quality.*

business rules are implemented using database technology as well as others. To the extent possible, we will use relational database structures, but to the extent the system constraints go outside such structures, we will have to extend the model to refer to programs that would do the processing.

## Sample Database Design

Figure 7–27 is a copy of a diagram originally presented in Chapter Two. It shows a sample database design that could be derived from the sample entity class model in Figure 7–11.

### *Unique Keys*

In the preceding section, one type of constraint was the UNIQUE IDENTIFIER. A UNIQUE IDENTIFIER is implemented in relational technology with a *unique key*, which may be either a *primary key* or an *alternative key*.

According to relational theory, each row in a table must be uniquely identified by the values of one or more columns in the table. Figure 7–28 shows the meta-model of this. In this model, each TABLE must be *organized around* one or more UNIQUE KEYS. Each UNIQUE KEY in turn must be *composed of* one or more UNIQUE KEY ELEMENTS, each of which must be *the use of* a COLUMN. A UNIQUE KEY must be either a PRIMARY KEY or an ALTERNATIVE KEY.

> **Business Rule**
>
> Each TABLE must be *organized around* exactly one PRIMARY KEY, but it may be *organized around* one or more ALTERNATIVE KEYS as well.

Note that in Figure 7–27 PARTIES, ORDERS, LINE ITEMS, PRODUCT TYPES, and SERVICE TYPES are all examples of the entity class TABLE shown in Figure 7–28. In that example, an ORDER may be uniquely identified by its "order_number". That is, the TABLE whose Name is "Order" is *organized around* a UNIQUE KEY (in this case, a PRIMARY KEY) that is *composed of* one UNIQUE KEY ELEMENT that in turn is *the use of* a SPECIFIED COLUMN whose Name is "order_number".

> **Business Rule**
>
> A COLUMN *used as* a UNIQUE KEY ELEMENT that is *part of* a UNIQUE KEY must be *part of* the TABLE the UNIQUE KEY is *on*.

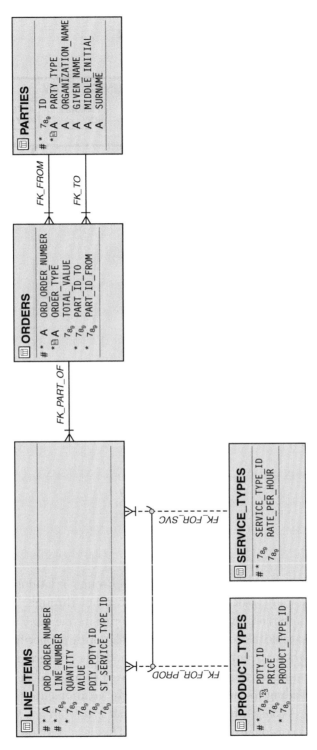

Fig. 7–27: Sample database design.

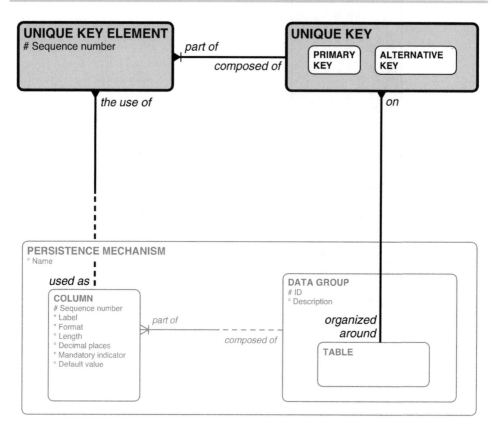

*Fig. 7–28: Unique keys.*

## Foreign Keys

Just as entity classes are related to each other through relationships, tables in a relational database are logically related to each other through *foreign keys*. A foreign key is the reference by one or more columns in one table to one or more columns in another table in order to represent a relationship. Specifically, as shown in Figure 7–29, when an entity-relationship model is converted to a database design, each one-to-many relationship is converted to a set of new COLUMNS in the TABLE corresponding to the "many" side of the relationship (the *child table*). This set of COLUMNS constitutes a FOREIGN KEY that is *a reference to* a UNIQUE KEY *on* a different (or, occasionally, the same) TABLE. That is, a FOREIGN KEY consists of

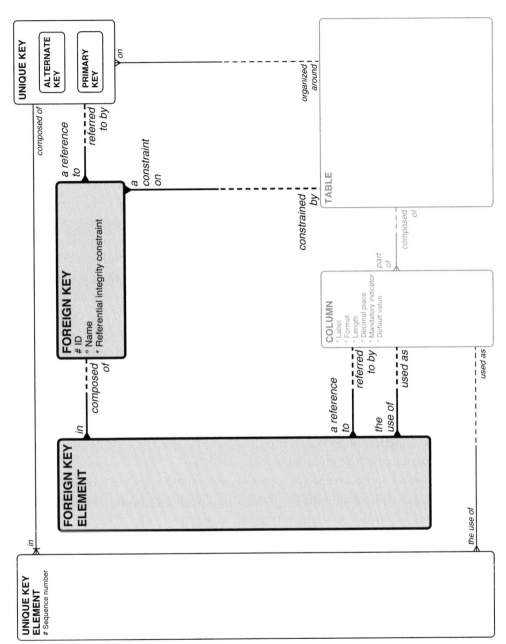

Fig. 7-29: Foreign keys.

COLUMNS that refer to the COLUMNS that constitute a UNIQUE KEY of the TABLE on the "one" side of the relationship (the *parent table*).

In Figure 7–29, then, each TABLE may be *constrained by* one or more FOREIGN KEYS. Each FOREIGN KEY, then, must be *composed of* one or more FOREIGN KEY ELEMENTS, each of which is *the use of* a specified COLUMN and *a reference to* another COLUMN. This second COLUMN must then also be *used as* a UNIQUE KEY ELEMENT *in* the PRIMARY KEY *referred to by* the FOREIGN KEY in question.

For example, as shown in Figure 7–27, "Ord_order_number" is a COLUMN in the LINE ITEMS table that is *used as* a FOREIGN KEY ELEMENT. It in turn is a *reference to* the COLUMN "Order number", *used as* a UNIQUE KEY ELEMENT *in* the PRIMARY KEY *on* the ORDERS table. This foreign key represents a constraint on the LINE_ITEMS table, in that a row usually cannot be created if it does not have a value in the foreign key column ("ord_order_number") that matches a value for the primary key ("order_number") in a parent table. Whether it can or not depends on the *referential integrity constraint* that is an attribute of the FOREIGN KEY.

A referential integrity constraint defines the extent to which a table is constrained by a FOREIGN KEY. The attribute "Referential integrity constraint" may have one of the following values.

- *Restricted*: Deletion of an occurrence of a parent table may not take place if the occurrence is related through foreign keys to occurrences of the child table.
- *Cascade delete*: Deletion of an occurrence of a parent table causes deletion of all related occurrences of the child table.
- *Nullify*: Deletion of an occurrence of a parent table may leave occurrences of the child table without parents. In this case, there is no constraint, and child occurrences may be created without specifying a parent.

**Business Rules**

1. A FOREIGN KEY ELEMENT is *a reference to* a COLUMN that is *part of* a TABLE. The same FOREIGN KEY ELEMENT is *part of* a FOREIGN KEY that is *a reference to* a PRIMARY KEY that is *on* the same TABLE.
2. A FOREIGN KEY ELEMENT is *the use of* a COLUMN that is *part of* a TABLE. The same FOREIGN KEY ELEMENT is *part of* a FOREIGN KEY that is *a constraint on* the same TABLE.

3. If the attribute "Referential integrity constraint" of an occurrence of FOREIGN KEY has the value "Restricted", then occurrences of the TABLE *organized around* the PRIMARY KEY *referred to by* the FOREIGN KEY may not be deleted if occurrences exist of the TABLE *constrained by* the FOREIGN KEY.

4. If the attribute "Referential integrity constraint" of an occurrence of FOREIGN KEY has the value "Cascade delete", and if an occurrence of the TABLE *organized around* the PRIMARY KEY that it is *a reference to* is deleted, then each occurrence of the TABLE that is *constrained by* the same FOREIGN KEY must also be deleted.

5. If the attribute "Referential integrity constraint" of an occurrence of FOREIGN KEY has the value "Nullify", then occurrences of the TABLE *organized around* the PRIMARY KEY that it is *a reference to* may be deleted. If this happens, the value of the COLUMN *used as* a FOREIGN KEY ELEMENT is set to "<null>".

## *Computed Columns*

In the preceding Row Three section, a DERIVATION was shown *to calculate the value of* an ATTRIBUTE. The DERIVATION was *composed of* one or more DERIVATION ELEMENTS, each of which was either *the use of* a constant, *the use of* another ATTRIBUTE, or *the use of* a SYSTEM VARIABLE, such as "Today's date". Because that was a conceptual model, the point was made that describing the derivation at that point made no assumptions as to whether the calculation was done when data were collected or on the fly when the derived value was requested.

In the system design represented here, any COLUMNS whose values are calculated before data are stored are no different from any others in this metamodel. They require no special treatment. If the design provides for the ability to calculate values dynamically when they are requested, however, a structure similar to the one seen previously is required. This is shown in Figure 7–30.

Specifically, a COLUMN may be *calculated via* one or more COMPUTATIONS, each of which must be *composed of* one or more COMPUTATION ELEMENTS. Each COMPUTATION ELEMENT in turn must be either *the use of* a constant, *the use of* another COLUMN, or *the use of* a SYSTEM VARIABLE, such as "Today's date". The Reverse Polish Notation approach described previously applies here as well.

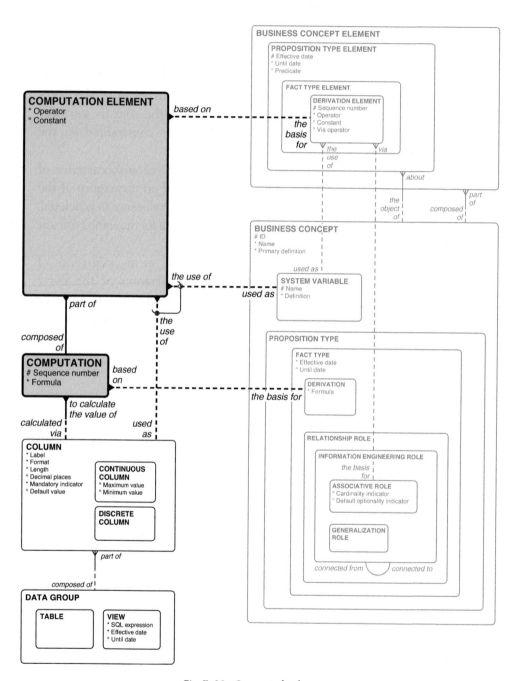

*Fig. 7–30: Computed columns.*

### Business Rules

1. The DERIVATION ELEMENT that a COMPUTATION ELEMENT is *based on* must be *part of* the DERIVATION that the corresponding COMPUTATION is *based on*.
2. If a COLUMN to be calculated is *based on* an ATTRIBUTE (using a COLUMN ATTRIBUTE MAPPING), the ATTRIBUTE must also be derived from a set of DERIVATION ELEMENTS that exactly correspond to the COMPUTATION ELEMENTS for the COLUMN.

### *Column Domains*

In Figure 7–31 we see that a COLUMN must be either a DISCRETE COLUMN or a CONTINUOUS COLUMN. A CONTINUOUS COLUMN can take as a value any real number, although this value may be constrained to be between its "Maximum value" and "Minimum value". A DISCRETE COLUMN, however, can only take as a value a VALID CODE that is *part of* a specified CODE SET. That is, each DISCRETE COLUMN must be *evaluated by* one and only one CODE SET.

Note that this is similar to the structure we saw for CONTINUOUS and DISCRETE ATTRIBUTES in the Row Three part of the model, shown previously. There, an ATTRIBUTE may be *constrained by* a DOMAIN that, if the ATTRIBUTE is a DISCRETE ATTRIBUTE, is a VALUE SET.

The difference between a VALUE SET and a CODE SET is that a PERMITTED ATTRIBUTE VALUE is the *concept* of the value. The PERMITTED ATTRIBUTE VALUE is *represented by* a VALUE CODE that in turn is *the use of* a SIGNIFIER, such as a WORD or ABBREVIATION.

For example, a VALUE SET may describe the states of the United States, but there may be multiple CODE SETS that actually describe the states. In one CODE SET (Postal Abbreviations), Alabama is *represented by* the VALUE CODE that is *the use of* the SIGNIFIER "AL". In another CODE SET (Obsolete Postal Abbreviations), it is *represented by* the VALUE CODE that is *the use of* the SIGNIFIER "ALA". In a third CODE SET (State Codes), Alabama is *represented by* the VALUE CODE that is *the use of* the SIGNIFIER "01".

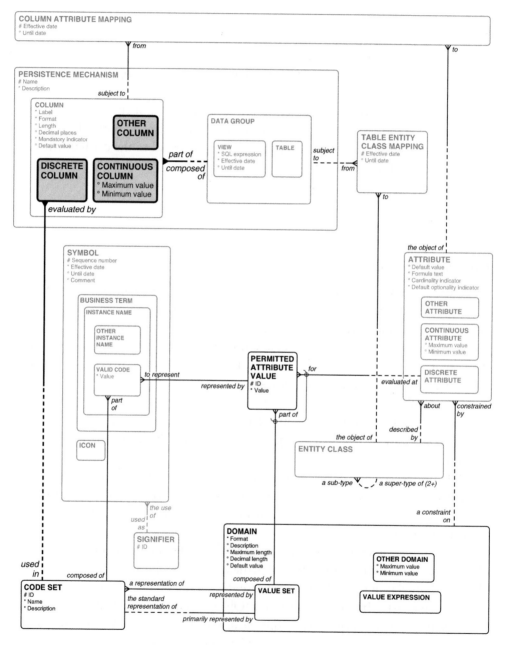

*Fig. 7–31: Column domains.*

The point is that when designing a COLUMN it will be necessary to identify which CODE SET is to be used for that implementation. As described previously, because PERMITTED ATTRIBUTE VALUES have to be identified somehow each VALUE SET must be *primarily represented by* one CODE SET. In the example, the VALUE SET "States of the United States" must be *primarily represented by* a CODE SET such as "State names". In this case, the VALID CODE for Alabama would be *the use of* the SIGNIFIER (a WORD) "Alabama".

### Business Rules

1. A VALID CODE may only be *to represent* a PERMITTED ATTRIBUTE VALUE.
2. If a DISCRETE COLUMN is *subject to* a single COLUMN ATTRIBUTE MAPPING to an ATTRIBUTE, then the ATTRIBUTE must be a DISCRETE ATTRIBUTE.
3. If a DISCRETE COLUMN is *subject to* a single COLUMN ATTRIBUTE MAPPING to an ATTRIBUTE, then the CODE SET that it is *evaluated by* must be *a representation of* a VALUE SET that is *a constraint on* that ATTRIBUTE.

## Database Constraints

Figure 7–32 shows that UNIQUE KEYS, COMPUTATIONS, and FOREIGN KEYS are but examples of the more general concept DATABASE CONSTRAINT. Having said that, we can postulate that there might be OTHER DATABASE CONSTRAINTS on either COLUMNS or TABLES.

## Object-Oriented Constraints

As with ATTRIBUTES and relational COLUMNS, object-oriented INSTANCE ATTRIBUTES are of two types, as shown in Figure 7–33. DISCRETE INSTANCE ATTRIBUTES (such as "State" or "Color") take values from a discrete list of the DISCRETE INSTANCE VALID VALUES. (See the description of DISCRETE COLUMNS earlier in this chapter and that of DISCRETE INSTANCE ATTRIBUTES in the material that follows.) An OTHER INSTANCE ATTRIBUTE, such as "Specific gravity", takes values from a continuous range and may have a "Minimum value" and a "Maximum value". A particular type of DISCRETE INSTANCE ATTRIBUTE, STATE, is described in detail in the material following. Note that a common usage of DISCRETE INSTANCE VALID VALUE is to record valid values for STATE, with the mechanism of LEGAL TRANSFORMATION (described in more detail in Chapter Six) to move CLASS IMPLEMENTATIONS from one STATE to another.

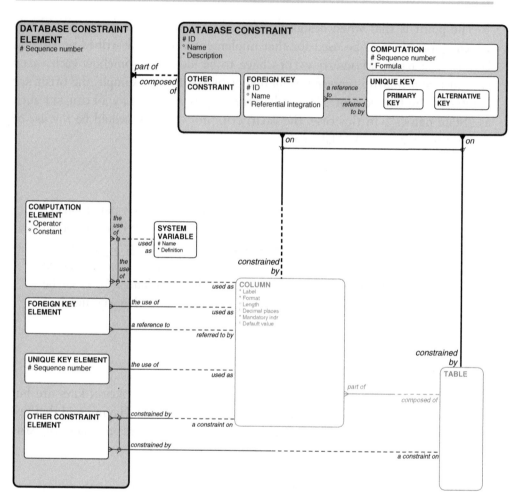

*Fig. 7–32: Database constraints.*

Although it is reasonable to suggest that domains could be specified to validate groups of INSTANCE ATTRIBUTES, as is done with conceptual ATTRIBUTES and relational COLUMNS, the literature about object-orientation does not mention them in this context. Instead, "domain" in the object-oriented community refers to an area of interest.* (See Figure 7–33.)

---

*Indeed, beyond the concept of a list of DISCRETE INSTANCE VALID VALUES, I have not been able to find any discussions of the validation of INSTANCE ATTRIBUTES.

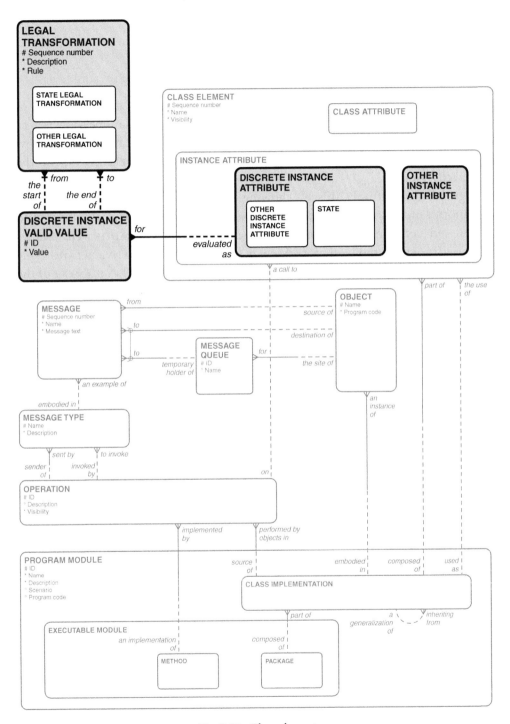

*Fig. 7–33: Class elements.*

## Links

### *The Architect's View (Row Three)*

Previously, we saw how ENTITY CLASSES in the Architect's View became TABLES in the database design and ATTRIBUTES became COLUMNS. Then we saw how COMPUTATIONS in the Designer's View are derived from DERIVATIONS in the Architect's View.

Figure 7–34 continues this by showing the connection between UNIQUE KEYS and UNIQUE IDENTIFIERS, between FOREIGN KEYS and INFORMATION ENGINEERING ROLES, and between OTHER CONSTRAINTS and SYSTEM CONSTRAINTS. This shows that FOREIGN KEY in the Designer's View is *based on* an ASSOCIATIVE RELATIONSHIP ROLE in the Architect's View. Similarly, UNIQUE KEY and UNIQUE KEY ELEMENT of the Designer's View are *based on* UNIQUE IDENTIFIER and UNIQUE IDENTIFIER ELEMENT, respectively, of the Architect's View. Note that where a UNIQUE IDENTIFIER ELEMENT may be *the use of* either an ATTRIBUTE or a RELATIONSHIP ROLE, a UNIQUE KEY ELEMENT is only *the use of* a COLUMN. This is because roles are in fact implemented as FOREIGN KEY columns in relational design.

And finally, each of one or more OTHER CONSTRAINTS in the Designer's View is *based on* a SYSTEM CONSTRAINT in the Architect's View. Note that in all of this linking between the Architect's View and the Designer's View, it is *not* assumed that the designer will simply take the default design implied by the entity-relationship model. That model is intended to describe the inherent structure of data, without regard to technology. When a database is built on a real computer with real database management system software, the structures often have to be modified based on the actual use to which the data will be put.

What is important, though, is to maintain the information about where the design came from. Even if one ATTRIBUTE is implemented as many columns, or vice versa, this model shows how the links can be documented. For the sake of future maintenance, it is important that this be done.

### *Programming Constraints*

Foreign key and primary key constraints can be implemented by database management systems. COMPUTATIONS require software to implement the Reverse Polish Notation approach. OTHER CONSTRAINTS certainly require software as well, whether in the form of database triggers, stored procedures, or other programs.

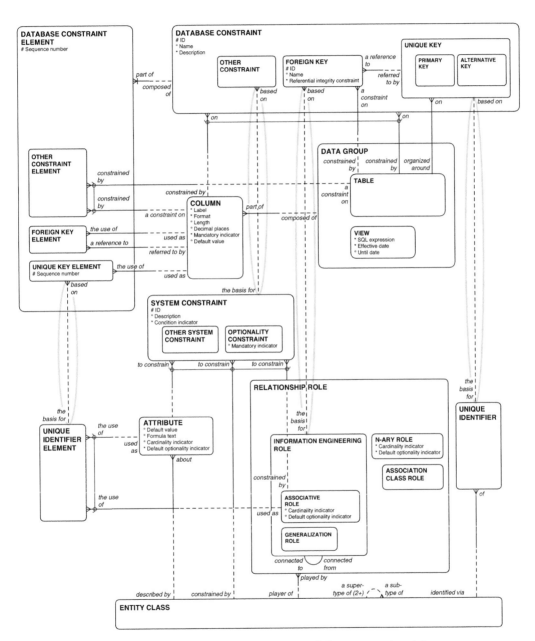

*Fig. 7–34: Unique keys, foreign keys, and the conceptual model.*

Figure 7–35 shows that each CONSTRAINT must be *implemented by* one and only one PROGRAM MODULE. Among the types of PROGRAM MODULES commonly employed at this are the DBMS itself, STORED PROCEDURES, and TRIGGERS, as well as OTHER EXECUTABLE MODULES.

## Data Quality

To the extent that quality standards are applied to ENTITY CLASSES and RELATIONSHIP ROLES, it is even more important that they be applied to the COLUMNS of an actual database. This, after all, is where data quality will be enforced. Figure 7–36 shows the extension of QUALITY STANDARD (shown in Figure 7–26) to apply also to a COLUMN. That is, each QUALITY STANDARD is *the use of a* VALID QUALITY CHARACTERISTIC VALUE *used as* a QUALITY STANDARD *for the evaluation of* a COLUMN.

---

### Business Rule

The VALID QUALITY CHARACTERISTIC VALUE *used as* a QUALITY STANDARD for *the evaluation of* a COLUMN *should be* greater than the VALID QUALITY CHARACTERISTIC VALUE *used as* a QUALITY STANDARD for *the evaluation of* either the ATTRIBUTE or the RELATIONSHIP ROLE that is *implemented as* the COLUMN.

---

## ROW SIX: MEASURING DATA QUALITY

As we have seen in the preceding chapters, Row Six is the view of actual systems as implemented. In the Motivation column, we have been concerned with, among other things, rules and constraints. To examine the full range of constraints in all systems is a bit too ambitious for this book, but it is possible to model the implementation of data quality constraints, as is done in Figure 7–37.

The definition of data standards as applied to attributes and relationships was shown in Figure 7–26 as part of the Row Three model discussed previously. This was extended to cover columns in the Row Four model in Figure 7–36. Here, we see that an actual QUALITY VALUE ASSIGNMENT is *the assignment of* a VALID QUALITY CHARACTERISTIC VALUE *to* a particular CELL INSTANCE.

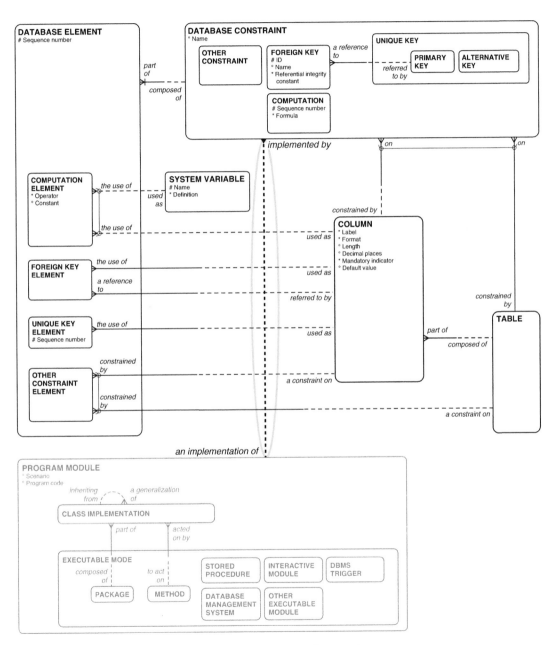

*Fig. 7–35: Constraint implementation.*

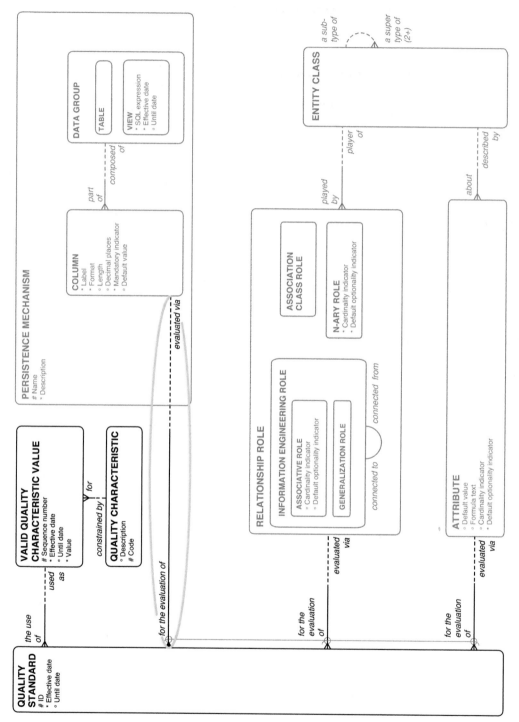

Fig. 7-36: Extended data quality.

340

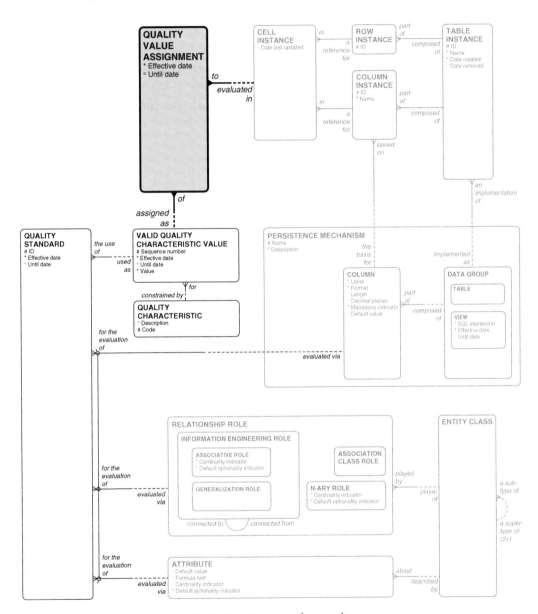

*Fig. 7–37: Measuring data quality.*

**Business Rule**

The VALID QUALITY assigned here for a particular CELL INSTANCE *should be* at least as high as the VALID QUALITY CHARACTERISTIC VALUE that was *for the evaluation of* all instances of the COLUMN that was *the basis for* the COLUMN INSTANCE that this CELL INSTANCE is *in*.

# GLOSSARY

The following pages contain definitions of the specialized words highlighted in the text of this book, as well as definitions of all the classes present in its models. In the definitions, other defined words are also highlighted. Words in SMALL CAPITALS are the names of entity classes in the model. Other words defined are simply various terms referred to in this book. To the right of each definition is a list of the chapters in which the term is discussed; the primary chapter is listed first.

| Term | Definition | Chapter |
| --- | --- | --- |
| *abstract model* | The universal data model that encodes everything into THING, THING TYPE, CHARACTERISTIC, THING RELATIONSHIP, THING TYPE RELATIONSHIP, CHARACTERISTIC, CHARACTERISTIC ASSIGNMENT, and CHARACTERISTIC VALUE. | 1 |
| ACCESS ROLE | The fact that a PARTY, POSITION, and so on plays a specified ROLE with respect to anything else in the model. | 5, 2, 3, 7 |
| ACCESS ROLE TYPE | The definition of a kind of ACCESS ROLE. By definition, the first of these must correspond to the sub-types of ACCESS ROLE: "Management role", "Enforcement role", "Permission role", and so forth. | 5, 2, 7 |
| *accessibility* | An *inherent* QUALITY CHARACTERISTIC that is a measure of the ability to access data when it is required. | 7 |
| *accuracy (to a surrogate source)* | An *inherent* QUALITY CHARACTERISTIC that is a measure of the degree to which data agrees with an original source of data (such as a form, document, or unaltered electronic data) received from an acknowledged source outside the control of the organization. | |
| *accuracy (to reality)* | An *inherent* QUALITY CHARACTERISTIC that is a measure of the degree to which data accurately reflects the real-world object or event being described. Accuracy is the highest degree of inherent information quality possible. | 7 |

*Continued*

| Term | Definition | Chapter |
|---|---|---|
| *action assertion* | A business rule that constrains data in explicit ways, such as requiring uniqueness, specified *optionality* and *functionality*, *referential integrity*, or *other constraints*. | 7, 2 |
| *activities* | The column in the *Architecture Framework* describing *how* an enterprise does what it does | 1 |
| ACTIVITY | A general term to describe something that is done. It is used when a more specific definition is not available. An ACTIVITY must be either a FUNCTION or a PROCESS. | 3, 1 |
| alethic proposition | An assertion of necessity (something must be true) or possibility (something can be true). This is the realm of the sciences. | 2 |
| ALTERNATIVE KEY | In *relational theory*, any UNIQUE KEY that is not a PRIMARY KEY. | 7 |
| ALTERNATIVE SYSTEM EVENT TYPE | One of a set of SYSTEM EVENT TYPES that are *part of* another SYSTEM EVENT TYPE. When the parent SYSTEM EVENT TYPE happens, it involves the triggering of only one of the ALTERNATIVE SYSTEM EVENT TYPES it is *composed of*. | 6 |
| APPLICATION CLASS | A CLASS IMPLEMENTATION in *object-oriented design* that is valuable for one application. Specifically this is either an EVENT RECOGNIZER CLASS or an EVENT MANAGER CLASS [Page-Jones 2000]. | 2 |
| APPLICATION SYSTEM | A collection of TABLES and PROGRAM MODULES developed together to address one or more business functions. | 2, 3 |
| *architect* | Someone skilled at deriving fundamental structures from the Business Owner's View. | |
| Architect's View | (Row Three of the *Architecture Framework*) A view of the underlying structures of Row Two, rendered in a more disciplined fashion, completing the conceptual model of the business. This is still without reference to any particular technology. | 1–7 |
| ARCHITECTURAL CLASS | A CLASS IMPLEMENTATION in *object-oriented design* that implements physical architecture, such as DATABASE MANIPULATION CLASS, HUMAN INTERFACE CLASS, or MACHINE COMMUNICATION CLASS [Page-Jones 2000]. | 2 |
| *Architecture Framework* | A scheme for representing a body of knowledge systematically. In this context, it consists of six rows describing the six perspectives of actors in the development of information systems, and six columns representing the six types of information involved: what, how, where, who, when, and why. Each cell represents a way of looking at one of these types of information from a particular perspective. | 1 |

| Term | Definition | Chapter |
|---|---|---|
| ASSESSMENT | A judgment about the implications of an INFLUENCER on either one or more MEANS (such as particular COURSES OF ACTION) or one or more ENDS, such as particular DESIRED RESULTS. | 7, 1, 4, 6 |
| ASSESSMENT ELEMENT | The fact that an ASSESSMENT concerns a particular END or MEANS. | 7, 4, 6 |
| ASSOCIATION CLASS ROLE | In UML, a RELATIONSHIP ROLE that relates an ASSOCIATION ENTITY CLASS to a RELATIONSHIP. | 2 |
| ASSOCIATION ENTITY CLASS | In UML, an ENTITY CLASS that records attributes of a RELATIONSHIP. It is connected to the RELATIONSHIP via an ASSOCIATION CLASS ROLE. | 2 |
| ASSOCIATIVE ROLE | An INFORMATION ENGINEERING ROLE that describes a relationship from one ENTITY CLASS to another that is not a *super-type* or a *sub-type*. | 2 |
| assumption | An INFLUENCER TYPE (a kind of "internal influencer") that is an assertion taken for granted or without proof. | 7 |
| attainable | A characteristic of OBJECTIVES: it is always possible to tell whether (and when) an OBJECTIVE has been achieved. | 7 |
| attribute | 1. (*UML diagram*) A descriptor of a kind of information captured about an *object class*.<br>2. (*Relational theory*) The definition of a descriptor of a *relation*. | 2, 1, 5 |
| ATTRIBUTE | A FACT TYPE ELEMENT (specifically a CHARACTERISTIC ASSIGNMENT) that is a descriptor of an ENTITY CLASS. | 2, 1 |
| ATTRIBUTE CLASS | A *business class* in *object-oriented design* that is a property of something. | 2 |
| ATTRIBUTE DEFINITION | The fact that an INSTANCE ATTRIBUTE in a Row Four object-oriented design is based on the definition of an ATTRIBUTE in a Row Three entity-relationship diagram. | 2 |
| ATTRIBUTE NAME | A BUSINESS TERM that describes a particular instance of an ATTRIBUTE in an occurrence of an ENTITY CLASS; probably its "Name". | 2 |
| ATTRIBUTE SELECTION | The fact that a particular ATTRIBUTE is included in the definition of a VIRTUAL ENTITY. | 2 |
| AUTHORSHIP ROLE | An ACCESS ROLE in which a PARTY is the creator *of* a RESOURSE. This is an ACCESS ROLE that is *an example of* an ACCESS ROLE TYPE OF "Authorship Role". | 5, 2 |

*Continued*

| Term | Definition | Chapter |
|------|------------|---------|
| *binary relationship* | A relationship between exactly two entity classes. | 2, 1 |
| *Boyce-Codd normal form* | In *relational theory,* a refinement of THIRD NORMAL FORM: No part of a primary key may be dependent on another part of that primary key. | 2 |
| BPR | (See *business process re-engineering.*) | 3 |
| *builder* | A person with the technological skills to create system artifacts such as program modules and databases. | 1–7 |
| Builder's View | (Row Five of the *Architecture Framework*) A view of the details of a particular language, database storage specifications, networks, and so forth. The *builder's view* is what ANSI called the *physical schema*. | 1–7 |
| BUSINESS CLASS | A CLASS IMPLEMENTATION in *object-oriented design* that is valuable for one industry or company, such as a RELATIONSHIP CLASS, a ROLE CLASS, an ATTRIBUTE CLASS, or a CLASS OF ENTITY [Page-Jones 2000]. (This Row Four entity class is linked to the appropriate Row Three entity classes via CLASS DEFINITION.) | 2 |
| BUSINESS COMMUNICATION LINK | The fact that there is a physical means of communicating from one SITE to another SITE. | 4 |
| BUSINESS COMMUNICATION LINK TYPE | The definition of a kind of BUSINESS COMMUNICATION LINK. | 4 |
| BUSINESS CONCEPT | Something we understand to exist or to be the case. | 2, 5 |
| *business event type* | The definition of a kind of thing that can happen. It may be an EXTERNAL BUSINESS EVENT TYPE (outside the enterprise's control) or an INTERNAL BUSINESS EVENT TYPE, which occurs within the enterprise and under its control. | 6, 5 |
| BUSINESS LOCATION | The fact that a particular BUSINESS EVENT TYPE or BUSINESS PROCESS is located *in* a particular SITE. | 4 |
| BUSINESS LOCATION TYPE | The definition of a kind of BUSINESS LOCATION. | 4 |
| *business metadata* | Data describing a body of information from a business person's point of view. That is, these are descriptions of what data are available and in what terms. | 1 |
| *business owner* | Someone who carries out the daily business of the enterprise. This could be a middle manager, an accountant, a shop foreman, or some such person. | 1–7 |

| Term | Definition | Chapter |
|------|-----------|---------|
| Business Owner's View | (Row Two of the *Architecture Framework*) Defines—in business terms—the nature of the business, including its structure, processes, organization, and so forth. There are usually multiple business owners' views of a given enterprise, and these may overlap or even contradict each other. | 1–7 |
| BUSINESS POLICY | A nonactionable DIRECTIVE that guides the activities of the business or governs them in a general way. Note that it "governs"; it does not control or shape COURSES OF ACTION. For example, to say that "We will not permit on-site visits" constrains the TACTICS available for meeting the STRATEGY to "Increase market share". It does not specify what those TACTICS should be. | 7 |
| *business process* | An ACTIVITY as carried out by business people, including the MECHANISMS involved. This is in the domain of Row Two, the Business Owner's View. Alternatively, the ARCHITECT in Row Three sees a SYSTEM PROCESS which is about the data transformations involved in carrying out a BUSINESS PROCESS.* In either case, processes can be viewed at a high level or in atomic detail. | 3, 5 |
| BUSINESS PROCESS DESIGN | The fact that a SYSTEM PROCESS is used for the design of a BUSINESS PROCESS. | 3 |
| *business process re-engineering (BPR)* | A technique for evaluating how an enterprise (or part of an enterprise) operates. This involves process modeling, specifically with an eye to identifying processes that do not contribute to the enterprise's profitability. | 3 |
| BUSINESS RULE | Either a set of conditions, a DIRECTIVE, or an "element of guidance". A constraint on a business's behavior.<br><br>There is not yet an industry standard definition of *business rule* although authors seem to be converging. Barbara von Halle defines it as "the set of conditions that govern a business event so that it occurs in a way that is acceptable to the business" (2002, p. 28). In its *original* | 7 |

*Note that, in spite of the use of the word* system *to distinguish what are Row Three activities from the "business processes" of the Business Owner's View, this is still not describing any particular computer system technology. It is only concerned with what processing of data might be carried out, and it remains completely independent of any particular technology that might be used.*

*Continued*

| Term | Definition | Chapter |
|---|---|---|
| BUSINESS RULE *(cont'd)* | Motivation Paper, the Business Rules Group defined a business rule as "a DIRECTIVE, intended to govern, guide or influence business behavior, in support of a BUSINESS POLICY that has been formulated in response to an OPPORTUNITY, THREAT, STRENGTH or WEAKNESS" [BRG 2005, p. 18].<br><br>In its submission to the Object Management Group, "The Semantics of Business Vocabulary and Business Rules", the Business Rules Team* defines a business rule as "an element of guidance that introduces an obligation or necessity, [and] that is under business jurisdiction" [BRT 2005, pp. 162–163]. | |
| BUSINESS RULE MAPPING | The association of a BUSINESS RULE to one or more DOMAINS, UNIQUE IDENTIFIERS, or SYSTEM CONSTRAINTS. | 7 |
| BUSINESS RULE MAPPING ELEMENT | The fact that a particular BUSINESS RULE MAPPPING is *to* a UNIQUE IDENTIFER, a DOMAIN, or a SYSTEM CONSTRAINT. A component of a BUSINESS RULE MAPPING. | 7 |
| BUSINESS TERM | The fact that a particular WORD or PHRASE can have a particular meaning. That is, it is the fact that a particular BUSINESS CONCEPT can be described by a particular SIGNIFIER (a *word* or *phrase*). | 2, 7 |
| *cascade delete* | A *referential integrity* constraint on a FOREIGN KEY that requires, upon deletion of a row in a TABLE, deletion of any rows in other TABLES with FOREIGN KEY values that point to the row in question. | 7 |
| *CASE* | (See *computer-aided systems engineering*.) | 1 |
| CELL INSTANCE | A physical datum captured in a ROW and COLUMN of a physical TABLE INSTANCE. | 2, 3 |
| CHARACTERISTIC | 1. An attribute or parameter in the *abstract model* that can be used to describe something of interest.<br>2. A FACT TYPE that is something you can measure about one or more BUSINESS CONCEPTS. The fact that a particular CHARACTERISTIC is about a particular BUSINESS CONCEPT is a CHARACTERISTIC ASSIGNMENT, a kind of FACT TYPE ELEMENT. | 2, 1 |
| CHARACTERISTIC ASSIGNMENT | 1. In the *abstract model*, the fact that a particular CHARACTERISTIC is appropriate to describe members of a THING TYPE.<br>2. The fact that a particular CHARACTERISTIC is about a particular BUSINESS CONCEPT. | 2, 1 |
| CHARACTERISTIC VALUE | (*Abstract model*) The fact that a particular THING has a particular value for a CHARACTERISTIC. | 1 |

*The Business Rules Team now includes vendors as members, while the Business Rules Group did not.*

| Term | Definition | Chapter |
|---|---|---|
| *Chen notation* | The first version of entity/relationship modeling, created by Dr. Peter Chen in 1976. It is noteworthy in its use of diamond shapes to represent relationships as things. | 2 |
| *chronosynclastic infundibula* | Places in the Universe where each Daddy could finally catch on to what the other Daddy was talking about. These places are where all the different kinds of truths fit together as nicely as the parts in your Daddy's solar watch [Vonnequt 1959]. | Preface |
| CLASS ATTRIBUTE | A CLASS ELEMENT that is a descriptor of an entire CLASS IMPLEMENTATION, such as "Number of instances". | 2 |
| CLASS DEFINITION | The fact that a BUSINESS CLASS in a Row Four *object-oriented design* is based on an ENTITY CLASS in a Row Three entity-relationship model. | 2 |
| CLASS ELEMENT | A component or characteristic of a CLASS IMPLEMENTATION. This may be either an INSTANCE ATTRIBUTE, which is a characteristic that is distinct for each occurrence (instance) of a CLASS IMPLEMENTATION, or a CLASS ATTRIBUTE, which is a characteristic that applies to the entire class and all of its occurrences. | 2, 7 |
| CLASS IMPLEMENTATION | The definition of a kind of OBJECT as implemented in program code. | 2, 3 |
| CLASS OF ENTITY | A *business class* in *object-oriented design* that is behaving as an *entity class* in an *object model*. | 2 |
| CLASS TYPE | The definition of a kind of CLASS IMPLEMENTATION. By definition, the first instances of this will be the same as the sub-types shown for CLASS IMPLEMENTATION: "Business class", "Architectural class", and so on. | 2 |
| CODE SET | The collection of VALID CODES that constitutes a *representation* of a VALUE SET. | 7 |
| *column* | An area of interest or a kind of information for each perspective in an *Architecture Framework*. Columns describe "Data", "Activities", "Locations", "People and Organizations", "Timing and Events", and "Motivation". | 1 |
| COLUMN | If a TABLE represents data about something, a COLUMN is the place in a TABLE to keep information about some aspect of that thing. Each *row* in the TABLE contains one value in each COLUMN. | 2 |

*Continued*

| Term | Definition | Chapter |
|---|---|---|
| COLUMN ATTRIBUTE MAPPING | The fact that a particular ATTRIBUTE in a Row Three entity-relationship model is implemented as a particular COLUMN in a Row Four database design. | 2 |
| COLUMN INSTANCE | An actual occurrence of a COLUMN as designed, but existing in a physical database. | 2 |
| COLUMN SELECTION | The fact that a COLUMN in a particular TABLE is part of the definition of a VIEW. | 2 |
| Common Warehouse Metamodel | A data warehousing and analysis domain metadata model created by the Object Management Group. | 1 |
| COMPANY | An ORGANIZATION recognized as a legal entity. | 5 |
| comparative evaluator | If this is an integrity constraint (condition indicator = "False"), it is a SYSTEM CONSTRAINT ARGUMENT to a SYSTEM CONSTRAINT, requiring that an object be greater than, less than, or equal to the constrained object. This is an example of an OTHER SYSTEM CONSTRAINT TYPE. | 7 |
| completeness (of values) | An *inherent* QUALITY CHARACTERISTIC that is a measure of the extent to which an ATTRIBUTE has values for all instances of an ENTITY CLASS. | 7 |
| COMPUTATION | An expression used *to calculate the value of* a COLUMN. | 7 |
| COMPUTATION ELEMENT | The fact that a COLUMN, a "Constant", or a SYSTEM VARIABLE is used in the COMPUTATION to *calculate the value of* a COLUMN. | 7 |
| computer-aided systems engineering (CASE) | An approach to developing systems that involve using computers to assist in modeling a *universe of discourse* and then to generate a system based on that model. | 1 |
| computer time-sharing | A technology developed in the late 1960s that permitted multiple people to use a single computer at the same time by dividing tasks and providing a split second of service to each user. | |
| conceptual data model (schema) | In the ANSI *four-schema architecture*, this is a description of a portion of an enterprise in terms of the fundamental things of significant interest to it. They are fundamental in that most things seen by business owners are examples of these. The model is constructed in a rigorous manner, being *fully normalized*, eschewing *many-to-many relationships* and is expressed in terms of *binary relationships* only. | 1, 2 |

| Term | Definition | Chapter |
|------|------------|---------|
| *concurrency* | An *inherent* QUALITY CHARACTERISTIC that is a measure of the information float or lag time between when data is knowable (created or changed) in one database and is also knowable in a redundant or distributed database. | 7 |
| CONSEQUENCE | An action or other implication of failing to follow a BUSINESS RULE. | 7 |
| CONSEQUENCE INVOCATION | The fact that a particular BUSINESS RULE can invoke a particular CONSEQUENCE. | 7 |
| CONSEQUENCE OF VIOLATION | Something that can happen as a result of data being entered that violates a SYSTEM CONSTRAINT. | 7 |
| CONSEQUENCE OF VIOLATION ASSIGNMENT | The fact that violation of a particular SYSTEM CONSTRAINT can invoke a particular CONSEQUENCE OF VIOLATION. | 7 |
| *constraint* | A BUSINESS RULE that constrains behavior in some way or constrains what data may or may not be updated. | 2 |
| *contextual clarity* | A *pragmatic* QUALITY CHARACTERISTIC that is a measure of the relative degree to which data presentation enables the knowledge worker to understand the meaning of the data and avoid misinterpretation. | 7 |
| CONTINUOUS ATTRIBUTE | An ATTRIBUTE whose values are taken from the set of real numbers. This is as opposed to DISCRETE ATTRIBUTES, whose values come from a list of permitted values. | 7 |
| CONTINUOUS COLUMN | A COLUMN whose value can be any real number. | 7 |
| *contributor* | According to the *Dublin Core*, a PARTY that participated in creating a DOCUMENT or other RESOURCE. | 2 |
| COPY | A physical representation of a DOCUMENT. This is either a PHYSICAL COPY (with a physical substance) or a VIRTUAL COPY (sent or stored electronically). | 2, 5 |
| *copy library* | A listing of data layouts constructed so as to be usable by many programs, usually in COBOL. | 1 |
| *corporate value* | An INFLUENCER TYPE (a kind of "internal influencer") that is an ideal, custom, or institution the enterprise promotes or agrees with. Each of these in turn must be an *explicit corporate value* or an *implicit corporate value*. | 7 |
| COURSE OF ACTION | An approach or plan for configuring some aspect of the enterprise. This involves the use of things, processes, locations, people, timing, or motivation. | 7, 3, 5 |

*Continued*

| Term | Definition | Chapter |
|------|-----------|---------|
| COVERAGE | 1. According to the *Dublin Core,* the extent to which a DOCUMENT or other RESOURCE describes a particular part of the earth.<br>2. The fact that a RESOURCE applies to a particular GEOGRAPHIC LOCATION. | 2 |
| *creator* | According to the *Dublin Core,* a PARTY that was instrumental in producing a DOCUMENT or other RESOURCE. | 2 |
| CUSTODIAL BUSINESS PROCESS | An ESSENTIAL BUSINESS PROCESS required to provide data to support a FUNDAMENTAL BUSINESS PROCESS. | 3 |
| *custodial process* | An *essential process* required to provide data to support a *fundamental business process.* | 3 |
| CUSTODIAL SYSTEM PROCESS | An ESSENTIAL SYSTEM PROCESS required to provide data to support a FUNDAMENTAL SYSTEM PROCESS. | 3 |
| *CWM* | (See *Common Warehouse Metamodel.*) | 1 |
| *cybernetics* | The science of communications and control. | 6 |
| *data* | The column in the *Architecture Framework* that is concerned with *what* things are significant enough to an enterprise that they require holding information about them. | 1 |
| *data dictionary* | In the days of mainframe computers, this was a listing of record layouts, describing each field in each type of file. | 1 |
| DATA FLOW | The fact that data, in the *form* of a VIRTUAL ENTITY CLASS, can be sent *from* a PARTY, POSITION, EXTERNAL ENTITY, or SYSTEM PROCESS *to* a PARTY, POSITION, EXTERNAL ENTITY, or SYSTEM PROCESS. | 3, 4, 5 |
| *data flow diagram* | A graphic representation of the interactions between different processes in an organization in terms of data flow communications among them. This may be a *physical data flow diagram* that describes processes and flows in terms of the MECHANISMS involved, a *logical data flow diagram* that is without any representation of the MECHANSM, or an *essential data flow diagram* that is a *logical data flow diagram* organized in terms of the processes that respond to each *external event.* | 3 |
| DATA GROUP | A *relation* that may be either a physical TABLE or a virtual VIEW. | 2 |

| Term | Definition | Chapter |
|---|---|---|
| DATA GROUP COLLECTION | A set of DATA GROUPS (TABLES or VIEWS) that are viewed together for some reason. They may have related meanings or related purposes. | 2, 3, 5 |
| data mart | A database in a *data warehouse* configuration that holds a subset of data specifically organized for a particular kind of reporting. | 2 |
| data model | A representation of the structure of data. As used in this book, the term refers to a *conceptual data model*, which describes data in terms of their inherent semantics, without regard to how they might be organized in a physical database. Some use the term to describe a *logical data model* that organizes data in terms of a specific data management technology, such as relational tables and columns, object-oriented classes, or ISAM hierarchies. | |
| data resource data | Michael Brackett's term for metadata [Brackett 2000]. | |
| DATA STORE | A medium for storing data temporarily. | 3 |
| data warehouse | 1. A centralized database for collecting the data from numerous other systems so that they can be made available for management reporting. The database is close to *3rd Normal Form*.<br>2. A system that includes the central database described in 1; *plus* procedures for *extracting, transforming, and loading* data from other systems; *and* one or more *data marts* that organize subsets of the data for particular reporting purposes. | 1 |
| DATABASE CONSTRAINT | In relational database design, a configuration that restricts the updating or deletion of data. This includes UNIQUE KEY, FOREIGN KEY, COMPUTATION, or any other encoded restriction on the updating of data. | 7 |
| DATABASE CONSTRAINT ELEMENT | Because a CONSTRAINT usually involves more than one COLUMN, this is the fact that a particular COLUMN is part of the definition of a particular CONSTRAINT. | 7 |
| DATABASE INSTALLATION | The fact that a TABLE INSTANCE exists in a particular DATABASE INSTANCE. | 4, 2, 5 |

*Continued*

| Term | Definition | Chapter |
|---|---|---|
| DATABASE INSTANCE | A VIRTUAL SITE that is a collection of tables managed as an identified group by a particular DATABASE INSTALLATION. | 4, 2, 5 |
| database management system | A software product used to create and manage data in a coherent fashion. Different DATABASE MANAGEMENT SYSTEMS are created and sold by different companies. | 3 |
| DATABASE MANIPULATION CLASS | An *architectural class* in *object-oriented design* such as "Transaction" and "Backup" [Page-Jones 2000]. | 2 |
| date | According to the *Dublin Core*, the point in time when a DOCUMENT or other RESOURCE was created. | 2 |
| DBMS VERSION | A particular edition of a DATABASE MANAGEMENT SYSTEM. | 2, 4, 5 |
| decussate | Intersect, cross. | 4 |
| definition conformance | An *inherent* QUALITY CHARACTERISTIC that is a measure of the consistency of the meaning of the actual value of each datum with its definition. | 7 |
| delimiting indicator | An attribute of CHARACTERISTIC ASSIGNMENT that determines whether this use of this CHARACTERISTIC is sufficient to identify occurrences of the BUSINESS CONCEPT being *described by* that CHARACTERISTIC ASSIGNMENT. | 2 |
| deontic proposition | An assertion of obligation (something is required to be so) or permission (something is permitted to be so). This is the realm of BUSINESS RULES. | 2 |
| derivation | A BUSINESS RULE (including laws of nature) that defines how knowledge in one form may be transformed into other knowledge, possibly in a different form. | 2 |
| DERIVATION | A DOMAIN that specifies how ATTRIBUTES *constrained by* that DOMAIN are calculated from other ATTRIBUTE variables. | 7 |
| DERIVATION ELEMENT | The use of a variable in a DERIVATION. This may be either another ATTRIBUTE, a "Constant", or a SYSTEM VARIABLE, such as "Today's date". It includes an "Operator" that tells a computing engine the role of this DERIVATION ELEMENT in the overall DERIVATION. | 7 |
| derivation integrity | A *pragmatic* QUALITY CHARACTERISTIC that is a measure of the correctness with which derived or calculated data are calculated from their base data. | 7 |
| derived fact | A *fact* whose value is derived mathematically from other facts. | 2 |

| Term | Definition | Chapter |
|---|---|---|
| *description* | According to the *Dublin Core*, full text description of the DOCUMENT or other RESOURCE. | 2 |
| DESIGN COMMUNICATION LINK | The fact that a communication link between two SITES is part of the system design. | 4 |
| *designer* | A person with sufficient knowledge of the technologies required to define the structure and nature of a proposed system. | 1–7 |
| DESIGN LINK IMPLEMENTATION | The fact that a particular PROGRAMMING UNIT COMMUNICATION will make use of a DESIGN COMMUNICATION LINK. | 4 |
| Designer's View | (Row Four of the *Architecture Framework*) A view of how technology may be used to address the information-processing needs identified in the previous rows. Here, object-oriented databases are chosen over relational ones (or vice versa), kinds of programming languages are selected (third or fourth generation, object-oriented, and so on), program structures are defined, user interfaces are specified, and so forth. | 1–7 |
| DESIRED RESULT | An END that is a state or target that the enterprise intends to maintain. There are two kinds of DESIRED RESULTS: GOALS and OBJECTIVES. | 7, 3, 6 |
| *detailed representation* | The model seen by the *builder* in Row Five of the *Architecture Framework*. | 1 |
| DIRECTION | A MEANS EFFECT that is the fact that a DIRECTIVE affects the operation of a BUSINESS PROCESS. It must be either a GUIDANCE or a GOVERNANCE. | 6, 7 |
| DIRECTIVE | A specification that constrains COURSES OF ACTION. It does this in two ways. First, it may simply be designed to *govern* one or more COURSES OF ACTION. For example, "A loan is not to be granted to someone whose credit rating is lower than B" governs the COURSE OF ACTION concerned with granting loans. A second effect is that sometimes a DIRECTIVE is itself the source of a COURSE OF ACTION. That is, a DIRECTIVE may be the *source of* those COURSES OF ACTION whose whole purpose is to enforce that DIRECTIVE. | 7, 5 |
| DIRECTIVE MOTIVATION | The fact that a particular ASSESSMENT ELEMENT (a STRENGTH, WEAKNESS, OPPORTUNITY, or THREAT) is the reason for a particular DIRECTIVE (BUSINESS POLICY or BUSINESS RULE). | 7 |

*Continued*

| Term | Definition | Chapter |
|---|---|---|
| DIRECTIVE ROLE | The fact that a particular DIRECTIVE (BUSINESS POLICY or BUSINESS RULE) is acting as the INTERNAL INFLUENCER. | 7 |
| DISCRETE ATTRIBUTE | An ATTRIBUTE whose value must be taken from an explicit list of PERMITTED ATTRIBUTE VALUES. | 7 |
| DISCRETE INSTANCE ATTRIBUTE | An object-oriented INSTANCE ATTRIBUTE that can only take a value from a list of explicit values. | 2, 6, 7 |
| DISCRETE INSTANCE VALID VALUE | A value that can be assumed by a DISCRETE INSTANCE ATTRIBUTE. | 6 |
| DISPLAY ELEMENT | An INTERFACE ELEMENT that simply displays text or a graphic. | 5 |
| DISPLAY GROUP | A collection of elements displayed on a screen that is *part of* a WINDOW. | 5 |
| DOCUMENT | A kind of RESOURCE usually embodied as either a representation of words and symbols on paper or as the virtual equivalent of that in electronic storage. | 2 |
| DOMAIN | A CHARACTERISTIC FACT TYPE that may be a *constraint on* one or more ATTRIBUTES. | 7, 2 |
| *Dublin Core* | An organization that has set out to standardize the way documents, recordings, web pages, and other media are described. | 2 |
| EFFORT | A MEANS EFFECT that is the *use of* a BUSINESS PROCESS to *achieve* a DESIRED RESULT. It is *invoked by* a COURSE OF ACTION. | 7, 3, 4, 6 |
| ELEMENTARY BUSINESS FUNCTION | A most atomic FUNCTION—one that cannot be broken into smaller FUNCTIONS. Once started, an ELEMENTARY FUNCTION cannot be interrupted before completion. | 3 |
| ELEMENTARY BUSINESS PROCESS | The most atomic BUSINESS PROCESS that cannot be broken down into smaller processes. Once started, an ELEMENTARY BUSINESS PROCESS cannot be interrupted before completion. | 3 |
| ELEMENTARY ENTITY CLASS | The definition of a thing of significance to the organization about which it wishes to hold information. This is as opposed to a VIRTUAL ENTITY CLASS, which is a composition based on other ENTITY CLASSES. | 2, 6 |
| ELEMENTARY SYSTEM PROCESS | The most atomic SYSTEM PROCESS that cannot be broken down into smaller processes. Once started, an ELEMENTARY BUSINESS PROCESS cannot be interrupted before completion. | 3, 6 |

| Term | Definition | Chapter |
|---|---|---|
| E-MAIL SITE | A VIRTUAL SITE identified by a domain name and an e-mail address. | 4 |
| EMPLOYMENT | A PARTY RELATIONSHIP that involves a PERSON working for an ORGANIZATION in a formal way, normally in exchange for pecuniary compensation. | 5 |
| ENABLEMENT | The fact that one COURSE OF ACTION makes another COURSE OF ACTION possible. That is, a particular COURSE OF ACTION enables the carrying out of another COURSE OF ACTION. | 7 |
| ENCAPSULATION | In *object-oriented design*, the principle that it should be possible to refer to an object with behavior and not know anything about how that behavior is implemented. | |
| END | Something that the enterprise sets out to accomplish. Primary among these, of course is the company's VISION, but the concept of END also includes various kinds of DESIRED RESULT. | 7, 4, 5, 6 |
| ENFORCEMENT LEVEL | A measure of the extent to which any BUSINESS RULE can be enforced. | 7 |
| ENFORCEMENT LEVEL IMPLEMENTATION | The fact that a particular BUSINESS RULE is *subject to* a particular ENFORCEMENT LEVEL. | 7 |
| ENFORCEMENT ROLE | A kind of ACCESS ROLE that is the fact that a PARTY, POSITION ASSIGNMENT, POSITION, and so on is responsible for the enforcement of business rules for a SITE, SYMBOL, a BUSINESS CONCEPT, a COPY of a DOCUMENT, a RESOURCE, a BUSINESS DESCRIPTION SPECIFICATION, an ACTIVITY, an INFLUENCER, a MEANS, an END, a SYSTEM PROCESS, a SYSTEM CONSTRAINT, a PERSISTENCE MECHANISM (a TABLE, a VIEW, or a COLUMN), a PROGRAM COPY, a DATABASE INSTALLATION, or a TABLE INSTANCE. This is an ACCESS ROLE that is *an example of* an ACCESS ROLE TYPE of "Enforcement Role". | 5, 7 |
| *enterprise model* | A comprehensive model (usually a DATA MODEL) of an entire organization, or a significant *part of* it, as seen by the *business owner* in Row Two of the *Architecture Framework*. | 1 |
| ENTITY CLASS | A thing of significance to the enterprise about which it wishes to capture information. | 2, 1, 5, 6 |
| *entity class* | (See ENTITY CLASS.) | 1 |

*Continued*

| Term | Definition | Chapter |
|------|-----------|---------|
| ENTITY CLASS NAME | A BUSINESS TERM that describes a particular occurrence of an ENTITY CLASS. Normally, this is also the value of the ENTITY CLASS's "Name". | 2 |
| ENTITY CLASS SELECTION | The fact that a particular ENTITY CLASS is part of the definition of a VIRTUAL ENTITY CLASS. | 2 |
| ENTITY CLASS STATE | An ENTITY CLASS typically moves through various states. Depending on the ENTITY CLASS, the state could describe its degree of completion, relevance of an activity, or a specific set of values for other characteristics. | 6 |
| ENTITY CLASS STATE TYPE | The definition of a particular kind of ENTITY CLASS STATE. | 6 |
| entity life history | A modeling technique that describes the events that affect an ENTITY CLASS STATE. | 1, 6 |
| entity-relationship model | (See conceptual data model.) | |
| entity-relationship modeling | A modeling technique that represents data structure in terms of the things of significance to an enterprise (entity classes) about which it wishes to hold information (attributes), and binary relationships between them. | 2, 1 |
| epistemological proposition | An assertion that something is known to be the case. These are the assertions of a typical data model. | 2 |
| equivalence of redundant or distributed data | An inherent QUALITY CHARACTERISTIC that is a measure of the degree to which data in one data collection or database is semantically equivalent to data about the same object or event in another data collection or database. | 7 |
| ESSENTIAL BUSINESS PROCESS | A BUSINESS PROCESS that is a collection of ELEMENTARY BUSINESS PROCESSES to constitute the complete response to an EXTERNAL BUSINESS EVENT TYPE. | 3, 6 |
| essential data flow diagram | A data flow diagram (consisting of either BUSINESS PROCESSES or SYSTEM PROCESSES) whose processes each represent the complete response to an external event. | 3, 1 |
| essential indicator | An attribute of CHARACTERISTIC ASSIGNMENT that determines whether an occurrence of a BUSINESS CONCEPT described by the CHARACTERISTIC ASSIGNMENT must have a value for the CHARACTERISTIC involved. | 2 |

| Term | Definition | Chapter |
|------|-----------|---------|
| ESSENTIAL SYSTEM PROCESS | A SYSTEM PROCESS that is a collection of ELEMENTARY SYSTEM PROCESSES to constitute the complete response to an external SYSTEM EVENT TYPE—that is, one whose External Indicator is "True". | 3, 6, 1 |
| ESSENTIAL SYSTEM PROCESS DIAGRAM | A representation of the processes carried out by an enterprise or a significant part of an enterprise, where SYSTEM PROCESSES are constrained each to be the complete response to an external SYSTEM EVENT whose External Indicator is "True". | 3, 6, 1 |
| *ETL* | (See *extraction, transfer, and load facility*.) | 1 |
| *event* | Something that happens at an instant in the world that causes a process to be launched. | 1, 2, 6 |
| EVENT MANAGER | An *application class* in *object-oriented design* that carries out an appropriate policy when an *event recognizer* signals the occurrence of a specific event. | 2 |
| EVENT RECOGNIZER | An *application class* in *object-oriented design* that monitors or checks for the occurrence of specific events. | 2 |
| *event type* | The definition of a category of events. | |
| EVENT TYPE SEQUENCE | The fact that one SEQUENTIAL SYSTEM EVENT TYPE comes *after* another SEQUENTIAL SYSTEM EVENT TYPE, in the context of a parent SYSTEM EVENT TYPE that it is a *part of*. | 6 |
| EXECUTABLE MODULE | A PROGRAM MODULE that describes processing of some sort. This is as opposed to a CLASS IMPLEMENTATION that describes the structure of the objects a program is to work on. | 3 |
| *explicit corporate value* | An "internal influencer" that is a corporate value explicitly stated. | 7 |
| EXTERNAL BUSINESS EVENT TYPE | A BUSINESS EVENT TYPE that is outside the enterprise's control. | 6, 5 |
| *external entity* | In a *data flow diagram*, this is an ultimate source or destination of data. Usually, this is a PARTY. | 3 |
| *external event* | Something that happens outside the control of the enterprise, and to which the enterprise must react. | |
| *external schema* | In the ANSI *four-schema architecture*, this is a description of a particular individual's view of the enterprise. Different individuals will see it differently, so these views may overlap or conflict. | 1, 2 |

*Continued*

| Term | Definition | Chapter |
|---|---|---|
| *extraction, transfer, and load facility* | Software that specializes in copying data from one place to another according to specifications. | 1 |
| FACT | An instance of a FACT TYPE. | 2 |
| FACT ELEMENT | An instance of a FACT TYPE ELEMENT. | 2 |
| FACT TYPE | An expression that links BUSINESS CONCEPTS together. Both the nature and the operating structure of an organization can be described in terms of the facts that relate the enterprise's terms to each other. A *fact* may be expressed in a sentence. | 2 |
| FACT TYPE ELEMENT | The fact that a BUSINESS CONCEPT is part of a FACT TYPE. | 2 |
| FIELD | An INTERFACE ELEMENT that displays a column from the database or accepts a typed-in value to be added to the database. (A FIELD may be the *use or display of* one and only one COLUMN in a database. It also may be a *trigger of* an EXECUTABLE MODULE when the "Enter" key is pressed.) | 5 |
| *fifth normal form* | In *relational theory*, the fifth of Dr. Codd's constraints on a relational design: A three-way (or more) relationship is redundant if all of its occurrences can be derived from combinations of two-way occurrences. | 2 |
| *first normal form* | In *relational theory*, the first of Dr. Codd's constraints on a relational design: Every *tuple* may have only one value for an *attribute* in a *relation*. | 2 |
| FOREIGN KEY | A combination of COLUMNS in a TABLE, where the value of each COLUMN is equal to the value of a PRIMARY KEY ELEMENT in another TABLE. The set of COLUMNS that constitute the FOREIGN KEY must correspond to the set of COLUMNS that constitute the PRIMARY KEY in the other TABLE. | 7 |
| FOREIGN KEY ELEMENT | The fact that a particular COLUMN is *used as* a component of a FOREIGN KEY. Each FOREIGN KEY ELEMENT is the *use of* a COLUMN in the TABLE containing the FOREIGN KEY, and *a reference to* a COLUMN in the TABLE that the FOREIGN KEY is pointing to (a PRIMARY KEY ELEMENT in that TABLE). | 7 |
| *format* | According to the *Dublin Core*, the physical nature of the DOCUMENT or other RESOURCE: newspaper, book, TV program, and so on. | 2 |
| FOUNDATION CLASS | A CLASS IMPLEMENTATION in *object-oriented design* that is valuable across all businesses and architectures, including FUNDAMENTAL, STRUCTURAL, and SEMANTIC classes [Page-Jones 2000] | 2 |

| Term | Definition | Chapter |
|------|-----------|---------|
| *four-schema architecture* | A view, developed in 1975 by the ANSI/X3/SPARC Study Group on Data Base Management Systems, which sees various business people as having different "schemas" in their heads and that each represents a particular view of the enterprise's data. These *external schemas* overlap and often conflict. A *conceptual schema* can be drawn up that integrates all these external views. This can then be reformed into one or more *logical schemas* to reflect particular database management approaches. Each *logical schema* is then rendered on physical media in terms of a *physical schema*. The point of this approach is that these views are relatively independent of each other. | 1, 2 |
| *fourth normal form* | In *relational theory*, the fourth of Dr. Codd's constraints on a relational design: No column within a PRIMARY KEY may be completely dependent on another column within the same PRIMARY KEY. | 2 |
| *framework cell* | The intersection of a ROW and a COLUMN in the *Architecture Framework*. Specifically, a particular kind of information ("Data", "Activities", and so on) from a particular perspective ("Planner's View", "Business Owner's View", and so on). | 1 |
| FUNCTION | A type of ACTIVITY to carry out a MISSION, GOAL, or OBJECTIVE of the enterprise. It is described solely in terms of what it is intended to accomplish, without regard to the technology used to carry it out or who is to perform it. This is also described without reference to time. | 3, 1, 5 |
| *functional verifier* | If this is an integrity constraint (Condition indicator = "False"), it requires an object to assume a function relative to the constrained object. For example, the value of an attribute may be required to be unique within an entity class. If this is a condition (Condition indicator = "True"), it tests to see whether this is so. This is an example of an OTHER SYSTEM CONSTRAINT TYPE. | 7 |
| *functioning system* | That which is seen in Row Six in the *Architecture Framework*. This describes existing programs, databases, procedures, and responsibilities. | 1 |
| FUNDAMENTAL BUSINESS PROCESS | An ESSENTIAL BUSINESS PROCESS that is used to directly *implement* a BUSINESS FUNCTION. | 3 |

*Continued*

| Term | Definition | Chapter |
|---|---|---|
| FUNDAMENTAL CLASS | A kind of *foundation class*. This is a basic class such as "Integer", "Boolean", or "Char" [Page-Jones 2000]. | 2 |
| *fundamental process* | An *essential process* that is central to the functioning of the enterprise. | 3 |
| FUNDAMENTAL SYSTEM PROCESS | An ESSENTIAL SYSTEM PROCESS used for the BUSINESS PROCESS DESIGN of a BUSINESS PROCESS (an ESSENTIAL BUSINESS PROCESS) that is directly *to implement* a BUSINESS FUNCTION. | 3 |
| GENERALIZATION ROLE | An INFORMATION ENGINEERING ROLE that is an ENTITY CLASS'S being a *super-type* or a *sub-type* of another ENTITY CLASS. | 2 |
| GENERATION | The fact that a PROGRAM MODULE was in fact generated via a GENERATION SPECIFICATION. | 3 |
| GENERATION SPECIFICATION | The fact that a PROGRAM MODULE can be generated according to specifications contained in a PERSISTENCE MECHANISM (for example, a TABLE or a COLUMN). | 3 |
| GEOGRAPHIC AREA | A GEOGRAPHIC LOCATION that is two-dimensional, covering an identified area. | 2 |
| GEOGRAPHIC LOCATION | Any identified place on the Earth* in one, two, or three dimensions. Sub-types can include GEOGRAPHIC AREA, GEOGRAPHIC POINT, and GEOGRAPHIC SOLID (although the last is not included in this metamodel). | 2 |
| GEOGRAPHIC LOCATION TYPE | The definition of a kind of GEOGRAPHIC LOCATION. The first occurrences of these must be the same as the sub-types of GEOGRAPHIC LOCATION in the model—"Geopolitical area", "Management area", and so on. | 4 |
| GEOGRAPHIC POINT | A GEOGRAPHIC LOCATION that is a point in one dimension. GEOGRAPHIC POINTS are used to define the boundaries of GEOGRAPHIC AREAS. | 4 |
| GEOGRAPHIC STRUCTURE | The fact that one GEOGRAPHIC LOCATION may overlap or include another GEOGRAPHIC LOCATION. The Attribute Inclusive Indicator is "True" if the first GEOGRAPHIC LOCATION is entirely contained within the second. It is "False" if they simply overlap. | 4 |
| GEOPOLITICAL AREA | A GEOGRAPHIC AREA whose boundaries are defined by law or treaty, such as a state or country. | 2 |

*Yes, it's true: This is a very geocentric book. The reader is encouraged to produce the inter-planetary (inter-stellar?) version.

| Term | Definition | Chapter |
|---|---|---|
| GOAL | A specific statement about a state or condition of the enterprise to be brought about or sustained through appropriate MEANS [BRG 2005, p. 8]. A GOAL is an *amplifier* of a VISION. That is, whereas a VISION describes a future state of the enterprise in general, a GOAL is one of the steps to be taken to accomplish that VISION. A GOAL, by definition, is more narrow than a VISION. | 7, 5, 1 |
| GOVERNANCE | A kind of DIRECTION *from* a DIRECTIVE describing the boundaries and direction for a BUSINESS PROCESS. | 7, 6 |
| GOVERNMENT AGENCY | An ORGANIZATION that is part of an international, national, state, or local government. | 5 |
| GUIDANCE | A kind of DIRECTION *from* a DIRECTIVE describing an overall supervision of a BUSINESS PROCESS. | 7, 6 |
| *guideline* | A kind of BUSINESS RULE that is suggested, but not enforced. | 7 |
| *habit* | An INFLUENCER TYPE (a kind of "internal influencer") that is a customary practice or use. | 7 |
| *homonym* | If a WORD or PHRASE is *used in* a BUSINESS TERM to *represent* a BUSINESS CONCEPT, and it is also being *used in* another BUSINESS TERM to represent a different BUSINESS CONCEPT, the two are "homonyms" of each other. | 2 |
| HUMAN INTERFACE CLASS | An *architectural class* in *object-oriented design* that is part of a human interface. This includes "window", "IconicTrigger", and so on [Page-Jones 2000]. | 2 |
| *ICAM DEFinition* | A collection of techniques originally developed as the "Integrated Computer Aided Manufacturing" (ICAM) initiative of the federal government. It encompasses techniques for modeling data, processes, ontology, objects, and others. | |
| ICONIC TRIGGER | An INTERFACE ELEMENT that, when touched on a display screen by a user, invokes an EXECUTABLE MODULE. | 5 |
| *IDEF* | (See *ICAM DEFinition*.) | 3 |
| *IDEF0* | An *IDEF* technique designed to model the decisions, actions, and activities of an organization or system. Although it does have provisions for explicitly describing mechanisms, it is organized in a sequence; the emphasis is on the functions being represented, not on processes [KBSI 2005]. | 3 |

*Continued*

| Term | Definition | Chapter |
|------|------------|---------|
| *IDEF1* | An *IDEF* technique for both analysis and communication in the establishment of requirements. IDEF1 is generally used to (1) identify what information is currently managed in the organization, (2) determine which of the problems identified during the needs analysis are caused by lack of management of appropriate information, and (3) specify what information will be managed in the TO-BE implementation [KBSI 2005]. | 3 |
| *IDEF1X* | An *IDEF* technique for designing relational databases with a syntax designed to support the semantic constructs necessary in developing a conceptual schema. Because it is a design method, IDEF1X is not particularly suited to serve as an AS-IS analysis tool, although it is often used in that capacity as an alternative to IDEF1. The IDEF1X system perspective is focused on the actual data elements in a relational database [KBSI 2005]. | 3 |
| *IDEF3* | An *IDEF* technique for collecting and documenting processes. IDEF3 captures precedence and causality relations between situations and events in a form natural to domain experts by providing a structured method for expressing knowledge about how a system, process, or organization works [KBSI 2005]. | 3 |
| *IDEF4* | An *IDEF* technique that views *object-oriented design* as part of a larger system development framework rather than an object-oriented analysis and design method that is ambiguous. IDEF4 stresses the *object-oriented design* process over graphical syntax, using the graphical syntax and diagrams as aids to focus and communicate important design issues.<br><br>IDEF4 is significantly different from other object design methods, primarily in its support of "least commitment" strategies and its support for assessing the design impact of the interaction among class inheritance, object composition, functional decomposition, and polymorphism [KBSI 2005]. | 3 |
| *IDEF5* | An *IDEF* technique designed to assist in creating, modifying, and maintaining ontologies. Standardized procedures—the ability to represent ontology information in an intuitive and natural form—and higher-quality results enabled through IDEF5 application also serve to reduce the cost of these activities [KBSI 2005]. | 3 |
| *identifier* | According to the *Dublin Core*, a unique identifier of a DOCUMENT or other RESOURCE. (See also UNIQUE IDENTIFIER.) | 2 |

| Term | Definition | Chapter |
|---|---|---|
| *implicit corporate value* | An INFLUENCER TYPE (a kind of "internal influencer") that is a corporate value understood by some or all in the enterprise, but it is not explicitly stated. | 7 |
| *infer* | An operation in a DERIVATION where a value in a "parent" is made available to a "child" ENTITY CLASS. | 7 |
| INFLUENCER | Something either within the enterprise or in its environment that affects the outcome of its END. | 7, 1, 4, 5, 6 |
| INFLUENCER TYPE | The definition of a kind of INFLUENCER. | 7, 4 |
| Information Designer's View | John Zachman's term for Row Three of his *Zachman Framework*; equivalent to the Architect's View in the *Architecture Framework*. | 1 |
| INFORMATION ENGINEERING ROLE | A RELATIONSHIP ROLE between exactly two entity classes. | 2 |
| *infrastructure* | An INFLUENCER TYPE (a kind of "internal influencer") that is the basic underlying feature of the enterprise. | 7 |
| INHERENT QUALITY CHARACTERISTIC | A QUALITY CHARACTERISTIC whose measurement is independent of the way data are used. These characteristics are measures of the data themselves, regardless of how they might be presented to knowledge workers [English 1999]. | |
| INSTANCE ATTRIBUTE | A CLASS ELEMENT that assumes a different value for every instance of the CLASS IMPLEMENTATION. | 2 |
| INSTANCE NAME | A BUSINESS TERM that describes a particular occurrence of an ATTRIBUTE, an ENTITY CLASS, or something else. | 2, 7 |
| *instance verifier* | If this is an integrity constraint (Condition indicator = "False"), it requires an instance of the constrained object to exist. This includes the OPTIONALITY CONSTRAINT. If this is a condition (Condition indicator = "True"), it tests to see whether an instance of the constrained object exists. This is an example of an OTHER SYSTEM CONSTRAINT TYPE. | 7 |
| INTERACTIVE MODULE | A program that is part of an APPLICATION SYSTEM's user interface. | 5 |
| INTERACTIVE MODULE | An EXECUTABLE MODULE that involves a human being entering or requesting data. | 3 |

*Continued*

| Term | Definition | Chapter |
|---|---|---|
| INTERFACE ELEMENT | An item appearing on a video display device that furthers the interaction between a human being and a system. It may be a DISPLAY ELEMENT, an ICONIC TRIGGER, a FIELD, or an OTHER INTERFACE ELEMENT. | 5 |
| INTERNAL BUSINESS EVENT TYPE | The definition of a kind of EVENT. Something that occurs within the enterprise and is under its control. | 6, 5 |
| INTERNAL ORGANIZATION | Any permanent or temporary department, section, branch, or other group within either a COMPANY or a GOVERNMENT AGENCY. | 5 |
| issue | An INFLUENCER TYPE (a kind of "internal influencer") that is a point in question or a matter in dispute between two contending parties. | 7 |
| ITERATIVE SYSTEM EVENT TYPE | A SYSTEM EVENT TYPE that can be triggered more than once in the context of its parent SYSTEM EVENT TYPE. | 6 |
| language | According to the *Dublin Core*, the natural language (English, French, Arabic, and so on) the DOCUMENT or other RESOURCE was rendered in. | 2 |
| LANGUAGE | A collection of spoken sounds and written symbols that represent a system for communicating a person's understanding of the world. | 2 |
| LEGAL TRANSFORMATION | The definition of a specific change in value of a DISCRETE INSTANCE ATTRIBUTE from one DISCRETE INSTANCE VALID VALUE to another. | 6 |
| locations | The column in the *Architecture Framework* that describes the places *where* the enterprise does business and how these places are connected. | 1 |
| logical data flow diagram | A *data flow diagram* that describes the flow of information in an enterprise without regard to any mechanisms that might be required to support that flow. | 3, 1 |
| logical data model (schema) | In the ANSI *four-schema architecture*, this is the organization of data for use with a particular data management technology. In a relational environment, this is in terms of *tables* and *columns*. In an object-oriented one, it is in terms of *object classes* and *attributes*. It could also be a COBOL record layout or a set of ISAM segments. | 3, 1 |

| Term | Definition | Chapter |
|------|-----------|---------|
| MACHINE COMMUNICATION CLASS | An *architectural class* in *object-oriented design* that participates in messages between machines. Examples include "Port" and "RemoteMachine" [Page-Jones 2000]. | 2 |
| *mailing address* | Often the description of a PHYSICAL SITE used to tell postal authorities how to deliver mail to the site. This usually includes a reference to one or more streets (plus the city, state, or province, and country where the site is located), but it could also be in terms of a post office box number. | 4 |
| MANAGEMENT AREA | A GEOGRAPHIC AREA whose boundaries are defined by the enterprise, as in "Southwestern sales region". | 2 |
| *management prerogative* | An INFLUENCER TYPE (a kind of "internal influencer") that is a right or privilege exercised by right of ownership or position in the enterprise. | 7 |
| MANAGEMENT ROLE | A kind of ACCESS ROLE that is the fact that a PARTY, POSTION, POSITION RESPONSIBILITY, and so on is responsible for the supervision of a SITE, SYMBOL, BUSINESS CONCEPT, a COPY of a DOCUMENT, a RESOURCE, a BUSINESS DESCRIPTION SPECIFICATION, an ACTIVITY, an INFLUENCER, a MEANS, an END, a SYSTEM PROCESS, a SYSTEM CONSTRAINT, a PERSISTENCE MECHANISM (a TABLE, a VIEW, or a COLUMN), a PROGRAM COPY, a DATABASE INSTALLATION, or a TABLE INSTANCE. This is an ACCESS ROLE that is *an example of* an ACCESS ROLE TYPE of "Management role". | 5, 2, 3, 7 |
| *mandatory* | A characteristic of an ATTRIBUTE or a RELATIONSHIP ROLE asserting that for each instance of the thing involved a value is required for this ATTRIBUTE or RELATIONSHIP ROLE. This is controlled by the "Default optionality" attribute and the OPTIONALITY CONSTRAINT that is a sub-type of SYSTEM CONSTRAINT. | 7 |
| *many-to-many relationship* | A *relationship* where an occurrence of each *entity class* may be associated with one or more occurrences of the other ENTITY CLASS. | 2 |
| *mathematical evaluator* | If this is an integrity constraint (Condition indicator = "False"), it specifies that an attribute be calculated according to a formula (or a function, such as SUM) for a constrained ENTITY CLASS. If this is a condition (Condition indicator = "True"), it tests | 7 |

*Continued*

| Term | Definition | Chapter |
|---|---|---|
| *mathematical evaluator (cont'd)* | to see whether this is so. This is a kind of OTHER SYSTEM CONSTRAINT TYPE. | |
| MEANS | Any capability that may be called on, activated, or enforced to achieve an organization's objectives. | 7, 3, 4, 5, 6 |
| MEANS EFFECT | The fact that a particular BUSINESS PROCESS is used to carry out a MEANS. This must be either a DIRECTION *from* a DIRECTIVE *on* a BUSINESS PROCESS, an EFFORT *invoked by* a COURSE OF ACTION *to achieve* a DESIRED EFFECT *through the use of* a BUSINESS PROCESS, or an OTHER MEANS EFFECT. | 7, 6 |
| MEANS EFFECT TYPE | The definition of a kind of MEANS EFFECT. Three MEANS EFFECT TYPES must be the same as the sub-types of MEANS EFFECT: "Guidance", "Governance", and "Effort". | 7, 6 |
| *measurable* | A characteristic of all OBJECTIVES: all OBJECTIVES contain in their expression one or more specific criteria that can be measured to determine when the objective has been achieved, such as "Increase sales by 10%". | 7 |
| MECHANISM | The fact that a particular BUSINESS PROCESS (such as "take order") is the *user of* a particular MECHANISM TYPE (such as "terminal attached to the Framis System"). | 3, 1 |
| MECHANISM TYPE | A system, form, or some other tangible tool required to carry out the BUSINESS PROCESS. | 3 |
| MESSAGE | A communication from one *object* to another, *via* a PROGRAM MODULE COMMUNICATION, which has the effect of *invoking* an OPERATION. | 3 |
| MESSAGE ARGUMENT | A parameter included with a MESSAGE to affect the behavior of the OBJECT receiving it. | 3 |
| MESSAGE QUEUE | A mechanism for storing MESSAGES when an OBJECT cannot receive them as quickly as they are sent. | 3 |
| MESSAGE TYPE | The definition of a kind of MESSAGE. | 3 |
| *metadata* | The data that describe the structure and workings of an organization's use of information, as well as the systems it uses to manage that information. | 1 |
| *metadata repository* | A database constructed for the purpose of storing, managing, and making available *metadata*. | 1 |

| Term | Definition | Chapter |
|------|------------|---------|
| *Meta Object Facility* | An Object Management Group standard defining a common, abstract language for the specification of metamodels [Poole et al. 2002, p. 40]. | 1 |
| METHOD | An EXECUTABLE MODULE that *acts on* a CLASS IMPLEMENTATION. | 3 |
| MISSION | An overall method for the ongoing operation of the enterprise (what the business is or will be doing on a day-to-day basis). | 7, 1, 3, 5 |
| *model of fundamental concepts* | The model seen by the *architect* in Row Three of the *Architecture Framework*. This perspective completes the conceptual model of the business, seeing the underlying structures of Row Two rendered in a more disciplined fashion. This is still without reference to any particular technology. | 1 |
| MODULE DATA USAGE | The fact that a particular PERSISTENCE MECHANISM (that is, a COLUMN, TABLE, or VIEW) is referred to by a PROGRAM MODULE. The MODULE DATA USAGE must be either "Create", "Retrieve", "Update", and/or "Delete". The settings of the attributes "Create indicator", "Retrieve indicator", "Update indicator", and "Delete indicator" determine which is the case. | 3 |
| MODULE DATA USAGE TYPE | This is a different way to show whether the MODULE DATA USAGE is "Create", "Update", "Retrieve", or "Delete". | 3 |
| MODULE LOCATION | The fact that an OBJECT, OPERATION, or PROGRAM MODULE is to be found in a particular SITE. | 4 |
| *MOF* | (See *Meta Object Facility*.) | 1 |
| *motivation* | This column of the *Architecture Framework* describes *why* an enterprise does what it does. This includes *mission* and *vision* at Row One, through *goals, objectives, strategies,* and *tactics* in Row Two. The *business rules* and *business policies* that also arise in Row Two feed the definition of constraints in lower rows. | 1 |
| MOTIVATION LOCATION | The fact that a particular INFLUENCER, OBJECTIVE, or EFFORT is *specific* to a particular SITE. | 4 |
| *multi-valued attributes* | An *attribute* that can have more than one value for a *row* in a relational table. | 2 |
| *multi-variate relationship* | A relationship between three or more ENTITY CLASSES. | 2 |

*Continued*

| Term | Definition | Chapter |
|------|-----------|---------|
| *n-ary relationship* | (See *multi-variate relationship*.) | 2 |
| N-ARY ROLE | A RELATIONSHIP ROLE that is part of a RELATIONSHIP that is among more than two ENTITY CLASSES. | 2 |
| *nihilartikel* | A fake word in a dictionary to prove copyright violations. | |
| *non-duplication* | An *inherent* QUALITY CHARACTERISTIC that is a measure of the degree to which there is a one-to-one correlation between records and the real-world objects or events being represented. | 7 |
| *normalization* | The process, originally articulated by Dr. E. F. Codd in his *relational theory*, for organizing data to reduce redundancy to the minimum possible. It involves guaranteeing that each attribute in a "relation" (*table* or *entity class*) is truly an attribute of that relation and none other. The process involves organizing data to follow the constraints of at least *first normal form, second normal form*, and *third normal form*. Additional value is found in *Boyce-Codd normal form, fourth normal form*, and *fifth normal form*. | 2 |
| *nullify* | A *Referential integrity* constraint on a table that permits deletion of a ROW, even if there are rows in other TABLES with FOREIGN KEY values that point to the row in question. Those values are replaced with nulls so that those rows no longer point to another TABLE. | 7 |
| OBJECT | An occurrence of a CLASS IMPLEMENTATION that is manipulated at runtime. In *object-oriented design* an OBJECT *encapsulates* data and only allows manipulation of data through controlled METHODS (also called "behavior"). | 2 |
| *object model* | A description of the structure of *objects* being assembled into a software product. The *object* may be a *business object* or a computer artifact. | 1 |
| *Object Role Modeling* | A form of representing the structure and constraints of an enterprise. It is similar to *entity relationship modeling* but uses a different syntax. | 2 |
| OBJECTIVE | A statement of an attainable, time-targeted, and measurable DESIRED RESULT the enterprise seeks to meet to achieve its GOALS. | 7, 5, 1 |
| *objectives/scope* | What is seen by the Planner in Row One of the *Architecture Framework*. | 1 |

| Term | Definition | Chapter |
|---|---|---|
| *object-oriented design* | An approach to program design that organizes a computer program's manipulations in terms of the "objects" being manipulated and the behavior of each. This is as opposed to more traditional approaches, which began with the program logic and collected data about things only as necessary to complete the logic. | 3, 2 |
| *occurrence* | A ROW in an ENTITY CLASS. An INSTANCE of the thing of significance represented by the ENTITY CLASS. | 2 |
| ONTOLOGICAL CLASSIFICATION | The fact that a particular SYMBOL (*the use of* a SIGNIFIER *to represent* a BUSINESS CONCEPT) is *part of* an ONTOLOGY. | 2 |
| *ontology* | 1. A branch of metaphysics concerned with the nature and relations of being [*Merriam-Webster* 2005]. <br> 2. A catalogue of terms describing the types of things that exist in an area of interest, with rules governing how those terms can be combined to make valid inferences [KBSI 1994]. If the relationships are hierarchical, it is called a *taxonomy*. <br> 3. "It is closely related to *semantics*, the primary distinction being that *ontology* concerns itself with the organization of knowledge, once you know what it means. *Semantics* concerns itself with what something means" [McComb 2004, p. 9]. | 2 |
| OPERATION | The fact that the behavior of objects in a CLASS IMPLEMENTATION is *implemented by* a METHOD. | 3 |
| *operational data store* | A database designed to integrate data from multiple sources to facilitate operations. This is as opposed to a *data warehouse*, which integrates data from multiple sources to facilitate reporting and analysis. | |
| *optionality* | A characteristic of an ATTRIBUTE or a RELATIONSHIP ROLE that asserts that for each instance of the thing involved a value is not required for this ATTRIBUTE or RELATIONSHIP ROLE. This is controlled by the Default optionality attribute and the OPTIONALITY CONSTRAINT, a sub-type of SYSTEM CONSTRAINT. | 7 |
| OPTIONALITY CONSTRAINT | A kind of SYSTEM CONSTRAINT asserting that if an ENTITY CLASS is in a particular ENTITY CLASS STATE then a particular ATTRIBUTE or RELATIONSHIP ROLE associated with that ENTITY CLASS either | 7 |

*Continued*

| Term | Definition | Chapter |
|---|---|---|
| OPTIONALITY CONSTRAINT *(cont'd)* | must (Optionality indicator = "False") or is not required to (Optionality indicator = "True") have a value. | |
| ORGANIZATION | A collection of people brought together for a specific purpose and generally recognized as such. | 5, 2, 3, 4, 6, 7 |
| *ORM* | (See *Object Role Modeling*.) | 2 |
| OTHER ACCESS ROLE | This is an ACCESS ROLE that is not a PROGRAMMING ROLE, an AUTHORSHIP ROLE, an ENFORCEMENT ROLE, a PLACEMENT ROLE, a PERMISSION ROLE, a SPECIFICATION ROLE, or a MANAGEMENT ROLE. | 5, 2, 3, 4, 7 |
| OTHER ATTRIBUTE | An ATTRIBUTE, such as a date, that is neither a DISCRETE ATTRIBUTE nor a CONTINUOUS ATTRIBUTE. | 7 |
| OTHER BUSINESS PROCESS | A BUSINESS PROCESS that is not an ESSENTIAL BUSINESS PROCESS or an ELEMENTARY BUSINESS PROCESS. | 3 |
| OTHER COLUMN | A COLUMN, such as a date, that is neither a DISCRETE COLUMN nor a CONTINUOUS COLUMN. | 7 |
| OTHER DATABASE CONSTRAINT | A DATABASE CONSTRAINT that is not a FOREIGN KEY, a UNIQUE IDENTIFIER, or a COMPUTATION. | |
| OTHER DISCRETE INSTANCE ATTRIBUTE | A DISCRETE INSTANCE ATTRIBUTE that is not a STATE. | 2, 6 |
| OTHER DOMAIN | A DOMAIN that is not a VALUE SET or a VALUE EXPRESSION. | 7 |
| OTHER ENTITY CLASS | An ENTITY CLASS that is not an ASSOCIATION ENTITY CLASS, a VIRTUAL ENTITY CLASS, or an ELEMENTARY ENTITY CLASS. | 2 |
| OTHER EXECUTABLE MODULE | An EXECUTABLE MODULE that is not an INTERACTIVE MODULE, a PACKAGE, a METHOD, a DATABASE MANAGEMENT SYSTEM, or a STORED PROCEDURE. | 3 |
| OTHER FACT TYPE | A FACT TYPE that is not a CHARACTERISTIC. | 2 |
| OTHER FACT TYPE ELEMENT | A FACT TYPE ELEMENT that is not a CHARACTERISTIC ELEMENT. | 2 |
| OTHER FUNCTION | A FUNCTION that is not an ELEMENTARY BUSINESS FUNCTION. | 3 |
| OTHER INSTANCE ATTRIBUTE | An INSTANCE ATTRIBUTE that is not a DISCRETE INSTANCE ATTRIBUTE. | 2, 6 |
| OTHER INSTANCE NAME | An INSTANCE NAME that is not an INSTANCE NAME, an ENTITY CLASS NAME, or a VALID CODE. | 2 |
| OTHER INTERFACE ELEMENT | An INTERFACE ELEMENT that is not a DISPLAY ELEMENT, an ICONIC TRIGGER, or a FIELD. | 5 |

| Term | Definition | Chapter |
|------|-----------|---------|
| *other internal influencer* | An *internal influencer* that is not a *habit*, an *assumption*, an *infrastructure*, a *management prerogative*, a *resource*, or *corporate value*. | 7 |
| OTHER LEGAL TRANSFORMATION | A LEGAL TRANSFORMATION that is not a STATE LEGAL TRANSFORMATION. | 7 |
| OTHER ORGANIZATION | An ORGANIZATION that is not a COMPANY, a GOVERNMENT AGENCY, an INTERNAL ORGANIZATION, a SEMANTIC COMMUNITY, or a SPEECH COMMUNITY. | 5 |
| OTHER PARTY RELATIONSHIP | A PARTY RELATIONSHP that is not EMPLOYMENT. | 5 |
| OTHER RESOURCE | A RESOURCE that is not a DOCUMENT. | 2 |
| OTHER SYSTEM CONSTRAINT | A SYSTEM CONSTRAINT that is not an OPTIONALITY CONSTRAINT. | 7 |
| OTHER SYSTEM PROCESS | A SYSTEM PROCESS that is not an ESSENTIAL SYSTEM PROCESS or an ELEMENTARY SYSTEM PROCESS. | 3 |
| OTHER VIRTUAL SITE | A VIRTUAL SITE that is not a DATABASE INSTANCE, a TELEPHONIC SITE, an E-MAIL SITE, or a WEB SITE. | 4 |
| *override with explanation* | An ENFORCEMENT LEVEL that can be assigned to a BUSINESS RULE: specifically, when the violation occurs there must be a comment justifying it. | 7 |
| PACKAGE | An EXECUTABLE MODULE that is a collection of CLASS IMPLEMENTATIONS. | 3 |
| PARTY | A PERSON or an ORGANIZATION of interest to the enterprise. This includes PARTIES who are playing roles of "Vendor", "Customer", and "Employee", among others. | 5, 2, 3, 4, 6, 7 |
| PARTY RELATIONSHIP | The fact that a PARTY is in some way associated with another PARTY. The nature of the relationship is defined by the PARTY RELATIONSHIP TYPE the PARTY RELATIONSHIP is *an example of*. | 5 |
| PARTY RELATIONSHIP TYPE | The definition of the nature of one or more PARTY RELATIONSHIPS. These include "Employment", "Corporate structure", "Union membership", "Husband", and so on. | 5 |
| *people and organizations* | This column of the *Architecture Framework* describes *who* is responsible for the various aspects of the enterprise's operations, as well as the population that constitutes its environment of vendors, suppliers, government regulators, and so on. | 1 |

*Continued*

| Term | Definition | Chapter |
|------|-----------|---------|
| PERMISSION ROLE | A kind of ACCESS ROLE that is the fact that a PARTY, POSITION, POSITION RESPONSIBILITY, and so on is responsible for granting permission to gain access to a SITE, a COPY of a DOCUMENT, a RESOURCE, a BUSINESS DESCRIPTION SPECIFICATION, an ACTIVITY, a SYSTEM PROCESS, a PERSISTENCE MECHANISM (a TABLE, a VIEW, or a COLUMN), a PROGRAM COPY, a DATABASE INSTALLATION, or a TABLE INSTANCE. | 5, 3, 7 |
| PERMITTED ATTRIBUTE VALUE | Either one of a list of values allowed to be specified by a particular DISCRETE ATTRIBUTE or one of a list of values allowed to be specified by any ATTRIBUTES *constrained by* a VALUE SET. | 7 |
| PERSISTENCE MECHANISM | A mechanism for keeping the values of CLASS IMPLEMENTATIONS (specifically, their INSTANCE ATTRIBUTES) after a program ceases execution. Typically, this is a COLUMN that is *part of* a DATA GROUP, specifically a TABLE. | 2, 3, 5 |
| PERSISTENCE MECHANISM LOCATION | The fact that a particular PERSISTENCE MECHANISM has been defined at a particular SITE. | 4 |
| PERSON | A human individual. | 2–7 |
| PHRASE | A collection of WORDS that form a single semantic meaning. | 2 |
| PHYSICAL COMUNICATION LINK | The fact that one SITE has the facilities to communicate with another SITE. | 4 |
| PHYSICAL COPY | A COPY of a DOCUMENT that has physical existence, typically on paper. This is as opposed to a VIRTUAL COPY, which exists only in the electronics of a computer system or network. | 2 |
| *physical data flow diagram* | A *data flow diagram* that identifies and represents data flows and processes in terms of the mechanisms currently used to carry them out. | 3, 1 |
| *physical data model (schema)* | In the ANSI *four-schema architecture*, this is the organization of data used to place it in specific storage media. This is in terms of "Tablespaces", "Cylinders", and so on. | 1 |
| PHYSICAL LINK IMPLEMENTATION | The fact that a particular PROGRAM COPY makes use of a particular PHYSICAL COMMUNICATION LINK. | 4 |
| PHYSICAL SITE | A SITE that is located in space—as opposed to a VIRTUAL SITE, which is only a location in an electronic network. | 4, 2 |

| Term | Definition | Chapter |
|---|---|---|
| PLACEMENT ROLE | An ACCESS ROLE that is the fact that a PARTY, POSITION, and so on is located at a particular SITE. This is an ACCESS ROLE that is *an example of* an ACCESS ROLE TYPE of "Placement Role". Sub-types of "Placement Role" could describe the nature of the placement, such as "Home address", "Work address", "Corporate headquarters", and so on. | 5, 4, 7 |
| *planner* | A person concerned with the overall direction and description of the enterprise. | |
| Planner's View | (Row One in the *Architecture Framework*) A view that defines the enterprise's direction and business purpose. This is necessary to establish the context for any system development effort. It includes definitions of the boundaries of systems or other development projects. | 1–7 |
| *polymorphism* | In *object-oriented design*, the principle that the same definition can be used with different types of data (specifically, different CLASS IMPLEMENTATIONS), resulting in more general and abstract implementations. | |
| POSITION | The definition of a particular category of work to be done by someone with a specific set of skills. | 5, 3 |
| position verifier | If this is an integrity constraint (Condition indicator = "False"), it requires a specific ranking of the constrained object relative to other objects ("lowest", "highest", "oldest", "newest", or a specified ranking, like "5$^{th}$"). If this is a condition (Condition indicator = "True"), it tests to see whether this is so. This is a kind of OTHER SYSTEM CONSTRAINT TYPE. | 7 |
| *post-justified override* | An ENFORCEMENT LEVEL that can be assigned to a BUSINESS RULE. Specifically, if not approved after the fact, there may be sanctions or other consequences, but if approved, the action is acceptable. | 7 |
| POTENTIAL IMPACT | Either a potential RISK or potential REWARD *revealed by* an ASSESSMENT ELEMENT. POTENTIAL IMPACT can be expressed in terms of the "Probability" of the RISK or REWARD, and its "Impact value". The value is in terms of a "Unit of measure". | 7 |
| PRAGMATIC QUALITY CHARACTERISTIC | A QUALITY CHARACTERISTIC associated with data presentation quality and how well data supports specific business processes and how well it meets both information producers' and knowledge workers' needs [English 1999]. | 7 |

*Continued*

| Term | Definition | Chapter |
|---|---|---|
| *preauthorized override* | An ENFORCEMENT LEVEL that can be assigned to a BUSINESS RULE. Specifically, the rule is enforced, but exceptions are allowed with prior approval. | 7 |
| *precision* | An inherent QUALITY CHARACTERISTIC that is a measure of an ATTRIBUTE's having the right level of granularity in the data values. | 7 |
| *predicate* | Something that is affirmed or denied of the subject in a proposition in logic [*Merriam-Webster* 2005]. | 2 |
| *primary key* | In *relational theory*, the set of columns whose values can be used to uniquely identify each ROW (*tuple* in Dr. Codd's original terminology) in a TABLE (*relation* to Dr. Codd). | |
| PRIMARY KEY | The UNIQUE KEY (normally) used for creating FOREIGN KEYS pointing to the subject TABLE from other TABLES. | 7 |
| *private* | A kind of *visibility*, where a CLASS ELEMENT can only be seen within the context of its CLASS IMPLEMENTATION. | |
| PROCESS | A kind of ACTIVITY performed by the enterprise to produce a specific output or achieve a goal. It may or may not be described in terms of the MECHANISMS used or the PARTIES performing it. A set of PROCESSES is usually described in sequence. | 3 |
| PROCESS CRITERION | A value or *set point* used *to determine the success of* a PROCESS OBJECTIVE *for* a SYSTEM PROCESS. | 7 |
| PROCESS IMPLEMENTATION | The fact that a SYSTEM PROCESS has been implemented either *as* an APPLICATION SYSTEM or *as* a particular PROGRAM MODULE. | 3 |
| *process map* | A kind of *data flow diagram* used in business process engineering to represent the tasks performed in an enterprise and the links between them. | 3 |
| PROCESS MEASUREMENT | An evaluation of the performance of a SYSTEM PROCESS. A measurement from the SYSTEM PROCESS is compared to determine whether it is below the "Minimum value" or above the "Maximum value" of the SUCCESS CRITERION *for* that SYSTEM PROCESS. If so, it is *the source of* a SYSTEM EVENT TYPE that is *the trigger of* another SYSTEM PROCESS to correct the situation. | 6 |
| PROCESS OBJECTIVE | Each SYSTEM PROCESS may be *directed toward* one or more PROCESS OBJECTIVES. Each of these in turn is *controlled by* one or more SUCCESS CRITERIA (set points). | 6 |

| Term | Definition | Chapter |
|---|---|---|
| PROCESS OBJECTIVE TYPE | The definition of a kind of PROCESS OBJECTIVE. | 6 |
| PROGRAM COPY | A PROGRAM MODULE is the logic of a program. It is *replicated in* one or more PROGRAM COPIES. That is, a PROGRAM COPY is the *physical manifestation of* a PROGRAM MODULE. | 3, 4, 5 |
| PROGRAM LOCATION | The fact that a particular PROGRAM COPY is to be found in a particular SITE. | 4 |
| PROGRAM MODULE | A unit of program code. | 3, 5 |
| PROGRAM MODULE COMMUNICATION | The fact that one PROGRAM MODULE can send messages to another PROGRAM MODULE. | 3 |
| PROGRAM MODULE STRUCTURE | The fact that one PROGRAM MODULE is a component of another PROGRAM MODULE. | 3 |
| PROGRAM MODULE TYPE | The definition of a type of PROGRAM MODULE. The first set of PROGRAM MODULE TYPES must correspond to the sub-types of PROGRAM MODULE: "Executable module", "Class implementation", and so on. | 3 |
| PROGRAMMING LANGUAGE | A scheme for expressing computer commands. | 3 |
| PROGRAMMING UNIT ROLE | An ACCESS ROLE *for* a PROGRAM MODULE that is played *by* a PARTY only. ACCESS ROLE TYPES that are a *sub-type of* "Programming unit role" could include "Programmer", "Designer", "Project manager", and so on. | 5, 3 |
| *projection controller* | Whereas other kinds of constraints prevent things from happening, a projection controller asserts that under specified circumstances something must happen. A STATE is enabled, something is copied, or an action is executed. This is a kind of OTHER SYSTEM CONSTRAINT TYPE. | 7 |
| *protected* | A kind of *visibility*, where a CLASS ELEMENT can be seen and used only within its CLASS IMPLEMENTATION and by classes that are inheriting from that class. | |
| *public* | A kind of *visibility*, where a CLASS ELEMENT can be seen and used by any other CLASS IMPLEMENTATION or operation. | |
| *publisher* | According to the *Dublin Core*, the company that physically produces the DOCUMENT or other RESOURCE. | 2 |

*Continued*

| Term | Definition | Chapter |
|------|-----------|---------|
| QUALITY CHARACTERISTIC | A parameter that describes a particular aspect of data quality to be measured. This may be an *inherent* QUALITY CHARACTERISTIC (independent of the way data are used) or a *pragmatic* QUALITY CHARACTERISTIC, associated with data presentation quality and how well it meets both information producers' and knowledge workers' needs. | 7 |
| QUALITY STANDARD | The assignment of a VALID QUALITY CHARACTERISTIC VALUE to a RELATIONSHIP ROLE or to an ATTRIBUTE. Note that the values of either of these will then be evaluated in terms of this QUALITY STANDARD. | 7 |
| *recursion* | (See *recursion*.) | 1, 2 |
| *reference data* | Data that describe the infrastructure of an enterprise. These comprise the "type" ENTITY CLASSES that provide lists of values for other ATTRIBUTES. | 2 |
| *referential integrity* | In a *relational database*, the quality of a table that all its associations are with real instances of other tables. | 7 |
| *relation* | 1. According to the *Dublin Core*, reference to a related DOCUMENT or other RESOURCE.<br>2. In Dr. Codd's original *relational theory*, an array of data consisting of rows and columns that describe instances of a particular thing of significance (implemented as a TABLE in a *relational database management system*). | 2 |
| *relational database management system* | A DATABASE MANAGEMENT SYSTEM whose architecture is based on Dr. E. F. Codd's *relational theory*. That is, it stores data in terms of simple, two dimensional tables. | |
| *relational theory* | The theory of data organization proposed by Dr. E. F. Codd that recommends organizing data in terms of simple two-dimensional structures called *relations*, consisting of uniform rows (called *tuples*), each of which is in terms of a specified set of *attributes*. The *attributes* must be specified according to a set of rules (*normalization*) that guarantee minimum redundancy. | 2 |
| RELATIONSHIP | The complete association among specific ENTITY CLASSES consisting of two or more RELATIONSHIP ROLES. | 2 |
| RELATIONSHIP CLASS | A kind of BUSINESS CLASS in *object-oriented design* that corresponds to a RELATIONSHIP ROLE in an entity-relationship model [Page-Jones 2000]. | 2 |

| Term | Definition | Chapter |
|------|-----------|---------|
| RELATIONSHIP ROLE | A FACT TYPE that describes the fact that instances of an ENTITY CLASS have a particular named association with instances of another ENTITY CLASS. | 2 |
| *RelationshipEnd* | The fact that instances of a particular ENTITY CLASS have a particular named association with instances of another ENTITY CLASS. | 1 |
| *resource* | An INFLUENCER TYPE (a kind of "internal influencer") that is the resources available for carrying out the business of an enterprise, especially their quality. | |
| RESOURCE | The physical source of information about BUSINESS CONCEPTS in the form of SYMBOLS. That is, each RESOURCE may be *the source of* one or more SYMBOLS. A RESOURCE may be a DOCUMENT, a video, a musical recording, or any OTHER kind of RESOURCE. | 2, 5 |
| RESOURCE DISTRIBUTION | The fact that a COPY of a RESOURCE has been (or will be sent) to a PARTY or a SITE. | 2 |
| RESOURCE STRUCTURE | The fact that one RESOURCE may be *part of* another RESOURCE. | 2 |
| RESOURCE STRUCTURE TYPE | The definition of a kind of RESOURCE STRUCTURE. | 2 |
| RESOURCE TOPIC | The fact that a particular RESOURCE may be *the source of* a particular SYMBOL. | 2, 5 |
| RESOURCE TYPE | The definition of a kind of RESOURCE. The first of these must correspond to the sub-types of RESOURCE: "Document", "Other resource", and so on. | 2 |
| *restricted* | A *referential integrity* constraint on a FOREIGN KEY that prevents the deletion of a ROW in a TABLE if there are rows in different TABLES with FOREIGN KEY values that point to the row in question. | 7 |
| *reticulate* | To divide, mark, or construct so as to form a network. | 4 |
| *Reverse Polish Notation* | A system of representing a mathematical formula, which involves organizing it in terms of variables and operations on each variable. | 7 |
| *rightness or fact completeness* | A *pragmatic* QUALITY CHARACTERISTIC that is a measure of having the right kind of data with the right quality to support a given process, such as to support a performance of the process or the making of a decision. | 7 |

*Continued*

| Term | Definition | Chapter |
|------|-----------|---------|
| *rights* | According to the *Dublin Core*, the ownership of some aspect of the DOCUMENT or other RESOURCE. | 2 |
| *role* | (See RELATIONSHIP ROLE.) | 1 |
| ROLE CLASS | In a CLASS IMPLEMENTATION, a BUSINESS CLASS that describes the role someone plays, such as "Employee" or "Patient" [Page-Jones 2000]. | 2 |
| *row* | 1. In *relational theory*, a set of values for a specified set of attributes.<br>2. In the *architecture framework*, representation of a perspective of a particular observer on the information management world. Observers include the *Planner*, the *Business Owner*, the *Architect*, the *Designer*, and the *Functioning System*. | 2, 1 |
| *Row Five* | (See *Builder's View*.) | 1 |
| *Row Four* | (See *Designer's View*.) | 1 |
| ROW INSTANCE | A physical example of a ROW as defined for a TABLE DESIGN. | 2 |
| *Row One* | (See *Planner's View*.) | 1 |
| *Row Six* | (See *Functioning System*.) | 1 |
| *Row Three* | (See *Architect's View*.) | 1 |
| *Row Two* | (See *Business Owner's View*.) | 1 |
| *second normal form* | In *relational theory*, the second of Dr. Codd's constraints on a relational design: Each attribute must depend on the *entire* PRIMARY KEY. | 2 |
| SELECTION CONDITION | The fact that a particular ATTRIBUTE or RELATIONSHIP ROLE is used to select occurrences in an underlying ENTITY CLASS to populate a VIRTUAL ENTITY CLASS. The value of each occurrence of an ATTRIBUTE or each occurrence of a RELATIONSHIP is compared with a "Value" using an "Operator" ("equal to", "greater than", and so on) to determine whether that occurrence is part of the VIRTUAL ENTITY CLASS. | 2 |
| SEMANTIC CLASS | In a CLASS IMPLEMENTATION, a kind of FOUNDATION CLASS that is a common term, such as "Date", "Time", "Angle", and so on. Semantic classes have a richer meaning than plain "Integer" and "Char" [Page-Jones 2000]. | 2 |
| SEMANTIC COMMUNITY | The set of people whose unifying characteristic is a shared understanding (or perception) of the things that they have to deal with. This includes, for example, "Doctors" or "Economists". | 2 |

| Term | Definition | Chapter |
|------|-----------|---------|
| *semantic web* | A machine-processable web of smart data, [where] smart data is data that is application-independent, composeable, classified, and part of a larger information ecosystem (ontology) [Daconta et al. 2003, p. 4]. | 2 |
| *semantics* | The branch of philosophy concerned with describing meaning. | 2 |
| SEQUENTIAL SYSTEM EVENT TYPE | One of a set of SYSTEM EVENT TYPES that will be triggered in sequence as part of a single other SYSTEM EVENT TYPE. | 6 |
| *set point* | In *cybernetics*, a value used in controlling a PROCESS. When the process returns a value that is above or below the *set point* (depending on the "Set point above indicator"), a specified other PROCESS is launched. | 6 |
| SIGNIFIER | A set of marks (either a GRAPHIC, or a WORD or PHRASE) that can represent one or more BUSINESS CONCEPTS. | 2, 5 |
| SITE | An address used for locating a person, resource, or other item. This can be a PHYSICAL SITE, which is a place on Earth that has a purpose, such as an office building, a home, or an oil well. Alternatively, it can be a VIRTUAL CLASS, such as a telephone number or an e-mail address. | 4, 2, 5 |
| SITE LOCATION | The fact that a particular PHYSICAL SITE is to be found in a particular GEOGRAPHIC LOCATION. | 4 |
| SITE TYPE | The definition of a kind of SITE. The first of these must be the same as the sub-types of SITE shown in the model—"Physical site", "Virtual site", "E-mail site", and so on. | 4 |
| *source* | According to the *Dublin Core*, another DOCUMENT or other RESOURCE from which this RESOURCE was derived. | 2 |
| SPECIFICATION ROLE | An ACCESS ROLE that is the fact that a PARTY, POSITION, and so on is empowered to design or specify the characteristics of a RESOURCE, PROGRAM MODULE, or other element. | |
| SPEECH COMMUNITY | Any group of people either inside or outside the enterprise whose unifying characteristic is the vocabulary it uses. At a general level, this could be "The population of the United Kingdom" or simply "English speakers", but it could also be as specific as a particular dialect. | 2 |
| STATE | A DISCRETE INSTANCE ATTRIBUTE whose VALUE for an OBJECT represents the current status of that OBJECT. It is defined for all OBJECTS in a CLASS IMPLEMENTATION. | 2, 6 |

*Continued*

| Term | Definition | Chapter |
|---|---|---|
| STATE LEGAL TRANSFORMATION | A LEGAL TRANSFORMATION that applies only to DISCRETE INSTANCE ATTRIBUTES that are STATES. | 7 |
| STATE TRIGGER | The fact that a particular MESSAGE can be used to initiate a particular LEGAL TRANSFORMATION. | 6 |
| *state-transition diagram* | A diagram that graphically represents the states an ENTITY CLASS (or a part of the enterprise) goes through in response to events. | 1 |
| STORED PROCEDURE | An EXECUTABLE MODULE stored in a database instance, to be invoked as *part of* the verification process for particular data elements. | 3 |
| STRATEGY | The essential COURSE OF ACTION attempted to achieve an enterprise's END—particularly GOALS. Moreover, a STRATEGY must be *to carry out* exactly one MISSION. In general, STRATEGIES address GOALS, and TACTICS address OBJECTIVES. | 7, 3 |
| *strictly enforced* (BUSINESS RULE) | An ENFORCEMENT LEVEL that can be assigned to a BUSINESS RULE. Specifically, if the rule is violated a penalty is always applied. | 7 |
| *structural assertion* | A BUSINESS RULE that is a *term*, a *fact*, or a *derivation*. | 2, 7 |
| STRUCTURAL CLASS | A kind of *foundation class* in *object-oriented design* that implements a structure. This includes "Stack", "Queue", "BinaryTree", and so on [Page-Jones 2000]. | 2 |
| *subcontractor's view* | John Zachman assigned the *subcontractor* to the Row Five perspective in his *Zachman Framework*. This is equivalent to the *Builder's View* in the *Architecture Framework*. | 1 |
| *subject* | According to the *Dublin Core*, a topic that categorizes this DOCUMENT or other RESOURCE. | 2 |
| *sub-type* | An ENTITY CLASS is a *sub-type* of another if an occurrence of it is also an occurrence of the other (called a *super-type*). The *sub-type* is a sub-categorization of the *super-type*. | 2 |
| SUB-TYPE ROLE | A kind of GENERALIZATION ROLE that is the fact that an ENTITY CLASS is a *sub-type* of another ENTITY CLASS. That is, all occurrences of the first ENTITY CLASS are also occurrences of the second ENTITY CLASS. | 2 |
| SUCCESS CRITERION | According to *cybernetic* theory, in a feedback loop the *set point* that determines the extent to which a SYSTEM PROCESS meets its PROCESS OBJECTIVE. This must be expressed in terms of either a "Minimum value" or a "Maximum value" of an ATTRIBUTE. | 6 |

| Term | Definition | Chapter |
|------|-----------|---------|
| *sum* | An operation in a DERIVATION in which the value of an ATTRIBUTE in a parent table is equal to the sum of the values of a specified ATTRIBUTE of all related instances in a child table. | 7 |
| *super-type* | A ENTITY CLASS is a *super-type* of one or more other ENTITY CLASSES, if an occurrence of the first is also an occurrence of exactly one of the others. | 2 |
| SUPER-TYPE ROLE | A kind of GENERALIZATION ROLE that is the fact that an ENTITY CLASS is a *super-type* of another ENTITY CLASS. That is, each occurrence of the first ENTITY CLASS is also an occurrence of one of several other ENTITY CLASSES. | 2 |
| SYMBOL | The fact that a BUSINESS CONCEPT may be represented by a SIGNIFIER (a WORD, PHRASE, or GRAPHIC). | 2, 5, 7 |
| SYMBOL CONTEXT | The scope for a BUSINESS TERM. For example, in a rental car company the word *site* means different things in the context of a rental than it does in the context of a repair. | 2 |
| *synonym* | If a WORD or PHRASE is *used in* a BUSINESS TERM to *represent* the same BUSINESS CONCEPT as another WORD or PHRASE *used in* another BUSINESS TERM, the two WORDS or PHRASES are "synonyms" of each other. | 2 |
| SYSTEM | A MECHANISM TYPE that consists of one or more linked computers, along with associated software. | 3 |
| SYSTEM CONSTRAINT | A BUSINESS RULE described in terms of its effect on data. Specifically, a SYSTEM CONSTRAINT must be *to constrain* either an ENTITY CLASS, a RELATIONSHIP ROLE, or an ATTRIBUTE. | 7, 5 |
| SYSTEM CONSTRAINT ARGUMENT | A qualifier for either a SYSTEM CONSTRAINT ELEMENT or a SYSTEM CONSTRAINT as a whole. | 7 |
| SYSTEM CONSTRAINT ARGUMENT TYPE | The definition of a kind of SYSTEM CONSTRAINT ARGUMENT. | 7 |
| SYSTEM CONSTRAINT ELEMENT | A component of a SYSTEM CONSTRAINT that identifies something doing the constraining—an ENTITY CLASS, a RELATIONSHP ROLE, or an ATTRIBUTE. | 7 |
| SYSTEM CONSTRAINT TRIGGER | The fact that a SYSTEM CONSTRAINT or a SYSTEM PROCESS may be *initiated by* another SYSTEM CONSTRAINT. | 7 |

*Continued*

| Term | Definition | Chapter |
|---|---|---|
| SYSTEM CON-STRAINT TYPE | The definition of a kind of SYSTEM CONSTRAINT. | 7 |
| SYSTEM EVENT TYPE | The definition of something that happens in the world that produces data affecting the business. | 6, 3 |
| SYSTEM PROCESS | The implementation of a BUSINESS PROCESS that consists of the conversion of data from one form to another. | 3, 5, 6, 7 |
| SYSTEM VARIABLE | A variable whose values are maintained by the operating system. It could be "Today's date", "Computer identifier", or something similar. | 7 |
| TABLE | A two-dimensional array of data, consisting of one or more *rows* representing instances of the thing the TABLE describes and one or more COLUMNS each containing a kind of data describing that thing. | 2 |
| table cell | A place for a datum in a TABLE: a particular *attribute* in a particular ROW. | 2 |
| TABLE ENTITY MAPPING | The fact that a particular ENTITY CLASS (in a Row Three entity-relationship model) is implemented by a particular COLUMN in a Row Four database design. | 2 |
| TABLE INSTANCE | The physical implementation of a TABLE design in a real database. | 2, 5 |
| TABLE SELECTION | The fact that a particular TABLE is a component of a VIEW. | 2 |
| TACTIC | A COURSE OF ACTION that represents one or more details of a STRATEGY. A STRATEGY, then, may be *implemented by* one or more TACTICS. In general, STRATEGIES address GOALS, and TACTICS address OBJECTIVES. | 7, 3, 1 |
| technical metadata | Descriptions of the physical technologies used to store and manage data. This includes database schemas as well as physical storage parameters. | 1 |
| technology model | The model seen by the *Designer* on Row Four of the *Architecture Framework*. | 1 |
| TELEPHONIC SITE | A VIRTUAL SITE that is a node on a telephone system, identified by a "Telephone number". | 4 |
| temporal event | The fact that time, as represented by a clock or a calender, passed a certain point. | 6 |
| term | A rule that describes how people think and talk about things. Thus, the definition of terms (that is, their underlying business concepts) establishes a category of BUSINESS RULE. See also | 2 |

| Term | Definition | Chapter |
|------|------------|---------|
| *term (cont'd)* | BUSINESS TERM—the fact that a particular WORD or PHRASE can have a particular meaning. | |
| *ternary role* | A RELATIONSHIP ROLE that is part of a RELATIONSHIP among three ENTITY CLASSES. | 2 |
| THING | Something of interest in the *abstract model*. | 1 |
| THING RELATIONSHIP | In the *abstract model*, the fact that something of interest is associated with something else of interest. | 1 |
| THING TYPE | In the *abstract model*, a classification of something of interest. | 1 |
| THING TYPE RELATIONSHIP | In the *abstract model*, the fact that a classification of something of interest is related to another classification of something of interest. | 1 |
| *third normal form* | In *relational theory*, the third of Dr. Codd's constraints on a relational design: Each attribute must depend *only* on the PRIMARY KEY. | 2 |
| *time* | (See *timing and events*.) | 1 |
| *timeliness* | A *pragmatic* QUALITY CHARACTERISTIC that is a measure of the relative availability of data to support a given process within the timetable required to perform the process. | 7 |
| *time-targeted* | A characteristic of OBJECTIVES: it is always possible to specify a specific date (such as "December 31, 2007") or a relative date (such as "within two years") when the objective is expected to be achieved. | 7 |
| *timing and events* | The column in the *Architecture Framework* concerned with *when* things happen and how they are triggered. | 1 |
| *title* | According to the *Dublin Core*, text briefly defining the content of a document. The name by which the DOCUMENT or other RESOURCE is commonly known. | 2 |
| TRANSFORMATION RUN | The actual running of a particular PROGRAM COPY on a particular date. This TRANSFORMATION RUN is meant to be used *to place a value in* a CELL INSTANCE. It may be composed of one or more TRANSFORMATION ELEMENTS, each of which must be *the use of* a different CELL INSTANCE. | 3 |

*Continued*

| Term | Definition | Chapter |
|------|------------|---------|
| TRANSFORMATION RUN ELEMENT | The fact that a particular TRANSFORMATION RUN is *the use of* a particular CELL INSTANCE. | 3 |
| *tuple* | In Dr. Codd's original *relational theory*, this was a ROW in a *relation*. | 2 |
| *type* | According to the *Dublin Core*, a general category—ideally selected from a controlled vocabulary. | 2 |
| *type verifier* | (OTHER SYSTEM CONSTRAINT TYPE) If this is an integrity constraint (Condition indicator = "False"), it requires an instance of the constrained object to be related to objects of a specified relationship to each other—mutually exclusive, mutually inclusive, and so on. If this is a condition (Condition indicator = "True"), this kind of SYSTEM CONSTRAINT tests to see whether this is so. | 7 |
| *UML* | A suite of modeling notations to support *object-oriented design*. Notations are available for modeling classes, states, processes, and other dimensions. The class diagram can be used to develop both *entity-relationship models* and *object (implementation) models*. | 1, 2 |
| *uniform resource identifier* | A means of identifying a DOCUMENT page or another kind of RESOURCE. It consists of a scheme name and a schematic-specific name. | 2 |
| *uniform resource locator* | A kind of *uniform resource identifier* used to define locations on the Internet. The term "uniform resource identifier" is a general term describing anything that can be used to identify a web site. *Uniform resource locator* (URL) is part of a formal identification scheme currently (2005) used for identifying sites on the World Wide Web. | 2 |
| UNIQUE IDENTIFIER ELEMENT | The fact that a particular ATTRIBUTE or RELATIONSHIP ROLE is part of a particular UNIQUE IDENTIFIER. | 7 |
| UNIQUE IDENTIFIER | The fact that the values of a specified set of ATTRIBUTES and RELATIONSHIP ROLES are sufficient to uniquely identify each instance of an ENTITY CLASS. | 7 |
| UNIQUE KEY | The specification of a set of columns, whose values can uniquely identify every ROW in a TABLE. This is the implementation of a UNIQUE IDENTIFIER in a relational database. | 7 |

| Term | Definition | Chapter |
|------|-----------|---------|
| UNIQUE KEY ELEMENT | The fact that a particular COLUMN is *part of* a UNIQUE KEY. | 7 |
| *universe of discourse* | The set of *concepts* that are the meaning behind the terms and *fact types*. | 2 |
| URL | (See *uniform resource locator*.) | |
| *usability* | A *pragmatic* QUALITY CHARACTERISTIC that is a measure of the degree to which the information presentation is directly and efficiently usable for its purpose. | 7 |
| *use case* | A model of human/machine interaction similar to data flow diagrams, in that it represents communications between external entities (here called "Actors") and processes, but the assumption is that the processes involved represent systems (typically shown only as a single process representing the entire system). The content of data flows are not documented and, rather than being decomposed into lower-level detail, these details are simply described in text as "steps." There is no notion of storing data in intermediate "data stores." | 3 |
| VALID CODE | The fact that a particular VALUE may be used *to represent* a particular PERMITTED ATTRIBUTE VALUE. Each VALID CODE must be *to represent* a PERMITTED ATTRIBUTE VALUE. VALID CODE is a BUSINESS TERM that is *to represent* the BUSINESS CONCEPT called PERMITTED ATTRIBUTE VALUE. | 7 |
| VALID QUALITY CHARACTERISTIC VALUE | A value for a QUALITY CHARACTERISTIC that may *used as* a QUALITY STANDARD for an ATTRIBUTE or for a RELATIONSHIP ROLE. | 7 |
| *validity or business rule conformance* | An *inherent* QUALITY CHARACTERISTIC that is a measure of the degree of conformance of data to its domain values and business rules. | 7 |
| VALUE EXPRESSION | A DOMAIN that describes a constraint in terms of a mathematical formula. | 7 |
| VALUE SET | A DOMAIN that is a set of PERMITTED ATTRIBUTE VALUES a DISCRETE ATTRIBUTE can assume. | 7 |
| VIEW | A virtual TABLE consisting of COLUMNS and selected instances from other TABLES assembled in a systematic way. | 2 |

*Continued*

| Term | Definition | Chapter |
|---|---|---|
| VIEW SELECTION CONDITION | The use of a COLUMN to determine which instances of a selected TABLE populate a VIEW. Each instance of a TABLE in a TABLE SELECTION for a VIEW is chosen based the "Value" of a selected COLUMN. That value is compared with the "Value" in the VIEW SELECTION CONDITION in terms of its "Operator". | 2 |
| VIRTUAL COPY | A COPY of a DOCUMENT that has no physical existence. Rather, it is stored and/or transmitted only in the electronics of a computer system or network. This is as opposed to a PHYSICAL COPY, which has a tangible existence. | 2 |
| VIRTUAL ENTITY CLASS | An ENTITY CLASS composed of other ENTITY CLASSES, ATTRIBUTES, and RELATIONSHIP ROLES. | 2, 6 |
| VIRTUAL SITE | A SITE that does not have a physical reality beyond bits in a computer somewhere. It is identified by an address that is meaningful only in an electronic environment. | 4, 2 |
| *visibility* | An attribute of OPERATION in *object-oriented design* that tells whether the OPERATION can be "seen" by any program, or whether it is "private"—only accessible within the model involved. | 7 |
| VISION | A description of a desired future state of the enterprise, without regard to how it is to be achieved. | 7, 1, 5 |
| WEB | (See *World Wide Web*.) | |
| WEB SITE | A VIRTUAL SITE that contains RESOURCES identified by *uniform resource identifiers*. | 4 |
| WINDOW | A defined, bounded region on a video display screen. A WINDOW has an identity, and can usually be manipulated—moved, changed in size, and so on. | 5 |
| WORD | 1. A speech sound or series of speech sounds that symbolize and communicate a meaning without being divisible into smaller units capable of independent use. <br> 2. Any segment of written or printed discourse ordinarily appearing between spaces or between a space and a punctuation mark [*Merriam-Webster* 2005]. | 2 |
| WORD USAGE | The fact that a particular WORD appears in a PHRASE. | 2 |
| *World Wide Web* | (Also called "the Web".) A system of Internet servers that support specially formatted documents. The documents are | 2 |

| Term | Definition | Chapter |
|---|---|---|
| *World Wide Web (cont'd)* | formatted in a markup language called HTML (HyperText Markup Language) that supports links to other documents, as well as graphics, audio, and video files. This means you can jump from one document to another simply by clicking on hot spots. Not all Internet servers are part of the World Wide Web. | |
| XML ATTRIBUTE | In an XML DOCUMENT TYPE DECLARATION, this *qualifier of* an XML ELEMENT is the definition an XML ATTRIBUTE VALUE that constrains an XML TAG. | 2 |
| XML ATTRIBUTE VALUE | The actual value of an XML ATTRIBUTE for a specific instance of an XML TAG. | 2 |
| XML BLANK TAG | An XML TAG that contains no data between its initial expression and its termination. | 2 |
| XML CONTENT TAG | An XML TAG that contains data between its initial expression and its termination. | 2 |
| XML DOCUMENT | A body of text organized in terms of XML TAGS. It has a specific structure defined by its creator to be understood in detail by its recipient. | 2 |
| XML DOCUMENT DECLARATION | A specification of the kinds of XML TAGS that can be used for any XML DOCUMENT based on this declaration. | 2 |
| XML ELEMENT | A component in an XML DOCUMENT TYPE DECLARATION that is the specification for a particular XML TAG. | 2 |
| XML ELEMENT CONTENT | The fact that a particular XML CONTENT TAG contains data that constitute a BUSINESS TERM (the use of a WORD or PHRASE *to represent* a BUSINESS CONCEPT). | 2 |
| XML TAG | A text label that identifies a portion of an XML DOCUMENT. | 2 |
| XML TAG DEFINITION | The fact that an XML TAG or an XML ELEMENT (in an XML DOCUMENT TYPE DECLARATION) is defined in terms of either an ENTITY CLASS or an ATTRIBUTE. | 2 |
| XML VERSION | The particular edition of the XML language used as the basis for a particular XML DOCUMENT. | 2 |
| *Zachman Framework* | The original *Architecture Framework* as defined by John Zachman [1987]. | 1 |

# REFERENCES AND FURTHER READING

*If I have seen farther, it is by standing on the shoulders of giants.*

—Isaac Newton
Letter to Robert Hooke, 1676

American National Standards Institute (ANSI). (1978). "ANSI/X3/SPARC DBMS Framework Report of the Study Group on Database Management Systems", *Information Systems*, Vol. 3, Number 3.

Aristotle. 350 BCE. *Posterior Analytics*, Book II, 1. Translated by G.R.G. Mure, 1962. Ninth Year Course, Volume 2. Chicago: The Great Books Foundation.

Ashby, W. R. (1956). *An Introduction to Cybernetics*, New York: John Wiley and Sons (Science Editions).

Barker, R., and C. Longman. (1992). *CASE Method: Function and Process Models*. Wokingham, England: Addison-Wesley.

Beer, S. (1979). *The Heart of Enterprise*. Chichester, UK: John Wiley and Sons.

Berners-Lee, T. (1998). "Uniform Resource Identifiers (URI): Generic Syntax," Internet Engineering Task Force/Network Working Group. Available at *http://www.ietf.org/rfc/rfc2396*.

Booch, G., J. Rumbaugh, and I. Jacobson. (1999). *The Unified Modeling Language User Guide*. Reading, MA: Addison-Wesley.

Brackett, M. H. (2000). *Data Resource Quality*. Boston: Addison-Wesley.

The Business Rules Group (BRG) (1995, 2000). "Defining Business Rules: What Are They Really?" (4th ed.), formerly titled the "GUIDE Business Rules Project Report" (1995). Available at *http://www.BusinessRulesGroup.org*.

The Business Rules Group. (2005). "The Business Motivation Model: Business Governance in a Volatile World," release 1.2. Formerly titled "Organizing

Business Plans: The Standard Model for Business Rule Motivation" (November 2000). Available at *http://www.BusinessRulesGroup.org*.

Cockburn, A. (2001). *Writing Effective Use Cases*. Boston: Addison-Wesley.

Codd, E. F. (1970). "A Relational Model of Data for Large Shared Data Banks," *Communications of the ACM* 13(6).

Daconta, M. C., L. J. Obrst, and K. T. Smith. (2003). *The Semantic Web*. Indianapolis: Wiley Publishing.

DeMarco, T. (1978). *Structured Analysis and System Specification*. Englewood Cliffs, NJ: Prentice-Hall.

Dublin Core Metadata Initiative (DCMI). (2004). "DCMI Type Vocabulary." Available at *http://dublincore.org/documents/dcmi-type-vocabulary*.

Dublin Core Metadata Initiative (DCMI). (2005). "DCMI Metadata Terms." Available at *http://dublincore.org/documents/dcmi-terms*.

English, L. (1999). *Improving Data Warehouse and Business Information Quality*. New York: John Wiley & Sons.

Eva, M. (1994). *SSADM Version 4: A User's Guide, Second Edition*. London: McGraw-Hill.

Feldmann, C. G. (1998). *The Practical Guide to Business Process Reengineering Using IDEF0*. New York: Dorset House.

Finkelstein, C. 1989. *An Introduction to Information Engineering: From Strategic Planning to Information Systems*. Sydney: Addison-Wesley.

Gane, C., and T. Sarson. (1979). *Structured Systems Analysis*. Englewood Cliffs, NJ: Prentice-Hall.

GUIDE. (1989). "Repository Data Model Addendum," GUIDE Publication No. GRP-336.

GUIDE. (1987). "Repository Data Model," GUIDE Publication No. GRP-254.

Hall, J. (2004). "Business Semantics of Business Rules," *Business Rule Journal* 5(4). Available at *http://www.BRCommunity.com/a2004/b182.html*.

Hay, D. C. (1996). *Data Model Patterns: Conventions of Thought*. New York: Dorset House.

Hay, D. C. (2003). *Requirements Analysis: From Business Views to Architecture*. Upper Saddle River, NJ: Prentice Hall PTR.

International Standards Organization (ISO). 2003. "Information and Documentation—the Dublin Core Metadata Element Set", ISO 15836:2003(E). Available at *http://www.niso.org/international/SC4/n515.pdf.*

Jackson, M. (1983). *System Development.* Englewood Cliffs, NJ: Prentice-Hall.

Jacobson, I. (1992). *Object-Oriented Software Engineering.* Harlow, UK: Addison-Wesley.

Johnson & Johnson, Inc. (1943). *Credo.* Available at *http://www.jnj.com/our_company/our_credo.*

Johnson, S. (1755). *Dictionary of the English Language.* Ceder City, UT: Classic Books.

Jupiter Media Corporation (JMC/URL). (2006). *Webopedia.* Available at *http://www.webopedia.com/term/u/url.*

Kemerling, G. (1997–2002a). *Philosophy Pages* (semantics). Available at *http://www.philosophypages.com/dy/s4.htm#sems.*

Kemerling, G. (1997–2002b). *Philosophy Pages* (ontology). Available at *http://www.philosophypages.com/dy/ix2.htm#o.*

Knowledge Based Systems, Inc. (KBSI). (2005). IDEF Web Site at *http://idef.com.*

Marco, D. (2000). *Building and Managing the Meta Data Repository.* New York: John Wiley & Sons.

Marco, D., and M. Jennings. (2004). *Universal Meta Data Models.* Indianapolis: Wiley.

Martin, J., and C. McClure. (1985). *Diagramming Techniques for Analysts and Programmers.* Englewood Cliffs, NJ: Prentice Hall.

McComb, D. (2004). *Semantics in Business Systems: The Savvy Manager's Guide.* San Francisco: Morgan Kaufmann.

McMenamin, S., and J. Palmer. (1984). *Essential Systems Analysis.* Englewood Cliffs, NJ: Yourdon Press.

Merriam-Webster. (2005). *Merriam-Webster Online.* Available at *http://merriam-webster.com.*

Miller, G. A. (1956). "The Magical Number Seven, Plus or Minus Two: Some Limits on Our Capacity for Processing Information," *The Psychological Review,* 63(2):81–97.

Object Management Group (OMG). (2007). *Semantics of Business Vocabulary and Business Rules (SBVR)*. Beta 3 Document. Dec/07-06-06.

Object Management Group (OMG). (2003). *UML 2.0 Infrastructure Specification*. OMG Adopted Specification ptc/03-09-15.

Olsen, D. H., and N. Forsgren. (2002). "A General E-Commerce Data Model for Strategic Advantage: Mapping Site Structure to Site Visit Behavior," *The Review of Business Information Systems* 6(1):17–24.

Page-Jones, M. (2000). *Fundamentals of Object-Oriented Design in UML*. Boston: Addison-Wesley.

Poole, J., D. Chang, D. Tolbert, and D. Mellor. (2002). *Common Warehouse Metamodel*. New York: John Wiley & Sons.

Ross, R. (1997). *The Business Rule Book: Classifying, Defining, and Modeling Rules, Second Edition*. Boston: Database Research Group.

Ross, R. (1994). *The Business Rule Book: Classifying, Defining, and Modeling Rules, First Edition*. Boston: Database Research Group.

Rumbaugh, J., I. Jacobson, and G. Booch. (1999). *The Unified Modeling Language Reference Manual*. Reading, MA: Addison-Wesley.

Rummler, G. A., and A. P. Brache. (1995). *Improving Performance: How to Manage the White Space on the Organization Chart*. San Francisco: Jossey-Bass.

Sowa, J. F., and J. A. Zachman. (1992). "Extending and Formalizing the Framework for Information Systems Architecture," *IBM Systems Journal* 31(3). IBM Publication G321-5488.

Tannenbaum, A. (2002). *Metadata Solutions*. Boston: Addison-Wesley.

von Halle, B. (2002). *Business Rules Applied*. New York: John Wiley & Sons.

Vonnegut, K. (1959). *The Sirens of Titan*. New York: Dell Publishing.

Zachman, J. (1987). "A Framework for Information Systems Architecture," *IBM Systems Journal* 26(3). IBM Publication G321-5298.

# ABOUT THE AUTHOR

**David C. Hay** is founder of Essential Strategies, Inc., a consulting firm dedicated to helping clients define corporate information architecture, identify requirements, and plan strategies for the implementation of new systems, including data warehouses. A pioneer in the use of standard data models for standard business situations, he is the author of *Data Model Patterns: Conventions of Thought*. Taking advantage of more than thirty years of experience helping companies identify systems requirements, he is also the author of *Requirements Analysis: From Business Views to Architecture*. Dave is a member of DAMA International and the Oracle Development Tools User Group and has spoken frequently at events sponsored by these groups and others.

# INDEX

Printed and bound by CPI Group (UK) Ltd, Croydon, CR0 4YY

03/10/2024

01040316-0008